THE LINE OF FIRE

Admiral William J. Crowe, Jr.

with David Chanoff

359.0092
Crd

SIMON & SCHUSTER
Simon & Schuster Building
Rockefeller Center
1230 Avenue of the Americas
New York, New York 10020

SIMON & SCHUSTER and colophon are registered trademarks
of Simon & Schuster Inc.
Designed by Pei Loi Koay
Manufactured in the United States of America

10 9 8 7 6 5 4 3 2 1

Library of Congress Cataloging-in-Publication Data
Crowe, William J., date.
   The line of fire : from Washington to the Gulf, the politics and
battles of the new military / William J. Crowe, Jr. with David
Chanoff.
       p.   cm.
   Includes index.
   1. Crowe, William J., date.   2. Admirals—United States—
Biography.   3. United States. Navy—Biography.   4. United States
—History, Military—20th century.   I. Chanoff, David.   II. Title.
E840.5.C76A3   1993
359'.0092—dc20
[B]   92-44122
                                                      CIP

ISBN 0-671-72703-6

For Shirley,
Blake, Brent, and Bambi,
But Most of All for Shirley

CONTENTS

1

When I was seven years old, around the time this photo was taken (with my loyal dog Czar), I read a book entitled *Annapolis Today*. It convinced me, once and for all, that I wanted to be a naval officer.

2

Not that many years later, I found myself at Annapolis as a proud midshipman. This picture is living proof that I once had hair.

The U.S.S. *Trout,* which I commanded from 1960 to 1962, in all her glory entering Charleston harbor. You can't distinguish me, but I'm on the bridge.

In 1971, I was photographed in Vietnam with my staff. At the time, I was Senior Adviser to the South Vietnamese Riverine Force. No one who witnessed or participated in the struggle in Indochina walked away unchanged.

In 1981, as Commander-in-Chief, Allied Forces Southern Europe, I spoke to NATO troops at Doganbey, Turkey, during a field exercise.

With President Ronald Reagan at the beginning of my term as
Chairman of the Joint Chiefs of Staff.

6

Marshal Akhromeyev and I talked with Army troops at Fort Hood,
Texas, during his visit to the United States in July 1988. While
observing tanks and artillery, he laughingly remarked, ''The laws of
physics apply to both sides.''

7

I reviewed an honor guard of Soviet sailors on board the cruiser *Kirov,* the pride of their fleet, off the coast of Murmansk, in June 1989.

General Moiseyev, my Soviet counterpart, and I sign the Dangerous Military Incidents Agreement in the Kremlin in June 1989.

Shirley and I are joined by our family at Christmas 1991: (sitting, left to right) Shirley, our dog Mele, granddaughters Amanda and Caitlin, Blake's wife Lynne; (standing, left to right) Brent's girlfriend Carol Clarke, Brent, me, Blake, and Bambi.

I was active as an adviser to Governor Clinton on military issues during the campaign.

AUTHOR TO THE READER

AMONG OTHER THINGS, this book is a record of the evolution of a sailor, from midshipman to Chairman of the Joint Chiefs of Staff. As such it has much in common with other stories of those who rose through the ranks. But one of the peculiarities of my career was that it overlapped almost exactly with the great Soviet–American confrontation that drove history from the end of World War Two until the beginning of the 1990s. A result of this coincidence was that my service intersected with some of the era's more dramatic encounters. As a staff officer in the Pentagon I found myself in the middle of the *Pueblo* affair. Later I fought in Vietnam, commanded NATO armies, oversaw the last years of America's preparation for strategic nuclear warfare, and helped brake the mad rush to SDI.

When I began looking back to write this book I had the satisfaction of noticing that my career described something of a nice, coherent entity. I had started off training for war against the Soviet Union and had ended up (almost five decades later) becoming friends with the Soviet chief of staff. But as I wrote, hoping to capture that picture in its neat frame, events insisted on accumulating. Like Tristram Shandy (and no doubt a crowd of other memoirists), I sometimes wondered if a living person could ever catch up with himself and finish writing an autobiography. Mine, anyway, seemed to go on. Francis Fukuyama might argue that history ended with the Soviet Union's demise; I did not find it so.

In particular, it seemed to me that with the end of Soviet antagonism the principal threat to America's health was no longer to be found in the outside world, but in the economic travail and social divisiveness that so disturb our domestic life. The post–Cold War scene has changed with startling speed. Although I formally retired in 1989, I found myself more and more taken with our need to understand and deal with a fundamentally different world. So strongly did I feel about this that I threw off the career officer's habit of silence and became involved in the election of 1992, advising and supporting Bill Clinton. Most of what follows concerns the experiences I had as a military man. But my participation in public affairs continued after I left the ranks, and these memoirs touch on that too. It may be the first time a former Chairman has entered the political fray. Almost certainly it will not be the last.

Come all ye bold seamen
Wherever you're bound,
And always let Nelson's
Proud memory go 'round.

And pray that the wars
And tumult may cease,
For the greatest of gifts
Is a sweet lasting peace.

May the Lord put an end
To these cruel old wars.
And bring peace and contentment
To all our brave tars.

A SEAMAN'S HYMN

INTRODUCTION

I WAS TRYING to get a good look at the Soviet nuclear-powered cruiser *Kirov,* but the window next to my seat was tiny and the helicopter pilot was complicating things further with a series of sharp turns as he circled to land. Suddenly the chopper steadied itself and hovered off the *Kirov*'s starboard quarter at about 150 feet. I could see her perfectly. The 45,000-ton flagship of the Soviet Fleet looked massive as it plowed through the sea with the Arctic summer sun glinting off gun barrels, missile silos, and a forest of antennas. The sleek lines and raked clipper bow gave the ship a silhouette that was graceful but also loaded with menace.

As the helicopter sidestepped over the afterdeck landing pad, I lost sight of the *Kirov,* but had a good look at an accompanying Soviet destroyer 2,000 yards off the port beam. In the distance I also thought I could make out the cruiser H.M.S. *London, Kirov*'s full-time NATO shadow—a reminder that despite this friendly visit I was paying the Soviets as Chairman of the Joint Chiefs of Staff, the danger was still alive. On this bright morning of June 15, 1989, there was much that had not yet changed.

It crossed my mind that I had given little thought to arrival formalities or to what might be expected of me. Nothing, I hoped. Of more immediate concern were the long johns and woolen drill sweater I was wearing. I had been determined to dress prudently. Summer or not, we were in Murmansk, well north of the Arctic Circle, and I expected the weather to be chilly. One of our Russian hosts had joked that in these latitudes there is only one good day each year, after the mosquitoes die and before the snows begin. But today it was unusually hot, the temperature already threatening to break ninety. The wind was a balmy summer breeze.

The helicopter landed with a jolt, and I worked to free myself from the safety harness. Sweating freely, I hit the deck, and my arthritic knees momentarily locked. The rotor blades were still turning, and for a minute I was caught in a flurry of noise and discomfort as I shed my life vest and silently cursed the long johns. In front I saw the *Kirov*'s captain beckoning me toward a ladder, and as I started climbing, the shrill scream of a bosun's whistle pierced the air, piping me aboard. Reaching the main deck, I walked through a cordon of side boys and looked up. There in front of me was a full-dress guard parade, two long ranks of Soviet sailors in blue uniforms and white leggings, bearing their rifles at an exaggerated present arms. Behind them was arrayed a large Navy band. I had requested no honors; my thought was to discard whatever ceremonies we could in favor of down-to-earth personal contacts between the two sides. I knew that the Soviet staff had not ordered this, nor had the Defense Ministry. Most likely the Soviet naval commander had simply been unable to resist the opportunity to mark the occasion.

As I cleared the side boys, the first notes of "The Star-Spangled Banner" rang out, catching me by surprise. Overhead a large American flag waved against the pale blue sky. I looked around and saw that the entire ship was at attention, saluting. Not only the honor guard, but everybody, my own small party as well as the Soviets. Scanning the superstructure, I saw Mike Wallace with his CBS camera crew—I had brought him along despite initial objections from both the Soviet and American bureaucracies. Wallace was brushing tears from his cheeks. Suddenly the weight of this moment swept over me, and I struggled to disguise my emotion. Nothing like this had occurred since World War Two. I had been a second classman at Annapolis in 1945 when Russian and American soldiers embraced on the Elbe. Since then my entire professional life had been lived in enmity with these people who were now standing stiffly at attention around me, their right hands raised to their caps.

That thought would not go away, even after I had reviewed the guard and climbed up to the bridge to meet the captain and talk to some of the crewmen. For forty-five years as an American military officer, nearly every thought, almost every single thing I had done had in one way or another been directed against the Soviets. I had used all my abilities to block and thwart and frustrate their efforts. Together with my colleagues I had planned to destroy them—not just our opposite numbers but their people, their weapons of war, their factories and resources, their very life as a nation. It was hardly an exaggeration to say that our conflict with the U.S.S.R. had given us our primary raison d'être. As a young man I had practiced running submarines against their surface ships. In graduate school I had studied their foreign policy and its implementation, how they were hurting us and how we could counter them. In all our games and exercises they had been our only serious adversary. I had fought a war against them at one remove in Vietnam. In the Persian Gulf I had bent every effort to build our strength and deny them access. In the Mediterranean and the Pacific, forces under my command were in regular unfriendly contact, always primed for hostilities. For almost half a century it had all been driven by our mutual animosity.

Through the wide bridge windshield I watched the exercises begin. Missiles streaked into their targets with a rush of flame and violent bursts of high explosives. I tried hard to concentrate on them with a professional's eye—to watch for weaknesses and strengths, to assess the ability of the Soviet sailors to handle their ships and weapons. But my mind kept wandering back to how much it had all changed. Like me, these men had shaped their lives largely in preparation for a single mission.

I thought of George Kennan, whom I had invited for lunch in the Pentagon a week before, just prior to my departure. Kennan, eighty-four years old, had written his famous "X" article more than four decades earlier. As much as anything, that document had defined the containment policy and shaped America's global posture in the post-war era (and in the process had informed the careers of almost two generations of American military men). Kennan was quite pleased, he said, to be invited to lunch by the Chairman of the Joint Chiefs. I felt the honor was mine. Kennan did not remember, but in 1967 as a doctoral candidate in politics at Princeton University I had audited a course he was teaching. He had been one of a group of faculty members there who had helped me focus my own thinking away from the narrow province of the professional warrior and toward the broader sphere where the political and military intertwined.

At lunch, Kennan had not wanted to speculate on the U.S.S.R.'s internal upheavals. Instead our discussion centered on the fundamental transformation we were witnessing in American-Soviet relations. I was not ready to believe that we could yet dismiss the Soviets as a threat. Almost always in the past our contacts with the Soviet military had been disastrous—nasty, uncooperative, and bellicose. Yet around me now the American vice chiefs were talking, laughing, and taking notes and pictures on board the Soviet flagship. Truly we were in the midst of a sea change.

The simple fact that I was in Murmansk was stunning enough. For years no American officer had visited this Russian Gibraltar—the home of the great Northern Fleet and site of the world's largest submarine base. During World War Two, Murmansk was the destination point of the Anglo-American Lend-Lease convoys, but for decades now the military traffic had been going in the other direction. From here Soviet men-of-war rode the current backwards, heading out to missions in the Atlantic and Mediterranean. From here the ballistic-missile and cruise-missile submarines played hide-and-seek with the American undersea surveillance network as they made their way to patrols off New York, Norfolk, and Charleston. This entire region was highly classified, a closed military zone. Yet here we were.

In October, three months from now, I would be retiring as Chairman. If ten years earlier someone had asked me to draw up a list of things I thought I might still do in my career, I would have put traveling on a space shuttle to Mars far ahead of visiting the Murmansk naval headquarters. Yet we had now been in the Soviet Union for five days—myself; my wife, Shirley; the vice chiefs of the Army, Air Force, Navy, and Marines; and a support team. In Moscow we had met with my counterpart, the new chief of the Soviet General Staff, Mikhail Moiseyev. We had been to the Supreme Soviet with its life-size bust of Lenin staring down at the delegates from behind. We had looked into the mouths of missile silos and inspected the Soviets' newest long-range nuclear bombers. The media were using the word "unprecedented" for what was taking place at a time when not everyone was yet convinced that the Cold War was really over. But "unprecedented" did not begin to capture the mix of feelings that I and my colleagues were experiencing on this journey.

Back in Leningrad at night, I had time to reflect on this day—in some ways the culmination of my forty-seven years in the military. The transformation in American-Soviet affairs was earthshaking, something that was already rearranging the conceptual foundations of international relations. The prospects were tantalizing: friendly rivals rather than two armed camps; resources allocated to development instead of warfare; a mutual approach to solving international problems, many of them inflicted on the world by the Cold War; nuclear standdown—moving the doomsday clock backwards and stepping away from the brink of holocaust. But uglier possibilities also threatened. Could the Soviets hold to this new course, or in the end would Mikhail Gorbachev fail (as Nikita Khrushchev had) and Stalinism reassert itself? And if they did hold steady, could a less militaristic U.S.S.R. keep itself together? Or would political relaxation lead inevitably toward violence inside the Soviet empire and even more danger for the world? One thing was certain: We were just now standing on a precipice, gazing out at a great unknown.

How ironic that this moment had arrived just as I was about to retire. As Chairman I had worked hard to decrease tensions. (In Moscow I had just signed a military-to-military contacts agreement and an accord on reducing dangerous activities when our forces operated in close proximity.) I had done my best to further arms limitations. The Intermediate Nuclear Forces (INF) Treaty had been concluded during my tenure, and START negotiations were moving ahead—both treaties had the support of the Joint Chiefs. Former Soviet Chief of Staff Sergei Akhromeyev and I had developed a warm (if unlikely) friendship and had made the most of it to break through a legacy of fear and misunderstanding. But soon the military side of these openings would be in other hands, and that gave me a twinge of regret.

But not much. I was certain that whomever George Bush chose as my successor would be politically astute and versed in foreign affairs. All of the candidates for the chairmanship I would soon be vacating belonged to a new breed of military leaders. Few officers these days made it into the higher ranks without a firm grasp of international relations, congressional politics, and public affairs. If many of the older generation of generals and admirals had narrow educations and mostly warfighting experience, that was no longer true. The old military was gone. But stereotypes die hard, and it could hardly be said that the public was aware of the extent of the transformation. Yet during my time the armed services had gone through a profound change, a shift in the military culture that had shaped my own professional life just as surely as had the confrontation with the Soviets.

The Navy I had entered in 1943 was in many ways a closed and insular society. Its officer corps was all male, lily white, distrustful of intellectuals and bureaucrats, and inherently suspicious of both the Army (there was no separate Air Force) and civilians. Women were unwelcome, blacks segregated, Hispanics and Filipinos typed as stewards. The Army, of course, was equally closed minded. During wartime the armed services absorbed large numbers of volunteers and draftees, but in peace they were small self-contained societies, monastic orders with their own peculiar mores, sustaining themselves on the fringes of the civilian world.

It was not until after World War Two that the change began, chiefly as a consequence of America's global conflict with the Soviet Union. Containing the Soviets required large standing forces and began consuming an eye-opening share of the federal budget. As a result, for the first time in its history the nation started taking a serious interest in the peacetime military. Such previously remote subjects as the services' handling of civil rights, integration, equal opportunity, and women in the military became newsworthy and fell under public scrutiny. A massive infrastructure of military bases was established throughout the country, deeply affecting local economies and politics. The military was propelled into a whole spectrum of problems it had never before faced, and it was forced to develop large numbers of people skilled at dealing with them, people at home in the civil and political arenas as well as on the battlefield.

At the same time, technology was revolutionizing the services (as it was the rest of society). Nuclear weapons, space programs, atomic reactors, computers, and sophisticated electronics brought military people into basic scientific research and created new, complex relationships between the academic, industrial, and military worlds. As the Cold War lengthened, the Pentagon emerged as a giant among public institutions, enmeshed as never before in the economic, political, and social life of the nation. It was one of the great and largely unconsidered alterations the Cold War brought to American society.

All this had happened in my time. I had watched (and participated) as foreign affairs and media relations became part of the military's province. Mike Wallace was filming this trip for *60 Minutes,* and when I returned I would be interviewed on the three major networks —something an earlier military would never have understood or condoned. I had seen an efficient working relationship evolve between the political and military sides of the American house. This entire visit had been carefully coordinated by the Pentagon, State Department, and White House as part of a broad effort to open up the U.S.S.R. The next day I was scheduled to meet with Mikhail Gorbachev; back in Washington I would brief Secretary of State James Baker and President George Bush.

Signs of the transformation in the armed forces were all around me—my staff included black, Hispanic, and women officers. They came from all the services: Army, Navy, Air Force, and Marines— normal enough now, but improbable in the not-so-distant days of bloody interservice rivalry. My executive assistant, Rear Admiral Joe Strasser, was a fighting officer with a doctorate in political science. The bulk of my own career had been lived in the political-military business, something that would not even have been possible in earlier times. I was on the verge of leaving a military that had become practiced in dealing with the globe's complexities, one that was intellectually and philosophically ready to function in the unpredictable reality that loomed after the end of the Cold War.

It was my good fortune to have lived during this era of epochal change in America's armed forces. My story, then, is that of a man whose professional life spanned the period—who was commissioned into the old world and watched the new one being born. And while I was not directly involved in the myriad transformations, I witnessed them all and was touched by them all. I was part of the process, and I was myself changed by it.

Chapter 1

THE
TRUE CHURCH

UNDERNEATH GRAY SKIES the superdreadnought U.S.S. *Pennsylvania* had a threatening look, humped in the middle where the bridge and steel conning tower bulked up at the foot of the foremast, weighted toward the bow by the two giant forward gun turrets. That's what it looked like as I stared at the picture that hung over my bed when I was a boy. My father had been a radioman on the *Pennsylvania* when she escorted Woodrow Wilson to France in 1918. Among his memorabilia were the ship newspapers that described each day of the voyage as the great warship and its charge made way through heavy seas toward Brest. I read them all, and everything else I could get my hands on about the Navy—histories, biographies, adventures. At night I pored over the photographs in our heavily illustrated four-volume history of World War One. I dreamed of Dewey and Farragut and John Paul Jones. The biggest body of water I had ever actually seen was Lake Overholser. But somehow, all the way out in Oklahoma City where I was growing up, the sea cast its spell on me. It had a magnetism about it, a feel, a mystery.

Over time I began to understand that there were special skills connected with running ships. There was complicated machinery to work, and navigation was an art of its own. But once you acquired the knowledge, you could handle the big ships, you could sail around the world and fire the great guns. Best of all, when you mastered these things you joined a special group; your life was set apart from those of ordinary people. I read about the majesty of fleets and battles at sea, about surviving storms and shipwreck and overcoming the wild elements. I read about heroism and leadership, and I knew that one day I myself would go to sea.

On June 20, 1943, at the age of eighteen, I found myself pacing outside the walls of the Naval Academy, fifteen hundred miles from home, wondering about life behind them. There was no doubt in my mind that I was about to cross a threshold, and the prospect both frightened and excited me. But I had no inkling that I was literally entering a different culture (some would say a closed culture), one that would do its best in the coming years to shape me to its own values and mores—even as I both took them to heart and struggled against their hold on me.

Plebe summer, the training period before the Academy's year began, was tense, full of talk and dark rumors about what the work would be like once we got started. Everyone knew the attrition rate was high, and as the fall semester drew near the fear level rose. One commander tried to reassure us. "No matter how dumb you might be," he said, "just remember, someone dumber than you has already graduated from here."

Once we got under way I was amazed by the speed at which I and my classmates were assimilated into the system. Oklahoma University, where I had spent a year before receiving my appointment, had given me a good academic preparation, but outside the classroom Annapolis had its own way of doing things. Midshipmen quickly got accustomed to being hollered at (so that when they finally got aboard ship it wasn't a new or unusual phenomenon). My peers and I found ourselves getting up at strange hours and standing long, inconvenient watches, even during exam periods when other things were on our minds. We learned to keep our rooms spotless and perform arbitrary chores required by people who seemed to care little about our academic loads. We were expected to do these things and succeed as students at the same time. We found out quickly that duty was important, rank was important, and doing what you were told was especially important. Other schools might furnish equally good naval officers, but an Annapolis man got into the necessary military frame of mind earlier in the game.

It took me a while to accept being bossed around, but I had wanted a place at the Naval Academy so long and so badly that at first it never occurred to me to do anything but what I was supposed to do. But by the time I was a first classman I was bridling under authority, going over the wall on occasion, and accumulating a hefty share of demerits. I knew even then that I was trying to protect my sanity by asserting my independence. At the same time I developed a talent for avoiding detection—great training, as it turned out, for surviving in the Pentagon. As my battalion officer (affectionately referred to as "Jug Butt") said one day, "Crowe, you may make a good officer someday, but you're a damned poor midshipman."

One thing I was good at, though, was arguing. The Naval Academy had recently started a debate program, which pleased me no end, since debate had been my favorite activity in high school. Even though the program was young we still made it to the Eastern intercollegiate tournament, held that year at West Point. My partners on the team were Jack Jones and Vernon Weaver. Jones was a fellow Oklahoman with whom I had debated for several years at Classen High. The two of us had been at it for a long time, so while Navy might have been new to the activity, we weren't. Our hardest debate was in the semifinals against Princeton, but we beat them. They couldn't believe it. How could Princeton have lost to Annapolis? After all, this wasn't football. Of course a lot of debating is experience and technique. You don't necessarily have to have the best arguments or the best mind to win. They knew that as well as we did, but it didn't soften the blow much.

In the finals we met West Point. Maxwell Taylor was the superintendent of the Military Academy then, and a strong supporter of debate. As a result there were several hundred cadets in the audience, which meant we were badly outnumbered. The subject was "Should there be compulsory military training," a loaded question in 1944. Taylor insisted that West Point argue the affirmative, but when the dust cleared, we had prevailed again.

When my senior year was over, I graduated 81st in a class of 816, twenty places under a midshipman from Georgia named James Earl Carter, fifty-five places below future CIA chief Stansfield Turner, but slightly ahead of my close friend Jim Stockdale, who would later spend seven years in a North Vietnamese prison camp and eventually run for vice president with Ross Perot. Carter and I were classmates again in submarine school, though after that we rarely saw each other. Much later in life, when he was President, he came to the Pentagon for a ceremony. "Bill," he said, "I'm happy to see you. [I was a vice admiral then.] It looks like we both surprised each other."

My first ship was the U.S.S. *Carmick,* a Benson-Livermore-class destroyer minesweeper that was one of the fastest ships the Navy had built to that time. The *Carmick*'s captain was Asa A. Clark III, six four, broad shoulders, and the best ship handler I ever served under. While Clark was a hard man, he also possessed a warm heart and a sense of tolerance, fortunately for the group of green officers I came in with. On our first voyage (around San Francisco Bay) Clark ordered the newly minted communications officer to show "stop," commonly indicated by running speed markers up the yardarm.

Without a clue, the unfortunate young man raised four flags which spelled out STOP. "What the hell is that, mister?" yelled Clark, but his voice registered more resignation than anger.

Many officers in the surface-ship Navy of those days did not share Asa Clark's more humane qualities. A warship is a crowded high-powered instrument that does dangerous things, and its master was likely to be quick-tempered and unforgiving. Running alongside a resupply ship at fifteen knots, or firing guns, or maneuvering at high speed in heavy seas demanded seamanship and discipline. Authority was rigorously enforced, and subordinates found nothing unusual about receiving peremptory treatment from their superiors.

After several of my own initial embarrassments, I found on a seven-month tour of the Pacific under my second captain that I had the makings of a sailor. But though I enjoyed the sea, I did not take easily to the caste system and the tight discipline. I reacted badly to it, the same way I had in my last years at the Naval Academy. I knew that I was not an authoritarian person, and I did not like living in an overly rigid environment. (In that sense I was never a very "military" individual—one of the reasons some people were amazed I made the progress I did in the Navy, none more so than myself.)

But while the surface Navy was a stringently hierarchical organization, the submarine force enjoyed a different reputation. Anyone looking for more camaraderie, more trust, and a less structured relationship between officers and enlisted men went into subs. Supposedly, submariners led an exciting, free-swinging sort of life. Even their dress code was relaxed, and since I was regularly accused of looking like an unmade bed anyway, I thought the habit might be overlooked on a "pigboat."

In fact, I had been reading about subs since high school. Submarines were a volunteer service, and submariners were an elite within the Navy. Like aviators, they had their own insignia, and what they did involved special daring and skill. I graduated Annapolis with the idea of going into pigboats just as soon as the Navy would let me, which meant right after two obligatory years on surface ships.

On July 1, 1948, I entered submarine school at New Haven, Connecticut, where I was instantly immersed not just in the mechanics of submarining but in the traditions and achievements of the force. During World War Two, submariners represented only about 1 percent of the Navy's strength, but they had sunk 60 percent of all Japanese shipping destroyed. When I started riding the boats, the men who had made this history were all around me.

In the ten years following submarine school, virtually all of my seagoing was on diesel submarines—the *Flying Fish*, the *Clamagore*, the *Wahoo*, and the *Trout*, my first command. People learned to live in tight quarters on a diesel sub. The eight officers and seventy-five or eighty crewmen were thrown together, working and living in spaces so small that resignation, humor, and a high tolerance for frustration were prerequisites to survival. Submarine life may not have created saints, but it surely made people more tolerant than they were to begin with.

For the crew, privacy was an alien concept altogether, though for officers there was a separate head in the forward torpedo room—a tiny compartment no bigger than a desk blotter. An officers' shower was there too, about the same size. But neither officers nor crew spent much time on showers. The equipment that made fresh water took space, weight, and energy and was not efficient. The whole procedure was more trouble than it was worth. So not only were we cramped in, we were cramped in with a lot of other people who were not bathing too frequently. It didn't pay to be too clean, if only on grounds of self-defense. Scarce water also cut down on shaving, and beard contests were common features of shipboard life. I entered, but my beard was so sparse that everyone laughed. I regularly won "most scraggly."

Preparing to take a four-hour watch on the bridge in cold weather, a submariner would put on as many layers as he possibly could. By the time he finished he looked like a penguin. Then he would go up and spend his time trying desperately to stay dry and keep from freezing to death. By the time he came off duty his outer clothes at least were drenched, and he would hang them in the forward torpedo room, where everyone else had hung theirs. Of course in bad weather nobody would completely undress to go to bed. It was too uncomfortable dressing and undressing in crowded quarters on a rolling ship. So people just took off their foul-weather gear and lay down on their bunks fully clothed. This added a certain pungency to the general aroma, already a melange of smells from diesel engines, sodden wool, and occasionally overflowing heads. Cleaning the ship was not easy, and sleeping could be a problem (one trick was to smear Mentholatum under your nose; it kept you from smelling anything else). There is a Navy chestnut about the admiral inspecting a group of officers. Stopping in front of one officer, he takes a whiff. "Fish, farts, and fuel oil," he says. "Young man, you must be a submariner."

The subs I sailed were small ships of about 2,100 tons (the German U-boats of World War Two were often half that size). When we cruised on the surface, the main deck was only six feet or so above the waterline, while an officer and two lookouts rode on an open bridge another ten feet higher. In a rolling sea the boat slid over the waves, slipping into the valleys and rising up the slopes. But when it was unusually heavy and the wind was screaming, you could watch mountains of water march by—bracing yourself for those that broke over the bridge and snatched the breath from your lungs. The bow would plow under and the sea roar up at you, smashing the conning tower and separating into sheets of salt spray. Then a forty-footer would sail by and then another. You seemed part of the ocean. To a diesel submariner, that made it all seem worthwhile.

Diesel subs did not like to submerge in that kind of weather, because ultimately they would have to surface, and surfacing in rough seas could be precarious. In the few minutes it took to pump the tanks and achieve buoyancy, a broadside could knock the ship forty or fifty degrees over. Fears of capsizing would shoot through everyone aboard. Every loose object on the ship would scoot around while battery acid splashed out of the batteries. If you opened the hatch too quickly, water poured down into the boat. I was in a boat when that happened, and two feet of water flooded the forward battery compartment. If the water actually got down into the batteries, you'd have a truly serious problem; seawater and acid turned to chlorine.

Even in good weather, diesels spent most of their time on the surface (operating underwater used the batteries, which ran down quickly). Today's nuclear subs go down and stay for months, often not surfacing during an entire cruise. But for a diesel man, real submarining meant diving and surfacing constantly in a boat that was both surface ship and undersea craft. A few years after I joined the force, the snorkel was introduced, which meant that a boat could stick a pipe out of the water and charge the batteries while submerged. But snorkeling was not easy under any circumstances, and in a rough sea it was brutal. In heavy waves, the snorkel pipe, twenty-four inches in diameter, was constantly going under. To prevent taking in water, the pipe was equipped with a sensor-operated valve; when the sensors got wet, the valve slammed shut. But the diesel engines needed air, and when the outside supply was cut they suddenly sucked at the oxygen in the boat. Inside the hull the pressure changed dramatically. Ears popped in and out. Those who tried to sleep while the boat was snorkeling were awakened by a sudden bang accompanied by pressure and pain. Eardrums could break.

But when you were down for a long time with no snorkel it was worse. After twenty-four hours the air starts to go foul. Stay down thirty-six and you can't light a cigarette. Forty-eight hours and people begin to suffer badly—each movement becomes an immense energy-draining labor. During World War Two when submarines were under depth-charge attack, they would stop all the equipment, seal the boat, and attempt to outlast the attack.

Some years into my career I experienced something near that, as executive officer of a boat that was on a reconnaissance mission off the Soviet coast. We had been in the area for several days, and although we were unaware of it, Soviet units had detected our presence. We decided to take our patrol close into shore just as they were sending ships after us. Nearing the beach, we saw through the periscope a division of frigates steaming out to sea, or so we thought. In reality they were searching for us.

It seemed a marvelous opportunity to take some close-up pictures, and we quickly worked out an intercept course. Coming within several hundred yards of one of the lead ships, we took one photo after another through the special camera-equipped periscope lens. As we got set for the last exposure, the sonar operator reported that he had picked up a sonar in search mode. Snapping the shot, I heard him announce, "They've locked on us." In the periscope the captain saw the frigates veer around and come bearing down.

A moment later we were going deep at high speed. Diving hard, we heard the sonar operator say with great calm, "Torpedoes in the water." On reviewing it later, we thought the chances were that he had not heard torpedoes but anti-torpedo gear that the lead frigate had dropped into the water. But at the time we were sure they were firing. Moments later, as we were evading, an electric explosion rocked the port motor and fire broke out in the maneuvering room.

The fire was soon smothered, but the port motor was out of commission, which meant we had lost half our propulsion. Above us we could hear what sounded like a significant portion of the Soviet Navy searching. Slowly we inched our way toward the open sea. In the early years of the Cold War, submarines from both sides commonly tried to get close to each other's shoreline, probing and reconnoitering. When a probe was discovered, the enemy submarine would be hunted until his batteries were exhausted and he was driven to the surface. Those involved in this cat-and-mouse game were never sure what the result might be. If a submarine surfaced out at sea, the chances were that he and his pursuers would exchange signals and go on their ways. But if a sub came up inside territorial waters, the consequences might be very different.

Inside the ship we prepared to destroy our documents and equipment. Not knowing how long we might have to stay submerged, we cut down all activity to save oxygen and conserve the batteries. There was no cooking, no smoking, nothing that would consume energy or air. Those not on watch were ordered into their bunks.

For the next two days we maneuvered at very slow speed seven hundred feet below the dragnet, the oxygen inside the sub slowly depleting. To replenish the batteries, we rose in the dead of night to poke our snorkel through the surface, only to retract it and sink down again after twenty minutes. In daytime we remained at depth. There was a limit, we knew, to how long we could keep this up.

After forty-eight hours we had put considerable distance between ourselves and the shoreline. For a while we were unable to hear the searchers' sonar and it began to seem that we had lost them. Finally we surfaced, to find ourselves alone on the open sea. We made some temporary repairs to the damaged motor; but when we dove, it shorted out again. Crippled, we limped toward home on the surface.

As was common in the Navy, my early sea duty was interspersed with tours ashore. In 1950, after my first tour of submarining, I was appointed personal aide to the head of the Atlantic submarine fleet at New London, Connecticut. Rear Admiral Stuart S. Murray, the commander, had led submarine divisions in the Pacific during World War Two. He had been on the retreat from the Philippines to Australia and had finished the war as captain of the battleship *Missouri,* on whose deck the Japanese had signed the final surrender. Admiral Murray was a nephew of Alfalfa Bill Murray, a famous character and former governor of Oklahoma. (It was said that Alfalfa Bill's voice was so loud and so profane it astonished politicians.) But where the old governor had been caustic and cantankerous, S. S. Murray was so considerate and cheerful that he was known throughout the Navy as "Sunshine." He was one of the kindest, most gracious men I had ever met; he stood out. In those days kindness was not a trait too many admirals favored.

Admiral Murray's successor was more to type. George Clifford Crawford was not one of the kindest men I had ever met. In contrast to the gracious Sunshine Murray, he was a stickler for protocol with an old-fashioned quarterdeck disposition. Skinny, with a prominent Adam's apple, he was known far and wide as "Turkey Neck." Crawford was a hard customer with a first-rate reputation from the war, where he had commanded a submarine division in action. He knew what he was doing, but he had a short fuse. His motto seemed to be Never Apologize. (Shortly after his arrival he flunked the entire base after giving its hundred-plus buildings a white-glove inspection. For three days personnel had nowhere to eat on base because he had closed down the mess hall.)

I had at that time the pleasure of being mess treasurer, a job that was always fobbed off on the most junior member of the staff. So in addition to being Crawford's aide I was now also his man in the staff mess hall, and among the deficiencies Crawford found in New London was the staff mess service; it was too sloppy. "I want banquet service," he declared. So I checked out all the etiquette books I could find in the New London public library and I mustered the stewards to explain how we were going to do things. I read to them out of Emily Post, then sat there while they practiced their "banquet service" skills on me. Knives, forks, spoons, linen, food presentation, all of it precisely according to the most demanding society standards. The Navy stewards had more or less been trained in that sort of thing. But they had never taken it seriously themselves, nor had they ever met anybody who did, especially in the submarine corps, a notoriously loose outfit.

Among the officers there was a substantial amount of glee over my discomfiture as mess treasurer. My brother officers, especially the younger ones, knew I was struggling with this "banquet service" etiquette, and they knew that I was not exactly qualified by background or inclination for the job of instructing anyone in the finer points of table manners. One day when we were right in the middle of this ordeal, a fish lunch was being served in the officers' mess. As the stewards served the fish, I was watching nervously, sure that something dire would erupt any moment and wondering what it would be this time. As I looked on, the admiral stared at his piece of fish, then said in his usual less than delicate tones, "Where's the ketchup?" "Sir," said the steward, turning white, "we don't have any ketchup." "Goddammit!" roared the admiral. "I want ketchup!"

With that the steward went running out of the kitchen to find some ketchup. As he passed my end of the table I held him back and whispered, "On a tray, on a linen napkin, in a saucer, just right—

understand?'' He nodded, then disappeared into the kitchen. Two minutes later he was back, walking in his best pseudo-butlerlike manner carrying a tray in one hand. In the middle of the tray was a white napkin, in the middle of the napkin was a saucer, and on the saucer was—I could hardly believe my eyes—a bottle of ketchup. I thought the admiral was going to have cardiac arrest; I was sure I would.

Whatever his rough edges, Crawford was imbued with the Navy ethos—the ingrained mores and tenets of this culture I too had wholeheartedly thrown myself into. For him, as for other Navy men, the United States was above all an island nation whose role in world affairs depended on maintaining a strong Navy. Not many officers had actually read Alfred Thayer Mahan,* but the entire corps enthusiastically agreed with his conviction that the Navy was America's "first line of defense." Nor was it clear to them why everyone else didn't think so too, or why the Navy might not be number one in defense expenditures. "Neptune was God," as Secretary of War Henry Stimson had put it, bemoaning Mahan's influence (and viewing the Navy through jaundiced Army eyes). "Mahan was his prophet, and the one true church was the U.S. Navy."

The conviction also reigned that the Navy was beleaguered, that the Army and Air Force were constantly trying to diminish their seagoing rival. That was why the Navy had traditionally fought against "jointness" (the current term for interservice cooperation). Not that any healthy naval officer felt a sense of inferiority. On the contrary, we were sure that we were better educated and more stringently selected than our peers in the other services. In our perhaps prejudiced view, we believed that our own profession was the most demanding, that the sea was a harsher master than either land or air. Even naval aviators thought so. After all, operating from a carrier was the most difficult of aviation feats. And what other service could boast anything similar to submarining?

We were intensely proud of our victories and heroes. The Navy's battle legacy was Manila and Midway, Mobile Bay, Leyte Gulf, and other equally glorious engagements. Its pantheon sparkled with heroes like Jones, Decatur, Farragut, Nimitz, Halsey, and Spruance. It can be easy to denigrate the significance of history, tradition, and common ideals, but these were the elements that inspired my generation to serve, to fight, and to die if necessary.

---

* The great nineteenth-century proponent of naval power. It's been said that Mahan was the most quoted and least read author of his day.

But despite the fascination with the sea that I shared with all my colleagues (and the conviction that if a man could successfully command a ship he could handle any job in the world), I also heard some kind of inner voice telling me there was something more I ought to be doing. In particular, I had the distinct feeling that my education was unfinished, that somehow I ought to get back to school.

As a result, I applied for postgraduate training, an opportunity the Navy made available to a certain number of officers each year. To be accepted I needed the approval of my commanding officer, but Admiral Crawford thought my intentions verged on lunacy. A young man, he believed, should be at sea. Why would anyone want to be anywhere else? Certainly he didn't. "What in the world do you want to do that for?" he said. "You don't really want me to sign this. It'll ruin your career." Then he took the Naval Academy Register out of his desk. As I stood there, he went through his entire class, pointing out with a triumphant laugh those who had gone to graduate school and what failures they had turned out to be. "This guy's retired," he said, "that guy's been passed over, this one's out in the middle of the Pacific doing nothing, that one's sitting around in Panama. They've all had postgraduate training. Just look at them! Are you sure this is something you want to do?"

Crawford's attitude toward education wasn't his alone. The fact was that the seagoing Navy of that day did not think the classroom was a proper place for a naval officer. What good would postgraduate training do a Navy man, unless perhaps it was in some relevant engineering field? More education wouldn't help you do your job better, and it certainly wouldn't advance your career. Few officers on promotion boards had advanced degrees, or thought much of them. But I wanted it anyway. I had been imbued by my father with the conviction that the more education the better, and I was not about to accept Admiral Crawford's opinion on the subject, whatever cogency it might have had in terms of my naval career.

With his reluctant signature on my application, I put in for the law school program and was accepted at Yale. But three weeks before the semester began, Congress deleted the funding, and instead of going to New Haven I found myself on the U.S.S. *Clamagore* based at Key West, a diesel submarine on which I was to spend the next year and a half.

I had been attached to the *Clamagore* for fifteen months when I got word that my father had had a heart attack. With the ship about to leave for Portsmouth, New Hampshire, I immediately took leave and flew back to Oklahoma to be with him. It was on that trip that a friend introduced me to Shirley Grennell, a stewardess with American Airlines who lived in Tulsa and flew back and forth between Oklahoma and New York City. When it was clear my father was out of danger, I flew to Washington, D.C., where I had left my car, then drove frantically to New York to meet Shirley's flight and spend a couple of hours with her before I had to rejoin the ship. Two weeks later I invited her to the Army-Navy game in Philadelphia, where I proposed. I had no doubt whatsoever that she was the person I wanted to spend my life with, and it seemed to me the most wonderful luck imaginable that she felt the same way.

Shirley's grandparents had come to Oklahoma in 1900 and settled in a sod house ninety miles northwest of Oklahoma City in a tiny community named Okeene. Both her parents were raised there, and her father eventually served as Okeene's mayor. Later he was elected state representative, then senator, a Republican at a time when there were only four Republicans in the Oklahoma Senate. While I was growing up, it was hard to find a Republican anywhere in Oklahoma—my father's conversion in 1940 had stunned neighbors and family alike. Until I met Shirley I had considered that having had a grandfather with the wisdom to make the great 1889 Oklahoma Land Run was the best thing that had ever happened to me. Suddenly that circumstance ranked a distinct second.

Shirley and I spent the next two and a half months meeting in New York City. Then in February 1954 I flew back home, met her parents, and was married twenty-four hours later—on St. Valentine's Day. For a while we set up house in Portsmouth, New Hampshire, then the ship returned to Key West, where we lived in a pink "Bahama" house. If the termites ever quit holding hands, I told her, the place would fall down. That June I was ordered to shore duty again—as assistant to the naval aide to President Dwight Eisenhower—and with that we packed our bags for Washington, D.C., for what would be the first of many postings in that exciting and unusual town.

Chapter 2

WHAT ARE
WE DOING
ABOUT AFRICA?

THE JOB OF NAVAL AIDE to the President has since disappeared. But in 1954 the President had three military aides, from the Army, Air Force, and the Navy. The Air Force aide flew the presidential airplane. The Army aide handled communications. The naval aide ran Camp David and the White House mess, along with the boats on the Potomac and any other jobs he could appropriate in the eternal Washington race to garner turf.

Commander Edward L. Beach was the naval aide when I arrived. Ned Beach had graduated number-two man in his Academy class, and during the war had been one of the fleet's youngest submarine commanders. (He would later command the *Triton* on the first undersea circumnavigation.) A writer as well as an officer, he had already achieved national fame for his best-selling novel about the submarine corps, *Run Silent, Run Deep*. Smart and aggressive, Beach managed to get hold of all kinds of miscellaneous jobs around the White House. But the position did not begin to challenge his many talents, and like his Army and Air Force counterparts he spent time trying to look busy. As Beach's assistant, I had to look even busier.

Because the job was not overly demanding, I found I was able to enroll at George Washington University Law School at night. (My father was a lawyer, and the profession had attracted me for years.) Even if Yale wasn't in my future, I was still intent on pursuing graduate studies. Five nights a week I went to class. During the day I worked at the White House, where my main job was being in charge of the White House bomb shelter, one of the many responsibilities Ned Beach had collected for the Navy. As the officer in charge of the bomb shelter I had a place I could disappear to when nothing was going on. There I could study undisturbed, then walk to the GW Law School when the day was over.

This was the early atomic era, the time when children were being taught to sit in school hallways with their heads between their legs and words like "epicenter" and "megaton" entered the household vocabulary. Civil defense had suddenly become a high-priority subject, especially in Washington, D.C., the nation's ground zero. All over town people were building bomb shelters, stocking emergency supplies in their basements, and generally preparing for the worst. As commander-in-chief of the White House bomb shelter, I was by definition the leading authority on shelters (a month earlier I had never heard of them). And as Washington's resident expert I got a stream of calls. "Lieutenant Crowe, would you please come over and tell us how to get ready for the attack. Will you tell us how we should build our bomb shelter? What should we have in it? What can we leave out?" Almost every day I was running around town advising people about bomb shelters, which in fact I knew very little about.

One night during the height of this bomb scare period I was at home. In our apartment I had a special phone connected directly to the White House. It had never rung since I started the job, and either Shirley or I had stashed it out of the way under a chair somewhere. All of a sudden this phone started ringing, and I went down on my hands and knees trying to dig it out from behind an accumulation of other things. When I finally answered it, Commander Beach was on the line. In guarded tones he said, "I think you'd better get down here." "O.K.," I said, "but why?" "I just think you'd better come in." Beach's voice was tense. "This is the real thing." With a rush of anxiety I realized he was talking about the atomic bomb.

Driving in to the White House from our apartment in Alexandria, I was thinking the whole time, Here I've been running around preaching that people should have food and flashlights and that they should know where to go. And I've just left Shirley in the apartment without a car, without food, without a flashlight, and it's started.

The moment I got to the White House I went down to the bomb shelter, where I found Beach, a taut, worried look on his face. "We've had an FBI report," he started, "that atomic bombs have been placed in Baltimore, Washington, Philadelphia, and New York City. They are going to be set off at eight o'clock." "That's very interesting," I said. "Do you believe it?" "No, I don't," he answered. "Neither does the President. I reported it to him and he laughed. He doesn't give it any credence at all. He's over at the Hilton Hotel making a speech. It just seemed to me,'' Beach went on, "that we would look awfully foolish if something actually did happen and nobody was here." So he and I sat in the bomb shelter until eight o'clock.

Though President Eisenhower did not take the report seriously, the FBI did; and while Beach was skeptical, he did not completely dismiss it either. Supposedly, Puerto Rican nationalists had stolen several bombs (this was just four years after several nationalists had shot up Blair House in an attempt to assassinate Harry Truman). Later I met an FBI agent who was part of a squad frantically searching suspected apartments in New York. "I was looking for a nuclear device," he told me, "and I had never even seen a picture of such a thing. If they had had one in the bedroom I wouldn't have recognized it." At eight-fifteen, Beach looked at me. We were both still there. "Well," he said, glancing at his watch, "I guess we can go home now."

Despite my job's lack of substance, I found working in the White House an adventure. It was exciting to learn the special mores and procedures of the place and to see Eisenhower on occasion. My duties took me all over Washington, so in addition to the White House I came to know many of the other government offices in the city. I was getting my first exposure to Washington's political life. I learned what an effort it is to get the President off on a trip, how complicated and costly the security and communications and other advance arrangements are. I learned to be careful of the White House secretaries, who fed off their bosses' reputations and patrolled their turf even more ferociously than the military aides.

I also got my first glimpse at the vastness of the governmental apparatus. Even from my modest perch in the White House basement, it was apparent that the fundamental challenge in Washington was to get the various pieces of this huge machine to function together. The notion grew in me that doing that kind of work would be a challenge—utterly different from the world of the submarine officer, with its focus on engineering problems and handling crewmen. Clearly, getting involved in government would require a kind of expertise that a submarine career was not likely to provide. For reasons I did not quite understand, I found myself thinking more and more about how one might acquire that kind of experience. From where I stood, education seemed the key. Graduate school (as I had learned from Admiral Crawford) did not necessarily fit in with the

Navy's expectations of what a young submarine officer ought to be doing. But school was the obvious avenue to a different set of horizons, and surely the Navy's needs went beyond seagoing and warfighting.

Commander Beach agreed that the Navy should have experts outside of the traditional naval categories (on this question he belonged to a distinct minority), and he encouraged me when I started looking into opportunities to further my education. I was already enrolled in night law school, but the only full-time graduate program the Navy had available at the time led to a master's degree in personnel administration at Stanford University, so with Beach's endorsement I applied and was accepted. It turned out to be a wonderful year. Shirley and I both loved Palo Alto and the San Francisco area, and Stanford was such an impressive place that I came away thinking I might like to go back there one day to teach.

More importantly, the program gave me the chance to read widely in group dynamics, sociology, and psychology, and showed me that at the age of thirty I was still capable of competing in an academic environment. Equally significant was the exposure to the civilian faculty and students. It was an education in itself to see how civilians viewed my profession. At first many of my classmates and professors seemed to share a suspicious, stereotypical view of the military that featured aggressiveness, mental rigidity, and benighted political convictions. I became convinced during that year that not only was it healthy for a military officer to live among his critics, but that everyday contacts seemed to moderate both parties' views.

To insure that I had not been permanently warped by academia, when I was finished at Stanford the Navy ordered me back to sea as the executive officer of the U.S.S. *Wahoo* in Pearl Harbor. I spent the next two years aboard ship serving under two fine captains, Lieutenant Commander Hank Hanssen and Lieutenant Commander Chuck Griffiths, both of them Midwesterners with a distinct talent for leadership.

Chuck Griffiths was an especially unusual teacher, so confident and clear about his role that he was able to break through one of the significant problems of Navy training. The highly competitive promotional system that pervades the service by and large produces able senior officers. But it also has its problems, one of which is the pressure to always perform at maximum efficiency. For ship captains this often creates an unfortunate conflict between the need to demonstrate their abilities and their role as teachers. The question every commander faces is whether he should perform the difficult procedures himself and show his ship to best advantage or concentrate on fostering the skills of his junior officers—with the inevitable mistakes and lower competition grades that will mean.

Griffiths, who eventually became vice admiral and senior officer of the submarine corps, knew that teaching was a commander's most significant peacetime function and never worried about what he disdainfully referred to as "cheap nonsense." A staunch advocate of learning through doing, he taught his juniors, myself among them, by allowing them to take responsibility. Even with his squadron or division commander aboard observing the *Wahoo*'s operations, Griffiths would say, "My third officer will be shooting the torpedoes today," or "My fourth officer will be bringing the ship into dock." That approach had a deep effect on subordinates, not only in helping them hone their skills but in demonstrating how a truly outstanding captain approaches his work. The lesson stuck when I became a submarine captain myself and later when as a division commander I had the job of grading commanding officers.

In the fall of 1958 an opening came up in Washington for personal aide to the deputy chief of Naval Operations for Plans, Policy and Operations, Vice Admiral Bernard Austin. I jumped at the opportunity. Plans and Policy (in Pentagon shorthand, OP 06) handled all the Navy's political-military relations with other branches of government—Defense, State, the Joint Chiefs of Staff, and the National Security Council. While yet another stint as a personal aide was not appealing, duty on the CNO's staff overcame any hesitation I might have had. Though I knew little about the plans and policy business, I was more than willing to learn. As it turned out, the appointment set me off on what was to become a rather unusual career path.

Austin, my new boss, was from an aristocratic South Carolina family, well-to-do and very courtly (his service nickname was "The Count"). His responsibilities fascinated me from the start. In his office you could observe at first hand how the Navy interacted with other elements of the Defense Department and other branches of government, how it fought with them and compromised and communicated and coordinated. Inside the Pentagon, the Navy was not a military force but a political animal, existing and striving in a landscape inhabited by other political animals.

In OP 06 you could also see the Navy participate in the world of international politics. One day, alarmed by something he had read in the newspaper, Austin came sailing out of his office up to the desk of his executive assistant, Captain Chuck Nace. "Chuck," he said, "what are we doing about Africa?" "Nothing," said Nace, and I breathed a sigh of relief. Till that moment I hadn't realized that Africa was any of our business. It never occurred to me that I should be concerned about that continent. The interchange had a certain humor to it, but what I really couldn't get out of my mind was the fact that my boss considered the whole globe his canvas.

In Austin's office I had my first opportunity to observe the workings of high command—even though it was from a seat in the back row. I watched Admiral Arleigh Burke, the Chief of Naval Operations (CNO); observed at second hand the Navy's dealings with the Joint Chiefs of Staff; saw the battle between the Navy and the Air Force over the Polaris missile submarine up close. Time and again the Navy was forced to fight for its future, and the decisions were made in Washington, not at sea. Who carried the day depended on who could best muster data, organize a case, and prevail in arguments with scientists, politicians, budgeteers, congressmen, and the other services. An officer's sea record did not impress such audiences; his ability to convince did.

Later, when I was a submarine captain, I was at a party in Charleston with a friend of mine, a division commander and lifelong submariner himself. A spirited argument started about some policy that Admiral Burke was having difficulties with, and in the middle of it I said, "You know, we do it all wrong." "What do you mean?" my friend asked. "Well, what we really should have as Chief of Naval Operations is not a Navy man at all. What we need is a good lawyer." "What?" He wasn't sure he had heard me properly. "That's right," I went on, aware the room had grown suddenly quiet. "The biggest things that happen in the Navy are winning the battles in JCS, the Secretary of Defense's office, the White House, and Congress. We have to convince all these people; otherwise we lose. What we need is a lawyer, preferably a New York lawyer." (I had never met a New York lawyer, but I had been given to believe they were the best.) "He doesn't have to know a lot about the Navy, he has to know how to win arguments."

My friend was furious. "You can't be serious," he said. "A lawyer! The worst people in the world, for Godsake. They don't know anything about us. They have no appreciation for what we do." "That may be true," I said. "But a lot of people who have a deep appreciation for what we do go up to Washington, and the Air Force ends up getting the money. I really think we ought to hire a professional advocate. If you want a Navy man, we can put a hat and a coat with some stripes on him." You could hear a pin drop. Everyone in the place was listening to this exchange, some I'm sure chortling to themselves at the idea of putting an admiral's hat with scrambled eggs on a lawyer, others horrified at what they were hearing.

Although I was exaggerating for effect, in fact I was not on such flimsy ground. What I was really saying, of course, was not that the Navy should go out and hire a CNO, but that we should train naval officers to be advocates, because the large peacetime decisions are made in dialogue, debate, and argument. That was true in 1960 and it is even more true today. That is the reason Colin Powell is such an effective Chairman. He may know nothing at all about the newest tanks (or he may know a great deal about them; it doesn't matter). He is a strong advocate with a sure understanding of the bureaucracy, both civilian and military, and that is the talent that makes him a tremendous asset to the services he represents.

When I left Austin's office it was to take command of the U.S.S. *Trout*, the Navy's newest diesel submarine—an appointment Chuck Nace had been instrumental in helping me get. Nuclear submarines were beginning to come along, but since I was not in the nuclear program this was a first-rate assignment.

I was exhilarated about receiving command of the *Trout*. The meaning of life for most Navy men is to go to sea, and the goal of 98 percent of young officers is command. That is what they aspire to, and despite my growing interest in the political-military world, that was my aspiration as well.

I couldn't help conveying my feelings to Austin. He himself had held many commands: a submarine, two destroyers during World War Two, a famous destroyer division in Arleigh Burke's "Little Beaver" squadron. "That's just wonderful," he said, after listening to me go on a bit. "But you'll discover that after you've had one command they're generally all alike and there isn't much more to learn. If you have seven commands it's like having one command seven times." God, I thought, what a statement! Heresy. How could a man of his talent and background say such a thing?

Whatever the truth of Austin's comment, an officer's first command is a high point. A young man receiving his orders to command can taste the excitement. Life seems free and intense and charged with purpose. There was a time in the Navy when a captain was truly an autonomous ruler, a king in his realm. Once he lost sight of land, he was literally on his own; nobody heard from him for months at a time.* Space-age communications have relegated that era to history, but a ship commander still takes his organization away from the rest of the world. He enjoys a sense of authority that few other people ever experience.

"The *Harder,* the *Darter,* the *Trigger,* the *Trout*/Always in and never out." Out of drydock, that is. They laid that to the *Trout* and her sister ships because they had been built around a lightweight high-speed engine that seldom worked properly. By the time I took command, though, the problem had been resolved—by cutting the ships in half, lengthening them eight feet, fitting a different engine in, then welding them up. Home port was Charleston, South Carolina, which gave Shirley and me our first brush with the Old South. In the early 1960s it sometimes seemed that Charleston was still fighting the Civil War; certainly nobody I met there ever admitted the North had won. As Oklahomans, Shirley and I were more or less neutral on the subject, but before we knew it our young children (three of them already: Blake, Brent, and Bambi) were talking to us in rich Southern drawls.

The *Trout* was blessed with an unusually capable and high-spirited crew who referred to themselves as the "Trout Tigers" and performed ferociously in every contest, even winning the squadron "E" (for excellence) at the end of my first year. Almost all the crew (except for a few grizzled chiefs) were young and cocky. It never occurred to any of them that someone from another ship might be better at something—not the training competitions, the deployments, the ball games, the charity drives, or anything else in the fiercely competitive atmosphere of the submarine force.

The *Trout*'s officers also shared an unusual closeness, though the bonds that tie submarine officers together are almost always tightly drawn. Every single day they worked together in close quarters and sat across the tiny wardroom table from each other. Even when the *Trout* was in port it was those same six or seven families that made up our officers' world. They did not finish work and go home to a different set of friends and neighbors. Instead the wardroom families

---

* In nuclear submarines today something of that still persists. Nuclear subs can receive messages from home, but the shore-based commanders don't hear from them unless they want a response, and something very unusual has to happen for that to occur. Submarines stay submerged for months, and ideally they never talk. They go out, accomplish their mission, and return without ever having communicated a single word.

constituted a closed circle. They ate at each other's houses, relaxed together, cared for each other, and supported each other. Their lives were knit together in a way most people never experience.

The ship had tremendous esprit, and pride was, in fact, one of the secrets of running subs successfully. As captain I did whatever I could to instill confidence and enthusiasm; in a sense that was my primary job. The executive officer ran the everyday business of the ship and the CO worried about how to make the crew better, how to raise and keep the morale up, how to take care of his people and make them feel good about what they were doing.

Under two superb executive officers, Bill Shaughnessy (who had stood first in his Annapolis class), then Bob King, we patrolled the Caribbean and the Atlantic Coast from Key West to Halifax. For almost two years we managed to avoid a major overhaul and spent most of our time at sea, sharpening our teamwork and skills, training, training, and training some more. It was hard work but never tedious. The days were filled; time disappeared. In good weather we'd steam on the surface through the morning, then make a dive to trim the ship, be down half an hour, steam some more, then make a midafternoon dive. On a diesel sub, once you have mastered the mechanics, life does not have to be stressful.

By the same token, though, the intellectual challenges on a diesel sub are limited. In the end you run out of them. The primary goal of junior officers on board diesels is to learn every single piece of equipment—where it is, what it does, how it might break, how to fix it. They keep huge notebooks, studying to qualify on everything, which they have to do to earn their "dolphins." At first that seems a prodigious task. But in time they master it. An experienced submariner acquires the impression (unusual in other walks of life) that he can know everything there is to know. For a captain, administrative and management problems are also limited. Like other sub skippers, I came to know my eighty-man crew as well as I knew the mechanics of my ship. Few things happened on the *Trout* that I was not aware of.

In 1962, after I had been on board for a year and a half, I noticed in the Navy's annual announcement of available graduate school opportunities that candidates would be considered for doctorates in the social sciences. This had never been done before. A master's degree was required. Application was by letter, and selected candidates would receive full tuition.

Although my master's was in personnel administration, I was particularly interested in international relations (a legacy of my tour in OP 06), so I wrote to Admiral Austin for a recommendation. Some months later I received notification that I was in contention, and some months after that, another letter announcing my acceptance. The Navy would support my studies at any institution that would have me.

I interviewed first at Yale, with the head of the graduate admissions committee, a world renowned expert in civic administration. But for some reason this brilliant man had the hardest time getting through his head what the Navy connection was. "Tell me again," he said. "You're in the Navy now?" (I wasn't in uniform.) "And you're on a ship now?" "Yes sir, I am." (I was still captain of the *Trout.*) "Let me get this straight. The Navy is going to put a ship out here in the harbor in New Haven? And you're going to live on it?" I couldn't imagine what he was thinking. "Well," he said, "you know our admissions are already closed for the year." "Yes, I know that," I answered, "but I've just now been accepted into the program and I'm doing the best I can." "I'm sorry." He shook his head as if still trying to understand what the United States Navy had to do with all of this. "I just don't see how we can admit you. I'm sorry."

Princeton treated my application very differently. They had been teaching Army graduate students for years (General Andrew Goodpaster was one of their graduates), and they had had an Air Force officer or two. But they had never had anyone from the Navy. I interviewed with Professor Edward Furness, who told me from the outset, "We understand what you want to do and we'd like to have you here. We think it's a fine opportunity for you and for us as well. Consider yourself admitted."

I couldn't wait for the summer to pass and classes to begin. I did not know precisely what I wanted to focus on, but I did know that it made sense to be as general as possible, so that afterwards I would be "detailable" anywhere. I had no desire to be pegged ever after as a specialist in some narrow area to which I would be confined for the rest of my career. I wanted to come out of Princeton with enough of a broad-based background so that I could go in any direction (which turned out to be wise, because sure enough, though most of my studies in graduate school concerned Europe, directly afterward I was sent to the Pacific and spent the next ten years working on Asian affairs).

Shortly after I had been accepted, I got a call from the submarine detail desk at the Bureau of Personnel. Admiral Hyman Rickover wanted me to come to Washington for an interview. I had applied to Rickover's nuclear submarine program almost a decade earlier. Several members of my class had been among the first officers in the program, but I had never been asked to join, nor had I ever received an encouraging response. By the time 1962 rolled around, the program had been under way ten years. We had a few nuclear subs at sea and quite a few people in the nuclear training program. My class alone had already contributed fifteen or twenty officers. Nuclear submarines were considered the cutting edge. For a submariner who wanted to succeed there was no place else to be. I had wanted it for a long time.

But now? Why does this have to happen, I thought, just when I have the opportunity to do something else I wanted to do so very badly? I talked it over with Shirley and asked her, "What if I go down there to Washington and they tell me they want me in the program?" And she said, "Then you tell them no. You don't want to go into the nuclear program, you want to go to school."

Most of the other people I talked to felt differently. My submarine squadron commander was adamant. "You have no choice," he said. "You can't turn down this chance. Every submarine officer wants to be in the nuclear program. Everybody in that program, Bill, their lives are going to be wonderful. They're all going to make flag and they're all going to go to heaven." And that was the general feeling among submarine people.

Of course, I had no assurance that I was going to be selected by Rickover; he had only asked me to come to talk. But I thought that I shouldn't go unless I was prepared to accept an offer—if he asked. I labored over the decision for four or five days, then I called up the detail officer and said I couldn't in good conscience come in. If I came up there I would just have to say that I had decided to go to graduate school. "That's horrible," he said. "You can't do this! You're a submarine officer." "Well, I appreciate how you feel," I said, "but it's my life and my career, and this is my interest. The Navy's given me another good opportunity, and I don't think it would be fair to either Admiral Rickover or myself to come to Washington. So thank you very much." "He won't like this at all," said the officer. "Well, he's had ten years to invite me and he just picked the wrong time. If he had invited me last year I'd be up there in a heartbeat. But he's waited too long." "O.K.," said the voice on the other end, "but I'm telling you he's not going to like it."

All that first year at Princeton I got feedback about Rickover from friends and acquaintances, all of it on the same theme: Boy, he really didn't like that. It was really dumb to do that. But that wasn't the end of it. The following spring, when I was well into my studies and enjoying them immensely, I got another call from the Bureau of Personnel telling me, "We want you down here next Thursday for an interview with Admiral Rickover." I said, "I thought we went all through this last year." "Yes we did," replied the desk officer, "but last year it was permissive, this year it's mandatory. Rickover's got a whole list of lieutenant commanders and he won't interview any of them until you come. If you don't come he doesn't go any further down the list." (That was vintage Rickover.) "So whether you like it or not, you are coming down here Thursday."

On the appointed day I got into my car and drove to Washington. I was interviewed by several of Rickover's subordinates first, then after sitting around until midafternoon I was finally ushered into the great man's presence. Rickover had a terrifying reputation. He was feared and disliked throughout the service—which he attributed to anti-Semitism (with more than a little justification). But he was also exceptionally cranky. Despite his brilliance, he had had a very hard time in the Navy and had early on become an engineering specialist or what was called an EDO—engineering duty only officer. He had gone to graduate school in electrical engineering, and when he came out he became a ship constructor. For a long time he labored in the vineyards fairly anonymously, though even in the Bureau of Ships he had developed a reputation as somebody who was extremely difficult.

Then all of a sudden he found a cause that turned him into one of the Navy's most public figures. In the late 1940s Rickover espoused nuclear propulsion, and with his forceful personality and iron will he drove that idea through the Bureau of Ships against powerful opposition. He fathered the nuclear program, and never afterward relinquished the slightest authority over it. He controlled the admission of candidates to his program personally.

My interview with Rickover started poorly, then deteriorated. He asked me first about my education, then told me he hated the Navy's doctoral graduate program; doctorates in social sciences especially made him sick. After that he said he also hated people who had been aides to admirals (I had been aide to three of them) and he gave me the business about that for a while. He verbally beat me up in every direction, and my experience in his office was in no way unique. Rickover's interviews were infamous. If you didn't happen to fit into one of the categories he hated, then he invented one you did fit into.

The whole purpose of a Rickover interview was to upset you. He didn't care how, as long as he did it. Ostensibly he did it to see how the interviewee would react, to judge his level of self-control. But some thought that was a rationalization, that in fact he enjoyed the outrageous browbeatings he gave people. Without question he carried a great deal of emotional baggage around with him.

At one point in our interview Rickover said, "Listen, if I accept you today, would that be okay? Would you take it?" And I said, "Well, Admiral, I wouldn't. I'd love to be in the nuclear submarine program, and just as soon as I finish my graduate studies I'd like very much to be accepted." "When will that be?" "Two years, sir." "What? Two years from now?" He got up and started storming around his office. "You stupid bastard! The very nerve of you to come in here and tell me that! You expect me to accept you and not come into the program for two years? Get out!"

I took the hint and sat in the waiting room for a while, then was told to go back in. When I was standing in front of him again he attacked me some more for not being a loyal submarine officer. I said, "Admiral, I understand how you feel about it, and I'm sorry. When I went into this program I had to make some tough choices and I think that what I'm doing up there is important enough to finish. I also think it will benefit the Navy as well."

"Goddammit!" he snarled. "A PhD isn't worth anything. Who gives a damn about a PhD? You just want something to secure your civilian existence. You're just looking to get out of the Navy, that's what you're doing." Then he threw me out of his office for the last time. I was one of five people Rickover interviewed that day. The only other one he turned down was Harry Train, who was several years behind me in the Naval Academy but was a great success there and afterwards. Harry eventually retired as a four-star admiral after serving as Commander-in-Chief, Atlantic. Harry and I shared at least two distinctions. We both made four stars and we were both rejected by Rickover.

When I left Rickover's office I was distraught. My prospects for a submarine career suddenly looked dismal, and I did not know how that would affect my Navy career as a whole. Most of my Navy friends agreed. There was no place else to go. I wasn't an aviator and it was too late to move to surface ships, so maybe it really was over.

In 1963 no nuclear submariners had yet made admiral; the program was still too young. But everyone assumed that with so many talented people in Rickover's program, before long they would take a disproportionate share of the admiral slots. But the Navy's non-submariners had their own opinion about that, and they didn't give a damn about Rickover. We don't care how many hotshots you have collected, they said. You represent 10 percent of the Navy, you get 10 percent of the flag (admiral) openings. As a result, when the nuclear program matured, only a small percentage of submariners who were up for admiral made it, which was a great loss to the service, because many of those who didn't were exceptionally able people. But the Navy was not going to let a sliver of the service rule the entire organization, not even a sliver led by someone as fierce and determined as Hyman Rickover.

Rickover, however, did maintain unchallenged control over who got into nuclear submarines, a qualitatively different kind of control than anyone else in the Navy exercised. Rickover had lobbied hard and had persuaded Congress to pass a law making the civilian Atomic Energy Commission responsible for the safety of the Navy's nuclear power plants. Then he succeeded in having himself named as head of the AEC's division of naval reactors. As a result, he wore two hats, a civilian hat and a Navy one. Once he had accomplished this, he informed the Navy that no one would be allowed aboard those submarines unless he said so. When the Navy's leaders told him that wasn't the way they did business, they learned that in his civilian hat he had the statutory authority to do exactly that. Rickover had outflanked them.

But Rickover could not impose his will on the promotion boards, which were also controlled by statute. Once the doors closed on a selection process, nobody went in the room. Even Rickover himself was not selected for admiral by the boards, but the nuclear submarine publicity had brought him into national prominence, and when the nominations came to the President's desk Truman said, "Where's Rickover's name?" When he was told that Rickover had not been selected, Truman said, "The hell he hasn't. I'm selecting him." And his subsequent promotions were mandated by Congress, not the Navy.

Interviewing with Rickover had been a wrenching experience for me in more than one way. Suddenly I had been snatched out of my new world of Princeton and was back in my old world, where everything revolved around submarines and the only thing worth doing in life was going to sea. From Princeton to Washington was only a few hours' drive. But psychologically and intellectually the distance was

vast, and while I was deeply attached to the submariner's life I had
led for a decade, I was now in the grip of something new.

The department that had accepted me at Princeton was called
"Politics," the university's name for political science, including international relations. I was even more attracted to history, but a
degree in that field would have taken at least one and possibly two
years longer, and I knew that even the three or four years minimum
I would need in Politics would seriously test the Navy's patience.

The Politics department at Princeton was headed by Professor
Harold Sprout, who was, coincidentally, a specialist in naval history
and policy. Harold Sprout became my adviser and sponsor, and
before long a friend. Although he had written extensively on the
Navy, I was the first Navy student he had ever had, and we developed a productive relationship from the very beginning.

I was a somewhat different graduate student in several ways.
There were only sixteen of us in my class, everyone other than
myself on scholarship. At age thirty-seven I was by far the eldest. I
also lived in a rented house. Our graduate group always had our
parties at my house, because Shirley and I were the only ones who
lived so grandly—that is, we had an unfinished basement that was
relatively immune to beer spills. I even drew a salary, a fact that left
my classmates in a state of wonder.

My fifteen fellow students were among the brightest people I had
met. A young man by the name of John Saul, from Canada, was the
quickest of the lot, but he didn't have the writing talents of Len
Miller, from Kansas, who could contemplate an assignment for a
week, then sit down and type out a finished draft. I had never seen
anything like that; I still haven't. Perhaps the most intriguing was a
boy named Rosenfeld, who had a long Russian first name and looked
like an anarchist. Painfully skinny, he always sported two or three
days' growth of beard. He not only looked like a radical, he was a
radical; his politics were extreme. He had gone to Columbia in math-
ematics, graduated with honors, proceeded through Columbia medical school, entered practice, then decided that medicine was too
crass. Now he had turned to political science. He was an expert
cellist as well and seemed always to be lugging around his cello case,
which looked like just the sort of thing a dedicated anarchist might
carry a large bomb in. For the first six months he didn't know I was
in the Navy, then when he found out he didn't speak to me for
weeks. He was infuriated. He had thought I was a friend, then I
turned out to be a commander. After a while we became friendly

again, but he had a hard time admitting to himself that he was the kind of person who could be friends with someone in the pay of the American military.

The intellectual atmosphere at Princeton was dramatically new to me. The university had gathered a dazzling constellation of scholars, and I was able to study with a number of them: Harry Eckstein in comparative government, Leon Gordenker in international organizations, James Billington (the current Librarian of Congress) on the Soviet Union. I audited courses with Marion Levy, one of the country's foremost sociologists, and George Kennan, who had just come back from Yugoslavia. These were people with superb intellects and the ability to conceptualize in a nuanced fashion, which I had never before encountered.

From an intellectual standpoint, Princeton was a world-shaking experience. It fundamentally changed my approach to life. The basic thrust of the curriculum was to give students an appreciation of how complex and diverse various political systems and issues are. The stress was not so much on political events as on fitting events into a theoretical structure and thereby developing a useful general understanding. The bottom line was that answers had to be sought in terms of the shifting relationships of groups and individuals, that politics pervades all human activity, a truth not to be condemned but appreciated and put to use.

This was a profound and at times unsettling change for a young man who had spent his professional life in the Navy. On a ship the world is compartmentalized and structured; decisions may be hard, but facts are most often clear. The Navy has a characteristic approach to life: Here, it says to its initiates, is a finite problem, and here is how to solve this finite problem. Repeated often enough, that approach tends to engender a cast of mind. Most Navy officers are engineers who can be marvelously creative in solving engineering problems and designing or redesigning operating procedures. If they have a problem they will get down on their hands and knees in the grease with a wrench and rearrange a piping layout or improvise an imaginative mechanical solution. But these very same people will go out and vote exactly the way their grandfathers did, because that's the way they voted. While in their professional sphere they will demonstrate a sometimes astonishing versatility and innovativeness, they tend to make an intuitive distinction between these matters and broader issues.

Clearly the Navy is more than a job; it is a way of life, a culture (as all the services are). And the culture captures its members, it encapsulates them. But that does not mean it is necessary to buy everything the Navy sells. Princeton forced me to become more analytical and more tolerant than I had previously been. It challenged me to reassess some of my more conventional and ingrained Navy views. It was one of the things that set me somewhat apart from many of my colleagues, that at times made my career so tenuous, but that also lifted it up. I became more willing to question, to reexamine, to argue for alternatives. Occasionally Navy friends would come through Princeton and spend the night. Inevitably we would discuss some of my courses, and more than once they left shaking their heads sadly over my transformation into a raving liberal. The next day I might venture the same opinion in class only to hear Rosenfeld sneeringly refer to me as Genghis Khan.

By 1964 I had finished my course work and had passed my oral qualifying exams. In previous years Harold Sprout had encouraged several Army officers to do their dissertations on the British Army and British Ministry of Defense. He suggested I write mine on some aspect of the Royal Navy.

The Bureau of Personnel thought about this and decided they would give me "permissive orders," which meant they would allow me to go, but they would not pay for it. Shirley and I took our savings out of the bank to buy tickets for ourselves and our children, and to sublet a flat in London. My dissertation topic was "The Political Roots of the Modern Royal Navy." In all I interviewed over a hundred people, former sea lords, naval officers, Admiralty civil servants, even Lord Mountbatten.

Almost everyone I approached was friendly and forthcoming. One who was not was the official historian of the Royal Navy, Stephen Roskill. When I wrote asking for an interview, he answered with an arch letter to the effect that my subject, the contemporary Navy, was not appropriate for a dissertation, and my work must be a sham since it was evident no serious university would sponsor such a thing. I had never met the man, and I was amazed to receive such a message from him.

Shortly afterward I was interviewing former First Sea Lord Caspar John, an old sea dog with huge bristling eyebrows. When I told him about the letter, he snorted and shook his jowls. "Get me a copy of that," he said. "I'll take care of it." A few days later I received the meekest note from the historian inviting me to meet with him, which I did, and had a useful interview too. Caspar John told me later that the historian hadn't really meant anything by the letter, it was just that he was a former Royal Navy captain who had hated Americans since World War Two because of Admiral Ernest King (the American CNO during the war). "You shouldn't let that bother you in the least," John said. "All of us hated Americans because of Ernest King."

I was in England for about five months. For learning about the British people, the Royal Navy, and British politics, it had been a priceless opportunity. I reveled in it, and so did Shirley and the children. Coming back to put my thoughts in order, though, was not a joy. One of my friends at Princeton told me that completing a dissertation is not an intellectual exercise but a moral exercise, and that is true. Above all it does test your determination.

While I was struggling to finish I was also wondering what might actually come of me, assuming that I did. It was now 1965 and I had worn my uniform twice in the last three years. Given what had happened with Rickover, I did not know how many bridges I had actually burned. And if I could not go back to submarines, where could I go? It was not clear to me how the Navy would react to a maverick with a PhD or how they would put my education to use. In terms of keeping my career alive, I knew it was imperative to fill a command billet, if only to keep the conventional channels open. I was just completing three of the most intense, productive years of my life, but the future looked anything but certain.

Chapter 3

REMEMBER
THE *PUEBLO*

DESPITE MY ANXIETY, the Navy did not seem to overtly acknowledge that any problem existed. (Of course, the unofficial rumor circuit had written me off.) After my three years away from duty, the Bureau of Personnel simply assigned me to a higher level submarine job—chief of staff to Commander, Submarine Squadron Three in San Diego—just as they would have if I had never been to graduate school and never incurred Rickover's wrath. In fact, my Rickover encounter was well known, but in the diesel submarine community a nuclear-power turndown was not unique. Some even considered it a badge of honor. The only sign that I had ever been away from the force was some good-natured ribbing, especially from my new boss, Captain Jack Bennett, who insisted on introducing me to one and all as "Dr. Crowe . . . but I wouldn't trust him with a Band-Aid."

At the end of the year I was promoted to command of Division 31, which (in a touch of irony) included two nuclear submarines, *Permit* and *Snook*.* *Snook*'s skipper was Jim Watkins, a young commander who was clearly a comer. Even then his evaluation ("fitness") reports were saying that he was four-star material. Watkins eventually rose to become Chief of Naval Operations and, after his retirement, Secretary of Energy. When I was Chairman, I once told him that I didn't know how he had done so well, considering that the fitness reports I had given him were in his record. "Oh, those," he shot back. "I had those destroyed when I was chief of the Bureau of Personnel."

Division 31 concentrated on anti-submarine operations, exploring the limits of nuclear-powered performance and perfecting our hunt-

---

* U.S. submarines were traditionally named for fish. But during World War Two we had built over 250 of them, and by 1964 only the more arcane fish species were still unclaimed. It took an ichthyologist to recognize some of the ship names.

ing and evading techniques. In tactical situations, what chiefly distinguished nuclear subs from diesels was their ability to maintain high speeds underwater. A diesel sub might sustain seventeen knots for forty-five minutes, but that would drain the batteries so badly that it would have to surface. An early nuke could stay at twenty or twenty-five knots indefinitely.

At high speeds, though, nuclear boats made so much noise that it was difficult to use their own sonar. The higher the speed the less the boat could hear, and the better the enemy could hear her. We had to determine which speeds allowed us to listen and which wouldn't, which would keep our noise level sufficiently low and which generated too much noise. The equations were complex and had never been tested. To work out the most effective procedures, the division's boats exercised against each other constantly.

We practiced tracking, in both nuclear subs and diesels, and we worked out tactics for losing a tracker. To do this it was not sufficient to simply go to high speed and run away. If the tail was a nuke he could go just as fast, and at high speed he could hear you at great distances. Instead we learned to run in bursts, then go quiet and evade. We had never before had submarines with these capabilities, and we experimented incessantly, learning and developing doctrine.

We also practiced dogfighting. Two attack submarines would close, each trying to pick the other up and get off a shot before the other realized he was detected. This often led to high-speed maneuvering very close in as each sub worked to get into firing position while avoiding his opponent. To prevent accidents the boats were assigned different depths, but everyone knew how difficult it was to maintain depth while putting one of these 5,000-ton ships into a hard turn. Sonar would track the other boat as it closed in. Then suddenly you would hear "Close aboard! Close aboard!" and a roar like a railroad train in a tunnel as your adversary passed just overhead.

In regular training exercises the boats would change both course and depth at speed, a delicate maneuver that required great skill. The control surfaces were so sensitive that at twenty-five knots a nuclear attack sub could change depth two hundred feet in a matter of seconds, almost before the conning officer knew what had happened. If the ship was near maximum depth to begin with, it could quickly find itself in trouble.*

Once we developed doctrine for nuclear operations, it became part

---

* The Navy may well have lost a submarine to exactly this kind of accident, though we never knew for sure. Underseas accidents are notoriously difficult to reconstruct.

of the submarine force's operating repertoire. Every boat utilized it as it went out to keep track of the Soviets. In this game, American submarines held a long-standing advantage. Our sonar was more advanced, and our quieting efforts far more successful. Compared to the Soviet nuclear subs, our propeller, shaft, and engine noise levels were muted, almost silent. Early on we established a decisive edge that we never afterward relinquished.

As division commander, I rode the boats regularly and participated in these pioneering efforts to build tactical doctrine. It was exciting work, but I knew that this job was my last hurrah in the submarine force. In the competition for promotions, the separate naval communities—surface, aviation, and submarine—dominate the process. But my background was in diesels and by this time they were a dying breed—dinosaurs, so to speak. Because I had not been accepted for nuclear training, I could not look to the submarine community for support, and a community sponsor is crucial if an officer wants eventually to make admiral. In earlier times a submariner could simply shift over to surface ships. But now the surface community was getting irritated at the rapid growth of the undersea force. Submarines were no longer an appendage to the surface fleet; they had come into their own as a partner, and a rival. The new reality was that anyone who changed over would probably knock a competing surface officer out of the running for promotions, so the welcome mat for wayward submarine sailors had been withdrawn.

I might, I thought, make captain, but after that my prospects were not good. The only way I might go beyond this in the Navy would be through my education. If there was anything that distinguished me, that was it. So I had to play to my strength. It was hardly the normal career pattern, but I had chosen long ago to be a maverick—what else was new?

As my San Diego tour wound down, I made inquiries through some friends in the Pentagon about an assignment to OP 61, the Navy's political-military branch, which I had observed firsthand when I worked for Admiral Austin. One of the main shops under the deputy chief for Plans, Policy and Operations, OP 61 included sections for each region in the world. It was also the office which sponsored graduate education in international affairs, so on both counts I was drawn to it. When orders came through assigning me to head the East Asian desk (which dealt with the entire Pacific region), I was ecstatic. My academic training had more to do with Europe, but this was close enough for government work.

Career people are ambivalent about the Pentagon, widely known as the "Puzzle Palace." (A Navy saying has it that "any duty outside the Beltway is great duty.") Many younger officers find their way there directly from the excitement of a sea command. Just yesterday they were giving orders on the bridge and suddenly they are sitting in a cubbyhole with a hierarchy over them so heavy it makes their heads ache. They had been free spirits, and now they live in the suburbs and commute to work, creeping through the rush hour traffic and staying late at the office. It can have a depressing effect.

Twenty-three thousand people work in the Pentagon's neoutilitarian rabbit warren of drab offices. The building has seventeen and a half miles of corridors. Architects who have studied it insist that a person can walk between any two locations in seven minutes, a statement that blithely assumes such a person knows where he or she is going. It is, to say the least, a hectic and confusing environment.

Nevertheless, the building is the nerve center for all the armed services. The operations and message rooms function around the clock. Roughly 116,000 messages come into the Pentagon from every part of the world each night, to be routed, read, and acted on. It is the one place where a determined and talented officer can develop a solution to a problem, shepherd it through the bureaucracy, and see it directly influence actions around the globe. If you land a "good" job, it is possible to truly lose yourself in it. You even begin to like your cozy office and the constant motion and frenzy around you. The building throbs with excitement, and in time it begins to exert a mysterious pull, though few will admit that, even to themselves.

OP 61 was a high-pressure, fast-paced shop. Working with complex international issues and dealing regularly with the State Department, we were involved with a constant stream of crises. Many of the people we worked with in other government agencies were experienced foreign affairs professionals. While that could not be said of OP 61 personnel, they were nevertheless a handpicked group, bright and quick studies. A few even had graduate degrees and the number was increasing every year. My own office, the East Asian Division (OP 612), consisted of four or five people, always working at full stretch on issues that were frequently of immediate interest to those above us.

Like Janus, OP 61 faced two directions. Meeting with State and other civilian agencies, we were advocates for the Navy position, which often was rigid and took little account of political imperatives. Facing the other direction, we made great efforts to educate our bosses about the views of outside organizations—often more sophisticated than our own positions. It was a tough act, with lots of opportunity to either impress or alienate our superiors.

I had not been there very long when I submitted a paper suggesting the Navy take some particular course of action that diverged from the standard approach. When my immediate boss, the four-stripe deputy director of OP 61, read it, he called me into his office and exploded. "For Chrissake," he said, "we didn't send you to Princeton so you could come back and tell us how to run the Navy. We sent you up there to learn how to argue for the things we want back here, not to listen to what you think are original ideas. We're not going to do a single one of the things you've got in here." Twenty-three years later I cannot even remember the subject of that paper, but whatever it was, the Navy wasn't going to do it. I had been sent away to learn how to write and express myself; nothing more was required, or wanted.

Perhaps because the graduate social science program was in its infancy, that gentleman (and many of his peers) had not realized that once the Navy started sending people to graduate school they were going to come back with new ideas (some sound, some impractical), and they were going to insist on a hearing. Today we send many officers for advanced education, and they do shake things up. They do not simply accept the standard hidebound ways. That's why we do it. But at the time, those shortsighted comments seemed to confirm my underlying fears—perhaps I had, as so many people had told me, made a ruinous mistake by going to Princeton. Though the Navy's old-time anti-intellectual biases were slowly dying, in some quarters they still retained a firm hold.

The head of Plans and Policy in 1968 was Vice Admiral Francis "Champ" Blouin, a former Naval Academy boxing champion (hence the nickname) who had spent his life as a surface officer but had picked up some political-military experience along the way. In the early days of Vietnam he had worked in the office of the Secretary of Defense and had made a number of trips to Saigon, where he had been when South Vietnam's President Ngo Dinh Diem was assassinated. Given the time he had spent in Vietnam, Champ had considerable knowledge about the American involvement in that country.

One day Blouin called me in and said, "You know, the North Vietnamese are blatantly violating the Geneva Accords. I don't think everybody understands what the Accords are, what they require, and what those people are doing. So I want you to write a paper that will describe the agreement, its history, and how it is being flouted."

I assigned the research for this paper to Dick Knott, a serious and thoughtful staffer. But the more he and I looked into it, the clearer it became that while the North Vietnamese were indeed violating the agreement, they were not the only ones. The United States had never actually signed the 1954 Accords, but we had pledged ourselves not to use force to disturb their provisions, and the fact was that in various ways we had not lived up to that commitment. In the end Knott and I wrote what we considered a balanced paper. Our conclusion was that though the Geneva Accords had temporarily resolved the war between France and Ho Chi Minh's Vietminh revolutionaries, neither Hanoi nor Saigon had intended to adhere to them at the time, and subsequently they had broken down. The North Vietnamese had done this and this and this, which were indeed blatant breaches, and as Saigon's ally the United States had done that and that and that. Then we submitted it.

Admiral Blouin erupted when he saw the paper. It was almost as if we had set fire to the flag in his office. The very idea that the United States might not be abiding by the Accords was unacceptable. He ripped me up and down, and the more he thought about it, the more it occurred to him that I might not be the only one in need of straightening out. The attitude this paper expressed might be prevalent in the whole organization. With that in mind he called a meeting of the entire Plans and Policy staff, which was quite rare. (Dick Knott and I took a certain amount of pride that we had precipitated the only 06-wide meeting in our time.) Blouin got up and talked about Vietnam to make sure that everyone was squared away on the subject, that we all knew the difference between the good guys and the bad guys and which side was which. The admiral never mentioned the East Asia desk, but everyone in the room knew who the culprits were who had brought the wrath down on the entire outfit. Knott and I became individuals of distinction. (To Admiral Blouin's credit, he never mentioned the incident again, nor did he hold it against me. We subsequently became fast friends and suffered through some thorny problems together.)

In fact, fourteen years had passed since the Geneva Accords, and they had long since ceased to be of anything but historical interest. But the tempest graphically illustrated the staff officer's dilemma (particularly the officer with graduate training). I was not about to write a puff piece maintaining that the United States was blameless. Nor was I going to alter the world or history to make sure they fitted with the Navy's naive views. Going to my immediate superior in OP 61, I said, "Look, Blouin's given me an impossible job. Whatever he thinks, the fact of the matter is he's wrong. If you want analyses and projections, we'll give them to you, but I'm not going to change facts just so they read comfortably." My boss, a two-star, was not sympathetic. Our job was to satisfy the guy above us. "I understand your problem," he said, "but I can tell you that I'm not part of your solution."

After this I knew without a doubt that Princeton had indeed changed something fundamental inside me. I was now serving two masters. I still had ingrained in me those Navy mores, views, and criteria that constituted the service culture. But every time I wrote a paper I found myself thinking, What would Professor Sprout think of this? How would the academic people in the field judge this piece of work? I was a career naval officer, yet I unexpectedly found that I now also owed allegiance to a canon other than the Navy's.

In OP 612 I had six officers working with me at one time or another, including Jim Elster, a young lieutenant commander who possessed one of the finest minds for the political-military business I had come across. Our lives in the shop were spent writing papers that addressed every issue that concerned the Navy in the Far East. We briefed our superiors about problems in the region and we tried to foresee developments which would impact American interests. I took several trips to East Asia, and at one point I escorted the Korean Minister of Defense around the United States. Our department supported negotiations to renew the Philippines base agreement, participated heavily in the return of Okinawa to the Japanese, and wrote a series of think pieces on the Micronesian Trust Territories.

Although much of this work had an urgency to it, OP 612 was only one small part of a giant Navy bureaucracy in which each shop fed a paper stream that flowed topside. By the time a proposal or analysis reached a decision maker, individual contributions were usually unrecognizable. It was rare for an important issue to emerge that cast a spotlight on particular people in the trenches—although all the workers were always hoping for such an eventuality. Our own light emerged from under the proverbial bushel at the beginning of 1968 when the *Pueblo* affair suddenly lit up the horizon.

The U.S.S. *Pueblo* was a light cargo ship which had been converted into an intelligence-gathering vessel. On January 23, 1968, *Pueblo* was cruising off North Korea on a listening mission (she had run similar patrols previously). Her captain, Commander Lloyd Bucher, had strict orders not to penetrate North Korean territorial waters. Just before noon the *Pueblo*'s officer of the deck noticed a North Korean submarine chaser approaching at high speed. A few minutes later the sub chaser was joined by several patrol boats, which surrounded the intelligence ship and signaled her to follow. When Commander Bucher headed out to sea instead, the North Korean ships opened fire with machine guns and cannon. Within minutes one American crewman lay dead and several others were bleeding from serious wounds. When the defenseless *Pueblo* hove to, a North Korean boarding party took control and sailed the ship into the port at Wonsan.

While these events were taking place, only the sketchiest information was coming into the Navy's operations center in the Pentagon. (It would be almost a year before the crew was released and the *Pueblo*'s capture could be fully reconstructed.) At my desk in the Plans and Policy section, the information was even skimpier. It was not until the next day that I learned the details, those few that were known. The *Pueblo*'s radioman had been in contact with the ship's shore base in Japan reporting the attack. The crew was destroying the intelligence manuals and codes, the radioman had said. But he was talking from his little radio office, and no one knew how far they had gotten before the Koreans boarded. A panicky message had come in from Bucher himself saying, "I've been shot in the anus." That was the last we had heard.

What was clear was that the American reaction was confused and indecisive. At first no one seemed to know what the *Pueblo* was, or even that an American ship was in those waters. (The intelligence command that was running *Pueblo* knew, but they had not widely shared that information.) When the carrier nearest *Pueblo*, the U.S.S. *Enterprise*, finally received a message about *Pueblo*'s plight, the group commander had hesitated to launch planes. He wanted more information. Throughout the Far East, commanders groped for facts and took no action. Nothing about the response was impressive, and the upshot was that no help arrived. Once the North Koreans had captured the ship, it was not clear what the planes might have done even if they had been able to reach the scene.

As it became obvious that this was going to be a political crisis for the Navy, my shop was dragged into the problem. I was just then about to leave on a round-the-world trip, but that was hastily cancelled. Predictably, the incident provoked a storm in the U.S. Congress, which wanted all the facts immediately and leveled volleys of hot criticism at the Navy. Congressmen and senators wanted to know why Bucher had not done this or that. But although we were beginning to flesh out the incident, we still did not know most of the answers—even to the critical question of whether the *Pueblo* had been inside North Korean territorial waters when she was attacked. I answered almost a thousand congressional letters on behalf of the Navy staff, often surmising and extrapolating from flimsy evidence. And each answer needed the approval of a dozen people in the Secretary of Defense's office, so worried was everyone about the political fallout. I also acted as the Navy's liaison with the State Department and sat in on meetings to consider the U.S. response to the North Koreans.

What response to make was on everybody's mind. In Lyndon Johnson's White House, economic penalties were considered, and there was talk of launching a military strike. But all the options were tempered by the fact that the North Koreans were holding the crew. Ultimately President Johnson made the decision to respond through diplomatic means. At that point the focus of the problem shifted from how to react to how to get the crew back. The fact that Washington had no formal relations with Pyongyang complicated matters. But before long, lines of communication had been established and negotiations commenced, although it was apparent from the start that the North Koreans were going to prove obstinate about returning their prisoners.

When these talks got under way, Vice Chief of Naval Operations Admiral Bernard Clarey decided that the Navy should draft a plan for repatriating the crew, whenever that might take place. American POWs in Vietnam were already a powerful issue, and against that background Clarey knew the return of the *Pueblo*'s crew from captivity would strike a particularly emotional chord. He wanted it to be done right. Initially Clarey assigned reponsibility to the Bureau of Personnel, but the bureau's plans brought a host of objections from other organizations that wanted to handle the release themselves.

The Bureau of Personnel wanted badly to make a show out of the repatriation in order to demonstrate that the Navy knew how to take care of its people. They wanted to transport all the families to San Diego to greet the crew, putting everybody up in hotels while the returnees were being medically examined, debriefed, and counseled. Essentially they were planning a hero's welcome.

When the Navy's legal specialists heard this, they were appalled.

From the beginning they had been concerned that Commander Bucher might actually have disobeyed orders and intentionally sailed into North Korean territorial waters. No one knew for sure if that had happened, but as soon as the incident took place we began examining Bucher's background, and the more we looked the more uneasy we became. Among his colleagues Bucher was reputed to be something of a cowboy; it was not completely implausible that he had sailed in closer than he should have to better monitor Korean transmissions. If it turned out that a man had been killed and several wounded as a result of Bucher's direct disobedience of orders, the Navy would have to take legal action. Beyond that we did not have the slightest idea if any of the crew might have acted improperly in captivity, giving away information, for example. But several elements of the Bureau of Personnel's repatriation plan were likely to jeopardize our ability to prosecute, and the legal people refused to go along with it.

We also had concerns about the *Pueblo*'s lack of resistance. The crew had not, for example, steamed away and forced the North Koreans to make a decision about sinking them. They had not put the engines out of commission, which would have forced their captors to tow them in (and would also have provided more time to mount a rescue mission). We suspected that the ship had not even destroyed all its codes and intelligence publications, which turned out to be the case. There were many unknowns.

For this reason, the intelligence people were adamant that they should be in charge of repatriation. We were dealing with a potential intelligence catastrophe, and they wanted the crew isolated from all outside contact until a thorough debriefing could be completed. This was a rather extreme option, directly at odds with the desires of both the legal and personnel departments. Nor were the medical spokesmen happy with the intelligence position. They too were now insisting on having first crack at the crew. After all, the hostages were living in North Korean prisons and quite possibly being subjected to physical and mental abuse in addition to disease and nutritional deficiencies.

Meanwhile the State Department had also injected itself into the fray. Early in the game Secretary of State Dean Rusk had declared that the *Pueblo* had not violated territorial waters. If Bucher was in fact going to confirm that, they wanted him to do it on television without delay, regardless of how a public statement might affect subsequent prosecution or anything else. (I wrote a long memorandum to the Secretary of the Navy describing how such a statement might jeopardize our ability to take legal action.) Public Affairs agreed wholeheartedly with State: Bucher should be put on television immediately (provided he was going to say the right things), but they did not want the release occurring late in the day when a press conference would miss "prime time." I had a hard time crediting this requirement, but Public Affairs was dead serious. Moreover, in the end they prevailed (which says something about where the real power resides in the Pentagon).

Clarey's attempts to mediate among the parties met with scant success. Loud arguments flared between organizations espousing irreconcilable positions. I had been sitting in on these meetings, more or less enjoying all the internecine conflict, since my shop was not directly involved. But after one particularly testy exchange between the personnel and intelligence people, a very frustrated Admiral Clarey suddenly turned to me and said, "You do it, Bill. You're the only one here who doesn't have a vested interest in the outcome. You write the plan."

Actually, I had listened carefully to the arguments, and while I did not think the task would be pleasant, I did believe that compromises were available and that we could resolve the problems before too long. A year later I was still working on it and looking back at my initial assessment with some wonderment.

We drafted the repatriation plan in my office, coordinating with all the interested parties, whose number grew until it sometimes seemed that every single organization in Washington was determined to have the final voice. Ordinarily, the Joint Chiefs would not have allowed the Navy to run a matter of this magnitude by itself, but this was such a hot potato that they opted out. From my harassed perspective it even appeared that they took a certain perverse pleasure in watching the various agencies beat the Navy up and send me back to the drawing board time and again.

Reconciling these quarreling wildcats was a painful process, but slowly we began making progress. One after another the main problems yielded when someone would come up with an imaginative approach, which I would then incorporate in appropriate language, then massage a dozen times until everybody could live with it.

In the process of moving toward a final version, I briefed the plan all over Washington. The National Security Council, Secretary of Defense Robert McNamara, and Secretary of State Dean Rusk were all interested. I saw Undersecretary of the Navy Charles Baird frequently, and was often on CNO Thomas Moorer's calendar. Concern about how the *Pueblo* affair would be resolved started off high and remained high. There were regular flurries of excitement when it seemed the crew might be released, then hopes would be dashed when negotiations hit yet another snag. Widespread public sympathy was reflected in Congress, where key representatives and senators expressed their concern for the captives' welfare. For almost a year the *Pueblo* remained a hot issue. It was not until December that the North Koreans finally agreed to release the hostages.

Curiously enough, agreement with the North Koreans on releasing the crew was accomplished through a strange piece of stageplay. In the government's early councils, many negotiating suggestions had been rejected as being too farfetched. One of these was based on the fact that despite worldwide publicity, the North Korean government had told their own people nothing other than their own version of the affair. With access to information so tightly controlled, the North Korean people were completely ignorant of any other side of the story. Since that was so, the suggestion was that our negotiators could say to the North Koreans, If it will help you with your own people, we will admit Bucher penetrated North Korean waters. You can use that in your domestic news releases. Then you give us the crew, and afterwards we will deny to the world press that we penetrated. That concept had originally been rejected out of hand by our planners, who did not believe that even the cynical North Koreans would ever buy such a two-faced concept.

But when months went by and nothing had worked, the American side resurrected this scheme. The North Koreans were told that for purposes of their domestic consumption we would admit the violation, then after they returned the crew we would deny it. Amazingly, the North Korean negotiators said that sounded reasonable, and the two sides reached agreement. The American admission of guilt appeared on North Korean television. The crew was released. Then denials were made for the world press—which of course were not shown on North Korean TV. To this day I am not sure the North Korean people know the true story.

In the end, with all the jockeying over who would actually control the repatriation procedure, Public Affairs was given the job. But in the course of bringing the planning together, a major problem developed over how to ask Bucher whether he did or did not violate North Korean waters. It turned out that if we so much as asked the question outside of the appropriate legal context, we would jeopardize any subsequent prosecution. On the other hand, if Bucher himself volunteered the information, a case against him would not be tainted.

The details of how we were going to get that information were worked out with great care. The man who actually had operational command at Friendship Bridge between North and South Korea when Bucher was turned over was Deputy Assistant Secretary of Defense for Public Affairs Richard Fryklund, a veteran reporter who was then in government. The plan was that Fryklund would greet Bucher, take him into a car, and begin a conversation. His object was not to ask Bucher anything specific, but simply to get him talking in the hope that he might voluntarily reveal what we needed to know. Bucher was known to be voluble, and sure enough shortly after he got into the car he started baring his soul. Within five minutes he said, "You know, we didn't go inside their waters at all; they came out after us." Fryklund put him right in front of the television cameras and with no coaching Bucher said all the things we wanted him to say.

The crew followed Bucher out and were flown to Clark Air Force Base in the Philippines for preliminary physicals and initial processing. Then they were transferred to San Diego. The families were also brought to San Diego, where the Navy put them up and allowed them a short time with their loved ones before the crew was removed to the Navy hospital for a week of medical examinations and tests. Once this stage was completed, they were isolated for several days of intensive intelligence debriefings. All of this was done under the supervision of Navy lawyers, with the hope of keeping the legal slate clear.

Even before the crew returned to San Diego, rumors had been circulating about torture and beatings by the North Koreans. As a result, President Johnson had announced that each member of the crew would be examined carefully for signs of maltreatment. If there had been any, Johnson declared, the North Koreans would be held responsible and we would take appropriate action.

Johnson had coordinated his announcement with CNO Thomas Moorer, and shortly after the crew was released he called Moorer and asked how the investigation into maltreatment was going. Moorer answered, "I'll have to look into it, Mr. President," knowing full well that there was no investigation under way yet. A minute later my phone rang with a frantic message for me to see the CNO immediately.

When I walked into Moorer's office, he described the call he had just received from the President. "What are we doing, anything?" "Not as yet," I told him. "Well, we've got to do something about it now. I told the President we'd have results at the end of next week." "Fine," I said. "I hope it's possible." "No, no," he said, "you don't understand. *You* are going to do the investigation." "What do you mean?" I said. (I had been working seven days a week on the repatriation as it was.) "I mean *you're* going to do it, and you're going to have the results for me by the end of next week. You can take anybody on the staff you want, but I want you to fly to San Diego, find out what happened to that crew, and be back in my office by Friday morning with a report."

I picked an attorney I had been dealing with, a young OP 61 commander named Bill Lynch—a wonderful wit and lawyer. Then I got hold of Lieutenant Don Hackett, who had done a fascinating intelligence study of the *Pueblo*'s activities just prior to her capture. (Hackett had been able to deduce quite a bit of information during the year and was fairly convinced that *Pueblo* had not penetrated Korean waters.) With these two and two yeomen I climbed on a plane the next day and flew to San Diego.

On Sunday evening I met with the crew, all of whom were in the Balboa Naval Hospital, and explained what we would be doing. The next morning we began interviewing, but none of the first five sailors we talked to would answer a single question; their lawyers had told them to say nothing. Oh boy, I thought, imagining President Johnson on the phone with Admiral Moorer asking about the report, we're not going to get anywhere like this. Calling Moorer's office, I told his assistant that we had a real problem. "These guys," I said, "have all got Navy lawyers who've advised them to keep their mouths shut."

By two o'clock that afternoon the entire crew of lawyers had been relieved and a new batch assigned. In addition, the district legal officer was personally supervising this new team. The lawyers were still expected to defend their clients properly, but they did point out to them that there were certain things they could talk about without endangering themselves.

The next morning we started in again. First the district legal officer gave a briefing in which he informed the crew members that whatever information came out in their talks with me would not be available to any future legal proceeding. When he was finished I confirmed what he had said, and assured them that nothing I heard would be used outside of my own investigation. I gave them my word on it.

At that point an older enlisted man stood up and said, "I don't give a damn about any of this. This crew is shot through with guilt. If there is anything we can do to make North Korea accountable, I'm going to try and help. I'll be the first one, so please question me."

That broke the dam. After that almost everybody started talking. It turned out the North Koreans really had maltreated the crew badly, and some of the members were bona fide heroes. One was a first-class quartermaster named Charles Law, a big strong man who had stood up to the questioning and given his interrogators nothing but defiance. He said nothing, even when they beat him bloody with a two-by-four. He even managed to get the North Koreans' wrath transferred to him from several other crew members. He was an exceptionally courageous man. The executive officer was another pillar of strength, but some weren't. There were four or five people, including an officer, whose conduct in prison was suspect. On advice of their lawyers they would not talk to me, and I never saw Bucher either; he was being treated for pneumonia at the time. But we did interview everyone else, and by Thursday we had gathered more than enough information to put together a report on North Korean abuses.

On Thursday night, Bill Lynch, the yeomen, and I caught the red-eye special (Hackett had left earlier), where we set up shop with a typewriter in a first-class row of seats we had gotten special permission to reserve. While Lynch and I talked from one side of the aisle, the yeomen took notes and pounded away on the typewriter they had unlimbered on the tray between their seats. We finished the report just before the plane landed at Dulles, then drove right over to my office to type up a clean copy. At nine o'clock we briefed Admiral Moorer on it. The report caused such a stir that I was called over to the White House to make another briefing to one of the President's assistants. The report was handed in to President Johnson on Saturday, but that was the last that was heard of it. Despite Johnson's promise to hold the North Koreans responsible, nothing was ever done. The fact was, of course, that there was precious little we could do. We did have good identification of the people who had tortured the crew though, by name, in case we were ever in the position to take action. But the report itself died a quiet death.

•   •   •

Several weeks later the Navy court of inquiry which was to examine the conduct of Commander Bucher got under way. The planning I had done on repatriation included everything up to an inquiry, but it stopped there in order not to impose on the court, which was by law protected from outside interference. Besides, five admirals were sitting as judges, and the consensus was that a high-level group like this would not need any hand-holding or play-by-play direction.

But while the admirals may have had a lot of experience, they were not quick to grasp that this would not be a normal court of inquiry. Bucher was by now a public figure and the subject of intense media interest. Moreover, his attorney was Miles Harvey, an astute San Diego trial lawyer who was also a captain in the naval reserve. Harvey knew both the law and the Navy; he also understood implicitly that whatever the Navy might think, this inquiry was going to be a national event and that congressional and public opinion were going to play a role.

The admirals were no match. Within forty-eight hours Harvey had persuaded them to agree to several motions that strengthened Bucher's hand and neatly hogtied the court. Among other things, Harvey won an agreement to permit Bucher to tell his story from beginning to end before being questioned. Then he used Bucher's emotional performance to put his client in a glowing light. It was an impressive display. In essence, Harvey was running the court.

Watching this, the Pentagon was aghast. The general feeling throughout the military was that Bucher deserved a court-martial. Had they been asked their unvarnished sentiments, many naval officers would have said that Bucher should have gone down with his ship. Guns or no guns, the *Pueblo* was a U.S. warship and he should not have given it up without resisting. Certainly not until he had destroyed all his documents, and then he should have destroyed his engines after that.

CNO Tom Moorer's understanding of the case was far more sophisticated. But he knew that if public opinion was in favor of Bucher, once it got rolling the Navy would never be able to do anything, no matter how much he might want to or how justified it might be. What Moorer really wanted was a fair review and fair treatment of Bucher's conduct, and he wanted to put the inquiry in some kind of neutral framework so that those ends could be accomplished. But attorney Harvey was winning decisions and positioning Bucher in just the right public spotlight.

Harvey was playing to a surge of public sympathy that many in the Navy and among the *Pueblo* crew itself did not completely understand. Three months earlier when the crew returned to San Diego they had been worried. They themselves were deeply distressed by their own conduct; on the whole many believed they had not performed well, not only in prison, but on the day of the capture. As far as they could tell, they were coming back to public condemnation. The United States had been humiliated and now, they thought, it would be taken out on them. Moreover, many of the crew believed that that would be just. They had spent a dismal year in prison stewing about their failures that day and about their subsequent conduct, and by the time they came out they were an anxious, dispirited group of men.

But instead of finding shame and disgrace in San Diego, they got off the plane to a hero's welcome—bands were playing, flags were flying, dignitaries lined up to shake their hands. Bucher was feted and people stood up in front of microphones and said unexpected things. It took a few days for the crew to digest the fact that they were not going to suffer further for what had happened. They could not really understand what everyone was talking about, until they put together that the public simply did not know anything about their experience other than what their hearts told them and what they had read in a few laudatory newspaper accounts. In essence the people out there were just good Americans who felt the crew had been mistreated and who wanted to welcome them back home and compensate them in some way for their year in prison.

When the court of inquiry came out with their report, they recommended a court-martial for Bucher. But despite the court's finding, it was obvious to everybody involved in the final decision— chiefly CNO Moorer and Secretary of the Navy John Chafee—that a trial was not in the cards. They had come to the conclusion that the Navy could not take public action against Bucher. While the court of inquiry was meeting, popular opinion had mobilized itself and brought in a verdict. The Navy had been outflanked; whatever the justice of the situation, a court-martial would do more harm than good.

The Navy's deeper concern, though, was not Bucher at all. The real problem was the impact a lack of action would have on the fleet's ship commanders. Regardless of what we did or did not do to Bucher, it was important in some fashion to get across the leadership's views on proper conduct. The CNO had to convey a forceful message to our commanding officers clarifying what was expected of them in light of the *Pueblo*. In a memorandum to Admiral Moorer summarizing this situation, I suggested that after the smoke cleared the CNO write a letter addressed to all commanding officers, spelling out his views on the incident and how it impacted their responsibilities. The main thrust of the letter would be that COs would still be held accountable for their ship's conduct and that the *Pueblo* inquiry had in no way diminished their responsibility. No doubt he received similar recommendations from others, and a short time later this was done.

Without a doubt, a court-martial on specific charges would have unambiguously conveyed the necessary message. But while in the enclosed world of the Navy that might have appeared as a feasible course of action, it was not an option in the real world. A court-martial for Bucher would simply have been unacceptable to the public, no matter how guilty he might have been. For most people, the overriding interpretation would have been that the Navy was looking for a scapegoat. Besides (and this opinion had made itself clearly heard), even if he was guilty, the man had done his penance. He had spent a year in a North Korean prison camp. Why pick on him anymore? So despite the court's recommendations, a court-martial was out.

This was not justice, perhaps, but justice was not the pole around which this event flowed. There was the public consensus; there were the needs of the Navy as a living organization. The conflict was between those two, and political necessity ordained the outcome.

Chapter 4

PERSUADER-IN-CHIEF

AFTER THREE YEARS AT OP 61 the problem of what to do next began breathing down my neck again. By this time I felt quite comfortable in the political-military world and I was aware that my work had been noticed. But a major command (preferably a ship command) was a prerequisite to any future prospects, and the outlook for that was dismal. The submarine force had only second-rate billets available for diesel types, and the surface community was not inclined to offer me any command at all. But one promising development had unexpectedly come up on the radar screen.

It was now 1970, and although the United States was reducing its presence in Vietnam, the war was still in full swing as far as the Navy was concerned—especially now that Elmo Zumwalt had been appointed CNO. Until Zumwalt's elevation the Navy (except for the aviators) had never given Vietnam its full attention. It was not, after all, the Navy's war. Earlier I inquired about an assignment there and the detailer said, "What in the world do you want to do that for? Do you want to ruin your career?"

But prior to his appointment as CNO, Zumwalt had been senior naval officer in Vietnam. While there he had tried to spark the Navy's interest, but with only modest success. As Chief of Naval Operations, though, Zumwalt's influence acquired significantly more weight. He personally encouraged officers to divert from traditional assignments and go to Vietnam. On his initiative the Bureau of Personnel created new incentives for those who did, one of which was to equate the more important posts in Vietnam to "major commands at sea." Not that Zumwalt's efforts completely changed the thinking. When I began considering whether to volunteer, the deputy chief of OP 61 called me in and said, "What do you think you're doing? You know how old you are? [I was almost forty-five.] You don't have to go to Vietnam. That's just Zumwalt up there talking. This is a young man's war. You've got a PhD, and you're in the political-military business. Don't do it.''

I volunteered anyway; I genuinely wanted to go. I had spent my life in an organization that was supposed to fight wars, and I had never experienced one at first hand. The more I thought about it in that light, the more important it became to me. My political-military experience too had been oriented toward the Pacific, and if in the future I was going to find myself analyzing Asian policy I would be far better prepared if I knew Vietnam firsthand. But while I found all of this persuasive, many of my friends didn't. ''That's a lot of trouble to go to,'' said one, ''just to get some more ribbons.'' Another put it more succinctly. ''Bill,'' he said, ''I think you're nuts.''

Of far deeper significance were Shirley's feelings. She knew that I did not have to go, but she also understood my reasons for wanting to. After our first discussion she thought about it for a week, aware that I would not take this step without her support. When we talked it over again she said she thought I ought to go. She did not have to say it, and I was not pressuring her. But her attitude was that I had good reasons for wanting to do it; it was my professional life. I think she reasoned that if I missed Vietnam I would always regret it. ''It will be hard on me and the family,'' she said. (Our children were then fourteen, thirteen, and eleven; they were, to say the least, a handful.) ''But I'll manage that. I don't want you to worry about it.'' I have always marveled at the strength this decision took, at her ability to see what it meant to me, and at her willingness to live with the potential consequences. I told her then, ''It's fine to say all this'' —I was deeply grateful—''but it's conceivable that I may not come back. I may be killed.'' In fact, not too many Navy people were being killed, but I would be in helicopters regularly, and between the Vietcong and the chances of an accident, there was a decent possibility. ''I assume you took that into account when you decided you wanted to go,'' she said. ''I think we both understand what it means. I think you will come back, but you know, every day you went to sea on those submarines I didn't know if you were going to come back.'' She had made a conscious decision to live with these burdens long ago.

Before leaving for Vietnam I was assigned as senior adviser to the Vietnamese Navy, with headquarters in Saigon. But like 90 percent of those who went to Indochina, when I arrived I was given a different job than the one I was slated for. My boss, Vice Admiral Jerry King, who had relieved Zumwalt as the senior naval officer in Vietnam, decided to extend the current adviser's tour and sent me into the Mekong Delta instead. Forty-eight hours later I was living in a godforsaken former French Foreign Legion post at the foot of the U Minh Forest, just outside the village of Camau.

My counterpart there was Captain Nguyen Thong, a hard-bitten career officer whose riverine task force kept the South Vietnamese 21st Division supplied as it fought the Vietcong up and down the mangrove swamps of the U Minh. Thong had been at war most of his life. He was a fighter, a tough, hard man. Most of his sailors were young draftees from Saigon who had to learn on the job, which meant in combat, and he taught them as quickly and effectively as he could. More than once I saw him punch enlisted men and administer other harsh punishments. It took us a long while to become friends, but from the start I knew he was a bona fide warrior who expected no quarter and gave none himself. In time I came to like and admire him.

I traveled all over the region with Thong. Almost every day we were together in a helicopter or on one of his riverboats. The two of us were in a helicopter over the U Minh the day before my forty-fifth birthday when we were either hit by ground fire or had a sudden mechanical failure. Whichever, the compensating bar flew off the aircraft and we started shaking violently. I heard the pilot say, "I don't know if I can get her down. I don't know if she'll stay together." It was really shaking, and I said to myself, I'll never live to be forty-five. The pilot started auto rotating in while the co-pilot was shouting "Mayday! Mayday!" on the circuit. We splashed right into a swamp. The first words out of the co-pilot's mouth were "Oh, shit, I had it on intercom." All his "maydays" had gone into our earphones rather than out over the air.

I learned constantly from Thong and his veterans. They could smell danger, and if a novice had any sense he picked up their body language fast. When they moved off the street in some backwater village, I moved off. Thong could read the villagers, the signs, the atmosphere. My counterparts had been fighting guerrillas so long they just did things instinctively. Like Old West gunfighters, they never sat with their backs to a doorway. They never took the same route twice, never talked on the radio at the same time every day. They always sent their security into a cafe before they entered. They distrusted everybody and were never separated from their weapons. I emulated them. When I climbed into a helicopter I had my paratrooper M-16, a nine-millimeter semi-automatic, a knife, and a small pistol tucked into my boot.

Thong had been putting up with a lot of things, including American advisers, for a long while. But that didn't stop him from being intensely pro-American. He treated advisers warily, particularly when they offered tactical advice (at least until they proved themselves), but he liked U.S. equipment and he appreciated our technical knowledge. He recognized that despite his fighting experience, our people knew a great deal more than his about preventive maintenance and how to keep machinery running. His own recruits had never done anything remotely resembling that kind of work.

The downside was that the Vietnamese developed the habit of letting Americans do it if there were any around. One day when I showed up at a command post deep in the U Minh and went aboard one of our boats, I found an American gunner's mate cleaning the machine guns. Alongside him were the Vietnamese crewmen, fast asleep. I said, "What are you cleaning the guns for?" "Well," he answered, "we're going into the forest tomorrow. We want the guns ready." "What are those guys doing?" I asked, jerking my thumb at the inert forms on the deck. "They don't like to clean guns, sir." "Well, that doesn't have anything to do with it, does it?" "No sir, but they know that if there's an American here he'll do it. You know, sir, when we get on the canals tomorrow they'll be great. They're good fighters and they'll man the guns. But they don't like to clean them." "What if you weren't here?" I said. "Then what'd happen?" "Well, sir, if I weren't here they'd either clean them or they'd die."

I took the gunner's mate off the boat. Then I took all the other Americans off and told Thong that when the boats were alongside the dock we would advise and train, and do whatever we could to help improve his units' capabilities. But I was not going to defeat our whole purpose for being there by doing their jobs for them.

Training Vietnamese was hard, primarily because so much of what they had to be taught went counter to their cultural background. From a sociological standpoint (though not from a military adviser's) the challenge was fascinating. Historically, family loyalties run deepest in Vietnam. Among other things, this meant that when the Army drafted a boy out of the countryside, put him in a unit, and told him, "If anyone shoots at your buddy, you shoot back," he asked, "Why?" Whatever the Army was saying, another voice was telling him that if people were shooting at a stranger, that was the stranger's problem. A fellow recruit was not his brother or his uncle. He wasn't from his hamlet or village. If he got shot at, let him take care of it.

To build the Vietnamese military it was necessary to tear down some of these family and village loyalties and substitute allegiance to the country, something the Saigon government never truly succeeded in doing. For many Vietnamese youngsters it was a struggle to grasp a concept such as loyalty to the government, let alone internalize it. The South Vietnamese Army was more experienced than the Navy, and they were further along in overcoming the problem. Some of their units were very good indeed. The Navy that I saw was training hard and getting better, but it still had its difficulties, which observers often attributed to a lack of discipline. But the underlying reasons were cultural ones.

These cultural patterns were ingrained and could not quickly be trained out. There were no shortcuts. The North Vietnamese had done it, but they had been at it a long time, and in addition they had communism on their side, a powerful ideology which they used as a wedge to drive between soldiers and their families. The Saigon government had nothing like that, so the job was that much harder. I was never convinced that the Vietcong—Hanoi's South Vietnamese allies—were completely successful at it either. The VC faced grave problems. They did not always hold together. They had high desertion rates and nightmarish recruitment difficulties, the same problems the Saigon Army was experiencing. They were trying to acculturate their people into the communist philosophy, and when they succeeded their fighters were very good. Until then they tended to be shaky.

South Vietnam's difficulties were exacerbated immeasurably by the fact that by 1970 (when I arrived) the Americans were pulling out, leaving behind warfighting methods ill-suited to Saigon's needs. When an American unit engaged the enemy, it expected and insisted on artillery support. There was no place in the Delta that was not covered by an artillery fan. We had batteries throughout the region, with established fields of fire, and wherever you were in the Delta you knew where the artillery was, what its range was, and what fire fan you were in. Americans also used helicopters lavishly—for attack, for search and rescue, for medical evacuation. All that made sense for the resource-rich United States military but not for the small and poor South Vietnamese Army. Yet that was how we had trained them to fight, and as we went away we took with us many of the resources on which they had grown dependent.

I was there during the period when the South Vietnamese were trying desperately to carry on using our methods. But where we had six guns, they had one or two, and they were not as adept at employing them or keeping them going. The same was true of helicopters and boats. We had established an elaborate maintenance system that was far too complex for the less well trained Vietnamese. As a result, shortly after our maintenance people began to leave, the boats and helos started suffering.

After five months I was promoted to senior adviser to the Vietnamese riverine force, with over two hundred boats, several thousand people, and a supporting base structure.* My first priority after taking over the senior adviser's job was to reorganize the entire maintenance and spare parts system for boat upkeep, making it much simpler. The simplification helped, but in the end the task required intensified maintenance training. I beefed up training, but it was still hard to get the Vietnamese to grasp the importance of these unexciting routines. Yet without good maintenance naval forces cannot function. And here again the problem was cultural. Vietnamese boys had not come of age driving cars; they didn't grow up fixing mechanical gadgets.

These kinds of deep-rooted problems could not be solved by pulling rank or exerting authority, especially not by advisers. Most of the American advisers had a straightforward approach. They were there to do a job, and they did not have a strong interest in the social mechanics of the country or the psychology of the people. They faced huge daily doses of frustration and aggravation. Things would just not work as they should have; the Vietnamese insisted on putting their own spin on everything. Young advisers would storm into my office livid with exasperation: Why are we helping these people? They won't do this and they won't do that and they hate the guy next door. They won't listen! Why don't we just go home?

I sometimes felt that way myself. One afternoon a convoy in the U Minh lost three boats in one mining attack. We had twelve advisers on board, and six of them were killed. I got a call that night from my immediate boss, Rear Admiral H. Spence Matthews, chewing me up and down. "What'd you let them lose those boats for?" "Well,

---

* My counterpart was the resourceful Captain (later Admiral) Dinh Manh Hung. At the war's end Hung was to participate in the remarkable but little-known odyssey of the South Vietnamese Navy. Though by that time many of their ships were in dreadful condition, the entire force sailed out of South Vietnam together, first reaching Subic Bay in the Philippines, then Guam. Hung himself was on a destroyer escort that carried 460 people. Afterwards Hung and his extended family lived with Shirley and me for three and a half months while the settlement agencies arranged a permanent home for them. For his sixty-seven-year-old mother, it was the fourth time in her life that she had become a refugee.

Admiral, you know I don't run this operation down here. I advise, but I don't command. If they want to send their boats in there against my advice they're going to do it." "Listen," he said, "I don't pay you to lose boats. You're not supposed to let them do that. You have another day like today and we're going to be out of business."

That episode and dozens like it (if less fatal) convinced me that the hardest job in the world is that of an adviser. His own people hold him responsible, but he does not have any of the authority of command. He is only as effective as he is persuasive.

Eventually I arrived at a rule of thumb for the advising business. An adviser's effectiveness is like a bank account. He can criticize his counterpart harshly and do anything he wants with him as long as he has a sufficiently large account in the bank. But if he exceeds his account his counterpart will stop listening and he'll lose his credibility. If I had to take Captain Thong to task about something, I would be very careful for the next week or so and build up my account again. I had to make sure he never lost face in front of anybody else. I had to make sure that no matter what I said, no matter how vehemently I said it, that he knew I was on his side, that I wasn't saying it to kick him around. That is hard to convey, so whenever I had to do something like that I worked very hard to replenish the account.

My adviser's position and its limitations mirrored the larger American role in Vietnam. In the end we could only be as effective as we were persuasive, and we never learned to be adequately persuasive. Field advisers were often exasperated by their difficulties, but Washington's political frustration with Saigon was far more serious (eventually it proved terminal). The underlying corruption, thuggishness, and cronyism of the South Vietnamese government strangled the war effort in a dozen ways, yet Washington seemed powerless to bring about any real change. We tried hard to pressure Saigon to be more honest and to move toward democracy. But we could not force the South Vietnamese to rationalize their government, and we did not have sufficient leverage to force them to do it.

Our ultimate leverage, of course, was the ability to leave if our advice fell on deaf ears. But though that might have sounded like an attractive option, its logic was more theoretical than practical. The fact was that after he had committed 500,000 troops, Lyndon Johnson was no longer a free agent—nor was Richard Nixon after him. The president's prestige was too heavily invested to simply leave. After such a massive involvement, no President could say to his constituents, We did not think very clearly about our strategic interests or about the nature of our South Vietnamese partners, and we have sacrificed thousands of your sons and daughters for something we did not assess adequately. Any party that admitted such a thing would have brought disaster down around its ears.

As a result, pulling up stakes was an empty threat, and the Saigon leadership knew it. I watched at first hand as we tried to force our ideas on them. But the kind of nation building we desired was not within our grasp. We were not successful at getting the various South Vietnamese factions to work together, or at stamping out corruption, or at introducing genuine democracy. And our ultimate leverage did not exist.

At times it was maddening. One was greatly tempted to say to hell with it. We're getting our young men killed, we're spending money, we're committed, and by God these people in Saigon are eating the heart out of their own country and alienating our support at home. We should not put up with this nonsense. Far better to run the show ourselves and let them know that if they get in our way we'll remove them. Just occupy this damned screwed-up country and straighten it out once and for all.

I think every adviser must have felt that way in his heart at one time or another. But of course it made no sense as a considered position. (John Kennedy had given in to this way of thinking in 1963, and after the CIA-backed coup replaced Ngo Dinh Diem the Saigon government got even worse.) Everyone knew well enough that the American people would not tolerate the idea of throwing out governments and installing U.S. high priests and proconsuls, and that doing so would have destroyed our ethical position for being there. But the frustration did run deep.

It took me a while to come to the conclusion that we really did not have ways to solve the problem. But once I arrived there I found myself caught in a kind of moral ambiguity. We were killing and being killed, in support of a government that did not deserve support, at the behest of our own government, which could not figure out how to win. While I did not start wringing my hands over the situation, I was not comfortable with it either.

In circumstances like these, the professional fighting man's attitude, including my own, tended to be that first of all there was a job to do and responsibilities to carry out. I was not going to refuse to do my duty because I was in the toils of these intellectual problems. At the same time, I was gripped by the age-old soldier's motive: You do not let down your friends and your mates. People all around you are laying their lives on the line, and those are the people you do things for and take risks for. I saw phenomenal feats of courage performed by youngsters who I knew did not believe in the war. But they would never put a buddy in danger or leave him out on a limb. When your cause seems unclear, that is what keeps you fighting.

It was also true that in 1970 in the Mekong Delta we were not being tested as some Americans had been in other times and different places. As frightening and tense as the canal and swamp war could be for those who fought it, for many Vietnam was a far darker experience. Veterans of heavy fighting in the Central Highlands, the Iron Triangle, and other fiercely contested areas sometimes went through profound emotional traumas. They saw the maiming and killing and said to themselves, I see no good reason for this; it is horrible and I am participating in the horror. I think there were many vets who did reach that point.

I did not suffer that kind of stress. In the Delta, death and destruction were sporadic; the fighting was rarely that intense, nor did it involve large numbers. The VC were there, but in small units—in the U Minh we may have occasionally had a battalion. Once in a while small North Vietnamese units turned up, but not often.* Moreover, we were making visible progress. During my tour the VC areas of operation shrank steadily and their tax revenues dwindled. I could see the local traffic coming back to the canals and commerce reviving. Perhaps success in the Mekong Delta was not going to win the war, but at least here we had tangible achievements to point to.

There was something else that short-circuited any serious doubts I might have had about the war. The Vietcong were a vicious enemy, purveyors of cold-blooded terror. Their deliberate policy was to murder local leaders and burn down villages. They did whatever they could to draw American fire into populated areas so they could use the destruction for propaganda. Almost twenty years after the fall of Saigon many Americans know of the anguish our veterans sometimes suffered because of their roles in the war. Fewer perhaps are aware how many American troops came out of Vietnam hating the enemy.

---

* It was hard to get a grip on numbers. Deep in the Camau peninsula, the U Minh Forest was South Vietnam's backwoods, its Ozarks. One got the impression that much of the violence was from local inhabitants who had always resisted the central government's writ. In these Mekong Delta backlands, fighting outsiders was a tradition, no matter who they were.

I knew those feelings from picking through burned-out villages. I saw what could happen when our soldiers were lost behind enemy lines. Early in my tour one of our helicopters was shot down, and for three days we couldn't locate it. Ultimately we did find the wreckage, and nearby the three dead crew members who had been unspeakably mutilated and dismembered. That kind of experience focused your feelings, not on doubt but on hate. It put you in a fighting frame of mind.

Vietcong atrocities were numerous in the guerrilla war that was fought in the Delta, but some incidents were almost too much to bear. One night a VC assault team infiltrated the little village across the river from the small South Vietnamese Navy base at Camau. There, from the shelter of the houses, they opened up a rocket barrage against the base, knowing full well that their fire would be returned. In the ensuing fight the thatched-roof bamboo huts caught fire and the whole village was soon ablaze. A number of the villagers managed to get across the river in small boats. Panicked, they gasped out stories of families and children caught in burning houses.

As the fighting slackened, a number of American Marines and sailors crossed to the village and, still under fire, pulled eleven children out of the inferno. By this time I had gotten to the scene, and we quickly bundled these terribly burned children into a truck and rushed them to the Vietnamese hospital in Camau. When the hospital claimed it was too overcrowded to take them, the men insisted that I intervene with the American hospital at Binh Thuy. Like all service hospitals, Binh Thuy was under emphatic orders not to accept Vietnamese civilians when there were Vietnamese medical facilities available.

Over a field radio I had a roaring argument with an overloaded American hospital administrator. But when I insisted that we had dying children on our hands he said, "What the hell, let's get them in here." A short time later two medevac helicopters were landing in our cluttered field in the middle of the night. The pilots did not know the area and there were power lines and other obstacles, but they came in anyway and we carried the children into the choppers.

When we got back to the base that night, it was the first time we had been in a lighted area since the firefight started. As we looked at each other, we realized that each of us had the skin of burned children clinging to his uniform. We were covered with shreds of blackened skin. That scene engraved itself on my memory, as I'm sure it did on the others. For me the horror was mixed with pride for what these American boys had done, and also a powerful animosity for those who had precipitated it.

In Vietnam I developed a deep respect for the younger generation of Americans, whom I watched perform heroically time and again. Much has been made of our problems in that war, but almost every commander also saw courage and patriotism that were the equal of anything the Vietnam veterans' forebears demonstrated in battle.

I still think of Vietnam daily and mourn for our losses there and for the tragedy of it. We had a good cause. The South Vietnamese people did not want a communist government imposed on them and they did not want to be ruled by the North. They still don't. In Vietnam today communism has failed, as it has virtually everywhere else. Most Southerners still resent Northerners and hate the ideology Hanoi has inflicted on them. From that point of view, we were right to have gone to Vietnam. But our great fault was in not understanding quickly enough that the fundamental dilemma of our adviser's role could not be resolved. We could not bring about a government in Saigon capable of motivating its own people or sustaining the support of the American people. And without that we could not win the war. It took a long time before we grasped that all our ingenuity and energy could not overcome this problem—time enough to incur 57,000 deaths ourselves and to mete out hundreds of thousands to our enemies. It was no crime that we were unable to resolve that dilemma. It was a crime, however, that it took us so long (and so much dying) before we understood the problem.

For many military people it was bitter to have fought for so long and at such cost in pursuit of a failed policy. It was even harder to discover that our efforts were not always appreciated and that blame for disastrous political judgments came to rest largely on the military's shoulders. I carried those scars out of Vietnam. I still carry them, as do so many others who fought there. But they also spurred thought; some of the most important lessons of my life were learned in Vietnam and put to use later.

After almost a year in Vietnam I received orders to report back to Washington—which seemed to be turning into the story of my life. I wanted badly to stay in my job and tried to put off the return. But despite all my maneuvering, I was unable to get any changes made. The United States was just then opening negotiations with the Micronesian islanders to end the U.N. Trusteeship which had been in place since 1964, and Admiral Moorer, who was now Chairman of the Joint Chiefs of Staff, wanted a military representative in the negotiations. My close friend and former boss, Vice Admiral J. P. "Blackie" Weinel, had recommended me for the job of deputy to the chief negotiator, Ambassador Haydn Williams.

While it was gratifying to have my political experience recognized in this way, the appointment seemed once more to have shunted my career into some impossible side eddy. What I really needed if I was to have a shot at making admiral was a significant sea command, and I had hoped that my work in Vietnam might put me in line for one, despite my diesel submarine background. But technically I was not working for the Navy now; I was working for a civilian whose office was located in the Department of the Interior.

As a result, my elevation to rear admiral in early 1973 was something like an electric shock. (One veteran admiral said it seemed incredible that someone from Interior had been selected.) Although the selection boards operate in secret, I later learned that my promotion had indeed been more than a little unusual. Admiral Bernard Clarey, who was head of the board, was interviewed after his retirement by the Defense Department's oral history program. He told them that of the fourteen hundred or so captains they were considering (for thirty admiral's openings), my name had dropped out before the final cut. But anyone on the board had the right to ask for a review, and Clarey himself requested additional discussion of my candidacy. The consensus was that I had not spent enough time at sea, but Clarey argued that my experience as an advocate was more important. He even ventured the unexpected opinion that one day I might make a good Chairman of the Joint Chiefs. What the other board members might have thought about that bold surmise has not been recorded. But they did keep my name in. Nor did it hurt that the iconoclastic CNO Elmo Zumwalt was just then pushing the Navy hard to promote more mavericks and dissidents.*

---

* The single most difficult problem in selecting top leadership in the military is how to insure that an individual who succeeds in the promotion process will have the independence of thought needed for high command. Zumwalt himself was the first I ever saw who achieved high rank and also managed to preserve a highly idiosyncratic cast of mind. In every military organization some mavericks do survive, but their numbers are extremely small. The great problem is to structure the organization so those people get promoted.

Zumwalt tried to attack the problem institutionally. He was CNO, and the CNO spends a large chunk of his time selecting flag officers to fill the required leadership roles. He does not personally promote flag officers, but he does convene promotion boards, and he lays down guidelines for them to follow. Though the boards themselves are statutorily independent, the CNO is still able to influence the general promotion policy. Nevertheless, in the

Professionals aspire to higher rank, but in most cases, and certainly in mine, you do not really expect to overcome the odds. Consequently, no matter how good your mental preparation, it still leaves you somewhat breathless. There is, of course, euphoria, reinforced by the congratulations from friends that pour in from all points on the compass. But there is also humility, if you have any sense. At this point I had never been promoted early for any rank, although quite a few of my classmates and contemporaries had enjoyed that distinction and had already made flag. Actually, my eligibility for consideration was already drawing to a close, so in that sense too my selection was a near thing.

Curiously, once I was selected, my unusual career pattern (which I had always viewed as a handicap in terms of promotion) turned out to be a strength. While I had had fewer seagoing commands than some of my peers, I did have experience in a number of areas high on the agenda of senior officers: joint positions, international affairs, strategic planning, political-military affairs. A large part of my career had been devoted to these fields, and now I found the demand for this kind of expertise was high. My promotion led to two tours in the Pentagon, a year as commander of the Middle East Force, then a three-year stint as deputy CNO for Plans, Policy and Operations, the same post that Admiral Austin had held when I was his aide seventeen years earlier.

In each of these positions my advising experience had relevance. But a decade after leaving Vietnam I found myself involved in a business that made greater demands on my persuasive abilities than anything I had previously imagined. In May 1980 I was appointed NATO Commander-in-Chief for Southern Europe. As a newly minted four-star with magnificent quarters in Naples facing Mount

---

Navy the selection of admirals is a rather clean, democratic process. Behind those closed doors the selection board members use their own values to pick flag officers. Consequently, in the end, Navy values dominate in reaching selections. Those values are hard to alter; you have to do it over years, like water on stone.

But the CNO's guidelines do have some influence, and Zumwalt tried to alter those values faster. He promulgated guidelines that said in essence, I want some iconoclasts. He'd say, "Last year we didn't have a single one of those kind of people! This year I want two! Don't give me all these peas in a pod." As a result a number of people who were outside the traditional patterns were selected, including myself. My impression is that since his departure the enthusiasm for "iconoclasts" has waned. But still Zumwalt made a heavy impact on the culture and it had some lasting effect—though certainly not as much as he desired. The CNO cannot just say, We're putting the rudder hard over. That doesn't do it. He can turn the helm, but the rudder doesn't necessarily go with it, because there are a bunch of people down in the bowels pushing it the other way.

Vesuvius, I had forces from four countries in my command in addition to American units. But despite my large office and the impressive title on my desk, not a single one of those forces would do what I wanted if their governments didn't feel like it.

My staff included Army, Navy, and Air Force officers from all the NATO countries with forces in the Mediterranean: Greece, Turkey, Italy, the United States, and Great Britain. The Southern Europe command also cooperated with France and maintained friendly contacts with Portugal. Spain too was in the process of coming into NATO. I had a French admiral on my staff, an Italian admiral in charge of the maritime command, an American Air Force general for the air units, a four-star Turkish general on the ground in southeast Turkey, a four-star Italian general in northern Italy, and a Greek commander for the Greek Army formations. I used to say that I wasn't the Commander-in-Chief, I was the Persuader-in-Chief.

The biggest problem on NATO's southern flank was the persistent enmity between Greece and Turkey. Among the many difficulties it caused, Greek-Turkish hostility immensely complicated the three or four regional military exercises we held each year. We needed both Greece and Turkey in those maneuvers, but getting them to agree on the ground rules was tough. Well before we could kick off, one or the other (or sometimes both) was more than likely to withdraw.

The focus of their antagonism was the Aegean. To the Greeks, the Aegean is a Greek body of water. Athens, they believed, should be responsible for its defense. They took vigorous exception to the presence of Turkish forces in what they insisted was their domain, even in exercises. The Turks felt otherwise. The way they looked at it, the defense of the Aegean should be split between the two nations, and split or not, Turkey had to have access.

My general approach to the problem was to hold separate exercises in each country under the rubric of a single larger exercise, so that they would not run afoul of each other. But that was not possible with amphibious, naval, or air exercises. The Greeks simply would not participate in anything in the Aegean at any time if the Turks were involved, and especially if they were given command—even symbolic command—for a few hours.

Ordinarily, planning for a major exercise would begin a year in advance. Perhaps the NATO plan for defending western Turkey needed updating, which would call for an amphibious operation involving naval units from all countries and a landing by Turkish troops on the Dardanelles. At this the Greek action officer on my staff would declare, "I can't agree to that. The ships will have to transit the Aegean, and Turkish troops have no business in Greek waters."

If the exercise was important, I would move ahead anyway, leaving the details of dispositions till later. But the objectionable specifics would gradually bubble up to the senior levels, and the noise level would rise accordingly. Arguments would flare over routes and numbers and who would furnish the air cover and how the areas would be divided and whether the air traffic would be controlled from Athens or Izmir. Each side laid down conditions they knew the other side would never accept.

About a month before D-day, the problem would make its way to the ministerial level and I would find myself sitting with the Greek minister of defense or even with Prime Minister Andreas Papandreou. There I might manage to get a tentative agreement—tentative because even if Papandreou concurred with everything I said, the minute I left his office he would change his mind—which I usually learned via a press conference or news release.

I did get one major war game off the ground with both Greek and Turkish forces. This was the result of an elaborate air control plan complete with separation zones. Every effort was made to keep the planes of either nation from flying over the other's territory and to compress the time spent in the Aegean to the absolute minimum. But still the exercise was marked by charges and countercharges. The theater echoed with Greek and Turkish claims that the other party had blatantly violated their sovereignty or flagrantly transgressed the exercise rules. Senior officers on both sides vowed never to participate in another, and I was personally accused of favoritism by both militaries. I told them that if only one of them had complained I would have been worried, but that since both did I must have done something right. The washup was high drama, and for me sheer pain.

The answer to the question of whether Greek-Turkish antagonism has any basis in today's reality, or whether it is simply a burden of history, can only be found in the minds of the Greeks and Turks. It did not appear to me that Turkey was preoccupied with this curse. Ankara had other problems, and it rather annoyed Athens that it did. But Greeks thought about Turks constantly. If theirs was not real fear, it was excellent theater. They regularly insisted that the Turks were massing forces to assault eastern Greece. The Turks of course denied it, and no such attack occurred. I always believed that when Papandreou was in power the main reason for kicking up dust was to win votes (intelligence reports seemed to confirm this view). But though the threat might have been manufactured, there was no question that it struck responsive chords throughout the Greek citizenry.

Papandreou himself was charming, on the surface a highly likable man. He spoke fluent English and could seem almost American. But though he was bright and articulate, he was also unscrupulous, capable of making one worthless promise after another. His ultimate standard seemed to be whether or not an action was to his domestic political benefit. Papandreou's attitude toward the United States depended entirely on whom he was talking to at the time. One moment he was a warm supporter of American policy. But then he would deliver a campaign speech and castigate the United States violently. His American-born wife was strenuously opposed to everything the United States stood for and made no secret of it. She was a prominent participant in anti-American rallies in Athens and made it clear she enjoyed them. To her credit she was consistent; she participated with equal enthusiasm in such protests in the United States.

Ironically, perhaps, given the deep national antagonisms, Greek and Turkish officers on my staff got along very well socially. When they were out of their own countries they were quite compatible because they had so much in common. But once they started talking officially, they fell to arguing. Of course, as the Greeks would say (and did say over and over), this all springs from their history.

It all started, I would invariably hear whenever a problem was on the table, with the fall of Constantinople in 1453. Then would follow a detailed historical review leading up to the difficulty of the moment. For four hundred years the Greeks were under Turkish rule, a time they refer to as "The Tyranny," which did not end until 1922. (Kemal Ataturk himself, the father of modern Turkey, was born in a small town in northern Greece.) Historically the two nations have shared one of history's great blood feuds.

My Italian deputy when I first arrived in Naples was Major General Gino Cacciola. Gino was one of the best educated, most knowledgeable individuals I had ever met, a remarkable historian with an intimate understanding of the history and politics of the Mediterranean. After I got to know him a bit and appreciate his abilities, I asked his advice about our Greek-Turkish problems. "I'm open to any suggestion you feel might be helpful," I said. "We shouldn't be confined by our past or by conventions or anything else. We need imagination, a whole spectrum of approaches. I want your help."

"You're absolutely right," he said. "We should have a whole

quiver full of arrows. But the very first thing we should try is extreme flattery." I was willing to try that (I was willing to try anything); I wasn't above it. For a while I went around flattering Greeks and Turks at every opportunity. The trouble was that they themselves had been at the same business for so long it didn't work. Every time I visited Greece they gave me a gift, and I quickly found out that if they gave me a big gift it meant I most certainly was not going to get whatever it was that I wanted. If it was a little gift, I might have a chance at it. When I finally departed NATO three years later, they gave me some truly wonderful gifts, which of course meant that I had failed utterly.

The Turks have a distinguished military background. In the early Ottoman days they were the terror of the world. They not only won battles, sometimes they won them in minutes, including several of the great battles of history. As soldiers they were awe-inspiring. That was when they were at the peak of their power, of course, but the modern Turkish Army has inherited the tradition and is intensely proud of it. Every officer knows the nation's military record in detail, right down to the Korean War, where they also had an outstanding record. General Necdet Oztorun, the deputy chief of staff, who served in Korea, often chided me about how his unit had saved an American company from defeat.

As a NATO commander I might not have been able to get the Turks to cooperate with Greeks, but at least I knew I could count on their discipline and bravery. In battle, they would do what they were told to do. The other side of the coin was that Turkish military thinking was highly stylized. Initiative did not extend down the ranks.

But there was never a question that they would fight tenaciously. The Turks have never hesitated to take casualties. It is embedded in their souls and in their history. On the Gallipoli peninsula in World War One they rushed the Allied trenches time and again. They lost hundreds of thousands of men, but they kept coming.* My instincts

---

* That was where Kemal Ataturk first distinguished himself. In my office I have a picture of him in mustache and helmet looking down on the Australian lines. Alan Moorehead wrote that rarely in history has a great campaign been so influenced by one man. Later Ataturk put together an army from practically no resources at all and succeeded in driving the Greek army from Turkey. Ataturk is utterly revered in his country. He was one of the two dictators in this century who turned societies completely around and who are still revered. Ataturk was the first. The other was an American. I mean, of course, Douglas MacArthur in Japan.

tell me that in the open field in this day of tanks and maneuver they would be strenuously tested. But if they were able to take a stand, they would be very difficult to uproot.

I am persuaded that the Greeks too would fight extremely well. It is a small military organization but with considerable punch for its size. Moreover, Greek troops are canny and natural scrappers. I never had any doubts about their staunchness, and I was convinced that if we ever had been confronted with Soviet and Warsaw Pact aggression much of the Greek-Turkish animosity would have disappeared—at least temporarily.

Although NATO incorporated substantial strengths, it was beset by problems. For years, prior to and including my period of tenure, the military had warned that Western capabilities were progressively deteriorating relative to those of the Soviets. In hindsight, we were undoubtedly overestimating Soviet strength, but at the time there were few dissenting voices. NATO commanders were painfully aware of their own weaknesses. Equipment tended to be obsolete and not uniform. Member governments often waxed eloquent about the coalition, but local politics severely limited the commitment of resources. While expenditures varied over time, few NATO members ever made even the goals they had set for themselves. Although through most of the 1970s and '80s the United States was spending from 5 to 6½ percent of its gross national product on defense, NATO as a whole spent in the neighborhood of 3 percent. U.S. aid was of some help, but by the 1980s it had markedly receded. This meant that NATO's military commanders struggled to prepare for increasingly unsettling worst-case scenarios with diminishing appropriations.

Grave strategic anxieties haunted NATO's commanders, although on the southern tier we were blessed at least in one respect. In my jurisdiction the sea tied together all the member states, and at sea we were dominant. The Sixth Fleet, together with the Italian Navy and British units, gave us control of the Mediterranean. As a result, we had a decent prospect of keeping open the lines between the southern nations and the sea lanes that connected our region to North America.

The land-based air and ground force balance was not nearly as encouraging. Of course uncertainties abounded in our calculations. It was not possible to predict how much of the Warsaw Pact's strength would be directed south in the event of war. Nor could we judge with any assurance how reliable Bulgaria, Hungary, and Rumania would be as Soviet allies, or whether our own reinforcement plans for the southern flank could be carried out in extremis. All these questions depended on unknowns, and very likely on what might happen in Central Europe.

But if the Kremlin decided to turn south in earnest, our lives would have been miserable. The early-warning networks in Turkey, Greece, and Italy were fragile and weak. Our air defense front was frighteningly thin. We would, of course, have attempted to compensate with seaborne air power and even assistance from Israel, but the options were shaky. On the ground, our situation would depend on how involved Russian forces were. (I never gave the satellites much credit.) If the Soviets gained air superiority, their ground capability could be fearsome.

The situation was complicated by the fact that NATO's three southern nations did not share borders; unlike Central Europe, the allies would be fighting in distinct areas with few land connections between them. Moreover, we had a potentially unfriendly North Africa in our rear. On the one hand, Libya was potentially a strategic hinterland, a place to regroup if we were badly pressed. On the other, it was a dagger poised. The prospect of Moscow shifting land-based air to Libya was a war planner's nightmare.

Facing this problem, in our war games I always wanted to secure Libya for the West. In addition to its strategic importance, Libya housed a huge inventory of modern air and ground equipment. But NATO sensitivities were such that even thinking along those lines in a game was not permissible. In one exercise simulating major hostilities with the Soviets, we had an American Marine division coming into the Mediterranean and I turned it toward Libya. Even though the game was completed before the task force could do more than turn southward, backs stiffened. The politics of NATO were predicated on the proposition that we had one enemy—the Soviet Union. Anything outside that assumption raised eyebrows quickly. Italy, for one, got the bulk of its oil from Libya. For Italian politicians, even a simulated war-game attack on Libya was intolerable.

Politics was the operative factor here, not strategic reality. But this was no isolated example. NATO had an unwieldy, excessively complicated command structure. But far more significant was the political machinery that sat atop it. Everything the alliance did had to be done unanimously, with the consent of all the members, and each member reserved the right to make its own decision to go to

war. The supreme allied commander had some authority to increase
the states of alert, and he did have a limited number of elements
directly under his control, air defense formations, for example. But
until troops were formally turned over to him by the respective countries, he was a general without an army. This was an essential condition of NATO's political unity, but there was always a strong dose
of skepticism among those in the military chain of command whether
in a crisis NATO could make the decisions that needed to be made
with the rapidity it needed to make them.

Given the wide disparity of interests among NATO's sixteen member nations, many thought it doubtful that a unanimous decision
would ever come out of the NATO political machinery. Theoretically, a sudden and massive Soviet aggression would generate a
common will to respond. But even during the most dangerous crises
of the Cold War that prospect was considered unlikely. The more
realistic scenario was one of increasing tension and Soviet mobiliza-
tion over time, allowing opportunity for NATO's disparate interests
to sharpen and clash. We never once played a war game where we
did not have that problem.

Even if a crisis was so severe that the NATO commander found
himself in actual command, the NATO system would be a great trial
for him. Member nations did not relinquish logistics responsibilities
to the supreme allied commander at any time. As I experienced
firsthand at NATO South, the NATO commander has only operational control. Logistics were the responsibility of the individual
countries. This meant that the commander would have a great variety of support troops operating behind his front lines, over whom he
had little control. Each individual nation's forces would have to
arrange their own logistics, with the result that routes and schedules
would have to be coordinated with each other and with the overall
commander, who at the same time would be moving operational
units around a large chessboard under extreme pressure. It would
have been a problem of gargantuan proportions. While I believed
that the pressures of war would quickly have created a more sensible
arrangement, logistics were nevertheless one of my serious concerns.

These were problems NATO had several decades to work
through. But the fact is that the member nations had no great desire
to sort them out. "Working it through" meant in essence giving the
military commanders peacetime control, and the coalition had no
intention of doing that. The United States was not the only nation

with strong political imperatives. The political difficulties were not resolved because the member states never wanted to resolve them.

These everyday problems that my colleagues and I experienced as NATO commanders have become more or less academic now with the demise of the Warsaw Pact. The world has breathed a collective sigh of relief that East-West tensions have dissipated. But no sighs have been more heartfelt than those of the military men who would have had to fight under NATO. More than anyone else, we know how fortunate it was that the allies never went to war.

Nevertheless, even with all its internecine conflicts and military difficulties, for over forty years NATO fulfilled its primary objective and deterred the Soviet empire from expanding westward. Although the Kremlin was constantly probing for weaknesses, NATO's fundamental coherence never cracked, and this, I am persuaded, was the prime factor influencing Soviet calculations. Challenging sixteen nations militarily is a sobering prospect, no matter what the balance of forces or the state of political arrangements.

America's great success, perhaps one of her greatest successes as a nation, was in providing the leadership that sustained NATO. Our military contribution underwrote the social and political cohesion of the coalition. Our political and military leaders consistently strove to shore up the alliance, to resolve or at least mediate the significant disagreements, and to project an image of allied determination. Although Americans are frequently castigated (and castigate themselves) for an apparent national desire for instant gratification and for an alleged inability to focus on long-term goals, it is no exaggeration to say that American willpower provided the glue that kept NATO whole and focused. The result was the longest period of peace that modern Europe has enjoyed and ultimately a decisive victory in the Cold War.

Chapter 5

CINCPAC

IN 1983 I WAS APPOINTED CINCPAC—Commander-in-Chief, Pacific forces. In some ways the nomination was out of the ordinary. If there was a pattern for those who reached the upper levels of Navy command, I did not fit it. I was not prominent in my warfighting community. I had had little direct experience in building the Navy. I was not an equipment specialist or a weapons technician. My career did little to stamp me as a traditional "Navy Man." On the other hand, I did have substantial joint, strategic, and command experience. The Pacific command was a major joint organization with broad political responsibilities in a region I knew well. I felt especially prepared for it.

But while my experience qualified me for the job, other factors had also conspired toward my appointment. A year earlier a different position had opened up—CINCLANT, Commander-in-Chief Atlantic forces. From my standpoint as commander for southern Europe, CINCLANT had seemed a logical move. Because it was a NATO job as well as a U.S. position, I would have been able to build on my three years of work with the alliance. A joint command as well as a Navy job, it would have exercised my bent for interservice cooperation.

My principal advocate inside the Pentagon was Richard Perle, assistant secretary of defense for international security policy. Among his various briefs, Perle had responsibility for Europe and NATO, and we had gotten to know each other during his frequent visits to Italy. Perle already had a reputation in Washington as a skilled strategist and gifted debater. He was, I thought, the brightest man I had met in government. The Atlantic Commander-in-Chief was the senior military man Perle had to deal with. We had experience working together and we saw eye-to-eye on many issues. We both felt it would have been an effective partnership.

But Perle did not make the decision; that was in the hands of the Secretary of Defense, who was advised by the CNO and Secretary of the Navy. John Lehman was Secretary of the Navy then, and Perle and Lehman did not get along. In point of fact, they did not even speak to each other. Prior to Ronald Reagan's election, they had been business partners, and the dissolution of their business had left the two men with a strong mutual dislike.

Whether because of my relationship with Perle or for some other reason, Lehman decided not to support me. There were, he said, too many submariners in high-level positions. I found that rationale curious. Although I still wore my dolphins, I had had nothing to do with the submarine force since my days with Division 31, sixteen years earlier. Many nuclear submariners, I knew, didn't even consider diesel veterans as submariners at all.

But although Perle and Lehman might not be speaking, Perle did have Caspar Weinberger's ear, and after some spirited dialogue Weinberger and the Navy Department worked out an agreement. Wesley McDonald, an old friend and classmate of mine was appointed CINCLANT. The quid pro quo was that when Admiral Robert Long retired as CINCPAC, I would be seriously considered for that post. A year later Long's term came to an end, and Shirley and I found ourselves on our way to Hawaii.

CINCPAC's area of responsibility extended from the west coast of the United States to the Far East, from the Aleutians to Antarctica, then into the Indian Ocean as far as the African littoral, the Bab el Mandeb, and the Strait of Hormuz. This immense and diverse area gives CINCPAC the largest unified command in the U.S. military structure. From his headquarters in Hawaii the Pacific commander enjoys a macro view of the entire Pacific Rim and beyond.

Historically, CINCPAC was the Paul Revere of the Pacific. He went around shouting, "The Russians are coming, the Russians are coming," and quoting alarming figures on the expansion of the Soviet Pacific Fleet and the Soviet buildup at Camranh Bay. His inevitable conclusion was that the Pacific should get more funds, more ships, and more weapons. But when I first reported to Hawaii I made a concerted effort to step back and look at the region with an objective eye. Of course it was not possible to completely discard my predispositions, but I made an honest attempt to assess our situation without emotion or greed. To what extent were we actually threatened by the Soviet presence in the Pacific?

In the course of my survey I found myself especially drawn to the work of Robert Scalapino, director of the Asian Studies department at the University of California, Berkeley. One of Scalapino's fundamental themes was that the Soviets were hardly players in the vast Asian marketplace. American trade with Japan alone at that time was reaching toward $80 billion a year. The Soviets did less than $10 billion in the entire region. Their products simply were not attractive enough to draw Asian buyers. The more I looked at it, the more it seemed to me that the Russians were bankrupt in East Asia. The single element that distinguished their position in the region was military strength, in particular their nuclear submarines based in Vladivostok and their units in Camranh Bay, which they had developed into a major base after the Vietnam War. In every other sphere they came off poorly.

On the other side of the ledger, by the early 1980s the United States had thrown off the humiliation of Vietnam and was solidly ensconced once again as the leader of the free nations of the Pacific Rim. Since the war, American political, social, and military policies had been tailored to the area and well integrated. Our presence in the western Pacific had prevented Soviet intimidation and allowed our allies and friends to nurture their interests in their own fashion and at their own pace. Most of our allies in the region were making political progress and moving toward pluralism (even if movement on this front was often not as fast or consistent as we would have preferred). At the same time they were experiencing tremendous affluence.

While Vietnam was still kicking up dust in Cambodia and spasmodically quarreling with China, East Asia was remarkably peaceful overall. Even North Korea had backed off from its more alarming rhetoric and except for the occasional verbal volley seemed uninterested in disturbing the waters. Our relations with Beijing were steadily improving, and the Chinese had made it clear that they favored American forces in the Far East as a counter to the Soviets. In essence, our forward deployed posture and network of alliances had neutralized the Soviets' penetration of the region. My general conclusion was that we were better off here than anyplace else in the world. In the Pacific our long-term policies had succeeded remarkably well.

National leaders throughout the region told me, when I began visiting them, that without our presence their achievements would not have been possible. It was, I thought, an excellent example of the utility of military force and how it can be productively employed in peacetime. George Shultz later said he felt that the diplomatic and military arms of the government worked together more closely in the western Pacific than in any other part of the globe. We were so successful, in fact, that other problems had become ascendant. Japan and Korea were already serious trade competitors and our future difficulties in the region were almost surely going to be economic. As a military commander I could not generate a particularly alarmist view of the Soviet threat in the Pacific.

This was not the traditional CINCPAC approach, and not everybody appreciated it, but that was my assessment. I was not in favor of reducing our armed forces, because I believed that American military capacity and cooperation with the Pacific nations was an important element of our success. Moreover, I thought our current posture was just about right. But I did not go around preaching that Soviet might there was growing out of control and would eventually overwhelm us. I did not believe it would.

Bob Long, my predecessor as CINCPAC, had initiated an imaginative reorientation of our Pacific planning that markedly increased the effectiveness of the forces we had in place. For years contingency plans for the Pacific called for substantial reinforcement in the event of war with the Soviet Union. But if we ever did find ourselves in a fight with the Soviets, it seemed clear to Long (as it did to me) that any early reinforcement of our Pacific forces would be doubtful. Western Europe would be the centerpiece of a massive conflict, and that theater would claim whatever resources were available.

Building on Long's efforts, my staff and I devised a whole new way of looking at a potential conflict in the Pacific and prioritizing missions so that we had a reasonable prospect of countering the U.S.S.R. without reinforcement. We reworked plans to take maximum advantage of American air and sea superiority. We prepared our forces to throw up a barrier across the northern Pacific and protect the communications lines between the United States, Japan, and China. We were ready to help build up Chinese capabilities and put pressure on the eastern Soviet Union. By the time we were finished reorganizing we were confident that we could box off Soviet forces and deal them considerable damage without detracting from the main effort in Europe. In my view it was a quantum leap forward both in terms of credibility and effectiveness.

The heart of our strength in the region was the forward presence we maintained. We were well placed to project influence, starting with Clark Air Base in the Philippines, working up through Okinawa,

the Korean peninsula, central and northern Japan. We were in an
excellent position to defend Korea, support Japan, and project immediate military power anywhere in the area. We did not have large
forces available, but we could react quickly. Our forward deployed
posture was part of our overall policy, in fact it was the heart of our
overall policy. As Shultz once put it, our "military provided the
umbrella underneath which all our diplomatic cards were played."

From a military perspective, the truth was that the Soviet Pacific
Fleet was never as powerful as many believed. They had (and Russia
still has) carriers, but they were anti-submarine and helicopter carriers that do not represent anything like the power of our attack
carriers with their squadrons of fixed-wing aircraft. Soviet ships
would have been hard pressed in any clash with the U.S. Fleet and
would not long survive. The Soviets did have a significant submarine
presence, though, and that was the main danger. But waging naval
warfare is in one sense similar to waging land warfare—you have to
deal from strength. War cannot be successfully carried on by a country that does not have the will or the economic base to support it. In
those areas the Soviet Union was clearly deficient, even in 1983.

The problem with the "Russians Are Coming" syndrome, as I saw
it then (and as is even more evident now), was that it distorted the
rationale for an American military presence in the region. If we
founded our presence on the need to counter the Soviets, and then
the Soviets dwindled or disappeared, we would have no argument
for staying. But the Soviets were never the only reason for us to be
there. Predictably, in the annual press for funds the Defense Department found the Soviet specter the most effective crowbar for prying
open government coffers. Unfortunately, this practice became habit
and created the impression that the Soviets were the sole reason for
our deployment. Now, with the U.S.S.R. gone and Russia more or
less prostrate, the traditional case is considerably weakened—many
say it has disappeared altogether.

Indeed, there is no tangible threat in the Far East at this moment.
But a rational policy is one that takes full account of the fact that this
world is replete with uncertainty. Developments of vast moment
have a habit of materializing unexpectedly. No one predicted the
Iran-Iraq war, just as no one foresaw Saddam Hussein's invasion of
Kuwait. Our policy of being forward deployed in order to deal with
unforeseen events and uncertainties and to express interest in our
friends' welfare has been consistently successful in the past and
should not be lightly cast aside.

If there is no Russian Fleet to contend with, we will not have to concentrate on protecting our blue-water lines of communication as we used to. But given our vital stake in the region, we still have to maintain a modicum of strength and use it thoughtfully. In essence, that was the keystone of the case for our military presence in the past (despite the rhetoric), and it still applies as we face new and changing circumstances. Perhaps the size, shape, and disposition of our forces will change—even be reduced substantially—but the merit of the basic argument remains unchanged.

Once I took up command in Hawaii I began regular tours of the region, accompanied by my executive assistant, Joe Strasser, and by John Helble, a first-rate foreign service officer and Asian expert who acted as my political adviser. I spent considerable time in Thailand, where we were quite concerned about the threat from Cambodia. General Kamlantek Arthit was the supreme commander of the Thai forces, and he and I continued the close cooperation that was in place when I took over, including joint military exercises. These were useful, although one occasion I observed was not carried out quite as I expected.

The highlight of the year was a combined exercise code-named Cobra Gold. Arthit invited me to observe the amphibious portion of this exercise, which involved a landing operation by Thai and United States Marines. We drove together to the beach where this landing was to take place. Gradually, the area seemed to take on a kind of county fair atmosphere. Leaving the car parked on the road above the beach, we made our way through an ever denser mass of people among whom ice cream vendors and other salesmen were plying a brisk business. When we got to the beach itself there was what looked to me like a cordoned-off royal pavilion, a raised dais covered by a thatch roof on which sat two elaborately carved high-backed wooden chairs. It took me a moment to realize that they were intended for Arthit and myself, and that it was from here that we would be observing the exercise.

Amphibious landings ordinarily take place around sunrise, but this one was set for midmorning. By the time the landing ships appeared offshore, the beach area was thronged with people, including what seemed to be a large number of very attractive young Thai women wearing the common slit skirts. There were so many people that when the Marines disembarked from their craft it was all the police could do to push the crowd back sufficiently for them to come ashore. Once they did make a lodgement they tried to follow the exercise objectives and establish a perimeter up near the road, but they were quickly engulfed by merrymakers and vendors. The operation had turned into a festive affair. Arthit and I were likewise immersed, and I was strongly tempted to buy a Popsicle, though in the end my dignity persuaded me not to.

The holiday atmosphere of Cobra Gold that year stood in stark contrast to the tense and dangerous situation along the border, where I visited a number of times to get a firsthand feel. Here the Vietnamese regularly attacked the border refugee enclaves that were run by the two non–Khmer Rouge opposition factions. Bombarding the hospitals and refugee camps with artillery, they wreaked indiscriminate slaughter. The sight of crippled and dismembered children was simply devastating. It was impossible not to feel the deepest sympathy for the Cambodians who were undergoing this heartrending ordeal. Nor could I get over the selflessness of the volunteers from around the world who manned the camps and hospitals, allowing some kind of order to emerge from horror and chaos.

Although the border situation was worrisome, the Thais seemed to contain it fairly well, even while they funneled supplies to the two factions of the resistance they were supporting. Of course Beijing was contributing the lion's share of support to the resistance, but their client was the Khmer Rouge, which had far the most effective fighting force. It was not a pleasant situation, and we did not like it. But neither did it appear to be getting out of hand. We had been worried that the Vietnamese, who had consolidated themselves in Laos, were going to do the same in Cambodia. In that event they would have emerged as a major regional power. But it was becoming apparent that Hanoi's leaders had already overstepped their resolve and resources and were not able to generate the staying power they had exhibited in South Vietnam.

My travels in Southeast Asia ranged widely. I visited our friends in Australia often and tried to improve ties with Malaysia and Indonesia. New Zealand was another port of call, but the agenda there was more eventful than I anticipated. (I did not start off on the right foot in New Zealand. I initiated my first press conference there by declaring, "It's good to be back in Australia." Although I corrected myself immediately, the slip made press copy for a week.)

When I first arrived, Prime Minister Robert Muldoon was in power. He had an oversupply of confidence and a disposition to match. Fiercely pro-American, he went to great effort to insure that the bilateral relationship remained healthy. But new elections in 1984 brought David Lange to power. Lange was a clergyman who had gone into politics but had neglected to bring the ethics of his church with him. He was not the first misrepresenter I had met in high places, but he was the most proficient. In his campaign he had bitterly criticized U.S. nuclear weapons and promised to prevent American ships from calling in New Zealand ports unless they declared that no nuclear weapons were aboard. There had always been a strong anti-nuclear faction in New Zealand's Labor Party, and Lange may have been a closet member of this group. In any event, he co-opted this plank from their platform.

That was well and good as long as Lange was in the opposition and merely scoring political points. But as so often happens in democracies, the political balance shifted and he managed to replace Muldoon as Prime Minister. The storm signals went up immediately, and Secretary of State Shultz quickly undertook a number of meetings with Lange. I likewise met with him. The new Prime Minister hinted broadly that the problem could be worked out and that he would engineer a solution satisfactory to both parties. But his actions did not bear out his words. I was appalled in my own discussions with him to find that Lange did not understand the difference between nuclear power (for propulsion) and nuclear weapons; moreover, he was entirely uninterested in the distinction. His confusion was accompanied by constant assurances that he was a firm ally of the United States. In his heart, though, he just did not want our ships in his ports, saw nothing inconsistent in the two positions, and could not understand why we were so exercised.

Shortly after Lange took office, New Zealand banned our warships from its ports unless we would give the desired assurances on nuclear weapons. This demand ran directly contrary to the "neither confirm nor deny" policy we had adhered to for over thirty years. We simply could not live with that ultimatum. As a member of ANZUS (the Australia, New Zealand, U.S. security pact) we were pledged to defend New Zealand, but Wellington was now refusing to welcome the American ships which would help carry out that defense. The result was that Washington withdrew its defense commitment and severed its ANZUS ties with New Zealand (though the term ANZUS remained in use as a shorthand for the residual Australian-U.S. relationship).

There was a serious public debate about whether we had taken the right course in canceling the commitment to an old ally. I, for one, believed it was the right thing to do. To the United States, having New Zealand as a formal ally made no military difference whatsoever. The Chicago police force is bigger than New Zealand's Army. The ANZUS alliance was originally formed to counter the Japanese military threat, which had disappeared almost four decades earlier. I am not even sure that it makes sense for New Zealand to be in an alliance with the United States. New Zealand is an isolated land, consumed with its domestic affairs and very little concerned with broad geopolitical issues. New Zealanders have an idyllic, beautiful country that is steaming along in its own semi-socialist way with an economy built around sheep. They have no great incentive to be involved in world politics. If they are ever attacked, the United States would likely support them for a variety of reasons, treaty or no treaty. With the demise of the Warsaw Pact and the U.S.S.R., their need for an alliance has now become even less evident than it was formerly.

But CINCPACs are not supposed to talk that way. Commanders instinctively want everybody in an alliance. My initial reaction was that the New Zealanders were putting themselves at risk, but that if they were imprudent enough to do it, it would serve them right. The more I thought about it, though, the more I thought that perhaps it was not a disaster. Maybe it was for the best, for New Zealand and for us. Why should they involve themselves, I thought, and why should we expend energy and resources to hold together an arrangement whose primary incentive had ceased to exist? It is unclear to me why we still talk so hard about New Zealand coming back into ANZUS. In the first place, they are not going to do it. In the second, I am not sure what the rationale would be today for a military relationship. In the third, aside from cosmetics, we have no reason to be worried about them. We have fashioned a new relationship with New Zealand now which is rather comfortable for both parties and we should leave it at that.

Japan was the main nation on CINCPAC's beat, and here a laissez-faire attitude was neither possible nor desirable. I believed it was wrong that the Japanese spent only 1 percent of their GNP on security while we financed their defense umbrella. I felt strongly that a country with Japan's economic strength and potential should share more of the burden. Consequently I argued vigorously at every opportunity in favor of Japan's increasing its defense appropriations. I am sensitive to the disadvantages inherent in a Japanese military buildup—chiefly the opposition of the other Asian countries that have such bitter memories of World War Two. But I still think Tokyo can and should take more responsibility for its own security and that we should continue to press them on it. If they cannot see their way to spending more on their own defense, then they should be providing more funding to assist our effort. There are imaginative ways to spend money indirectly in support of American help—especially when the Japanese GNP is more than $3.5 trillion.

Surprisingly enough, considering the long relationship, operational cooperation between Japanese and American forces was almost nonexistent until the early 1980s. There was good rapport, but the two militaries did not work much with each other. That situation began changing during the tenure of Bob Long (my predecessor) as CINCPAC. Since then we have engaged in joint planning and exercises, a budding cooperation I did everything in my power to foster.

While U.S.-Japanese military ties have strengthened, we have not succeeded in breaching the barrier between the Japanese and Koreans. Both governments have given considerable lip service to the idea of moving closer together, but the animosities still run deep, and close military cooperation is more than the relationship can bear. Nevertheless, until these two nations are willing to plan and operate bilaterally, fashioning a realistic, cohesive security planning for the area will remain a serious problem.

While Japan is the key American interest in East Asia, Korea provides the starkest illustration of our role in the region's power balance. My first visit there as CINCPAC was a bone-chilling introduction to the hatred that has divided the peninsula since the conclusion of World War Two.

The bus that transports personnel from Camp Kittyhawk, the U.S. base in the Demilitarized Zone, to the Joint Security Area at Panmunjon passes through the small village of Tassondory, the one South Korean settlement permitted in the DMZ by the truce agreement. Each of the farmers of Tassondory has seventeen acres to till, as compared to the average South Korean farmer, who has one. The extra sixteen are compensation for living so close to the northern border.

Camp Kittyhawk itself is home to 166 American and South Korean soldiers who serve as guards and observers in Panmunjon, the meeting place between the two sides since the Korean War. Established at the end of that conflict as a neutral site for the airing of truce violations and other differences, the Joint Security Area is today a half square mile where both sides have built compounds for their delegations and where strict regulations govern life. Each side is allowed no more than five officers and thirty enlisted people in the area at a time; visitors must be escorted; automatic weapons are prohibited.

The regulations have not prevented angry clashes over the years and, in several instances, fatalities. In June 1975 the North Koreans attacked Major William Henderson in the JSA and inflicted permanent brain damage. In 1976 the infamous "poplar tree" incident took place, in which two American officers, Captains Art Boniface and Frank Dorrett, were beaten to death with hoes and clubs. North Korean guards frequently seek opportunities to insult or even shove their American counterparts.

On the bus from Camp Kittyhawk I was accompanied by the colonel in charge of the American detachment, who briefed me on the conduct that would be required while we were in the Joint Security Area. We were forbidden to speak to northern personnel, to make any gestures that might be interpreted as threatening, even quick movements. During our stay we would be under constant observation from northern guard posts. We could expect them to be taking our pictures.

The moment we got off the bus, tension descended. Standing on the other side of the road, North Korean soldiers and officials had hatred written all over their faces—almost as if they had rehearsed for hours to project contempt and revulsion. Everyone moved slowly and deliberately, careful not to provoke some unintended reaction. In few other places in the world was the East-West conflict reduced to such tangible antipathy. For anyone who visits Panmunjon it is hard to forget the atmosphere that oppresses that historic junction. It penetrates right to the marrow.

To this day the regular meetings of the Korean Armistice Commission are distinguished by shouting and invective.* "Running dogs" and "capitalist pigs" are only two of the epithets frequently in the mouths of the North Koreans, while the Americans respond with icy silence and the coldest formality. An officer assigned to this unpleasant duty has to have an iron stomach, also an iron bladder. Neither

---

* This was written at the beginning of 1992 just as signs of decreasing tension between the two Koreas were emerging. One hopes that continued progress will at least moderate the bitter antagonism of the past four decades.

side displays weakness by using the latrine during the marathon meetings.

Militarily, South Korea was one of my major responsibilities as CINCPAC. The threat from the North, although it was receding to a degree even in the early 1980s, could not be ignored. Like all U.S. commanders in the region (past and present), I followed events in northeast Asia closely and was sensitive to the potential for having to close the peninsula quickly if tensions heated up.

Dealing with the South Koreans regularly as CINCPAC, it seemed to me that they had their minds firmly set on their own welfare (not surprising in light of their northern neighbor's historic aggressiveness and concentration on building military muscle, including atomic weapons). Their intention then, as well as now, was to keep the United States committed as fully as possible for as long as possible. I have been associated with things Korean for over twenty years and have been told time and again that if the South could just be assured of our presence for another five years they would become independent and have no further need for American support. They were saying that in 1970. They are saying it today. The South Koreans have been extremely successful at wooing Americans to their cause. But the fact is that their situation is not as bad as they picture it. They are, for example, much better postured militarily than they would have the outside world believe.

Nevertheless, the South Koreans dread the prospect of an American retreat or withdrawal so acutely that they can hardly contemplate it. Regardless of shifts in the region's actual balance of power, Seoul has an insatiable appetite for American support. But it is also true that the support has borne fruit; on the military, diplomatic, and political fronts our joint efforts have met with substantial success.

The Korean fixation on American support concerned me because, having responsibility for the entire region, I did not like the idea of committing my limited forces exclusively to one mission. I especially resisted pressure to pre-position materiel there. I knew that things had a tendency to disappear into the Korean maw and never be seen again. This syndrome was often aided and abetted by our commander in Korea, who looked at it much the same way as the Koreans did. He wanted everything in there he could get, which has been one of the perennial conflicts between CINCPAC and the Korea command.

There was nothing particularly sinister in all this. On the contrary, it was a natural phenomenon. All governments and organizations work this way; it's just that the Koreans were more skilled than most. Korea is a successful, prosperous country today primarily because of its relationship with the United States. I do not believe we owe the Koreans any apologies whatsoever if we want to keep our forces available for other contingencies in other locations, or devote more resources to different regional objectives. That does not mean that in the event of aggression across the DMZ our support would be diluted. On the contrary, the full weight of our capability in the Pacific would be brought to bear with no reservations.

The South Koreans, of course, believe in their hearts that while American interests might be global, there is in fact only one true threat to peace, and that threat lies across their northern border. They are correct to the extent that Pyongyang's thinking is not particularly rational, though probably the Kim Il Sung government is not quite as crazy as we often declare. If the Northerners could get a large return on their investment by attacking Seoul, they would do it. But the world has changed since Kim Il Sung came to power, and of course the moderating trends have accelerated with unexpected suddenness in the last several years. Throughout the world, countries which once relied on support from Moscow and its allies in pursuing confrontationalist objectives have had to thoroughly reassess their policies, and North Korea is no exception. At this writing, Pyongyang may be undergoing just such a reappraisal, and while the signals are still mixed, we are at least seeing the beginnings of a relaxation in the peninsula.

Without a doubt, the most troublesome ally with whom I dealt as CINCPAC was the Philippines under Ferdinand Marcos. At the time, the country was in the midst of a progressively more dangerous insurgency, fed by ethnic groups in the southern districts and communist guerrillas in the central islands. I visited often to assess the state of the Filipino armed forces and to advise my counterparts on steps to increase their effectiveness. But the situation deteriorated continually, and there were no signs that any turnaround was likely.

Despite consistent diplomatic support for Marcos from Washington, by the fall of 1983 I became convinced that he had lost touch with the realities in his country. He persisted in actions that were damaging to his cause and was impervious to advice. His continued presence at the helm, I thought, could lead only to a quickening breakdown and ultimate disaster. Eventually I concluded that the longer we waited to move Marcos out of power the worse it would be for both the Filipinos and for our own position in that country. Once I was fully persuaded of this I began voicing my assessment in cables and reports to the Pentagon and the Secretaries of Defense and State. As one message expressed it, "I think there is no way that working through Marcos we can expect the government to prevail in the insurgency or to get the policies we want to have in place. The time has come when we must begin considering ways to have him step down or to remove him from office."

I had not come to this point easily. My visits to the Philippines always began with a personal call on Marcos, and he was invariably courteous and friendly. Normally he received me at the Malacanang Palace in the heart of Manila, a collection of baronial buildings that in colonial days had housed the American high commissioner but which had served as the official residence of Filipino presidents since independence. The spacious grounds were surrounded by an imposing cast-iron fence and replete with beautifully tended exotic tropical plantings. But everywhere, it seemed, the lush shrubbery partially concealed heavily armed security people.

Marcos's office was on the second floor and opened onto a spacious hall with a series of meeting rooms on either side. It was in these rooms that visitors were kept until they were called for. The President's windowless office was filled with artificial plants, which seemed to confirm the story that Marcos suffered from a wide variety of allergies. Inside his office, Marcos had installed his desk in the middle of a dais, elevating it above floor level. Callers always found themselves looking up at the President, like supplicants. Behind the desk was a large screen, and it was obvious that someone was behind the screen. Often no pretense was made and the persons behind the screen scurried in and out without any attempt to hide their presence. I had no idea what was going on behind the screen. My assumption was that they were providing security or recording conversations, or perhaps both. I did know that refreshments were often prepared back there, then brought out to Marcos on order. My curiosity about the people behind the screen never flagged, nor was it ever satisfied.

Marcos was a very sick man. For some time we were not sure what was afflicting him, though we eventually learned that he was on kidney dialysis. The first thing I would look for at our meetings was his condition that particular day. Was he alert or woozy? Sometimes his eyes were glazed over and he was barely able to speak. When he was up to it, Marcos would be sociable and expansive, talking at length about World War Two. But always he sounded imperial, like a man who was running the country, and running it very much for his own benefit.

Over time I became quite familiar with the Philippine military, and I felt I had a good handle on what was wrong with it. I studied their operations and spent a substantial amount of time with various commanders. I met often with Chief of Staff General Fabian Ver to discuss the general state of the insurgency and the various military assistance projects the U.S. had under way. I had known his deputy, Eddie Ramos, since 1975, when I was serving in the office of the Secretary of Defense and he was heading the Philippine constabulary. Ramos was easy to talk to, straightforward, and a solid military professional.*

Ramos seemed to have a feel for the problems and a practical-minded approach to dealing with them. But his boss, Ver, was a farce, an intelligence officer who had been chief of the Palace Guard (Marcos's personal security) for years and had been appointed to head the military because of his loyalty to the President rather than because of any expertise in commanding troops. He was corrupt and unscrupulous; the rumor was that he had murdered people who stood in the way of his advancement. I had no idea if this was true, but it was certain that he was widely feared. It was also certain that he had almost no concept whatsoever of military affairs. He was presiding over the dissolution of the Philippine military as it suffered under Marcos's stifling grip and struggled to hold off the rebels in Mindanao and the southern district.

In my meetings with Ver I would always start off with a list of things I thought they should be doing. I would note the training and other improvements they needed, and I would describe what the United States would do to support them as they took these steps. Ver would always agree with me on each point and assure me that he would see to it. But he would do nothing. I soon concluded that he had no intention of accepting advice. His chief personal interests were in delivery dates for American equipment and in developing avenues for direct money inputs from the United States. He seemed to believe that the secret to military success lay in extracting as much American assistance as possible—preferably in the form of gifts.

Meanwhile, the Philippine Army had battalions that had been out in the field for six or seven years straight and that had never had any

---

* In May 1992 Ramos was elected President of the Philippines.

training courses at all. They couldn't shoot, they couldn't move, they couldn't communicate. They needed trucks, basic communications equipment, and all the training in small-unit tactics they could get. But though they desperately lacked the fundamentals, the Army was so beleaguered that they could never afford to bring troops out of the line. There was not even a rest and recuperation system or a leave schedule. Even worse, the Army did not reward the people who were doing the fighting. If an officer wanted to advance in the Philippine military, he did not go to the battlefront; he went to work at a headquarters in Manila, if possible for Fabian Ver.

With Ver unwilling or unable to move, I began going to Marcos directly with my unaddressed agenda. I always took a gift along, which I would present while we exchanged amenities. Then I would start off with what he really wanted from me—a worldwide tour d'horizon. I would describe for him what the Soviets were doing and what our analysis was of their various moves, particularly in the Far East. I would tell him how the arms control talks were proceeding and brief him on other international developments. Marcos was quite interested in all this and frequently interrupted with questions or comments. In fact, it was always evident to me that he would have far preferred for me to stop when I was finished with my global assessment and then go away.

Instead I would start talking about the Philippines. I would tell him where I intended to go and what problems had arisen since my last visit. "Mr. President," I would say, "I must tell you that you are not doing very well with this insurgency. If you want to prevail, you have to take some positive steps, and this is what I recommend that you do." Then I would list my top four or five agenda items.

At this Marcos would invariably get a little testy. "I appreciate your thoughts, Admiral. I know your heart's in the right place. But what's of more significance, I think, is when you are going to deliver those helicopters you've promised us." Or those mortars or APCs. He always knew precisely how much equipment he was getting from the United States and what the delivery schedules were. "And, you're also behind on your training money," he'd continue, side-tracking the conversation even further. Marcos was not even remotely interested in advice about how to run his Army. (I had a certain amount of sympathy for his attitude; no doubt it is demeaning to have a foreigner insist on injecting himself into your business. But affairs had deteriorated to such an extent that I felt I had no choice, and of course the United States had a significant stake in the out-

come of the insurgency and the health of the Philippine military.)
Finally he would start discoursing about the time he spent as a guerrilla during World War Two, the clear implication being that he was
the one who knew how to fight guerrillas, while we had amply demonstrated in Vietnam that we did not.

He would also convey to me how well he knew the present situation. I know that young lieutenant colonel so-and-so down there,
Marcos would say. I put him in that job. He'll do just fine. You're
wrong, Admiral. We're doing well down there. I know, I talk to that
lieutenant colonel every day. And the fact was that he did talk to his
young officers every day by phone, often bypassing their commanders. One day while I was in his office he was on the phone with
a junior officer. "You know," said Marcos, "I'm going to promote
you. I wanted you to know that, and I want you to remember who
promoted you. Your boss doesn't know about it yet, but I'm going
to call him shortly and tell him." The whole system was personal-
ized, and it was clear to me that nothing was going to change that;
neither Ver nor Secretary of Defense Johnny Enrile had any desire
to confront Marcos. I called on Enrile once just after he had returned
from a trip to Mindanao—where his army was fighting for its life. He
told me it was the first time he had been there in eight years.

Occasionally Marcos's conversation would veer off in other directions, discourses about the communists or ruminations on the stupidity of anyone running against him in future elections. "Nobody can
run this country except me," he would say. "I'm the only one who
knows how to save this country. It's nonsensical to think differently." Then he would turn to the evil and mistaken notion that he
was corrupt, growing increasingly excited until his speech was little
more than ranting and raving. I would report these exchanges with
my assessment in some detail to the Chairman and to State and
Defense.

On my final call to the Philippines in September 1985, I carefully
prepared my litany of observations on the Philippine military and a
series of recommendations. It was my intention to bear down hard.
Even though I had not succeeded in breaking through Marcos's
armor in almost three years, I was determined to make a valiant last
effort. But he completely outflanked me. He canceled our appointment at the last moment, then called back to invite Shirley and me
to have breakfast with him and Imelda the following morning.

When we arrived at the palace we were ushered into a sumptuous
private dining room lushly carpeted and heavily decorated with artificial flowers. Enrile was also there, but with Imelda and Shirley

present it was clearly not appropriate to embark on an argument about military matters. Besides, neither Shirley nor I could get a word in edgewise. On the wall behind us was an imposing painting of a young Marcos addressing the Philippine Parliament. The conversation immediately turned to "the old days," specifically to how Marcos had bested the forces of evil and corruption and had pulled the country back from disaster singlehanded. Enrile sat silent while this was going on, but Imelda found an opportunity to deplore the dirtiness of politics, announcing with a straight face that she was a "simple housewife" who did her best to stay away from that kind of thing. On the other hand, the press had publicly accused her of many deeds of which she had absolutely no knowledge, and so it was not altogether possible to keep her distance.

Imelda was articulate and had an impressive presence, but suddenly the breakfast was over and we were ushered out, as if Marcos had divined that despite the setting I might be about to break in with my usual unwelcome remarks. In saying goodbye, I told him that I did have a number of items I had wanted to discuss. Since time did not permit, I would put them in a personal letter to him. His demeanor did not change, but it seemed to me he was thinking, Will this damned admiral never quit harping at me.

Shortly afterwards I sent him a written assessment of the Philippine Army and my view of what must be done if the military was to survive as a viable organization. I did this, emphasizing the need to decentralize authority so that the commanders in the field had some authority and latitude. Nobody in the military was doing a thing unless Marcos said they could do it, and the man was only working half days. The whole country was at a dead stop. But, predictably, this effort, like my previous ones, had no effect.

Over a period of time a few others were arriving at points of view similar to mine, in particular the American ambassador to Manila, Michael Armacost, and his successor, Stephen Bosworth. When Armacost left the Philippines, he returned to Washington as undersecretary of state for political affairs, so his voice had special significance. Secretary of State George Shultz had an open mind on the subject, and he listened with increasing responsiveness to Armacost's arguments, especially since Assistant Secretary Paul Wolfowitz was also drawing similar conclusions.

But the Marcos problem was undeniably complex, and not everyone was swayed. There was, after all, no assurance that with Marcos gone the Philippines would not descend into civil war, or that a new, even less palatable dictator might not emerge. Iran was a recent and

painful example of the unexpected and potentially disastrous consequences that could attend the fall of an entrenched strongman. This
was Secretary of Defense Caspar Weinberger's basic position.
"Who will replace him?" he wanted to know. "At least Marcos is
ours. Before I espouse anything like what you are suggesting I want
to know who is going to replace him."

I had no answer to that, but I was convinced that we were in a
steadily deteriorating situation. The more time passed, the less
chance there was for some form of democratic or even stable succes-
sion. "I don't know who is going to replace him," I argued. "But
one thing I can say is that the longer we wait the more traumatic it's
going to be, and the more problematic it's going to be. The Philippines are going to be lost to this insurgency. As long as Marcos is
running the country there is no way to reverse it. We cannot save
him. We cannot make him healthy and enable him to do what is
necessary to run that country. It just cannot be done."

Weinberger was reluctant to accept that, as were many others in
the administration. That line of thought did not become policy for
many months, in fact until after I came back to Washington as Chairman. At that point I regularly expressed myself in policy councils,
joining my voice with those of others who had arrived at the same
conclusion.

The growing sentiment put President Reagan in a bind. He and
Marcos were friends. They attended parties together and socialized.
Imelda was friendly with Nancy. And Reagan, of course, was a
member of the school that said you give your friends the benefit of
the doubt. You stick with them to the end if you possibly can. But
by now George Shultz had taken up the cudgel, encouraged by
Armacost, Assistant Secretary for East Asia Paul Wolfowitz, State
Department Director of Intelligence and Research Mort Abramo-
witz, Assistant Secretary of Defense Richard Armitage, and myself.
Eventually the National Security Council discussions began to shift.

In reaction the administration began sending envoys to see Marcos, which I considered a waste of time though probably a necessary
part of the political minuet. Each of them encountered the same
problem I had: They found themselves talking to an irrational man.
The last envoy was Senator Paul Laxalt, an old political colleague
and close friend of the President's. Reagan told Laxalt that he
wanted him to undertake a delicate political mission to the Philippines and invited him to a National Security Planning Group meeting
in the White House. In addition to the President, Vice President
Bush was there, along with Weinberger, Shultz, Armacost, Wolfo-

witz, Armitage, National Security Adviser John Poindexter, and my-self.

Looking at Laxalt, the President started the meeting off. "Paul, we have some serious problems in the Philippines. We've just got to get a handle on Marcos and I want you to see him. I trust your capability, Paul, and your diplomacy. It's a sensitive mission." Laxalt looked suitably flattered by this assessment and it seemed to me that he did not completely hide his satisfaction. "Now we've been meeting," Reagan went on, "and all these people know Marcos and have been working on this problem for quite some time. I'd like them to describe the situation for you, so you can get the sense of the table here and some idea of what we want you to do."

Shultz then took up the discussion and made some comments along the same lines, indicating how severe the Marcos problem had become, though never saying outright exactly what the nature of Laxalt's mission would be. Then they got to the working people, Armacost and the rest of us. When my turn came I told Laxalt that we had arrived at the point where there was no alternative but for Marcos to leave. "You've got to convey to him that he can come to the United States if he wants to, there are many other places he can go, but you've got to tell him that he has to step down."

As the discussion went forward, Laxalt's expression transformed itself. Reagan had invited him in to discuss a diplomatic mission, but this was turning into something quite different. By the time we stopped talking, his countenance had taken on a different cast altogether. "You want me," he said, "to go over there and tell a head of state that he's got to step down and get out of his own country?"

"Well, yes, Paul," said Reagan. "I guess that's what we're say-ing." Laxalt had not bargained for this and he was obviously ap-palled by the prospect. I had great sympathy for him; I was glad Reagan hadn't chosen me. In the end Laxalt did visit Marcos, but though he implied and hinted and made veiled allusions, I do not believe he ever delivered the explicit message.

It was not until after Marcos's attempt to subvert the presidential election in February 1985 that President Reagan finally made it clear that he would have to give up power. In the end a deal was cut in which we guaranteed Marcos's safety and evacuation in return for his abdication. I always felt, then and afterwards, that I had played a role in freeing the Philippines of Marcos and allowing the Aquino government to come in, although I am not sure that Mrs. Aquino ever looked at it quite that way.

Chapter 6

BAPTISM
UNDER FIRE

AS THE SPRING OF 1985 ROLLED AROUND, my attention was once more drawn back to Washington. On April 12, General John Vessey, the Chairman of the Joint Chiefs of Staff, announced his forthcoming retirement, despite pressure from President Reagan and Secretary Weinberger to finish out his second term.

The service newspapers always love the prelude to the nomination of a new Chairman; the potential for speculation is boundless. I was aware that my name was occasionally being mentioned in their columns, and I also started getting a lot of "hot dope" through the grapevine. Friends coming through Hawaii from Washington felt impelled to pass on the latest. It looks like you're a contender, they'd say, or else, It's not looking so good. Either way I'd ask for specifics and they would answer, Well, I don't really know. I'm just hearing rumors.

At first I did not take the talk too seriously. It seemed to me that I was too far from the flagpole and that in any event not being a chief of service was probably a fatal handicap. Jack Vessey had been the vice chief of the Army Staff and Admiral Arthur Radford in 1953 had come directly from CINCPAC. Otherwise, all the chairmen had been chiefs of service before their elevation. Theoretically, it was the Navy's turn to provide the Chairman, but then again there was nothing sacred about service rotation.

Still, as time passed I began to see my name grouped with that of Chief of Naval Operations Jim Watkins as possibilities. On one visit to Washington, Jim asked to see me, and when I came into his office he said, "What's going on?" We both laughed, and I answered that I knew nothing at all. Neither did he. Evidently, being close to the flagpole did not necessarily insure that one was well informed. The only person from whom I heard anything specific was Secretary of the Navy John Lehman, who made a point of telling me, "Bill, I just want you to know, I am not supporting you for Chairman.'' That I found odd—not that Lehman wasn't supporting me but that he felt compelled to say so. Lehman was famous for his skill at maneuvering behind the scenes and playing the angles. It made no sense for him to announce he was opposing me, an act that would inevitably affect our relationship in the event I was selected. It seemed to me a mistake that he did not have to commit. To this day I cannot figure out what he had in mind, although when I did receive the appointment at least I knew whom I wasn't beholden to—though unfortunately it was never obvious to whom I was beholden.

I had estimated in my own mind that the decision would be made by the beginning of May. When I heard nothing by then, I crossed the idea off (at least I attempted to), assuming that I had not been chosen. But silence prevailed for another month, and early in June Colin Powell (then military assistant to Caspar Weinberger) called and asked that I speak to the Secretary. When I did, Weinberger offered me the post. I asked for some time to consult Shirley, and after talking it over we decided to accept. At heart I felt more ambivalent than enthusiastic. We both knew the demands the job had made on Jack Vessey, and we were already too familiar with Washington's frantic atmosphere (such a contrast to peaceful Hawaii). When the appointment was announced publicly, one newspaper reporter described what he saw as my resemblance to George Shultz. Apparently I too looked "like an amiable Irish bartender." When I showed Shultz the clipping, he laughed and said, "That's the last good thing they'll say about you."

Although I did not know who had said what to whom in the selection process, I did know that I had gotten the President's attention. The previous Easter I had had the opportunity to give President Reagan an extended briefing on Asia, and our meeting had gone well. Reagan had stopped over in Hawaii on his way to a state visit in China, bringing with him George Shultz, then White House Chief of Staff James Baker, and National Security Adviser Robert McFarlane. On the Monday after Easter I was to call on the President in his hotel suite. I had never met him until he landed that Sunday morning, and I was quite nervous. I was told I would have thirty minutes with the President and that I ought to cover anything I thought important for him to know before he left for China.

I labored over this presentation. Instead of giving a traditional military briefing, I wanted to address what I considered a President's needs. I personally do not like slide or board presentations, but I did take along a big cardboard with a map. As I was walking up to the President's suite with the board under my arm, one of his aides said, "You know, the President doesn't like those kinds of things." That's nice, I thought. Why didn't you tell me that yesterday? Shultz, McFarlane, and Baker were already inside, and a moment later President Reagan came in, looked at the board, and said, "What are we going to do here, see a bunch of slides?" "No, Mr. President," I said, mentally crumpling up the briefing notes I had put together the previous night. "What I had in mind was that you and I would just sit down on the couch and talk for a few minutes." "That's great," he said, "let's do that." "All this thing is," I said, quickly shoving the board behind the couch, "is a map of the Pacific in case we need it."

The few minutes turned into an hour and a half. Shultz, McFarlane, and Baker all asked questions as we went along, as did President Reagan. In broad strokes I painted the military picture in the Far East, putting the emphasis on China—how the Chinese were posturing themselves, what direction they were moving in, how they viewed the various problems they faced, and what issues most concerned them. The President was attentive and interested; we even got the map out from behind the sofa and studied it for a while.

That night I gave a dinner at my house to which Shultz came. The Secretary was extremely upbeat, and while we were sitting down in the backyard having drinks, he made some complimentary remarks about the briefing. "The President," he said, "was very impressed." It later got back to me through the grapevine that when the President returned to Washington, Weinberger asked, "How did my commander do out in Hawaii?" Reagan told him that if they needed another Chairman, he had found him. (I have no idea if that story was true.) So while I did not expect the appointment, when it came I was not entirely shocked either.

On October 1, with my family around me, I was sworn in as the eleventh Chairman—once in the Oval Office by President Reagan (who could not make the formal ceremony) and once on the Pentagon mall by Secretary Weinberger. Later I overheard one of my aides wondering if there was any significance in making me swear twice to uphold the Constitution. After Weinberger and I inspected the honor guard we adjourned to the reception in the Secretary's office. But before I had a chance to greet everyone I was informed that I was already late for the afternoon meeting of the National Security Council in the White House. When I finally tiptoed into the cabinet room, the conversation stopped and everyone stared as I found my seat and attempted to fade into the background. It was not an auspicious beginning.

Later in the afternoon I had my first chance to actually sit down in my new office on the second floor of the Pentagon's E Ring. It was spacious and pleasant and would have afforded a magnificent view of the Washington skyline if the windows had not been made of opaque bulletproof glass. I couldn't see out at all. The effect reminded me of my submarine days.

A week later, in the late evening hours of October 8, the first crisis of my tenure broke. I was alerted at my home that an Italian cruise ship had been hijacked in the eastern Mediterranean. The *Achille Lauro* was commandeered by Palestinian terrorists just after it departed from Egypt. My first thought was that an Italian ship carrying mostly Egyptian tourists was more or less an Italian responsibility. They had a navy and they were in the Mediterranean; they would handle it. My second thought was that we had better be prepared to react ourselves.

When I arrived at the Pentagon I went straight to the command center, which is in twenty-four-hour-a-day contact with our major headquarters around the world. The terrorists had issued a warning: If anybody followed them they would start killing passengers. A decision had been made in Europe not to trail them. It was a serious mistake. Warnings like that have to be ignored. The fundamental ground rule is that somehow or other you keep track of your prey. Despite all the sophisticated surveillance technology, it is possible to lose things at sea for short periods, particularly if you are not in contact when an incident occurs. And that had happened. We did not know the liner's location.

One of our destroyers was in Haifa, and we ordered it to begin searching. We were fairly sure the *Achille Lauro* was somewhere off the Israeli or Syrian coast, but other than that there was little to go on. Without much air capability east of Cyprus, we started flying long-range reconnaissance patrols out of Greece. A report came in that the hijacked ship had approached a Syrian port but was denied entry, then had sailed toward Cyprus. But our initial search around Cyprus revealed nothing.

That was an embarrassing way to begin a job, and Weinberger let me know about it. We were going to investigate what had gone wrong, but subsequent events overtook the decision. My assistant,

Vice Admiral Art Moreau, was an old hand at such incidents. He had been General Vessey's assistant for three years and he had lived through quite a few crises. With his counsel, I realized that locating the *Achille Lauro* was the least of our problems—we would find her soon enough. More significantly, the administration might decide to launch a rescue operation. If that was the decision, forces had to be ready.

We put several special-operations units on alert, forces with the know-how to storm the liner and kill the terrorists. The problem with special-operations units is that foreign governments are always nervous about being identified with such forces and do not allow us to base them permanently on their soil. As a result, when crises arise these forces have to be transported from the United States, which takes many precious hours. In this case we dispatched people from their east coast bases into the air base at Sigonella, Sicily, then approached the British about moving them to Cyprus. Meanwhile the Italians were doing little beyond engaging in diplomatic talk with the governments of Egypt and Cyprus. It was becoming apparent that if any military action was to be taken, we were the ones who would have to take it.

In short order, the British granted us entry to a base on Cyprus, but with the condition that all movements would have to be made under cover of darkness, a time-consuming restriction. Meanwhile we had dispatched from the Sixth Fleet an amphibious group that was rapidly approaching the eastern Mediterranean and would soon be ready to receive the special attack units.

Shortly after daybreak the next day we located the *Achille Lauro* south of Cyprus, moving slowly. An assault team was quickly transferred to an LST, which began to close in on the liner. Their job would be to board so suddenly and decisively that the terrorists would not have time to kill hostages. For this to work a night approach and attack was called for, which would have to be carried out with split-second timing. While our forces and equipment were at sea by the second night—a remarkable accomplishment considering they had come all the way from the United States—it would be the third night before everything was ideally positioned.

But late afternoon on the next day, the *Achille Lauro* steamed back into Alexandria. There the terrorists surrendered to Egyptian authorities and released the hostages, except for Leon Klinghoffer, whom they had already murdered in his wheelchair and pushed overboard. The crisis was effectively over before we had had a chance to act. When the terrorists were taken into custody by the Egyptian government, we stood our special operations people down, and they began to pack up for the flight home.

To our dismay, the next day brought news that the Egyptians had released the hijackers to the PLO. The United States made strong protests, but to little effect. In their negotiations with the hijackers, the Egyptians had made dramatic promises—none of the terrorists would be subject to punishment so long as no one else was hurt. We were even more upset after we received information that the PLO official taking charge of the terrorists was Abul Abbas, whom we believed had planned and ramrodded the hijacking. Abbas was chief of the Palestinian Liberation Front, which had been responsible for a number of airline hijackings and attacks on civilians. After this latest event we would have been more than eager to lay our hands on him, and instead the Egyptians were releasing their prisoners to him.

The following day an unexpected piece of intelligence came in, not via regular channels but through a separate political connection maintained by the White House. Apparently originating with the Israelis, the information advised us that an aircraft carrying Abul Abbas and some of the terrorists would be leaving Egypt's al Maza military airport, bound for Tunis. The intelligence was detailed; it provided not only the takeoff time and make of plane but even its tail number.

Almost as soon as this information came in, Deputy National Security Adviser John Poindexter called to ask if we might be able to intercept the plane and force it down at an American base.* Abbas's airliner, a chartered 737, would be in the air soon, likely within the next quarter hour. Could we be ready to take it down? Yes, I told him. If we had an air group close enough to the flight path, we could do it.

Putting in a flash call to our European command, I was told that the carrier *Saratoga* was in the general vicinity and would be able to intercept. I went right back to Poindexter and confirmed that we could manage it. All this happened in minutes; as far as we knew, the plane would be taking off at any time. "We can do it," I said,

---

* Oliver North later asserted that the idea was his. It did originate in the National Security Council, and he may have participated in the early deliberations. But he also claimed that he ran the operation that subsequently developed, which is entirely untrue. It was a Pentagon operation from start to finish.

"but I need a go-ahead from the SecDef [Secretary of Defense]." In the brief time that had gone by since the information came in I had not had a chance to call the Secretary's office. Weinberger was traveling that day, so I went upstairs to inform Deputy Secretary of Defense William Taft. "I've checked the forces," I said, "and we can intercept. I've told the Navy to assume they are going to do it and to make arrangements to put interceptors into the air corridor." "That's fine," said Taft. "I think it's a good idea, but I have to let Weinberger know." A few minutes later Taft reached Weinberger. Back in my office I got a frantic call. "Weinberger's on the phone," said Taft, "and he's against it. In fact, he's irate."

The Secretary, it turned out, was in an airplane. When I got on the phone, he said, "What the hell's going on?" I was brand-new and it was not comfortable to hear this. "That's a terrible idea," he barked. "I'm dead set against it, interfering with civilian aircraft. We'll be castigated all over the world." "Well," I said, "the original request came from the White House. We've responded, and if those terrorists are aboard I'm for getting them and taking the heat." "Just stop everything," he said. "I'll call the President." "All right," I said. "I can call it off, but my information is that the aircraft may be taking off momentarily. It may even be in the air already. If we're going to intercept, we've got to do it with dispatch. We're going to have to get at it!"

Some stiff words passed between us. I did not think Weinberger should be interfering, since he wasn't there. My opinion (and my own approach) was that if you are away from the scene of action you just have to go with your subordinates' judgment and support them. But the Secretary wanted control. That was his privilege, and nobody questioned it. But I didn't buy his decision for a minute.

A short time later Weinberger was back on the phone telling me to go ahead. He had had a discussion with the President, who told him, "I want to do it." When I said I hoped we had not missed our opportunity, Weinberger's tone changed. He seemed apprehensive about the delay he had caused. I was irritated enough to let him stew, though I felt there was a good chance we were still ahead of the power curve. Hanging up the phone, I released the whole operation. It was a go. Within minutes the *Saratoga*'s F-14s were up above the corridor in position to intercept the charter plane and bring it down to Sigonella (a NATO facility the United States used with Italian permission)—the only readily available friendly place to force a landing.

My main concern now was that the charter pilot might not obey the F-14s. There was considerable discussion as to what we might do if that happened. As badly as we wanted the terrorists, it was clear that we were not going to shoot down an Egyptian plane with their nationals aboard. But we were spared any additional measures when the pilot signaled his compliance as soon as he saw the fighters, followed them toward Sigonella, and voluntarily fell into the landing pattern.

By now I was in contact with Major General Carl Stiner, the commander of the special forces that had been brought over from Fort Bragg. Stiner and some of his men had stopped in Sigonella on their way home from Cyprus, and just as they thought the hijacking saga was over, there they were, right in the middle of its next installment. With the Egypt Air 737 circling above the base, Stiner's voice came over the phone asking for instructions. What steps, he wanted to know, should he take now? The Italians had just denied the plane permission to land.

That was the first indication I had that this operation might not go smoothly. We did not want trouble with Italy over this, but we also wanted the terrorists; and our only chance was to get them on the ground and into our custody as fast as possible. I ordered Stiner to have the plane land, no matter what Sigonella control might be telling them.

As the 737 was coming in for a landing, both State and Defense were trying frantically to get people out of bed in Italy (it was early in the morning of October 10), to inform them and solicit agreement to let us have the hijackers. I finally reached my Italian counterpart, General Lamberto Bartolucci, but not until the plane was on the ground. There was considerable confusion. Bartolucci said he would do what he could, but he was vague and didn't promise anything. This reply did nothing to inspire my confidence. Nobody seemed to quite understand the problem, and working through interpreters on a transatlantic phone line made it even more difficult.

When the plane landed, Stiner had it vectored to an out-of-the-way area of the airfield where he was waiting with his special forces. There they surrounded it and blocked it in with some military vehicles, but the terrorists refused to come off, and we knew they were armed. Stiner and I were talking via a satellite phone he had with him on the tarmac, deliberating about what action to take, when suddenly he said, "It just got a lot worse. The Italian Army is driving up; it looks like there's some colonel in charge. They seem to be surrounding us."

I groaned. Ten days on the job and we were about to start a war with Italy. The terrorists were in the airplane, which was blockaded by jeeps so it couldn't move, the special forces were ringing the plane, and now the Italian Army had surrounded the special forces. By this time we had confirmed our earlier information that Abul Abbas was on the plane, and we were attempting to make the point with the Italians that this was a major terrorist, a man the whole Western world was after and we needed to take him.

It was a tense situation. There was always a possibility (although remote) that one of the Italian or American soldiers facing each other might get nervous and fire off a round. Furthermore, Carl Stiner was not famous for his diplomatic skills. On the contrary, he was an aggressive hell-for-leather type with a reputation for being both superb in combat and headstrong. I was not positive he understood all the dimensions of this situation. He had had little experience with Italians, and he was clearly determined to keep the terrorists in his gunsights if he possibly could.

Stiner's sentiments were shared by almost everyone involved. What we really wanted was to grab Abul Abbas and his henchmen, and get them to the U.S. That was an aggressive plan to carry out in a foreign country, but that was what we had in mind. I believed that unusual means were called for, since to this point we had had no success in bringing Palestinian terrorists to justice. Had Sigonella been an American air base, we would have just done it. As it was now, if we wanted the terrorists we would have to storm the plane in the face of our hosts. From the moment the Italians intervened it was obvious that we were neck deep in a swamp of international politics.

From the start we had been playing a bit fast and loose with the norms of the game, and once the Italian Army arrived on the scene we were also playing from weakness. At that point it was clear that if anything was to be done at all, it would have to be done by Italian authorities. But they were understandably quite upset. They did not at all like our having contradicted the control tower and forced the plane down, though they probably could have tolerated that. But now we were pressing them hard to let us take these people into our own custody, or if they wouldn't allow that, at least to arrest them themselves.

Naturally, the Italians would have preferred to evade this problem; arresting Abul Abbas was not a pleasant prospect. Threats of terrorist reprisals were obviously in the air. The Italian officials on the scene were not forcing the hijackers off the airplane and instead had embarked on negotiations. The problem appeared to have paralyzed them. Shultz, Weinberger, and I were all talking to our opposite numbers, but none of us was making significant progress. Finally an Italian general arrived in Sigonella and ordered the Egyptian pilot to fly the plane to Rome.

It was apparent the Italians were trying to move the problem away from us and out of the media spotlight. They wanted to make their decision in peace, free from these irritating Americans. We briefly considered shooting the plane's tires so it couldn't take off, but we quickly decided against it. We knew we were walking a tightrope. It was not just a matter of being cute or figuring out something obstructive to do. We had already put the American-Italian relationship under a sharp strain and we anticipated there might be repercussions. (In fact, the next day the Italians began making noises about having us leave Sigonella because of our alleged violation of Italian sovereignty.) The question was: How far did we want to push this situation? The United States had suffered a great deal at the hands of terrorists, with little opportunity to strike back; so had the Italians, but Italy is closer to the Arab terrorist bases. We wanted these people, or lacking that, we wanted to make sure they were brought to justice elsewhere.

When the Italian general ordered the plane to Rome, Stiner said, "Well, I've got my own aircraft here. Do you want me to follow and make sure they actually go to Rome?" "Yes," I said, "that's a good idea. Do it." The Italian Air Force was going to escort the 737, but we were afraid the terrorists would veer off in flight and that their escort wouldn't do anything about it. Sigonella control, though, would not clear Stiner to take off; they would not permit him on the runway. But Stiner didn't let a little thing like that stop him and he took off anyway, from a taxiway. He followed the 737 all the way to Rome and ascertained that it did indeed land there.

At this juncture the Italian government was seized with the problem in earnest. One of the factors that by now had come into play was the growing Italian feeling that their pride would not allow them to do what we were asking, even if it meant letting Abul Abbas go. They did not want to be considered American puppets. In addition, they had recently gone through a sticky trial of terrorists in Milan, and they were receiving an array of threats from Arab groups. There was little question about their reluctance to face possible retaliation for holding and trying Abul Abbas. Despite their lip service to anti-terrorism, this was a man they did not want to have on their hands.

Ultimately, the Italian government took counsel of its fears and permitted Abul Abbas and the other PLO official who was escorting the hijackers to fly to Yugoslavia (which had close ties with the PLO), although they did hold the four *Achille Lauro* terrorists themselves. Abul Abbas no doubt spent an uncomfortable night in the plane while Rome decided what to do with him, but that was precious little consolation. Both Italy and Yugoslavia had extradition treaties with the United States, but in the end these were disregarded. The affair left us frustrated and more than a little disgusted at our friends' lack of resolve, though no doubt they allowed themselves to feel aggrieved by what they considered our own high-handed conduct.

For a new Chairman this was a dramatic way to break in. The end result was not what we wanted, but the military side of it at least had gone almost without a hitch. We had been able to shuffle through the stream of traffic in the air corridor, pick out the Egyptian plane, and force it down on very short notice. With a little luck we would have succeeded in bringing Abul Abbas and his colleagues back to the United States in chains.

The incident started off my association with Caspar Weinberger on a bit of an anxious note. But that quickly dissipated. I soon learned to value the Secretary's abilities. Weinberger had an exceptional mind, characterized by a phenomenal memory and instant recall. As I got to know him better, I also discovered that in spite of his somewhat dour public persona, in private he was an exceptionally humorous man. Out of the spotlight he had the ability to see the funny side of events and people and to laugh at himself as well. But he was determined not to let this aspect of his personality show through in public. Russ Rourke, the assistant secretary of defense for legislative affairs, told me that once he had mentioned to the Secretary that humor could be a great political advantage and that he ought to incorporate more of it into his speeches. Weinberger had answered that he wouldn't do anything of the kind. "I am not," he told Rourke, "going to be the Henny Youngman of this administration."

Weinberger was a stubborn man. Once the Secretary had reached a conclusion, there was little hope for a review. The art in working for him, then, was to keep minutely informed so that I could make myself heard beforehand. He was also fiercely ideological. He considered himself a representative of the right, and he approached every problem from that standpoint. If the conservatives did not feel strongly about a particular issue, then Weinberger would be willing to consider various approaches. But if it was an issue dear to them, there was no way to sway him.

Weinberger and I had only one major problem. By law, the Chairman of the Joint Chiefs is the principal military adviser to the National Security Council, as well as to the Secretary of Defense and the President. To me that meant I was available to anyone on the council who wanted to consult with me. But Weinberger was not happy about my talking to people outside the Defense Department without him being present.

It particularly upset him that as time passed George Shultz began to ask for my advice directly. Weinberger took strong exception to this. He and Shultz virtually never saw eye-to-eye. The two men had been competing for a long time; they had both worked for the Bechtel Group, and they had brought their rivalry with them into the Cabinet. In National Security Planning Group (NSPG) meetings I saw the friction at close hand as they disagreed on a wide variety of issues. Often it seemed that the subject was less important than prevailing in the argument. Their contention was one of the most serious problems within the Reagan administration.

This situation aggravated my difficulty with Weinberger. I had to feel strongly about an issue before I contradicted the Secretary. I had to be careful how I did it, and I had to be sure he knew I was going to do it. I had none of those problems with Frank Carlucci, Weinberger's successor. Carlucci understood that I had independent views, and he thought that was as it should be. As far as he was concerned, I could go directly to the President and disagree any time I wanted. But Weinberger was concerned that any difference between us would weaken his hand when we were taking issue with outsiders. This fear was legitimate enough, but I felt that in the inner reaches of the government, out of public view, I did not have to support positions I did not agree with. I had a responsibility to speak up.*

_____

* The business of giving advice can be more delicate than it might appear. Congress debated this subject during the Defense Reorganization hearings in 1986, often unrealistically. A common attitude was: When the Chairman has independent views, of course he has to express them. Who cares if the Secretary of Defense doesn't like it? But the Chairman does have to care, because if the Secretary of Defense loses confidence in him, he will simply cut the Chairman out of the loop. The congressman will angrily declare, He can't do that. It's not legal. But he can. The Secretary is in the chain of command; the

Shultz and Weinberger never did completely resolve the question of the Secretary of State's independent access. But eventually the chiefs and I began to have regular meetings with Shultz, and occasionally I would meet with him by myself. Weinberger was always invited but sometimes he did not attend. He was not altogether happy with this arrangement, but neither did he ever tell me not to do it.

Despite the occasional frictions, the working relationship between Weinberger and myself developed quickly and functioned rather well. That was fortunate, because scarcely two months later the Defense Department was again confronted by events in the eastern Mediterranean, and this time the challenge was considerably more substantial. In December of 1985 terrorists precipitated a chain of events that moved the United States toward a military confrontation with the Libyan dictator, Muammar Qaddafi.

Chairman is not. The Secretary can throw a fence around him, and if he chooses to do that he will. As a result, the Chairman must render his independent advice with caution and tact if he wants to keep playing in the game.

Chapter 7

THE SHORES
OF TRIPOLI

EACH QUARTER Vice Admiral Frank Kelso's proposal for the Sixth Fleet's next exercises included the Gulf of Sidra—south of latitude 32°30', Muammar Qaddafi's publicly declared "Line of Death." The proposal always triggered a wrestling match between State and Defense. Military exercises in sensitive diplomatic areas require State Department approval, and Foggy Bottom had little interest in exacerbating tensions with Libya, despite the fact that Qaddafi's line was a hundred miles offshore, far outside Libyan territorial waters. The line was a challenge aimed straight at Washington, and Washington was reluctant to pick up the gauntlet.

But by the end of 1985 the political atmosphere had changed. The *Achille Lauro* mastermind had escaped, and in December terrorists invaded the Rome and Vienna airports, killing and injuring nearly 150 people. Four Americans were among the dead. Libya's role was not clear, but Qaddafi's comments were outrageous. The attacks, he said, were "a noble act." In Washington the anger was palpable, though with no firm evidence of a direct link to Qaddafi, no one considered retaliation politically feasible. But this time when Frank Kelso proposed his fleet exercise, State's mood was confrontational; any aversion to a challenge below the Line of Death seemed to have vanished like smoke in the wind.

With this new round of exercises approaching, I proposed a change in our rules of engagement—the procedures that define what actions American military forces may properly take in a confrontation. For years U.S. policy had allowed units that were attacked to respond with "appropriate force." If a plane fired at one of our ships, the ship could shoot it down. But other targets (the airfield that launched the plane, for example) were off limits. Retaliation had to be proportionate and directly related to the incident. The emphasis was on preventing escalation and limiting the commanding officer's discretion. But in recent years sophisticated weapons had proliferated. Many Third World countries now had air-to-surface and surface-to-surface missiles that could reach their targets in seconds. Requiring our units to wait until they were actually fired on put American lives at great risk—our experience in Lebanon being the most recent example. I wanted them to be able to defend themselves as soon as a threat was apparent.

Weinberger agreed. We both wanted the Libyans to know that they could expect a forceful response to overt threats as well as to hostile acts. When President Reagan concurred, I flew to Europe to brief Frank Kelso on the new rules and emphasize that we were entering a new ball game. The thrust now would be that anybody adopting a menacing posture did so at his hazard. This entailed a substantial shift in orientation, not only in the Gulf of Sidra but worldwide. It marked a reduction in American tolerance for military provocation, a different psychology about violence others might direct at us. But thirty years of habit do not instantly disappear merely because someone promulgates an order. Operational commanders would naturally ponder the Pentagon's intentions. They would be asking themselves, If I shoot someone down and people are killed, will I be backed up? Do those guys in the Pentagon really mean it? I wanted them to understand that we were dead serious.

The exercise did not begin until March 22, a week behind schedule. Unsure what Qaddafi's response might be when we crossed the line, I delayed until then so that a third carrier had time to join the fleet. If anything did happen I wanted to have the additional strength on hand both to counter an attack and to strike back.

When the exercise did start, we took pains to insure that no particular action of either planes or ships could be construed as threatening Libyan land, sea, or air forces. Of course, we would be operating south of the "Line," and this could be interpreted by Tripoli as provocation. Nevertheless, we were clearly within international waters and within our rights as we saw them. In fact, one of our objectives was to assert the right to navigate in the Gulf so that Qaddafi's claims would not ripen into customary law.

For two days the Libyans watched, occasionally putting planes in the air, but always remaining over their own territory. Then on March 24, batteries at Syrte launched two surface-to-surface missiles toward the American ships. It was a long shot; the nearest targets were almost seventy-five miles offshore—at the missiles' extreme range. Our radars tracked them as they lifted off and lumbered out in our direction, then splashed harmlessly into the sea.

There had been little chance for the missiles to cause any damage. But the message flashed through the fleet that we had been fired on, and with the new rules of engagement in effect the commanders moved to retaliate. Return missile fire destroyed a number of Libyan acquisition radars while ships and aircraft began to hunt down the few Libyan patrol boats that were out in the Gulf.

Time passed, but in the Pentagon we heard no reports of any renewed attacks. The Libyans were not following up their initial launches; there was no news either of any success against their ships. As I waited, a phone call came in from John Poindexter at the White House. Why, he wanted to know, hadn't we sunk anything yet?

"John," I said, "it takes a little time. I'm not running the operation. You know I don't tell those guys what to do once the shooting starts." Poindexter, an active-duty vice admiral, understood this well enough, but he sounded tense. "You and Cap better come over here and talk to the President," he said. "He's pretty hot."

A few minutes later Weinberger and I were in a car speeding across the Fourteenth Street Bridge to explain to an angry President Reagan why we had failed to destroy any Libyan ships. As we walked through the President's outer office, a secretary called me aside and said, "A message just came through for you." Unfolding the note she gave me, I read, "We have attacked and sunk two patrol boats." By this time Weinberger was already inside the Oval Office. When I came in, we both sat down opposite an obviously unhappy Ronald Reagan. The President's grim look contrasted sharply with his normally pleasant demeanor. "Well, Cap," Reagan said, "I just don't understand it. American forces have been fired at. I want something done about it. I want something to happen!"

"I'm not sure what you have in mind, Mr. President," I began. "But we just sank two patrol boats." Reagan's frown changed instantly to a big grin; Weinberger was as surprised as he was relieved. "Oh, really?" the President said. "Tell me about it." I told him what I knew, trying to embellish the sparse message with nautical details, though even then there wasn't much I could add. Nevertheless it was vastly better than trying to explain why a fleet of American warships had been unable to sink a few lightly armed patrol craft. By the end of the day we believed we had destroyed three or four of them, but one was only damaged and another turned out to have been a radar shadow. Still, we felt that the Sixth Fleet had made its point.*

A week later, on April 5, a terrorist bomb blew up the La Belle Disco in West Berlin. The La Belle was a popular club, crowded with American soldiers. One serviceman was killed, along with a Turkish woman, and 230 more people were injured, including fifty Americans. Initial intelligence pointed to the Libyans. One high Defense Department official called it a "smoking gun." † The President decided that this time Libya's conduct would not be overlooked.

Three months earlier, shortly after the Rome and Vienna airport attacks, the Joint Chiefs had put together contingency plans for a raid on Libya. If we uncovered hard evidence linking Qaddafi and a terrorist action, we were prepared to retaliate. Investigation of the disco bombing seemed to yield that link.

We wanted to send an unequivocal signal that Washington was serious and that terrorist actions would not go unpunished. But opinions differed about how to do it. The military was assigned the task, but guidance was vague. It is always difficult in this kind of crisis to pin politicians down. Did we, for example, want to scare Qaddafi, or kill him, or destroy part of his war machine, or stop his oil production? There were a variety of views. Each interested government agency seemed to have a different concept of the mission and of what constituted appropriate targets.

Initially I met with our J-3 (Operations) and J-2 (Intelligence) people. Rear Admiral Tom Brooks, my staff intelligence officer, presented an exhaustive list of potential Libyan targets, which we then narrowed down in my office. Focusing on military targets, we identified the most suitable, determining which could be hit effectively in a single-pass raid.

Then my assistant, Lieutenant General John Moellering (accompanied by Brooks and JCS operations chief Lieutenant General Richard Burpee), went to the White House to present and defend my views in interagency discussions presided over by John Poindexter. At these meetings every agency with an interest laid out its priorities

---

* This action marked the first time that Harpoon missiles had been fired in action. While our performance was not flawless, the missiles themselves performed well. Any doubts about this weapon, which had experienced significant developmental problems, were dispelled.
† Recent information has thrown a cloud over the facts of this incident, but at the time strong indicators marked Libya as the perpetrator.

and campaigned vigorously for its own target choices. CIA, NSC, OSD, State, and others all had their favorites.

Some argued that for political reasons the strike had to clearly announce itself as a response to the disco bombing. According to this argument, we had to hit the people responsible for that attack. I did not agree. No one knew unequivocally who had done it. More to the point, finding a target that was demonstrably related to the bombing was next to impossible.

Alternately, the political types argued, we should go after terrorist targets in general. It would ease the public presentation if we could link the targets directly with terrorism. No one disagreed with that, but the problem was finding a worthwhile terrorist target. Intelligence would report that a particular site had been used for training terrorists, but when we took an overhead picture of it we would see an abandoned shed, an empty firing range, and a road. We could bomb the place out of existence and all we would have to show for it would be some holes in the sand. Fervently as we might have desired it, there was no main terrorist headquarters waiting for us to annihilate it.

I thought that we were too concerned with choosing an allegedly "appropriate" target. If we were going to attack Libya, to commit an act of war, I wanted to focus on Qaddafi's military capability, his tank parks, air bases, missile and radar sites. I wanted to destroy his capacity to harm us in the event we had to come back, or if we found ourselves engaged more deeply than we expected. Not a single bomb, I maintained, should be dropped solely to make a public relations impression. I opposed terrorist targets where there were no terrorists. The point, in my judgment, was not to justify our attack according to some abstract doctrine of fairness but to punish Qaddafi, to hit him where it would hurt and where it would do us the most good. To me that meant focusing on military targets, particularly those that might cause us future casualties.

But that did not convince everybody. We would recommend what we considered reasonable targets, and voices would be raised that there had to be a clearer connection with terrorism. "We're attacking a country here," Moellering would argue, "not slicing baloney. It makes no sense to think that if we get a terrorist target they won't be mad because it's only just and fair retribution. I'm sorry, but they are going to be mad. Once you bomb somebody, you've ripped your jeans. We've decided to commit a hostile act, and we are going to be criticized for it, regardless of what we hit. So if we're going to cross that line, let's take out something meaningful." I was continually amazed at how difficult that case was to sell.

Some thought the one really meaningful target would be Qaddafi himself. I thought that trying to kill Qaddafi made little sense. The man never slept in the same place two nights running. He moved; airfields and headquarters buildings didn't. Even those who were most eager to get Qaddafi accepted the validity of that argument, especially given the spotty intelligence and the limited resources we would be able to bring to bear. The notion that we should try to target Qaddafi never got past a few initial discussions. In the end we did injure him, but that was sheer accident; he happened to be sleeping that night in a tent next to a headquarters building that was a target. Seymour Hersh and several other journalists later accused us of designing the raid as an attempt to assassinate Qaddafi, but it was an accusation based on ignorance. Hersh wrote as if he had access to secret inside information. In fact he and the others were simply wrong, or at best had listened to the wrong sources.*

In the final analysis, our tactical decisions were based largely on political considerations. The first requirement was to keep American losses to an absolute minimum. We did not want casualties, and we did not want the Libyans parading prisoners through the streets of Tripoli. This limited us considerably, a point I emphasized in NSPG discussions. It necessitated a quick nighttime raid to reduce the reaction time of the Libyan air defenses. We could not mount successive waves or send planes in more than once. The other major political goal was to minimize Libyan civilian casualties. We certainly wanted to discredit any subsequent claims that our objective had been to attack noncombatants.

We sacrificed a number of the best targets because of our determination to avoid civilian casualties—particularly some military and intelligence targets in the center of Tripoli. Had we really wanted to pinpoint them, we would have had to go in the daytime, or linger for more time than we deemed wise. That in turn would have increased the risk to our pilots. We ended up choosing targets located so that if our planes missed, they would be unlikely to hit populated areas by accident.

I worried that the attack might not be substantial enough to wreak

---

* One interesting characteristic of the Pentagon is that a journalist who looks long and hard enough can find an "inside" source to support any premise. Everyone knows this, and reporters interested in accuracy take it into account.

tangible damage. People tend to remember pictures they have seen of bombed-out cities in World War Two, or more recently of the destruction in Iraq. But a six-plane attack making one pass does not have that kind of effect. A strike on that scale is lucky if it puts a bomb in the middle of a building and does some visible damage. More often the only sign will be a hole in the hangar roof or a few craters in a runway. Given our self-imposed limitations, structuring the attack was tricky. Since political decisions ruled out a preliminary assault on the air defense network, the last planes of an overly large raid would run a high risk from anti-aircraft fire. But if the raid was too small, the damage would be insignificant. When political conditions come into play so heavily, military planning becomes a series of hard compromises.

In the end my team managed to get about half our target recommendations accepted, among them the Tripoli and Benina airfields. We wanted to hit aircraft at those fields, and we wanted to put the runways out of business—at least temporarily. The Benina airfield especially was usually crowded with Migs. The intelligence people also prevailed; they insisted on something that would look as if we were hitting the control mechanism of the Libyan military. The way Qaddafi's command system was set up, there was not much control, so I harbored considerable skepticism about the significance of striking a command target. But intelligence persisted, so we picked out the headquarters compound at Azziziyah in the middle of the city. This would increase the risk of civilian collateral damage, but it was one of the few targets that lent itself to precision bombing at night.

We also did end up identifying one bona fide terrorist target, a complex at Murrat Sidi Bilal used in training SEAL-type commando operations. The equipment was kept in a large building right on the beach that had a barracks connected to it. From the aerial photographs we could see a few boats and what looked like torpedoes. There weren't too many people around, but here we could at least say with a straight face that we had found a terrorist target. We gave considerable thought as well to hitting key economic installations. But economic targets like pipelines or oil terminals require repeated raids. The attacker must be persistent and willing to take losses, and this we had decided against.

Given all the restrictions, I was not confident about our ability to hurt Qaddafi meaningfully. In essence the raid would be a political not a military operation. Consequently, I was not especially happy with the strike that was planned. I would have preferred one that would have made our point more decisively, a position my people argued a number of times during the debate.

At the final NSPG meeting I again went over the parameters of the attack, making it clear that the political constraints severely limited our capabilities and that it would be difficult to guarantee damage levels. My own preference, I reiterated, was for military targets and a more substantial effort. Otherwise, why cross the Rubicon in the first place?

But the political priorities were set. "If we get in and out fast," said one State Department representative, "we won't lose anybody, will we?" My answer to that was that if we were insisting on zero losses, then we had better not go at all. I did not believe our casualties would be high, but there was a good probability that we would lose one or two planes. It was naive to misunderstand the inherently uncertain nature of combat.

Without a doubt, I thought, the raid would boost American domestic morale and signal our displeasure; it might also have some positive effect around the world in demonstrating our seriousness. But I was not optimistic it would have any long-term impact on Libya's support of terrorism. On the other hand, I did feel the time had come to strike back and to test Qaddafi's determination.

Qaddafi's likely response was a mystery we couldn't plan for. There might be nothing. On the other hand, he could accelerate terrorism or even send kamikaze assaults at our ships in the Gulf of Sidra. Some thought there was a possibility he might launch an attack on Egypt. The CIA's psychological profile indicated Qaddafi was irrational in some ways and therefore unpredictable. The report depicted a man of overweening vanity, high temper, and tremendous ego, a man who would not allow himself to be intimidated under any circumstances. The suggestion was that if he lost face he would dedicate himself to revenge. Frankly, the analysis seemed shallow and highly speculative, and in the end it did nothing to influence decisions. But no one was making predictions with any certainty.

Once the decision was made to go, Air Force F-111s based in England were brought into the picture to complement the attack planes of the Sixth Fleet. We had two sets of targets, one around Tripoli and one around the Benina airfield in eastern Libya. We knew the Libyans would expect an attack to come from the carriers, and the fleet was deployed too far to the east to easily strike at Tripoli. Undoubtedly, they would have early warning of any carrier strike.

But we did not believe they would be expecting us to fly through the Strait of Gibraltar.

After the raid some criticized us for using the F-111s on such a long, difficult run. The charge was that they had been included solely to give the Air Force part of the action. That criticism always disturbed me. The number of services involved was irrelevant. The significant factors were the element of surprise and the firepower we could bring to bear. Given that we would be permitted only one strike, the Sixth Fleet was too limited in the weight of ordnance it could deliver. The element of surprise combined with the F-111s' superb fire control ideally suited them for a low-level one-pass night attack against heavy flak. In my mind, these advantages were decisive.

Air Force participation depended on Margaret Thatcher's willingness to permit the use of English bases. At the same time requests were made to allow us to overfly France and Spain, but those governments kept us hanging by our teeth. We especially wanted to go across France, which would have shortened the flight by two or three hours. Without French permission we were looking at the F-111s spending seven hours in the air and refueling five times on the way down. The aviators were prepared for it and had worked out alternate flight plans, but we put final decisions on hold until we knew if we had permission.

We bickered with France until the last minute, when General Bernard Rogers, the Commander-in-Chief of U.S. forces in Europe (and NATO's Supreme Allied Commander), called to tell me that Mitterrand had refused. Spain for its part was noncommittal. We might overfly, they said, as long as we did not ask permission—their theory being that if anything untoward happened they could deny participation. Rogers and I decided that with that sort of response we should go around Spain rather than over it. The question was, given the difficulties of the flight, should we go ahead at all? We had the tanking equipment in place, but would the severe fatigue of the marathon flight place the mission at too much risk? When the pilots themselves expressed absolute confidence that they could do it, Rogers and I decided to go ahead.

As time ran down, I became increasingly concerned about information leaking out to the Libyans. They suspected we might come and they were taking steps to augment their defenses. One serious problem was that people in Washington were doing their best to find out if anything was in the wind. For weeks the press had been speculating about an attack and the Pentagon correspondents were working overtime to substantiate rumors and break whatever details they could uncover.

I took a jaundiced view of this effort. My own psychology on such matters had been shaped during my early days in the Navy, when ship operations were classified right across the board in peacetime as well as wartime. When I first went to sea, it was drummed into us that you did not discuss operations. That was a holdover from World War Two, but I thought it was a rather good holdover.

But as the government opened up more and more over the years, the old approach eroded. Now the press assumes they have the right to operational details, at least in peacetime. Of course, when we decided to raid Libya we were determined to keep every bit of information secret—if we were going to attack, when, in what fashion. Despite all the speculation, we released nothing. But the press tried very hard to break our silence.

The journalist most successful at ferreting out information was George Wilson, the veteran military correspondent for the *Washington Post*. Not only was Wilson an aggressive and experienced investigator, he had also written a book on aircraft carriers, and in doing the research he had lived for six months aboard the *John F. Kennedy*. In the process he had made many Navy friends. He was obviously receiving operational details—where ships were going, what kind of operations they were training for, and other hard information. He was determined to break a story on when and how we were going to raid Libya, and I was not terribly confident that he couldn't do it.

I had so little success keeping operational details of the Libyan raid out of the papers that I set a false date for the attack and classified it "secret." Then at the last moment I switched the date to two days earlier. It was the sort of deception military people used to practice on their enemies.

The War Powers Resolution requires congressional consultation prior to any commitment of American troops to a war zone. But the problem with consultation is that congressmen often hold press conferences immediately afterwards and issue statements about what they have just heard. Of course they are asked not to, but on such matters they are their own bosses. With this in mind, President Reagan decided to schedule the consultation on the Libya raid as late as he could make it. In fact, after talking it over with his advisers, he decided to hold the meeting *after* the F-111s had taken off on their long run from England.

The meeting was held on April 26 in the Executive Office Building at four in the afternoon. A large group attended, the entire House and Senate leadership rather than just the majority and minority leaders. The atmosphere was friendly but strained; everyone understood that Libya was the subject.

The President was the last to arrive, accompanied by his Chief of Staff Donald Regan and National Security Adviser Robert Mc-Farlane. McFarlane led off, explaining the purpose of the meeting. Then President Reagan briefly described the situation, wording his remarks in such a way as to indicate that he was not asking for approval but simply telling the congressmen what he was going to do and requesting their views. He was followed by Secretaries Shultz and Weinberger, who painted the general political background and outlined the decision to mount the strike. Then McFarlane asked me to brief the attack.

When I finished, the floor was opened for comments. Predictably, the Republican leadership supported the President. Senator Robert Dole's brief comment perhaps reflected their sentiments most concisely: "That's fine," he said. When it was the Democrats' turn, Senator Robert Byrd differed. "I don't think that's fine at all," he said. "Where are these planes anyway? What time is the strike?"

"Seven o'clock," said McFarlane, "something like that."

"What if we decide not to do it?" said Byrd.

"Well," McFarlane replied, "we can always call them back."

"What do you mean call them back?" said Byrd. "Are they in the air now?"

"Yes," I answered, "they're in the air now. They're flying toward Tripoli."

Byrd hit the ceiling. "This doesn't sound like consultation to me," he said. "This sounds like you're just informing us. You've already decided what to do."

A spirited discussion ensued, during which the President, seconded by McFarlane, insisted the planes could be recalled and that too much was being made of this point. But Byrd was not interested in calling them back. He was angry, and despite only lukewarm backing from his Democratic colleagues he pressed on, denouncing the President's failure to confer. As an accomplished politician, the senator was not about to say whether he liked the idea of the raid. (Actually Byrd has been fairly consistent in his political life as not favoring forceful or violent options.) He was focusing on the ''consultation process,'' and he launched into an impassioned speech about how surely there were some congressmen who could be trusted enough to be brought in early on the planning process and kept informed throughout so that there wouldn't be any surprises at the last minute, when planes were already in the air.

In the administration's mind, planning of that sort is not Congress's responsibility, and there are few opposition congressmen who could be trusted with such information. That was the real answer to Byrd, though those things were not said out loud. Reagan, Shultz, and Weinberger treated him with kid gloves, but they didn't give an inch either.

''Right here in this room,'' Byrd declared in exasperation, ''are people who are trustworthy.'' Those words had a strong ring to them, but immediately after the meeting Byrd met with reporters and practically announced that an attack was under way. Two or three other congressmen went out and made statements that were also fairly transparent, but Byrd's was the most worrisome.

Both sides obviously had a point. Waiting until the planes take off to confer with Congress is hardly in the spirit of the War Powers Resolution. (Of course, no President has conceded the resolution's constitutionality.) As Chairman I would have felt far more comfortable if such operations were launched with at least the implicit approval of the legislature.

But the executive branch does have sound reservations. The use of force becomes politicized quickly; the President cannot expect Congress to confront issues impartially, nor to respect his confidences. Many congressmen are unable to resist the temptation to appear knowledgeable and influential once they have access to important military information. Senator Byrd's suggestion regarding the selection of a few congressmen to be privy to the planning process might have merit, except that it is hard to imagine Congress allowing the President to make those choices himself. Given the adversarial nature of our system, there is little chance that the argument can be resolved amicably or that the War Powers Resolution can be made to work. As presently practiced, it is not achieving its goals and serves merely to bring the two branches into conflict. Needless to say, it also severely complicates the role of the military planner.

The meeting in the Executive Office Building went on for an hour, and by the time it ended I wanted badly to be somewhere else. We were getting close. The moment I got back to the Pentagon I went into the command center. Everyone was on radio silence, but I knew that Sixth Fleet communications would be piped directly into the Pentagon Navy center while the Air Force center would very likely be monitoring some of the Air Force battle nets. I had the choice of putting it all through to the Joint Chiefs command center, but I decided against it. Listening to the talk from the planes and ships, the temptation to butt in is too great. It is hard enough for experienced commanders to keep from injecting themselves into their field officers' affairs, and I thought it might be particularly hard for the Secretary of Defense if he was exposed to raw reports in the heat of action. Consequently I elected to make do with our phone links to the European and Mediterranean commanders.

Once an operation is under way it is the responsibility of the men on site who know the situation intimately and are attuned to the moment-by-moment happenings. The senior commanders back at the Pentagon should not be interfering. Nevertheless, some do listen in and they often talk to their local commanders, which tends to greatly annoy the people in the field. They don't think any of the real-time exchanges are the rear echelon's business.

I had thought a good deal about questions of command and control, but quite apart from the theoretical side I had myself heard some startling conversations between rear headquarters commanders and field commanders. One memorable instance had taken place on April 30, 1975, during our evacuation of Saigon. I was in the Pentagon on that grim night when an amazing exchange was piped into the JCS command post.

The command center in Saigon was six or seven floors below ground, a miniature Pentagon. The commander there was Army Major General Homer Smith. As Smith was evacuating his headquarters, we heard him talking to the Pacific commander, to whom he was responsible. Smith was saying, "Helicopters are due in three minutes. I'm starting to evacuate." Then some other last-minute talk, then, "O.K., Admiral, I'm signing off here. I'm going up to meet the helicopters." There was a two- or three-minute lag, and then we heard this voice, "Homer, Homer!"—the voice of the Pacific commander. From Saigon, a radio operator said, "Admiral, General Smith has gone up to meet the helicopters. I'll get him right down." The man sitting beside me in Washington moaned, "Jesus Christ, that's seven floors up." Then there was a long delay, very long—eight or ten minutes. Then Smith's somewhat breathless voice: "Yeah, go ahead, I'm on the circuit." "Homer, Homer, tell the people going out to those helicopters to keep their heads down!"

Homer Smith was in the middle of evacuating his command—the most important event in his life. He didn't have room in his head for all the headaches he had. The last thing in the world he or anybody with him had to be told was to keep their heads down. It was a marvel that Smith was able to keep his self-control when he received this helpful piece of advice. I resolved right then and there that I was not going to interfere with commanders in the field, if at all avoidable.

At six-thirty on the night of the raid, Weinberger came into the command center, a small room off the main OPCON center where I was monitoring events with four or five others. Dick Burpee, the J-3, had stationed himself there and was in constant phone contact with CINCEUR headquarters in Stuttgart. I had been scheduled to attend a cocktail party that night at the Washington Marina. Not wanting to arouse questions, I had not cancelled. Shirley would make some vague excuse on the spot.

The strike was scheduled for midnight Tripoli time, seven o'clock in Washington, but with radio silence there was nothing to do but sit and look at each other. We would not know what happened until the planes cleared the beach and reported back to their respective headquarters. As usual, we were following CNN, and moments before seven the newscaster came on. "The tension in Libya is palpable tonight," he said. "Now we take you to our correspondent in Tripoli."

From Tripoli the correspondent's voice said, "I am at the [so-and-so] hotel, standing on the balcony outside my room looking out over Tripoli at night. The quiet and calm of the city belies the tension that has been building steadily here." He went on in that fashion for a minute or two, then said, "Wait a minute, I'm hearing bombs and gunfire. Yes, over there I can see rockets. I think there's an attack going on." Weinberger and I smiled at each other. The strike was on the minute.

Sitting there in the command center was gut-wrenching. We knew the attack had gone in, but nothing else. Then suddenly after twelve or fifteen minutes a report came from the European command— "Raid commander reports all aircraft feet wet"—followed by a report from the Sixth Fleet, "Feet wet, no casualties."

A short time later a second signal came in, less comforting. "First report possibly not correct. We cannot account for one aircraft.

Polling our group again.'' At that moment the F-111s were quite busy. The instant they cleared the beach they had to join with refueling tankers offshore, an operation that requires minute judgment at any time but was especially nerve-racking after the crews had just completed an extraordinary flight and been through the excitement of a low-level night attack. It wasn't until the third or fourth report that they were able to confirm that an aircraft was in fact missing.

At the time we did not know what had happened. In the debriefings, two other pilots reported having seen a ball of flame and something go into the water just as they were crossing the beach. Putting their reports together with bits and pieces of communications, we pretty well determined where we thought the plane had hit the water, though we did not know if he had been struck by an anti-air missile or if the pilot had become disoriented and lost control. We never were able to find out, though we thought a missile unlikely because this happened before the raid had actually hit home and we did not believe their air defense system had been alerted that quickly. In any event, there was an explosion and the plane went down in flames. Later the Libyans recovered two bodies and we heard rumors that they were going to do terrible things to them. But nothing of that nature happened. Eventually they offered to return the bodies, and after some on-again, off-again negotiations they did so.

For the next several days the weather over Libya prevented aerial photography. When we finally did get good pictures, I was upset at the apparent lack of damage. We had not exactly disfigured the Libyan landscape. The pilots had reported Libyan planes exploding on runways and other good hits; we even had gun camera film confirming some hits. But the pictures were not as clear as we would have wished. Later overhead shots showed burn marks on runways, but otherwise there was little debris at the main Tripoli airfield.

But then, to our surprise, Qaddafi himself went on television, showing people through the damage at the Azziziyah barracks. We had hit the command and control building we were after pretty severely. The tent Qaddafi had been sleeping in that night was close by, and he had apparently been wounded by several pieces of shrapnel. Qaddafi claimed his adopted daughter was killed, but we could find no record of the girl or their relationship.

Gradually intelligence began receiving reports from intercepted Libyan communications about plane damage. We were also able to more closely analyze the laser videotapes from the lead planes. From these we could make out the explosions the pilots had described, and when we counted the runway burns it was clear we had indeed wrought some havoc. A number of planes had blown up on the taxiways, which was what we had intended, but the Libyans had removed and hidden the wreckage before the weather permitted decent photography. At Benina, though, our success had been more modest. Most planes on the airstrip had been removed to other sites just prior to the raid, although several that were still there had been destroyed and airfield installations damaged.

Despite all our precautions, it also turned out that we had caused some collateral damage. War is not like everyday life; plans can go to hell in a moment. In a low-level high-speed attack at night it is inevitable that people will make mistakes. Only two of the Tripoli raid pilots had ever been in combat before. The raid commander was a Vietnam veteran, as was one other pilot in his group. But none of the rest had ever fired a shot in anger.

The planes that had bombed the Azziziyah barracks had used laser-guided "smart" bombs. With these weapons the pilot locks his laser on the target, then releases the bomb, which follows the laser home. But traveling at a jiggling 600 mph just about ground level in the heat of combat, the pilot sees the target at the last second and the crosshairs might be off a bit the moment he fires. Of course the bomb will still follow the laser wherever it happens to be pointing. A very slight error can send the bomb a long way from its target.

Shortly after the raid we knew that there had been some damage to the French embassy, which was nowhere near any of the objectives. Given the Quai d'Orsay's refusal of overflight rights for the attack, some observers drew the hasty conclusion that an annoyed F-111 aviator might have been expressing his resentment. But this was not the case. When Weinberger was asked about it during the press conference that he and Shultz held immediately after the raid, he opined that it was impossible we had hit the embassy. That was the Secretary of Defense's standard approach—admit nothing, don't speculate, emphatically deny. It could not have come from our aircraft, said Weinberger, who knew that we had no targets near the embassy. With all the anti-aircraft firing, some of the spent weaponry had likely fallen back down and hit the building.

But it turned out to be a U.S. bomb after all. When the pilots were debriefed, one of them volunteered that when he hit the pickle he was not on target. He estimated he was about a quarter of a degree up, which would have lofted the bomb about a mile and a half beyond the target. When we plotted it out, there was the French embassy, right in the glide path.

When I informed Weinberger, he said, "Well, we don't know for sure, do we?"

"No," I said, "but the evidence is pretty good."

"Well, as long as we don't know for sure, I'm sticking to my story." And until he left office he was talking about Libyan anti-aircraft fire coming back down on the French embassy. It got to be a kind of standing joke between us.

In the many discussions we held prior to the attack there was a general consensus that at the very least Qaddafi would retaliate by heightening the terrorism level. Many people had ideas about what he might do and how extensively he might do it; speculation abounded. But nobody predicted what actually did happen.

Instead of reacting violently, the Libyan leader went to cover. He did not do any of the things that had been considered likely.* His raving and ranting became remarkably subdued, and his investment in terrorism tailed off. Instead he went into the desert and meditated, as some reports had it, or attempted to recover his composure and overcome his embarrassment, as was more likely. For quite some time he was not seen in public. We had reports from people who had been in his presence that he seemed shaken—depressed and confused. We guessed that if he was in truth the extravagant egotist he seemed, perhaps the very fact that someone had attacked and almost killed him had been a devastating blow to his pride and balance. Instead of making him fighting mad it had shocked him profoundly. For the next few months we heard nothing from his military; they did not come out and probe as they had previously. They did not even cross the coastline anymore. His forces went into hibernation.

From our standpoint the attack was eminently successful. I had not expected it; I thought it likely we would be compelled to inflict more destruction. But it turned out that we hadn't needed it, that modest raid was sufficient. It had a major personal impact on Qaddafi and it achieved what we wanted—to make him reconsider his terrorism policy and to impress him personally with Washington's determination not to be intimidated. Beyond that, it demonstrated our capabilities and the fact that we had an open option to do the same, or worse, again. In retrospect, the return on the investment was extremely high—much higher than I had personally anticipated.

---

* Although, as this is being written, there is some suggestion that Pan Am 103 might possibly have been a Libyan retaliation.

Chapter 8

GOLDWATER-
NICHOLS

AIR FORCE GENERAL DAVID JONES took considerable criticism
as Chairman of the Joint Chiefs of Staff during the Carter administration. In the eyes of many in the defense establishment, the worst of
his various sins was that he had bought into Jimmy Carter's commitment to downgrading the armed services. They insisted that he had
conspired with Carter and Secretary of Defense Harold Brown in
slashing budgets and programs.

During his tenure, Davey Jones had spoken publicly about problems within the Joint Chiefs of Staff. In his view, the chairmanship
was not strong enough. The JCS organization precluded efficiency;
it typically produced slow responses and inclined toward the least
common denominator among the services. The system, he maintained, was badly in need of reform. The defense leadership (both
military and civilian) dismissed Jones's criticism out of hand. To
them it was a classic case of sour grapes—a disgruntled Chairman
venting his spleen.

But Jones was a determined man, and when he left the chairmanship he began to write and comment about the JCS, pressing the
need for reorganization. Whenever one of his articles appeared, reporters would get hold of it and rush over to interview people in the
Pentagon, especially the service chiefs and Jones's successor as
Chairman, General John Vessey. But the unanimous response was
That's nonsense. The Pentagon does not need reorganizing.

Eventually, though, retired Army Chief of Staff Edward Meyer
broke ranks and came out on Jones's side. Despite the Pentagon
denials, Meyer claimed that Jones was right; the Joint Chiefs were
indeed overdue for a major restructuring. "Shy" Meyer had been a
very young Army Chief of Staff with some rather innovative ideas
and the courage to challenge ingrown beliefs. He was also a man of
affairs about Washington, an articulate intellectual individual with a

reputation for knowing what he was talking about. No one concerned with the military was likely to dismiss his opinions outright.

Among those who listened was Sam Nunn, senior Democrat on the Senate Armed Services Committee. Nunn, who liked and admired both Meyer and Jones, then began to examine the situation himself. Before long he too was convinced that some type of defense reorganization was in order. Nunn knew that achieving this would be no minor challenge. A comprehensive analysis would have to be undertaken and ultimately legislation written and shepherded through Congress.

Nunn's first problem was that reorganization was a highly unpopular topic at the Defense Department; General Vessey and his fellow chiefs had already expressed themselves on the subject, and their opposition was echoed by other influential figures in the defense establishment. The political barriers to achieving any significant reform were daunting. Nunn's solution—a brilliant one—was to co-opt the support of Barry Goldwater, Chairman of the Armed Services Committee. Goldwater's lifelong espousal of the military would assert the legitimacy of reform as nothing else could. Goldwater himself had little energy left for battle. Fast approaching retirement, he was in constant physical pain, and his forceful personality was no longer what it had once been. But his stature and reputation were still very much intact. Moreover, as retirement approached he wanted to leave some mark that would outlive his own tenure.

Nunn's initial step was to persuade Goldwater that there was indeed something amiss and to endorse a working group of Armed Service Committee staffers to launch an in-depth study of defense organization. Then he appointed Jim Locher to head the group. A West Point graduate who had left the Army but had chosen to stay in the bureaucracy, Locher was smart and dynamic, almost driven. He had worked his way up to head of the committee staff under former Chairman John Tower and had stayed on under Goldwater. Attacking his task with relentless enthusiasm, in eighteen months Locher succeeded in producing an exceptionally interesting, 650-page report, a historical chronicle of American armed forces organization and decision making that was one of the best ever compiled. (I use it as one of my basic texts in the course on national defense organization I teach at the University of Oklahoma.)

In the process of compiling this report, Locher also succeeded in alienating a great many people. He was a good scholar, but he was young and quite convinced of the rightness of his views. Brash and often arrogant, he was a bulldog when it came to issues he felt strongly about, and he felt strongly about many. The chiefs were not pleased by the whole undertaking in the first place, and they were irate at Locher's far-reaching conclusions and at the antagonism toward the JCS they sensed from him.

In the year and a half it took to produce this report, Locher interviewed service people around the world. He had come to see me three times in Hawaii, where I was stationed at that time as Commander-in-Chief of the Pacific forces. I happened to be one of the people who agreed that some reorganization was appropriate. For three years, from 1977 to 1980, I had served as the Navy's JCS deputy, and during that time I had done a lot of thinking about the subject. The main problems with the Joint Staff were not enough jointness and too much compromise. Each service habitually saw every issue exclusively from its own standpoint and in many instances held up the release of papers until its concerns were accommodated in some fashion. This typically resulted in watered-down positions that took too long to formulate. I was likewise convinced that the quality of officers detailed to the Joint Staff could use substantial upgrading. It was unusual to find the most highly regarded officers laboring in the Joint Staff vineyard; many considered a tour there as a hurdle on the career path.

These views were not popular in the Navy. The fact was that the Army did support the Joint Staff fairly well. The Army had discovered when it was deployed in Vietnam that the command structure was organized so that they could not run the war, even though they were doing the lion's share of the fighting. CINCPAC ran it, and he reported to the Secretary of Defense through the Joint Chiefs. In maneuvering to insert itself into the command process, the Army found that the most productive approach was to put effective Army officers on the Joint Staff. Consequently, the Army began assigning some of their better people there.

In essence, the war forced the Army to scrap some of its parochialism and to take jointness more seriously. It seemed to me that the Air Force was also reorienting its approach to the Joint Staff, although they were not moving with the speed of light. Still, the Air Force effort was far better than the Navy's. The Navy has traditionally opposed anything that looked, sounded, or smelled joint.*

---

* The overarching aim of jointness is to expand officers' loyalties from a single service to the military as a whole. But it is hard for a youngster who has been trained, brought up,

I questioned that view. It seemed to me that whenever naval officers competed with their counterparts on committees and working groups they compared favorably. As a general rule they were quite well equipped to take care of themselves. Partly, the Navy's inferiority complex derived from its relative inexperience in the Washington bureaucracy. The Army and Air Force both tended to assign more officers to Washington tours and to keep people in the capital for longer periods. They had accumulated a reservoir of officers who were adept (or at least practiced) at negotiating the tricky Washington terrain. These individuals made formidable opponents in the bureaucratic wars.

There were good practical reasons for the Navy's relative inexperience in Washington. In peacetime the Army and Air Force have always had substantial slack in their organizations, which has enabled them to send large numbers of people to non-warfighting posts. The Navy, though, keeps fleets deployed in peace as in war. A high percentage of its officers have always been needed in seagoing billets. While the Navy also has brought its officers ashore for tours in Washington, they often stayed for only a couple of years before returning to sea. The maritime culture reinforced this practice. In the Navy's eyes, shore duty did not develop the important skills—a shortsighted perspective, but deeply held.

But whatever the reasons, the Navy's objections to jointness were legendary—going back to 1949 with what is usually known as "the Revolt of the Admirals." That incident (in which Chief of Naval Operations Admiral Louis Denfield was replaced after his authority was challenged by a group of senior admirals) followed a showdown between the Air Force and the Navy over the postwar role of nuclear weapons. In the course of a battle that raged in Congress as well as in the JCS, the Navy found itself opposed not only by the Air Force but by the Army as well. When it was finally over, the Navy's carefully nurtured plans for a supercarrier had been scrapped and the Air Force's strategic B-36 bomber funded. The Air Force concept of

---

and acculturated in one service to make this transition. To a layman that may seem odd. He or she may think that the Navy plays a vital role in the nation's security, but no more so than the Army or Air Force. While in the broad perspective that may be true, a career serviceman sees it differently. When I was on the Navy staff I spent much of my time making the case that the Navy does more important things than the Army. I did not mind that the Army was around or that it got a certain amount of money, but I did not want it getting too much. The heart of the matter is that military budgeting is a zero sum game. A dollar given to one service has to come from somewhere else.

strategic defense was vindicated and the Navy's concept discarded. Adding insult to injury, a new position of JCS Chairman was created, over the Navy's heated opposition.

Ever since then the Navy has been the least eager among the services to endorse any move toward unification; anything that might give someone outside the Navy control over maritime forces is instinctively opposed. Over the years a number of small steps toward reform have been taken, and every time the Navy has been against them, like the proverbial old man who said, "I've seen a lot of changes in my life and I've been agin ever one of them." The Navy too has been "agin ever one," to the extent that it became a standing joke in the Pentagon that the Navy would always be the last to vote for anything that smacked of more jointness.

I had gradually developed my own conviction of the need for reform when I served as head of OP 06. By the time Jim Locher came to see me, I was CINCPAC—unified commander of all forces in the Pacific theater, with a different set of problems and a redoubled interest in the subject. Like every other unified commander, I could only operate through the Army, Navy, Air Force, and Marine component commanders who stood between me and the forces in the field. The problem with this arrangement was that though the unified commander had all the responsibility, he did not have sufficient authority. His component commanders reported to their own service chiefs for administration, logistics, and training matters, and the service chiefs could use this channel to outflank the unified commander. There was a sizable potential for confusion and conflict.

The Vietnam War had been a tragic example of the harm a convoluted command structure could cause. There were more recent illustrations too. In the Beirut Marine operation the structure was long, complex, and clumsy. No provisions had been made for tailoring the command chain to circumstances. Grenada also suffered from lack of coordination among several layers of command. In fact, command difficulties seemed to surface in every operation we undertook.

In my meetings with Jim Locher I discussed the need to streamline the cumbersome command setup. I was even more vocal about the need to assure the loyalty of the component commanders to their unified commander rather than to their service chiefs. Component commanders had to have a single boss. I also favored more jointness throughout the operational world and a further centralization of authority under the Chairman of the Joint Chiefs. Others were also raising these same themes with Locher, and several of them found their way into his final report.

When the dust settled after publication of the Armed Services Committee's reorganization report, it was clear that everyone's ox had been gored and some were gored badly. Few liked it. In keeping with naval tradition, Secretary of the Navy John Lehman vehemently opposed the whole business, and so did most of his senior lieutenants. But the Navy wasn't alone—all the service chiefs rejected one or more parts of the proposal. JCS Chairman John Vessey maintained there was no need to reorganize and Cap Weinberger was fiercely hostile to the scheme. He had been Secretary of Defense for five years already. He simply was not going to subscribe to changes that seemed to reflect negatively on his administration.

But Sam Nunn went ahead anyway. When I came to Washington as Chairman in the fall of 1985, he was already drafting the Goldwater-Nichols Defense Reorganization Act. (William Nichols was a leading member of the House Armed Services Committee.) The sponsorship of these two highly respected legislators gave it a political aura and assured that, when and if it passed, the act would serve as a monument to them. But despite the formal sponsorship, the bill had been fathered by Nunn, and he was the one seeing it through from beginning to end.

Once defense reform was in the air, a number of Washington think tanks undertook their own studies, including the Center for Strategic and International Studies. For a time defense reorganization seemed to be the capital's leading cottage industry. These studies complemented Jim Locher's Armed Services Committee staff report, and consequently Nunn was able to draw on analyses done by groups of scholars and defense analysts with various points of view.

Interestingly, most of these reports addressed problems with Congress as well as with the JCS, Secretary of Defense's office, and the services. Practically everyone who looked at the problems of defense organization came out with a long list of recommendations concerning how Congress should change the way it did business with the Defense Department. Although Congress eventually passed the defense reorganization bill, it limited itself to addressing JCS and DOD shortcomings while ignoring completely the recommendations regarding its own structure and practices. This although most of the studies stressed that the recommended reforms were interdependent. There was not that much to be gained from restructuring the Pentagon without at the same time reshaping the congressional machinery. It has been cogently argued that congressional reforms are the most fundamental of all, and equally cogently pointed out that Congress will enthusiastically reorganize everyone but itself.

As the momentum for reorganization gathered steam, the administration asked former deputy Secretary of Defense David Packard to lead a study of the defense "acquisition structure" and make recommendations accordingly. The behind-the-scenes purpose of this initiative was to undermine the reformers and fend off Goldwater-Nichols. Ultimately, however, the Packard Commission issued a report which went substantially further than the sponsors intended and more or less confirmed the theory that improvements were called for, especially in regard to a stronger chairmanship. In any event, Congress was not so easily derailed. The Armed Services Committee had been ready to treat the Packard report as the administration gambit it was. Instead they were emboldened by it and went full speed ahead with the development of Goldwater-Nichols. Hearings on reorganization went on for months, and I found myself spending much of my time that year testifying before the various committees examining the subject.

It was an interesting period for me, and a delicate one. Weinberger's opposition to reorganization was determined, and the chiefs had a number of strong objections. All of them took issue with the Locher report, which I had contributed to in some measure. Of course, during my meetings with Locher I had had no suspicion that I would be named Chairman of the Joint Chiefs. But here I was. Somehow, despite the opposition within the military establishment, I had to do what I could to encourage Goldwater-Nichols. At the same time I had to fashion a good working relationship with the chiefs—which seemed like squaring the circle. Above all, I wanted the chairmanship strengthened. But if I was too adamant about that, there was no question the services would interpret my advocacy as a matter of transparent self-aggrandizement. I might think I was above such motives, but few others were likely to give me that much credit.

It was a tough position to be in. I did think there were some items in Goldwater-Nichols I could safely press for out in the open. I wanted a vice chairman, for example, which the chiefs initially opposed. But every chief had a four-star deputy, so it was hard for them to argue that they needed the help a deputy provided but the Chairman didn't. The chiefs did not want a change, because under the current system, when the Chairman was out of town one of the chiefs became acting Chairman. This gave them a modicum of extra authority and informed them of the Chairman's business. It kept the Chairman under better control, which they all favored, including Weinberger.

Changes that directly increased the Chairman's authority were harder for me to formally endorse. My approach on these was to stay out of the public debate while doing what I could behind the scenes to further them. In this delicate process I relied largely on the deft touch of Captain Rick DeBobes, chief legal counsel to the JCS and the most effective lawyer I worked with during my career. Serving as my representative, DeBobes found himself in the middle of several complicated fora. On the one hand he was meeting regularly with Jim Locher and his colleagues on the Senate Armed Services Committee staff, helping them draft language for Goldwater-Nichols. At the same time he attended meetings of the Defense Department and service representatives, who were assiduously providing point papers for use by opponents of the bill. Among the service representatives DeBobes strove to maintain a low profile, not an altogether easy task considering the intensity of emotions (John Lehman's Navy representative in particular seemed obsessed by the evil of the strong chairman provisions). Because i did not take a public position on these items, many people assumed that I, like the other chiefs, was against reorganization. That was not true. But I had to tread carefully.

I also tried to reduce some of the heat by introducing and implementing changes in advance of the legislation. I urged the chiefs to address the criticisms ourselves, in our own terms, rather than waiting until Congress forced new procedures on us. This suggestion met with resistance, but when it became clear that we were going to get a bill, like it or not, the attitude began to moderate. This was easier than it might have been, because over the course of the year the chiefs' opposition to the bill in general became less adamant. As time went on they began to conclude that some of their early objections had not been well founded, and they started considering specific issues more dispassionately. We were, in fact, able to make a number of modifications that many military people previously considered impossible.

Some of the procedures we changed were so hoary and sacred that I occasionally thought the Tank was going to explode from the effort.* We rewrote Pub One, for example ("Joint Chiefs of Staff Pub-

---

* Near the Chairman's office in the Pentagon's E Ring, the "Tank" is the room where the Joint Chiefs normally meet. The nickname is a holdover from the original meeting room, which was located in the bowels of the old Army Munitions Building among the boilers. The current chamber was formerly entitled the "Gold Room," after the hue of its carpet and curtains, but the term is now seldom used.

lication One," the document that spells out the command structure of the United States military), eliminating per dictum much of the parochialism that was drawing such stinging criticism from Congress. But sometimes it was a dogfight. In four years as Chairman, the closest I came to seeing punches thrown in the Tank was during our discussion of the Pub One section concerning the control of Marine air.

Marine air has always been used as flying artillery. Marine pilots are trained in the art of providing close support for their ground troops, who typically do not have the tanks and big guns that Army units do. To assure that this support will always be available, the Corps has tenaciously guarded the command of its air arm, an arrangement sanctified by Pub One. But unified commanders see the world differently, as I found out firsthand when I was head of NATO in southern Europe. In war games where we practiced reinforcing Europe in the face of a Soviet attack, Marine air would often arrive quickly. Marine troops, though, sometimes took several weeks. But though the aircraft were unemployed, the Marine command would not relinquish control. Their position was simple: Those squadrons were for the troops; when the troops got there we would marry them up and they would do what they were supposed to do. The unified commander's theory was: I don't care what they're for. If they're not working and we're engaged, they should be put to work in the war. But to his immense frustration, JCS Pub One gave the authority to the Marines.

One of the Joint Staff's proposed changes was to assign ultimate control of Marine air to the unified commander, and when the chiefs took up the revision a brouhaha erupted. Control of their air arm had been a pillar of Marine philosophy for decades, and it wasn't just active Marines who felt strongly about it, it was retired Marines and the ghosts of earlier generations of leathernecks.

I argued that giving the unified commander control did not mean the Marines were not going to have air. Theater commanders understood that air support is a necessity, and once Marine ground units arrived in theater they would have it. But in the interim Marine air could be used for other missions, and in emergencies it could be taken away from them. I knew some Marines felt that if anybody other than a Marine was the theater commander, he would be prone to declaring emergencies when there were none and take away the air. But we were not in the business of developing petty warlords who jealously guarded their fiefdoms. We were developing high commanders with good sense and integrity. And if we weren't, we were doing something wrong.

On the first day of this discussion tempers were high. Army General John Wickham had been a joint commander in Korea and he strongly supported change. The Air Force's Charlie Gabriel agreed, but he was more restrained. Admiral Jim Watkins temporized, but it was clear his sympathies were with the Marines. Marine Commandant P. X. Kelley was vehemently opposed to any change, and he made sure no one mistook his position. As the temperature rose, it became crystal clear that nothing would be achieved that day unless it was shedding blood or scattering teeth. I adjourned the meeting.

When we took the issue up again two days later, I was prepared for the worst. But by then tempers had cooled and people had had time to reflect. What followed was one of the most statesmanlike discussions I ever witnessed in the Tank. That day the chiefs were not men fighting for turf but military leaders thinking of the larger picture and determined to make whatever accommodations were necessary to bring the system up to date. The proposed change was adopted quietly. I was never prouder of the chiefs. The entire group —Generals Kelley, Wickham, Gabriel, and Admiral Watkins—demonstrated exceptional broad-mindedness and control. They had spirited arguments, but in the end they acted in a responsible and collegial fashion. The incident gave good evidence that the critics had underestimated the chiefs' ability to lay aside their partisanship when necessary. Jim Locher would not have believed it.

The fact was that the problem of interservice rivalry had indeed been overdramatized. In a sense, this was the criticism that had gotten Goldwater-Nichols off the ground, and congressmen who were pushing the bill kept it in the forefront for their own political purposes. Nichols especially painted interservice conflict as a rampant force. The chiefs, meanwhile, felt strongly that they were being unjustly maligned by critics who attacked them for never agreeing and stubbornly pursuing parochial positions at every turn. An exacerbating factor was that a good deal of committee testimony came from retired officers, and it was true that those who had served during the Carter era had experienced a strenuous interservice atmosphere. Jimmy Carter had cut back on military spending, and whenever funding decreases, interservice rivalry increases. But Watkins, Wickham, Kelley, and Gabriel had come to the Joint Chiefs in more relaxed and harmonious times. Much of what they were hearing in their forebears' testimony sounded foreign; it did not seem to apply to the organization they knew.*

To accomplish this agreement and others, the chiefs had to overcome some difficult and genuine service concerns. Marine Commandant Kelley was worried about his retired community, the attitude of his young aviators, and a host of other pressures which burden leaders who must retain credibility with the men and women they lead. (This was not a sin; it was a fact of life for all the heads of service.) All the chiefs faced serious dilemmas. On the one hand, they were constrained to act objectively and reasonably, in the best interests of the nation. But they also felt great pressure to function as the stalwart leaders of their own services.

Each service holds certain parochial beliefs dearly. These ideas may not be rational by some criteria, but that is irrelevant. Service communities expect their leaders to protect and cleave to their traditional viewpoints, or provide very good reasons for not doing so. It is a fact that if a service chief is to be effective he must have some type of consensual base in his own service to work from—just as a president, cabinet member, CEO, or congressman must have his base of support. Of course, he can on occasion depart from the norms, but he must do it skillfully and educate the troops as he goes. Otherwise he risks losing his credibility and his strength.

The retired military communities keep a close watch over what goes on in their services' upper levels. If they do not like what a service chief is doing, they tell him they don't like it, and they do not mince words. The retired community sponsors a large number of organizations that meet often and provide a social milieu for members and their families. Much of what they do involves the continued health and well-being of their particular service. Every chief knows that he is going to move out into that world in a very few years. He has many friends who are retired, soon enough he himself will retire, and he understands where so many of his ties will ultimately be. This is another one of the pressures which high commanders must balance, and it takes judgment and personal courage to do so.

While I was chairman I was quite fortunate not to have had much pressure from the retired community, mainly because I did not really

---

* At the same time, Congress more readily believes testimony from retired people than from active duty officers. The active officer, they think (with some justification), will toe the party line, while the retired person is more likely to be candid. The chiefs used to joke that they looked forward to retirement; it would make honest men of them.

have a retired community. I was not a nuclear submariner, I wasn't a surface officer, I wasn't an aviator. In the Navy, aviators pressure aviators, surface people pursue surface people, and submariners call submariners. Because my career did not follow any of the usual routes, I had just floated through those worlds. Thomas Hayward, the CNO from 1978 to 1982, used to kid me about it. An avid and committed aviator himself, Hayward would say to me, "You damned submariners." And I'd say, "Admiral, don't talk to me like that. I'm the only flag officer around here who doesn't have a community and the only one you can get an opinion from that doesn't have a community flavor." Hayward would just grin.

Moving the service chiefs to accommodate themselves to aspects of Goldwater-Nichols was a challenge. Convincing Caspar Weinberger to loosen his stance was even more difficult, although I had several allies in this effort, including Assistant Secretary of Defense Russ Rourke. The challenge here was to persuade Weinberger that if he continued to resist as strongly as he was, the bill would be even worse. To achieve a bill that hurt the least, he should get out in front of it. "Tell them," I urged, "that you want to cooperate with the legislation, that you know there are some things wrong, and you are willing to work with Congress to get them fixed." That would be, I thought, an effective approach, one that would have enabled the Secretary at least to influence the legislation and soften the more objectionable provisions. It would have put him in a position to argue that A, B, and C might be problems that needed addressing, but that other areas should be left alone.

Weinberger accepted that position intellectually, but when it came down to actually committing himself, he could not bring himself to do it. His problem was that he simply did not want Congress to butt into his business, a point of view that is easy to understand, but not one that is always wise. Conceptually the approach made sense to him, emotionally it was impossible.

It was clear early on that Goldwater-Nichols was going to run over its opponents, which it did. Anyone who could read the tea leaves knew we were going to have a bill, for better or worse. The Defense Department could decry it, denigrate it, condemn it, and criticize it, but we were going to have a bill. So the argument was not about whether we were going to have a bill or not, it was about whether we could make the final legislation better. When all was said and done, Weinberger preferred to go down fighting rather than cooperate with the enemy. And that is what he did.

Weinberger's feelings toward Goldwater-Nichols were similar to those of the chiefs in certain areas. He did not, for example, like the idea of increasing the Chairman's authority. A Chairman with more authority would be in a better position to frustrate the Secretary, for whom, after all, he worked. And in a sense that has happened. With the passage of Goldwater-Nichols the balance between the two has shifted somewhat, although that was not Congress's intent. The bill's strongest backers insisted it was primarily designed to strengthen the authority of the Secretary of Defense.

One element of Goldwater-Nichols that I opposed strongly was Title Four—the establishment of a distinct cadre of officers who were to specialize in joint assignments. The concept per se was not objectionable. But the detailed legislation that mandated every aspect of the "Joint Corps" from the selection process and the number of billets to promotional requirements was, I believed, a serious mistake that threatened a horrendous case of congressional micromanagement. In this instance the chiefs were unanimous in their opposition, and I agreed with them wholeheartedly. Congressman Nichols was the driver here. His staff had convinced him of the need for detailed and specific guidance, and the chiefs were unable to make a dent in his determination. Nichols was convinced our reluctance was yet another manifestation of anti-jointness.*

Goldwater-Nichols ultimately developed its own emotional momentum. As feelings heightened, it became increasingly difficult on both sides of the table to distinguish the wheat from the chaff. This was never more apparent than during the last week of debate on Goldwater-Nichols when I invited Nichols and the House Armed Services Committee to the Pentagon for breakfast with the chiefs. My hope was that we could persuade Nichols to back away from some especially onerous provisions—mainly regarding the proposed Joint Officers Corps. "This is your last chance," I told the chiefs, "the last shot we have at changing anything." In the congenial atmosphere of the breakfast I thought that the chiefs might succeed in at least moderating some of the more egregious elements. Congressman William Nichols was from Alabama. A World War Two veteran, he had lost a leg in combat and was a strong supporter of the U.S. Army, and especially its ROTC program, which he had come up through at Auburn University. Nichols was a courtly Southerner,

---

* Ultimately Title Four passed and we did our best to implement this poorly designed piece of legislation. But as predicted, administering the new code has been a nightmare.

intensely proud of his military record and sensitive to any slight, actual or perceived, to his patriotism.

As the breakfast proceeded, CNO Jim Watkins was expressing his objections. He started off moderately enough, but as he warmed to his subject he threw caution to the winds. Finally in an emotional burst he said, "You know, this piece of legislation is so bad it's, it's . . . in some respects it's just un-American!" Nichols's face went rigid; it was obvious he was profoundly offended. Whatever progress we might have made up to then went up in smoke. Nichols never said another word, and at the first opportunity he got up and walked out. A few weeks later Watkins retired on schedule as CNO, but I spent the next three months apologizing to Nichols, trying to coax him back into a reasonable frame of mind.

In the end the legislation passed as expected and was signed into law on October 1, 1986. We did get most of the major changes that were so badly needed; we even got the vice chairman, though a major battle ensued over what his seniority would be. The committee proposed that the vice chairman would rank number two in the U.S. military, an idea the chiefs vigorously opposed. Personally I didn't care if he was two or six. I just wanted a vice chairman so that when I was not there he would be running the JCS, no matter what his seniority was. (In spite of the obvious resentment, Congress finally decided the vice chairman would be number two.)

Given the sharp battle and the residual resentment over the vice chairman's rank, the first man to hold the position was going to face a delicate task. Air Force General Robert Herres seemed to me an ideal candidate. A former SAC pilot who had graduated from the Naval Academy before taking up a commission in the Air Force, Herres was perhaps the leading expert in the United States military on electronics, early warning, and space (he was Commander-in-Chief of the Space Command). His scientific and technical background would, I thought, complement my own experience, while his analytical brilliance would be especially welcome in dealing with some of the problems (like SDI, the Strategic Defense Initiative) we would soon be facing. Equally important, Herres was temperamentally suited to the job. A patient, low-keyed individual who gave little thought to ceremony or status, he was not in the least flustered by the chiefs' initial determination not to acknowledge his rank if they could help it. Instead he established himself through skill and hard work, without allowing friction to develop, which was exactly what I needed.

Once Goldwater-Nichols became law, the biggest job I had as Chairman, and probably the most important, was to implement its provisions with as little trauma and disruption as possible. The question was how to put reorganization into effect without shattering the cooperative atmosphere in the Joint Staff and alienating those who had opposed it. Technically and statutorily I had all the necessary authority. I could hold meetings, ask the chiefs their opinion, then go ahead and recommend whatever course I believed best.

But it wasn't quite that simple. No matter how much authority he has, the Chairman needs the chiefs' expertise and support. His responsibilities are beyond the knowledge of one man, and the data he requires in making many of his decisions are within the control of the individual services. Consequently, his relationship with each chief is crucial. This fact of life puts the Chairman on a tightrope through his entire tenure, no matter what legislation Congress passes. This was no time for a heavy hand. The chiefs could circle the wagons at any time. Moving too abruptly might well inspire a destructive insiders' campaign against the Goldwater-Nichols provisions that could have severe future consequences.

On the other hand, if I did not take swift, authoritative action, I knew the Armed Services Committee would be saying, What's wrong with this guy? We've given him all this power and he refuses to use it. He is not carrying out the changes we want carried out. Nevertheless I made a deliberate decision to move gradually in inaugurating the new format. Rather than baldly asserting my authority, I would allow the chiefs to accommodate to the new bill by degrees. I felt all the time that this would be critical in lifting Goldwater-Nichols off to a smooth start and preparing the way for an effective and decisive JCS, not just during my tenure but into the future—exactly the thing that would not happen if the chiefs set their jaws against it.

In fact, 95 percent of the issues before the chiefs are solved without the need for a "strong" chairman. But two areas especially are divisive in interservice relationships. One is money. When budgets are expanding, as they did during Reagan's first term, the chiefs can remain genial and concur easily on programs and expenditures. But when the budget is going down and everybody digs into his foxhole to defend his own, the Tank can be a battleground.

The second area is people. People arguments in the JCS are fierce. The chiefs feel even more strongly about personnel issues than they do about money questions. Congress sets the number of service personnel and limits the number of flag and general officers the armed forces can have (and as a result, the number of less senior officers). When the chiefs start dividing it up among the services, the conflicts can become vicious. There is a traditional ratio, but nobody is satisfied with it. Everyone is sure he is getting the short end. Although these issues are primarily the province of the service secretaries who deal directly with the Secretary of Defense, the JCS views are sought and the Chairman is asked for his personal input. As a result, they are discussed at length in the Tank ("screamed about" may be more accurate). Fortunately, Goldwater-Nichols empowered the Chairman to draw independent conclusions, without agreement from the chiefs. It was one of the legislation's more welcome advances.

I started gently, but as time passed and the chiefs grew used to the idea of the new arrangements, I exerted my authority more and more. Among other things, I was able to clear out the entire JCS docket, which had been backed up for years. When issues arose that we could not agree on, I did not just procrastinate and leave them around, I said, O.K., this is what I'm going to do. This is the advice I'm going to render to the Secretary (or the NSC, or the President). I want you to be aware of it before I sign off on it. Also, if there is any language you want me to include in my memorandum to express your opposition or to explain it, I'll be happy to put it in verbatim. And if any of you want to accompany me to see the SecDef and express your disagreement in person, you're welcome to do that too. But they never once took up the offer.

Chapter 9

BACKGROUND
TO THE GULF

SHEIKH ISA BIN SULIMAN AL KHALIFA, the Emir of Bahrain, was not at home during the summer of 1974. There was nothing unusual about that, but several events unrelated to the sheikh's travels conspired to turn his absence into a small crisis for American interests in the Persian Gulf.

One of these events had taken place only a few weeks after the Emir's departure when, for reasons now hard to fathom, the United States had decided to send the aircraft carrier *Constellation* into the Persian Gulf. No war was going on in the area at the time, and although we had maintained a minor naval presence at the old British base in Bahrain since 1949, American capital ships were not in the habit of visiting the region. The Arab states of the littoral were hypersensitive to any suggestion of gunboat diplomacy.

Although the Gulf's local rulers by and large were personally well disposed toward Americans, the same could not be said for a large portion of those over whom they ruled. For many local Arabs, as for Palestinians, Pakistanis, and other partially enfranchised "guest" populations, American friendship for Israel was an emotional trigger. Moreover, anti-colonialism was high on every Arab's emotional agenda. The *Constellation*'s intrusion fired anger.

A second important event had taken place the previous December. At that time Sheikh Isa, one of the region's more progressive rulers, had decided to experiment with democracy and had established a Bahraini Parliament. Now, with the Emir out of town, anti-American editorials began appearing in the newspapers, and before anyone had a chance to react, the Parliament passed a resolution calling on the United States Navy to leave its base. When the Emir returned home he was horrified. Within the year he had dissolved his Parliament, thus putting an end to Bahrain's only experiment with popular government.

Sheikh Isa would have liked to simply overrule the Parliament, but he was receiving contrary advice from his circle of advisers, including his cousin Sheikh Mohammed al Khalifa, the sophisticated and highly intelligent Foreign Minister. This advice ran more or less as follows: You may not like the Parliament's decision, but to reverse it by fiat would be a grievous error. You will anger and alienate every government in the Gulf, most of whom want you to eject the Americans. Your own people will also resent it. The damage is done; trying to undo it now would create serious problems. We must be cautious.

The Bahraini decision about the base did not raise a huge storm of protest in Washington. State did initiate an effort to have the lease cancellation reversed, but since there was no clear understanding about why we were there in the first place, it lacked conviction. In a sense, we were in the Gulf more as a matter of habit than policy.

Bahrain in earlier times had been a British protectorate, and the naval base at Jufair was originally theirs. After World War Two, American ships came into the Gulf, working with the British and eventually sharing the facilities. But in the early 1970s Whitehall decided to draw down its forces east of Suez, despite objections from Washington and other allies concerned about stability in the Middle East. At that point the United States had to decide whether to retain its own token force in the region—a tiny squadron consisting of four destroyers and an old seaplane tender that served as flagship. Eventually a decision was made to remain, and arrangements were worked out with the Bahrain government to lease about twelve acres of the old British base.

The small Gulf states were just then gaining independence, and the future of the area was unsettled. Bahrain itself was scheduled to become part of the newly formed United Arab Emirates but at the last minute decided not to join. At the same time, Teheran was making irredentist noises in Bahrain's direction. To the Bahrainis it seemed like a good idea to encourage the Americans to stay. Washington was willing, although State would have preferred doing so under a treaty relationship. While this did not materialize, in 1972 a lease was signed, making it possible for the Navy to maintain its presence—an admiral and five ships. With no ambassadors as yet, the admiral was the only American representative that people in the region saw. In his seaplane tender painted hospital white he steamed up and down the coast making courtesy calls on emirs, sheikhs, and sultans.

The general feeling in Washington was that an American presence in the region was a good idea. Our oil interests counseled us to stay, and the Navy Department considered the force a signal to our friends that we would be there if anything untoward happened. The United States would, the admirals reasoned, watch over the sea lanes; our presence would insure freedom of the seas and the uninterrupted flow of commerce. This was largely rhetoric. From a warfighting standpoint it was hard to justify the Middle East Force; it was essentially a "showing the flag" squadron. But on general principles alone the Navy did not want to leave a place where they were already established; its approach was that it is never a bad idea to have forward deployed forces.

Bahrain's unexpected decision to cancel the lease upset Washington's policy inertia about the Gulf. It also put a kink in my own plans. At that point I was serving in the office of the Secretary of Defense dealing with East Asia and Pacific affairs. Prior to that I had been deputy director of the Navy's Plans and Policy division, and before then I had represented the Defense Department at the Micronesian Status negotiations. All of these were political-military jobs, good experiences that had allowed me to pursue my bent for international affairs. But at the same time they had kept me away from a major sea command. In practical terms, this deficiency threatened my prospects for further promotion, but the Middle East Force was one opening I thought my resumé fit nicely. The position had heavy representational responsibilities and required a feel for foreign affairs. It was in an area of the world that interested me greatly, and if I received the appointment I would be able to combine command with my political-military experience. I wanted the position badly, and began to jockey accordingly, but with the lease cancellation it was about to disappear. Rear Admiral Tom Bigley, who took the post in 1975, assumed he was going out there to wind up American activities and close down our presence.

As Bigley was making arrangements for the Middle East Force to leave Bahrain, the Emir's government unexpectedly granted a year's extension, a bonus of sorts for past friendship. Now, they said, American forces would have until June 30, 1977, to complete their withdrawal. Suddenly Tom was promoted and ordered to Hawaii as deputy commander of the Pacific Fleet and I received a call from Vice Admiral David Bagley, Chief of Naval Personnel, inquiring whether I was still interested. I jumped at the opportunity. Five weeks later Shirley and I were in Bahrain. My main instruction was to work with the American ambassador to reverse the Bahraini decision on cancelling the lease.

The ambassador was Joseph Twinam. Though it was never completely clear to me, in my own mind I did not believe that the ambassador's heart was in the project. He would not say that, of course, because the official policy was to try to stay. But many career diplomats in that part of the world felt that keeping American bases in Arab countries was a mistake, and that our presence at Jufair put the Bahraini government at a disadvantage and jeopardized our own interests. I think that underneath, Twinam agreed with that, though on the surface he was trying to carry out government policy.

Shortly after I arrived, however, Twinam was replaced by Wat Cluverius, whose father and grandfather had been naval officers. (In the 1920s his grandfather had served as superintendent of the Naval Academy.) Cluverius came from a Navy family and he himself had served as a naval intelligence officer. He strongly believed the Navy ought to be in the Gulf. So did I. We quickly became close friends and the negotiations took on new life. We started working hard to turn the Bahraini government's mind around.

After the first six months we felt as if we had been batting our heads against a brick wall. The Bahrainis didn't have an argument, they had a position, which was that the lease stipulated that the United States had to leave if given proper notice. We've decided for political reasons that you have to leave, they said, and we've given notice. So now leave. What's all the talk about? Whatever we said, the Bahrainis answered simply that they found our case unconvincing.

Nevertheless, Cluverius and I were not entirely discouraged. Despite what we were hearing officially, we were besieged by people telling us they did not want us to go, particularly business people. A large element of the Bahraini population was Shiite, primarily of Iranian origin, though now largely Arabicized. Much of the commerce and trade was in their hands, and they were an important reason Bahrain had prospered. These people importuned me. You may read the Arab press, they said, but don't necessarily believe it. It is imperative you stay. Your presence is a moderating force, a force for stability. We are businessmen. We want you here. From what Cluverius and I could tell, many Arab Bahrainis also were pro-American, but the Israeli policy kept getting in their way. Their ambivalence was almost painful to watch.*

---

* Despite their anger at American friendship toward Israel, there is a great deal of popular Arab sentiment in favor of the United States. Arabs like Americans as Americans, and they love what Americans make. In Bahrain there was a franchise for every major Amer-

With popular sentiment favorable and the officials unfailingly polite (even as they dismissed our arguments), we were never quite
sure if the government might not at some point change its mind.
Were they indeed looking for a more persuasive case, or were they
perhaps just making it hard for us in order to demonstrate their
independence? Those in the Bahraini hierarchy knew that the business class and others with vested interests wanted the United States
to stay, and they knew the Emir liked the Navy and also wanted us
to stay. But the professional politicians and others in the ruling circle
were faced with a dilemma. In their view it was not a wise idea.
Bahrain would be put in a disadvantageous position vis-à-vis Kuwait, Qatar (their traditional enemy), and the other emirates. It
would look as if Bahrain was a lackey of the Americans. I suspected
they might want to reverse their position, but they needed a face-
saving formula. Clearly they were in no hurry.

Our conspicuous lack of success in that first half year was capped
off in January when Deputy Secretary of Defense William Clements
sent us a message that he would be traveling to the region. The signal
implied that Cluverius and I had not done much of a job, and that
Clements could not see why it had not been settled by now. He was
coming to Bahrain and he would wrap it up so that we could finally
put this little problem behind us.

A short time later Clements showed up with his entourage. We
met him at the airport, then went directly to the government offices.
Clements was not even going to stay an entire day. He arrived in the
morning and intended to leave in the evening. Waiting for us at the
Prime Minister's office were the Emir, the Prime Minister, the For-

---

ican company. The country was flooded with Westinghouse ovens, Carrier air conditioners, and GE products of every description. When I visited Saudi Arabia, the Saudis' oil
income was exploding and they were buying merchandise so fast they could not absorb it.
In the port of Jidda, acres and acres of goods were sitting outside: refrigerators, air
conditioners, ovens, automobiles, and almost anything else you might think of. The back-
log for unloading ships was nine months. Ninety or a hundred freighters sat in the road-
stead functioning as warehouses. Companies could not get them unloaded, so they would
send them down there, get in line, get their name on the unloading list, anchor the ship,
and rotate a skeleton crew every thirty days or so. The only other time I had ever seen
such affluence was after World War Two in Guam, where the American Pacific forces had
shipped all their equipment and supplies. I remember standing on a hill and looking out on
an area that extended as far as the eye could see, all of it covered with American vehicles.
That's what it looked like in Saudi Arabia. The Saudis could not distribute it or install it
or service it or do anything with it. The waste was unbelievable. After several months in
the open many items no longer worked. But the Saudis didn't care. They were buying
every piece of American goods they could lay their hands on.

eign Minister, and most of the other leading government personages, which made it an unusual gathering. More typically the Bahrainis preferred to meet visitors individually, at least at first. That way host and guest could exchange appropriate greetings and small talk and enjoy a cup of strong Arab coffee together. But Clements would not have time for that. So here we all were, and the conversation went straight to business—much to the annoyance of the locals.

Deputy Secretary Clements was a Texas oil man (he later served as Governor of Texas). He had made a great deal of money constructing oil platforms in the Persian Gulf and he was quite familiar with the Arab world, especially the Gulf states. But he was still a stereotypical Texan, fiery and aggressive. With Bill Clements, there was no hidden agenda and no under the table bargaining. Everything was shoot-from-the-hip directness. "We want to stay for these reasons," he said, looking the Bahrainis straight in the eye. Then he listed his arguments. "Above all we think it's important for your security," and he told them why he thought so. When he was finished he settled back in his chair and his face assumed a self-satisfied look that said, Well, I guess that's taken care of that. And he waited to hear the Bahrainis agree with him.

The first bad news was that the Emir didn't say anything except, "Thank you. The Foreign Minister will speak for us." When he said that, I thought, Well, here we go again. (I had just been through six months of this.)

The Foreign Minister was not about to be bullied by Clements. He was a shrewd customer with a keen mind and a history of international experience. The American deputy secretary did not particularly impress him. On the contrary, he himself was urbane and sophisticated, and quite at home facing down pushy Westerners. "We appreciate your coming to visit and speak with us," the Foreign Minister began. "We certainly understand your position and the sincerity of your feelings. But you do know, Mr. Secretary, that we have asked that the American base be closed in accordance with our agreement, and to be frank, we have not heard anything today that is any different from what we have been hearing since 1975. Nothing has changed in the circumstances that led us to make the original decision, and you have not brought us anything new. We have, as you know, given notice in accord with the agreement, and while we are grateful for your visit, I'm afraid our decision still stands."

Clements huffed and puffed for a while, but there was nothing of substance left to say. Finally he announced that his schedule was such that he had to go, so he would be leaving. "But I'm sure," he said, "that with more reflection you'll change your mind." Then we beat a hasty retreat with our tails between our legs. Clements, Cluverius, and I got into the same car for the ride back to the airport. In my book it had been a disaster. In Clements's book there were no disasters, at least none that he would admit participating in. "Well," he said, "we didn't get everything we wanted today, but we certainly sorted out the issues and cleared the air. I'm sure we're substantially better off now than we were before." Then he flew away. To Cluverius and me it seemed he had been tarred and feathered and ridden off on a rail, and the two guys who had had the problem previously still had it, except now it was worse.

The Clements episode persuaded me that the Bahrainis were not under any circumstances going to swallow the status quo, no matter what arguments we made. If we wanted to stay, we would somehow have to make it look as if we were decreasing or modifying our already quite limited presence. We would have to convey a convincing picture of change. From our hosts' political standpoint, it was imperative that they be able to demonstrate at the very least that they had imposed severely revised terms on us. The Foreign Minister had to be in a position to talk as if we were leaving, even if in fact we were not leaving. With this in mind I began considering ways in which we could reduce our presence to a degree but at the same time maintain our operational capacity. As Shirley said one day when I came home, "Just what are we doing? I heard the Foreign Minister on the radio announcing that we are leaving. But you talk as if we're staying." "You've got it," I said. "That's exactly what we're going to do."

But I had trouble convincing my immediate boss, Admiral David Bagley (the former Chief of Naval Personnel), who was stationed in London. Even though I made it clear that the Bahrainis would not back down and we were truly going to have to leave, I could not seem to convey the urgency of trying another approach.

I knew I had to find a way to take the matter up at the Pentagon directly. To arrange this I called my old friend and classmate Jim Stockdale, who was then a two-star admiral working on the Navy staff. "Jim," I said, "I need to come back to Washington, but my boss thinks he should be doing all the dealing with Washington himself, so I can't just fly in. The only way I can figure to get back is if somebody would send me a message ordering me home. I do think I can make some proposals that will help this problem."

Shortly after this conversation I received a message from the vice chief of naval operations informing me that my presence was required in Washington to consult on the Bahrain situation. With this in hand I called Bagley and said, "I just got a message," and he said, not happily, "I know. I saw it." "I'll stop and see you on the way," I told him. "You'd better," he growled. Bagley, like everyone else, was concerned with turf. My ambassador was so excited about my returning that he also arranged to go back "for consultations." He didn't want me interjecting myself in Washington without him there.

I saw Bagley in London and explained to him why I believed we had to change our strategy and make it look as if we were dramatically reducing our presence. We could do that by moving the dependents of the flagship crew back to the United States and putting the crew itself on a one-year rotation schedule. "That is terrible for a ship," Bagley said. "We can't really do that." "If we want to stay there," I said, "we are going to have to do exactly that, or something very like it." Then I suggested various other base facilities we could draw down to make our presence less conspicuous. "If we do these things," I said, "I can go back to the Foreign Minister and make a proposal that might be acceptable."

Bagley was not enamored of the idea, but he finally said, "If you can sell that, then O.K." And when I presented the idea to the CNO's office back in Washington, they bought it without hesitation. Cluverius was brought in on the details of my discussions and we returned to Bahrain together, smiling for the first time in months. We were actually looking forward to taking the offensive.

From that point on our approach to the Foreign Minister was "We understand your needs on this, and we are willing to work with them. If you desire, we can consolidate the functions on the base"—I kept it as vague as possible, and they didn't ask for specifics—"so that we will have a substantially decreased presence here. What we do have will be of a different character from what we have had in the past."

The guts of the concept was that most of the dependents would move out of Bahrain. The flagship was a 31,000-ton amphibious landing ship (the U.S.S. *LaSalle,* a "landing platform dock," had taken the place of the old seaplane tender) which accommodated a crew of about twelve hundred people. Of the twelve hundred, three or four hundred had families that would normally be living in Bahrain. But in fact all but about a hundred and fifty families had already left since the Bahraini announcement about closing the base. Now we were preparing to move all the remaining families except those of people manning the base facilities. Over half of the base personnel were young and single, and when we were finished there would be only about thirty or forty families left.

These proposals notwithstanding, we acted as if we were going to be staying, on the assumption that that would make the negotiations go better. To rationally close down the base we would have had to begin six months in advance, but launching that process would have conveyed the idea that we were resigned to the inevitability of closure, something I did not want to do. It was, of course, a gamble. If we really did have to leave on June 30, we could say at that point, O.K., we're on our way out, but please give us time to complete the departure—and hope they agreed.

It was an interesting time for me. Shirley and I were part of a tiny, close American community living in the middle of an Arab lake. Our lives rotated around the naval facility. The families did not know if they were going to leave on June 30 or not, and if they did leave, where they were going to go. And I couldn't tell them because I did not know myself. I had a meeting once a month with all the dependents, even children, to relate what had happened that month and how the talks with the Bahrainis were proceeding. And always one of the wives would stand up and say, If I'm going to be moving in June, I've got to know now. But I didn't know.

Once we went to the Foreign Minister with our new proposals, the tone of the discussions changed. It turned out that in fact he knew next to nothing about the details of our facilities. Although he had grown up in Bahrain, he had never been to the naval base. "Is there an airstrip out there?" he asked one day, leaving me speechless for a moment. The point was that he was not concerned in the least about specifics. What he cared about was cosmetics and how he could portray the negotiations. He was dealing strictly in perceptions, and I was assuring him that we could provide what he needed.

Our rent for the base was $4 million a year, which Bahrain had always maintained was merely symbolic and had nothing to do with their fiscal needs. One day the Foreign Minister was insisting that he needed more signs of reducing the American presence than we were proposing to give him. There was not enough appearance of change. Hearing this, Cluverius was struck by an inspiration. "Well," he said, "it would certainly look like we were curtailing the force if you reduced the rent from four million to two million. Why don't you lower the rent?" And the Foreign Minister answered, "That's an excellent idea. We'll do it." When we cabled State that the rent would be two million, Cluverius received a phone call from the Middle East desk: "In the last forty years of American diplomacy no one has ever lowered the rent. This is unprecedented in the annals of the State Department."

By the time we got down to the final stage of these negotiations it was already May and the upper levels of Bahraini officialdom were taking early vacations. My own life was consumed by these talks, but the people I had to get hold of were in Switzerland or London or the Aegean. They did not share our urgency about the negotiations. Before I knew it, the end of May was upon us, and the principals were still waterskiing in the Greek isles. Nobody changed their plans for our little problem. Still, by early June we were talking again, and by June 15 we had the agreement nailed down.

When we finally arrived at a conclusion, the Foreign Minister gave several press conferences to announce it. Anyone listening to him would have assumed the U.S. Navy was going home. For all the world that was what it sounded like. Then once in a while a reporter would come by and talk to me, and I'd say, "No, everything's fine, we're staying." The two trains had managed to pass each other in the night on what looked like the same track.

I always felt that in terms of service to the country, that was probably my most important contribution. If we had lost our access to facilities in Bahrain in 1977, we would not have been able to accomplish what we did in the Earnest Will convoying operation during the Iran-Iraq war. Desert Storm would have been more difficult. We would have been unable to establish our commitment to our friends in the region on a rock solid basis, which proved so essential during the events that followed Iraq's invasion of Kuwait. Without that facility still there, we would have been at a severe disadvantage. Bahrain was to prove the cornerstone for all our subsequent naval operations in the Persian Gulf. Pound for pound, Bahrain has been about the best ally we have had in recent times.

Chapter 10

A KUWAITI
OVERTURE

MY TOUR IN THE GULF exposed me to many of the internal problems of the littoral states and also to the vast strategic significance of the region. Despite three decades of surface quiet in the region, it was likely, I thought, that the United States might one day be called on to protect the petroleum lifelines. The potential for Soviet encroachment was a constant concern, and local instability or regional warfare could quickly create openings for the Russians or one of their clients to exploit.

In 1978 I analyzed the problems in an article for the *Naval Institute Proceedings*. Kuwait, I wrote, was a trouble spot. Kuwaitis were outnumbered two to one in their own kingdom, and Palestinian pressure there was intense. This volatile situation made neighboring Iraq a critical factor. The Ba'athist government would certainly welcome trouble in Kuwait as an excuse to interfere or even overthrow the ruling Emir, Sheikh Jabir al Ahmed al Sabah. Iran might inhibit Iraq's ambitions, but Baghdad was unlikely to consider Saudi forces a deterrent. If Iraq were to receive support from the Soviets, or if the Iranians were preoccupied, Kuwait (and its Western oil customers) might well face a serious threat.

If that happened, I noted, the critical challenge for the United States would be to insure that the Soviets or their clients didn't gain an irreversible military advantage before we could bring the weight of our power to bear. The Navy was ideally suited for exactly this kind of task. Our ships in the Gulf could be used to signal U.S. concern if a crisis started to build. They could provide protection for the flow of allied military support to our friends in the region. They could assist local states with air defense and land Marines as a preliminary to the arrival of Army divisions. The small Bahrain-based Middle East Force could not do all this on its own, but it would constitute an absolutely vital lodgement and adjunct to a larger scale American naval presence in the western Indian Ocean.

A year after this article appeared, the world of the Persian Gulf began to shake. In 1979 our longtime ally, the Shah of Iran, was overthrown. With an aggressive fundamentalism gripping Iran, the United States increased the Middle East Force and dispatched a carrier task force into the Indian Ocean. Slowly the turbulent events in the region led Washington to pay more attention to the Gulf squadron. These ships had always been considered a "presence" force, never a warfighting command. Yet it was becoming imperative to define a new role for them. What could or could not be expected of this force if hostilities broke out in the region?

Then came the Iran-Iraq war in 1980. We quickly reinforced the Indian Ocean carrier presence, afraid that the conflict would spill over and embroil other Gulf nations. When that did not happen, the tension lessened and we reduced our deployment slightly, breathing easier when it seemed that the Iranians and Iraqis would be satisfied with shooting each other.

But in 1986, the war's sixth year, the occasional attacks on shipping in the Gulf that had been going on since 1983 stepped up dramatically. First the Iraqis began attacking Iranian merchant shipping. Then the Iranians countered with their own maritime campaign against Iraq and her friends, in particular the Kuwaitis and Saudis, both of whom were providing large-scale financial support to Saddam Hussein and also transshipping arms Iraq acquired from Eastern Europe and the Soviet Union. The Saudis were clandestinely offloading arms and ammunition at the Red Sea port of Jidda and trucking them across the desert. Tanks, artillery, ammunition, and even Migs bound for Iraq from various Warsaw Pact countries were delivered through Kuwait City.

Before long the Iranians were hitting almost any neutral shipping that presented itself as a ready target. Iranian Navy units were involved, as well as heavily armed patrol boats manned by fanatic Revolutionary Guards. We were never quite sure how much of this was directed by the central government. The Revolutionary Guard boats seemed to be under the control of a group of semi-independent mullahs, and for a while even some of the Navy units appeared to be operating autonomously.

The American Middle East Force was right in the middle of this battleground. Its commanders were operating in what was essentially a war zone (though the administration, myself included, tried hard to avoid labeling it as such) without a well-defined role, and as the attacks on merchant shipping exploded around them the frustration level skyrocketed. Officers and crews hated to stand around and watch, forbidden to intervene as Iranian naval and air units shot up unarmed tankers and freighters. As one destroyer commander put it, he felt like he had "followed Alice down the rabbit hole."

Typically, an Iranian frigate or patrol boat would pull up alongside a neutral oil tanker, often at night, and ask for port of embarkation, cargo, and flag. When the answers came, the Iranian captain would thank the tanker master and circle away. A few minutes later he would turn off his running lights and come back at full speed. From point-blank range he would blast the tanker's living quarters with three-inch guns, machine guns, rockets, even anti-air missiles fired in surface mode. Most often there was no attempt to sink the ship, only to inflict casualties on its crew. From ten miles away an American destroyer would be listening to all this over VHF Channel 16, the bridge-to-bridge frequency. They'd hear the chaos and the screams, the frantic calls for help from Greek or Turkish merchant captains. At night they would see the gunfire and flames light up the sky.

Limited by our rules of engagement to rendering humanitarian aid, the American warships would steam toward the action, knowing that once they arrived the Iranians were likely to give it up and disappear. Some of our skippers, I knew, skirted the gray area of their orders and tried to position themselves between Iranian attack craft and unarmed neutrals. They also escorted their own resupply ships up to Bahrain and watched over American-flag shipping. Amid the violence the Middle East Force was walking a fine, perilous line.*

For Washington, there was no clear and obvious resolution. The fact was that the administration simply did not have a consistent point of view on the region. In particular, there was no coherent approach to the Iran-Iraq war, beyond a devout hope that it would go away. Nor was there any desire to jeopardize the Middle East Force's traditional neutrality. Even the Navy was not inclined to inject its units into the storm. The general feeling was that we did not want to complicate the problem further by American intervention. No one could predict where that might lead. But as the intensity of hostilities at sea built, the need to provide a definition sharpened.

In December 1986 a cable arrived in Washington from the Ameri-

---

* Just how perilous was demonstrated on May 17, 1987, when an Iraqi Mirage fired two Exocet missiles into the U.S.S. *Stark*, killing thirty-seven crewmen. As best we could determine, the attack was an accident, a case of mistaken identity. But it highlighted in tragic colors the vulnerability of our ships and the difficulties of their captains.

can embassy in Kuwait. The ambassador there reported that he had received a feeler from the Kuwaitis, very discreet and unofficial, but clearly a probe. What, his contact wanted to know, might the U.S. response be to a request to put part of the Kuwaiti tanker fleet under the American flag? When the cable came across my desk at the JCS, I thought I could see an opening we had been looking for for almost a decade.

On the upper curve of the Gulf littoral, Kuwait, for all its insignificant size, was the third largest oil producer in the world, exporting largely to Western Europe, Japan, and also America. But despite the robust trade in oil, Kuwait's relations with the United States were touched with ice. Kuwait's arm's-length attitude toward the United States had its origin, as does so much else in the Middle East, in the Israeli-Palestinian conflict. After 1948 a tide of Palestinian refugees arrived in Kuwait, many of them highly educated people. The influx was encouraged by the country's ruling family, the al Sabahs, who were already looking ahead to Kuwait's complete independence from Great Britain. These desert sheikhs understood that they would soon need trained, experienced people who could manage twentieth-century governmental and technical bureaucracies, people with skills the traditional Bedouin families did not possess. And here, suddenly, a raftful of technicians, lawyers, engineers, and accountants had washed up on their shore.

In the years that followed, Palestinians created and managed a bureaucracy that did indeed transform Kuwait from a desert sheikhdom into a modern state. But although the Palestinians were so significant in building Kuwait and had their hands on so many levers of governmental and economic machinery, they were still considered outsiders. For the Kuwaitis, while valuing their skills, had never accepted them as equal partners. Palestinians had never been given full citizenship. They could not vote; they were not permitted to own certain kinds of land; they were not allowed to ascend past a certain level in the government. All their prospects were carefully defined and limited. Second- and even third-generation Palestinians had grown up contributing their talents and efforts to Kuwait, knowing no other homeland. Yet they were kept apart. They did not have a full stake in the country. So even while Kuwait prospered, resentments fermented beneath the surface.

Prominent in the Palestinians' emotional makeup was a deep antipathy for the United States because of American support for Israel. For Sheikh Jabir al Sabah, the Kuwaiti Emir, this was a bias that demanded a high level of sensitivity. Palestinians at that time numbered 300,000 out of a total population of slightly over a million, and they were already a volatile element. Despite the sheikh's personal friendliness toward the West, the Palestinians had a heavy impact on government policies. And that meant, in particular, avoiding any alignment with the United States.

The Palestinians were Kuwait's problem. The American problem, as I saw it, was to find a way to circumvent the barriers, to demonstrate our good intentions and include this oil-rich nation within our circle of friends. As Middle East Force commander I had made great efforts to convey friendship and offer Navy services to the Kuwaitis whenever it was appropriate. Ambassador Frank Maestroni and I were almost hungry to find something we could do for them. But our overtures had gone unacknowledged, and so had those of our successors. In the years following my tour there were occasional signs of encouragement but no breakthroughs. Kuwait continued to adhere to a rigidly neutral policy. The sheikhdom enjoyed a thriving military assistance relationship with Moscow, and though her economic ties were with the West, her leaders remained aloof and distant.

But now with the escalation of Iranian hostilities the Kuwaitis were suffering. Although the Iranian gunboats spread their chaos around liberally, they paid special attention to Kuwaiti and Saudi shipping. For its part, Saudi Arabia did not actively look for ways to counter these assaults. No one who knew the Saudis expected them to confront the Iranians directly. They traditionally sought quieter methods of solving their problems, and in that period they had little confidence in their armed forces. The bottom line for Saudi Arabia was that even if a ship was lost now and then, with their vast wealth they could absorb the loss. Better not to incur a dangerous enemy who might be in a position to injure them significantly later on.

By 1986 the Kuwaitis had begun to feel differently. Unlike most other oil-producing states, Kuwait kept a fleet of ships under its own flag, giant tankers that could be easily identified by the Iranians. The destruction of even one of these ships would be a costly, time-consuming affair, and it would exacerbate the Gulf situation for both the oil-consuming and oil-producing nations. It was their search for protection that had led to the Kuwaiti feeler and (as we learned shortly afterward) to a similar inquiry to the Soviets.

To my way of thinking this was an opportunity we had to grasp. It also brought a positive response from Caspar Weinberger. The Secretary's main interest was in countering the intrusion of Soviet power and influence. We should, Weinberger felt, agree to reflag the Kuwaiti tankers, and we should do it soon. If we did not, the Soviets would be in a position to fill a vacuum created by our own negligence.

In short order Weinberger raised the question at an NSPG meeting, not as a formal agenda item but incidentally, flying a trial balloon to judge how heavy the weather might be on this issue. "Mr. President," he said, "we're looking at this reflagging request carefully, but at first glance it seems like a pretty good idea."

Ordinarily, if Weinberger believed an idea had merit, President Reagan would not express any reservations, nor would he explore it in depth at the meeting. Instead he would say, Cap, that sounds very interesting, then he would talk about it to his National Security Adviser and one or two of his old guard afterward. Consequently, whenever Weinberger expressed himself, the meeting was likely to turn toward George Shultz to ask his opinion. And Shultz, when asked, did not express any opposition.

Shultz's reticence suggested the administration's problem in making such a decision. U.S. Gulf policy was fuzzy at best. Decision makers knew more about what they did not want to happen than what our goals in the region were. We did not want the Iran-Iraq war to spread, nor did we want to get heavily involved in the fighting. Popular sentiment certainly did not favor an Iranian victory, but no one seemed sure how far we should be willing to go to prevent that outcome. The administration was not enchanted with the idea of helping Iraq's Saddam Hussein, but he was supported strongly by Saudi Arabia, a vital ally. The Soviets were potential players here too, and they had to be kept from taking advantage of the confusion. At the same time, unchecked seaborne terrorism from Iran was making this Gulf brew increasingly volatile. The situation presented President Reagan with perplexing choices.

Despite the lack of a clear focus, the consensus within the administration was to move ahead. Reflagging, though, proved a more complicated issue than anyone expected. Technical law regarding the merchant marine is not widely understood, and although people were ready enough to bandy around terms like "reflagging," there was mass ignorance about what that might actually entail.

At first it seemed there was a serious legal question as to whether reflagging was even possible. Lawyers and Coast Guard officials were in and out of National Security Council meetings explaining technicalities and requirements and expressing the gravest reservations. People were describing these things in excruciating detail who had never been near the council before and haven't been since.

With the Kuwaitis expecting a response, Weinberger was a frustrated man. Here we were engaged in high policy, and suddenly a crew of technicians had appeared out of nowhere and was telling us what could and couldn't be done. As time passed, pressure from Weinberger and the NSC mounted on the lawyers to find a way through the morass. But their job was to guard these regulations, and while the NSC might have been telling them, Don't bother us with details, just find a way, their response was What do you mean? Cut corners? This is *law* we're talking about, United States *statute!* As these discussions proceeded slowly toward resolution, we sent a signal back to the Kuwaitis informing them we would be willing to entertain a formal proposal to reflag their ships.

To our surprise, the Kuwaitis did not immediately respond. By this time the issue had received lengthy consideration in the National Security Council and we were eager to move ahead. Conditions were continuing to deteriorate in the Gulf, where almost every day brought new attacks on neutral shipping. In my own daily talks with Weinberger he would invariably ask, Have we heard anything from the Kuwaitis yet? We simply did not understand the delay.

In March 1987 I was scheduled to visit the Middle East. My old friend Sheikh Isa of Bahrain had invited me, and I wanted to stop in Pakistan, the United Arab Emirates, and Saudi Arabia as well. With no answer yet from the Kuwaitis, arrangements were also made for me to visit Kuwait City to take the question up in person with Kuwaiti officials.

On March 17 I arrived in Kuwait. Sitting down that afternoon with Sheikh Jabir, I told him that the United States government was prepared to go along with the reflagging of Kuwaiti ships. We would also, I said, be willing to provide escort protection for them. The Defense Minister, who was my official host, was clearly in favor of a joint undertaking, as was the Emir himself. But the Foreign Minister was not particularly happy with the idea. He was the leader of the anti-American faction in the government and seemed intent on discouraging anything that went beyond the traditional arm's-length relationship.

Leaving Kuwait that afternoon, I was convinced that they were still arguing the question among themselves. I also thought that one of the reasons for the Kuwaitis' delay was their desire to see what ϗind of chord the reflagging proposal would strike in Congress. They suspected that such a decision was not the President's to make alone, that others would be involved, and in that situation there could be no foregone conclusions.

As Congress prepared to hold hearings, reflagging was also being discussed and argued in other venues. Weinberger was pressing the President hard, arguing the strategic merits as he saw them, and also the emotional issues. These people, Mr. President, he'd say, referring with disgust to the Revolutionary Guards, these people are insurgents. They're bandits, pirates. Their government has no control over them! They're rushing around out there and attacking good people, unarmed merchants and innocent oil carriers. The President, not overly familiar with the region, or terribly inquisitive about it, responded positively to Weinberger, as he most often did. Not only did the geopolitical reasoning seem sound, but the Gulf presented a vivid picture of right versus wrong.

While my thoughts on reflagging diverged from Weinberger's (in ways that would become clear during the upcoming hearings), I thought there was a lot of good, justifiable emotion in his arguments. During my recent Gulf visit I had heard firsthand from the Middle East Force's commanders and men about the unprovoked murderous attacks they were witnessing. They were a frustrated group of sailors; they hated to have to restrain themselves while atrocities were carried out in front of their eyes.

Not everyone in the Navy saw the situation as those in the Gulf did, including many high-ranking officers. Some veteran commanders were not happy about the prospect of operating blue-water ships inside the Persian Gulf, which they regarded as little more than a lake. The Navy's modern warships had been designed for the open ocean, where their sophisticated radar and weapons systems could identify and destroy targets at long distances. But in the Gulf everything was compressed. Aircraft and missiles could hit ships in a moment, fast-moving patrol boats could emerge from nowhere and strike almost before they were noticed. In the Gulf, commanders would have only seconds to make life-and-death decisions (as the *Stark* would make so abundantly clear). These were not the conditions our ships were designed to fight in. This was not a mission our officers were trained for. If we went into the Gulf in force, we would be placing some of our best warships at risk.

In early June the congressional hearings on reflagging and convoying began, the start of what turned out to be a series of long, often heated encounters with the Armed Services and Foreign Affairs committees. I attended these in company with Weinberger, sitting on his right and watching the debate shape up between the Secretary and various congressmen who had conceived a strong dislike for the reflagging proposal.

Weinberger's underlying rationale for reflagging was the principle of freedom of the seas. It was right and necessary, he believed, for the United States to protect the free passage of innocent neutral commerce in international waters, particularly vital international waters such as the Gulf. But under attack, this argument soon began to betray weaknesses. The United States has been crying "freedom of the seas" for over two hundred years, but in truth, since the War of 1812 we have not always been willing to support the doctrine. On this particular principle our tradition has been long on talk, short on action.

Weinberger was an effective advocate, a skilled debater blessed with a near photographic memory. He could drag details out of his head from a document he had read in the distant past or from some obscure precedent that no one else had heard of. He was especially adept at weaving arguments together on the spur of the moment that could knock his adversaries into a cocked hat. But he was not always that impressive, I thought, at formulating solid, durable positions. Tenacity was his great strength, but once he had staked out a position he would not let go of it, regardless of where it led him or how much damage it did him. He was absolutely impervious to arguments that challenged his assumptions, and that antagonized many on the committees, even some who were basically sympathetic.

Sitting there next to Weinberger, I did not consider it my job to enter into the political arguments that were shaping up. As Chairman of the Joint Chiefs, my role, as I saw it, was to answer questions and explain the military requirements of the mission. What dangers we might face, how many ships we would need, what kind of logistical support, what sort of weaponry—those were the subjects I was happy to speak to. But though it was not my intention to get involved in the political issues, every time I went to the Hill the questioners led me deeper and deeper into the underlying debate.

The fact was that I had searched my soul on the reflagging request. I had done more agonizing over this issue than over any other since my appointment as Chairman, and I was committed to going into the Persian Gulf. But I came at the question from a different direction than Weinberger did.

The linchpin of our position in the Persian Gulf was our relationship with Saudi Arabia, and in recent years our ties with the Saudis had frayed badly. During my time as Chairman, Congress had already rejected a number of Saudi arms proposals, and each incident eroded the relationship further. Prince Bandar bin Sultan, the Saudi ambassador to the United States, watched as Congress dealt negatively with one request after another. Congress had also turned down further arms to Jordan's King Hussein. When I began my tenure in 1985, we had enjoyed excellent military-to-military contacts with Jordan, but those had now practically disappeared. At the same time, the United Arab Emirates were distancing themselves even farther from us, and Oman had made it abundantly clear that whatever its stance toward the United States might be, they would not risk unduly offending Iran.

Given this situation, it seemed to me that reflagging would go a long way toward mending our fences in the region. It was also the first opportunity we had had to make a real advance in our relationship with Kuwait. My conclusion, then, was that we should go into the Persian Gulf, not because of freedom of the seas, and not because we didn't want the Soviets there, but because it was the best chance we had to repair our Arab policy and to make some significant headway in an area where it was absolutely crucial for us to forge the strongest ties we could manage—despite the congressional undermining.

The strength of that position, I thought, was that it allowed us to make a discrete decision on this issue rather than getting bogged down in questions of moral imperative, which was what was happening now that the congressional opposition were getting their teeth into Weinberger. If we are so interested in freedom of the seas, Mr. Secretary, someone would ask, then doesn't that apply to the Iranians as well? Aren't the seas free for them? They're getting hit by the Iraqis in international waters. Does that mean we are going to escort Iranian ships too?

The hearings were intense. Weinberger carried on a furious debate with Congressmen Tom Lantos, Les AuCoin, Ted Weiss, and other liberals. The Secretary was relentless, insisting that we were dealing here with a matter of principle—freedom of the seas—and also that we were facing a crux in our worldwide conflict with the Soviets. His adversaries were equally combative; they picked out every opening, every vulnerability in Weinberger's arguments and pounded on them. Behind their no-holds-barred assault was the shadow of the Israeli problem. Some were obviously concerned that if we committed forces that would cooperate with the Saudis to maintain free passage through the Gulf and keep the Iranians in their box, there would then be a stronger case for arms for Saudi Arabia, and they did not want to enhance Riyadh's claims. When I said that "one of the reasons we have to improve our political position over there is the damage you have done to our Arab policy," they did not like it at all. But I did say it, time and time again, even though I had to admit that there weren't many congressmen who enjoyed hearing it.

Some were, of course, genuinely upset about the possibility of involving the United States in the Iran-Iraq war and were not confident that we could convoy and still remain outside the conflict. This argument was a much more legitimate one and, of course, impossible totally to dispatch.

From my vantage point it seemed that many of those who opposed our going into the Gulf had done so as a gut reaction, without first carefully examining the merits of the case. They had made the decision not to go in, then had to find public reasons to support their decision. In the process of casting around for a rationale, they asked, as Congress always does, What does the intelligence community say about it?

The fact was that while we had sought intelligence advice, the experts in the intelligence community did not believe they had been formally and adequately consulted. It seemed to me that up to this point our problem was more political than military, and I did not think intelligence types should control the decision. But this was a matter I should have handled more carefully. Congressmen have a strange but ingrained prejudice that intelligence is always right, to such an extent that they tend to treat generals' and admirals' assessments with more than a touch of disdain, unless they are strongly supported by those of the intelligence action officer (or in accord with the congressman's point of view). It's not that *your* opinion is worthless exactly, they intimate, but what does the *intelligence* community have to say about it?

The critical question in this case was not a matter of capabilities but of what Iran's willingness would be to engage in a sea war. On this issue there was little history to follow, and the intelligence experts were speculating. They did not know, though they certainly had opinions.

When the appraisals came in, they offered highly alarming "worst case" scenarios. The Iranians would be so upset by our reflagging that they would do anything they could to hurt Americans, not only in the Gulf but around the world. We would light an inferno we could not control. The prospects of success were nil; the whole Gulf would be aflame. That, in general terms, was the intelligence estimate, and our opponents in Congress loved it.

Personally I took the appraisals with a large grain of salt. I knew that they were partially conditioned by the intelligence community's pique. I also knew that they were not based on hard intelligence of, for example, Iranian contingency plans. They were merely estimates. And to judge these estimates it was important to understand several intelligence tendencies.

First, in building an intelligence capability, people who know something about specific areas are needed, preferably people who speak the language. For many of the world's regions the only people readily available with linguistic capability are individuals disaffected from the local regime. That had been, for example, a serious problem with our Soviet intelligence. When the Soviet part of the world started changing, for some time we could not get many of the people in the intelligence organizations to acknowledge the change. Often they had come to the United States in the 1950s and hated the Soviets deeply. Their general reaction was Don't tell me the Soviets are changing! I know more about it than anybody, and the Soviets aren't changing! Well, the fact was that the Soviet world was in flux, but they were not able to keep pace. Iran too had changed dramatically in the previous decade; it had gone beyond the scope of many of our analysts.

Second, during its history the intelligence community has been stung often, and consequently they have developed a vigorous tendency to cover their bets. For this purpose, surmising a worst-case scenario works best. It does not help the principal decision makers, but neither does it create future trouble for the providers. If the worst case materializes, they were right. If it does not, relief is the order of the day and no one has too much cause for complaint. In uncertain situations, it is always safe to predict that the world is going to be worse than it is. There was a strong element of this in our intelligence assessments on the Gulf. The CIA and DIA did not know what the Iranian reaction would be, and instead of saying, We don't know, they provided alarming predictions.

These estimates, together with our congressional opponents' desire to believe them, made it more difficult to carry the day. In response I argued that the intelligence conclusions were mistaken in two key areas. The view that Iran would counter reflagging with terrorist attacks on us around the world—what I called the terrorist explosion scenario—might well be right, but that was a problem we already faced. The Iranians were trying to hurt us wherever they could anyway, and if their abilities increased we were going to hear about it, regardless of whether we went into the Gulf. We could not permit ourselves to be intimidated by that threat to stop doing what was in our national interest. If they wanted to stir up the world like that, so be it. It seemed to me that in the long run it would hurt them more than it would hurt us.

As far as military action in the Gulf itself was concerned, my position on that subject was that in essence it didn't matter how angry the Iranians got. As long as we stayed at sea and in the air, we could manage the problem at reasonable cost. They may be furious, I thought, but they won't be nearly as furious in boats or planes as they would be in tanks. It was easy to attack unarmed merchantmen, where nobody shoots back. But the Iranians would not be eager to get into a real naval scrap. They had neither the technical sophistication nor the nautical background. They also knew that if they dealt us serious damage our carriers were capable of destroying their installations on shore, a threat that was likely to have deterrent value. If we were to go into their country with ground forces, that would be a different problem; Iran is a long way from home and the difficulties would be immense. But the sea was not their element, nor was the air. In those venues I was convinced our predominance was secure.

Congress was torn; this was a complex issue that aroused passion as well as political and intellectual debate. There was the usual Democrat-Republican problem—the Republican administration was proposing a controversial action, so the Democrats saw an opportunity to make political capital. The pro-Israeli congressmen didn't like the prospect of aligning ourselves with the Arabs. Others opposed the whole idea, fearful of the Vietnam syndrome. We were just asking for trouble, they declared, committing forces off the shore of a hostile country engaged in war. We stood the chance of losing many of our people in a hopeless cause. At one point Senator John Warner took me aside and said, his voice raspy with emotion, "If you lose one man over there you'll have to come out of the Gulf. One man!"

Still other congressmen were unhappy about surrendering our neutrality. That was a legitimate criticism, and I believed we should admit it—reflagging and convoying Kuwaiti tankers would not be a neutral action. But our political interest here was not to demonstrate our neutrality, it was to try to court Kuwait and the Gulf oil states, consistent with our historical pro-moderate Arab policy. My approach made sense to some congressmen. It was congenial as well to others who were attracted to the freedom of the seas argument, and to still others who just plain did not like Iran. The idea of Iranian renegades attacking unarmed ships made many Americans see red— a prominent reaction among the chiefs, for example. Among many civilians as well as military people there was a residue of deep resentment toward Iran left over from the embassy hostage period.

So the argument raged on both sides, though it was especially hot on the subject of the War Powers Resolution. Ted Kennedy, Alan Cranston, and others insisted that what we were proposing to do fell under the resolution, which meant that our convoying activities in the Gulf would be restricted to a ninety-day period after which Congress would determine whether we would stay or go. For its part, the administration maintained that the Gulf was not a war zone in the accepted sense of that term; large-scale commercial shipping was going on, oil rigs were operating normally, commercial air traffic was continuing with only slight route modifications.

What irritated me increasingly as the hearings dragged on was that despite the sharp opposition and the endless harping on the War Powers Resolution, there was no sign that either the committees or Congress as a whole would ever come to a vote on reflagging, as in fact they didn't. Too many in Congress simply did not want to be held accountable. If they prevented us from going in they would share the blame for whatever catastrophe our presence might have prevented. If they endorsed the mission, then they would be associated with its consequences. I often found myself wanting to shout, Look, let's quit talking about it. If you don't want us to go, pass a motion or a law that we can't go. Invoke the War Powers Resolution. Do *something!*

In due course the congressional hearings ended but endorsed no action. The congressmen in opposition had not influenced us, nor, as far as I could tell, had we swayed them. Consequently, we determined to move ahead as originally intended. The fact of the matter, however, was that while the administration's spokesmen had made a number of arguments, no specific set of prioritized objectives had ever been established. In particular, the effect our reflagging policy would have on the American relationship with Iraq was purposely left unarticulated. We did not want Iran to win this war, but few in the administration felt warmly about Iraq either. In essence, we had chosen to support our Arab allies and keep Iran from gaining an advantage at their expense. No one at the time had the presence of mind to foresee the ultimate impact our actions would have on the future of Iran or Iraq. We did not divine that Saddam Hussein would one day turn on his Arab allies.

As the hearings wound down, we finally heard from the Kuwaitis, accepting our offer. So after months of effort we were under way. We now began serious military planning for this operation, which was given the code name "Earnest Will." The military goal of the mission was to demonstrate our strength of purpose and our willingness to extend a protective arm to those we considered our friends. What happened here was likely to affect our position in this region for years to come, and that would have profound consequences. Success would depend on the effectiveness of our preparations and on our determination to see this through. But if we encountered serious problems, the precedents, at least in regard to our determination, were not comforting.

In recent times we had forsaken our Vietnamese allies and abandoned the Shah; we had withdrawn the Marines from Lebanon after the barracks bombing. This was a background our friends in the region alluded to often. You, they said, are here now. But you might leave at any time. We live here permanently, and so does Iran.

No one had to remind me that the success or failure of Earnest Will did not depend on us alone. The Iranians were a volatile and uncertain adversary. My assessment of them was that they would not challenge us head-on at sea. They would understand the power we were ready to bring to bear and our seriousness about using it. They would be angry, but in the end—when they saw the weakness of their options—they would swallow their anger and blink. But if my assessment was wrong, if they chose to make the Gulf a battleground, the danger could escalate dramatically. There was a chance I would emerge from this as one of the men who had unleashed the furies.

Chapter 11

OPERATION EARNEST WILL

IN PLANNING EARNEST WILL I was fortunate to have Vice Admiral Jonathan T. Howe as assistant to the chairman. Howe was an innovative strategist with extensive experience in the political world. He had been Vice President Nelson Rockefeller's military adviser, Henry Kissinger's NSC aide, and director of political-military affairs for the State Department.* During the course of a busy naval career Howe had managed to acquire a PhD in international law from the Fletcher School at Tufts University. His work habits were legendary, so much so that I wasn't the only one who sometimes wondered how he had ever found the time to father six children. Another great help was Vice Admiral Powell Carter, the director of the Joint Staff. Powell was something of an anomaly among the upper-level military, a self-effacing, quiet individual who seemed to have almost no ego. But behind the plain facade lurked a brilliant mind that was unmoved by anything but cold logic.

The fundamental problems of this operation broke down into two areas. We had to devise measures to protect our convoys from the Iranians, and equally significant, we had to tailor an appropriate command structure for our own forces. Years of experience with military turf wars warned me that getting the right command structure in this situation was going to be troublesome. Fortunately, the Goldwater-Nichols Defense Reorganization Act had passed the previous year, giving the Chairman and the unified commanders the authority to design command and control mechanisms to fit special circumstances. This was going to be the statute's first test.

The chief difficulty was that Earnest Will would require coordinated operations by the Middle East Force inside the Gulf and a

---

* Howe later served as deputy national security adviser under Brent Scowcroft.

carrier group outside the Strait of Hormuz. But the Persian Gulf was under the jurisdiction of the U.S. Central Command, while the Indian Ocean (where the carrier group would be located) fell under Pacific Command. That meant the operation would be taking place on the seam of two unified commands, a recipe for trouble. To complicate matters further, the Commander-in-Chief of the Central Command was a Marine general, George Crist (Norman Schwarzkopf's predecessor). The prospect of a Marine commanding an almost exclusively Navy mission was deeply disturbing to many in the naval community. A maritime operation of these dimensions, they believed, was far too significant to be left to a Marine, regardless of what the command structure of the United States called for.

When this conflict started to brew, I pointed out to the Navy hardliners that Hal Bernsen, the Commander of the Middle East Force inside the Gulf, was an admiral. But that did not satisfy them. Behind the scenes they were saying, He's not a first-line man. He's a rear admiral and a helicopter pilot. What they were really implying was that under no circumstances did they want the Marine general at Central Command running this operation; they wanted the admiral at Pacific Command to run it. "But it's not in Pacific Command's area," I insisted. That doesn't matter, they said. We need real expertise here, Navy expertise, not amateurs.

But I was not under any circumstances going to let this operation be taken away from Central Command, and I was equally determined to establish a single operational commander. After consideration, I combined the Middle East Force inside the Gulf and the carrier group outside into one task force assigned to General George Crist. This was the most effective way to insure a clear, short chain of command. It also had the advantage of keeping any action that involved this complex tangle of nations under the jurisdiction of those who knew them best. To satisfy the Navy's sensibilities, within the special task force I initially gave the carrier group admiral ("One of your own," I told the Navy staff) command over the Middle East Force admiral. I also saw to it that the Navy gave General Crist one of their most highly regarded officers as his chief for plans so that Crist would have high-level naval advice constantly at hand.*

---

* In the event, the carrier group admiral gave us a very hard time. He wanted strict schedules; he wanted to know six weeks ahead of time where every ship would be, where the convoys would meet, and how they would get to where they were going. Exactly the

While I was resolving the command situation, Howe, myself, and our staff were also working on the technical and military problems we would be facing. We quickly found that the Kuwaitis (like everyone else) thought convoying was a grand idea but had given little thought to the modalities of actually doing it. For years they had operated their giant tankers on schedules determined by the volume of oil ready for shipment and the delivery destinations. Kuwait would have, for example, contracts for delivery in an array of European and Asian ports and eleven ships available for transportation. The schedulers factored in the oil production rate, storage capacity, voyage times, loading times, and docking space so that the storage tanks were never full and oil production was never interrupted, the whole design determined on a strict cost basis.

But now the criterion would be security, not cost, and that did not sit well with the Kuwaiti oil bureaucracy. Refinery managers, oil company executives, and tanker masters were all unhappy with the new schedules we established. At the same time, the Navy commanders knew little about the special problems of running tankers. It took a while before everyone had adjusted to each other, which wasn't surprising. This was the first convoying operation we had conducted in almost forty-five years.

Because we were so uncertain about what the Iranian response would be, we decided to deploy a substantial task force: ten ships inside the Gulf with the carrier battle group nearby in the Indian Ocean. The carrier was there primarily in case the Iranians did something so formidable we had to retaliate against targets inside Iran. The carrier's escort ships would also be available to reinforce the Middle East Force in the event we needed more ships for convoying work. Subsequently, we also deployed the battleship U.S.S. *Missouri* to the area for a few weeks. I did not believe the Iranians were going to challenge us seriously, but I wanted to make sure that if they did we could hit them with overwhelming power. The Iranian arsenal included Chinese-made Silkworm missiles, a mix of missile

---

kind of predictability I did not want. In addition, he formulated a series of instructions to make sure the convoying ships did not get into trouble with the Iranians. I didn't mind trouble with the Iranians. If they behaved we would not bother them, but if they challenged us we were not going to back down.

With this approach, the carrier group admiral and the Middle East Force commander were at constant loggerheads. General Crist, who was a man of great patience and tolerance, eventually got fed up. In the end we adjusted the structure again and made the man inside the Gulf the boss.

frigates and corvette-type Swedish Boghammer patrol boats, and a capacity for mining. If they were willing to take the risks, they could create some serious mischief.

Among our special preparations, we armed the escort ships with a variety of small-caliber weapons. We were not worried that the Iranian patrol boats might actually sink a ship, but fifteen or sixteen highly maneuverable small boats carrying rocket-propelled grenades and 20-mm machine guns could mount hit-and-run raids and play a lot of hell with a warship. Curiously enough, modern American naval vessels have no small weapons for close-in combat against this kind of adversary. Many, in fact, have no small-caliber guns at all. They have missiles instead that are designed to shoot at aircraft and warships at a long range. The capability of our ships to handle multiple targets in close was limited. And they would be operating in shallow waters adjacent to an enemy shoreline dotted by islands—ideal ambush territory.

In addition to installing an array of machine guns and rapid-fire cannons on the escorts, we expected our seaborne helicopters to help counter the small-boat threat. But this too required some ingenuity. The Navy's regular shipboard helicopters were primarily ASW (anti-submarine warfare) types, loaded with the gear necessary to hunt down submarines but not appropriate for the mission at hand. They could extend the eyes of the ship out twenty miles or more, but we needed aircraft that could do more than just say, "There they are and here they come." We wanted helicopters out there that could engage in a shooting match. But the Navy had nothing with that capability.

In the search for the right helicopter I ultimately went to the Army Special Forces at Fort Bragg, which used two-man choppers equipped with infrared sensors and rapid-fire guns. Their engines were so quiet they could not be heard at more than one or two hundred yards, making them ideal instruments for nighttime observation and surprise attack. Best of all, their maintenance was simple and we could operate them from frigates as well as from the larger destroyers.

Here another little turf commotion sprang up. Though there was no overt Navy opposition to using the Special Forces helicopters, a kind of fog of resistance formed. Here and there objections surfaced to going outside the Navy for help. Not that these voices mattered much; they were residues of service jealousies whose day was over as far as I was concerned. We had been ordered to carry out a mission and we were going to do it with whatever we had, whoever owned it. I ordered the Navy to take the Army helicopters with their Army pilots and put them aboard the ships.

As Jon Howe and I continued our preparations during the late spring of 1987, we faced one Iranian threat for which we had no easily available counter: mining. We knew the Iranians had a large stock of contact mines, many of Russian origin and World War Two vintage. But while they had some minelaying capacity, they had not used it much. Whether they would now was an open question.

Ideally, we would have liked to deploy minesweepers, but the unfortunate fact was that the Navy possessed no modern mine-sweepers (though we were building several). Those we did have were World War Two wooden-hulled ships being maintained in reserve status. It was our intention to take some of them to the Gulf, but it would be a long, slow journey.*

Given these circumstances, the question was whether we should postpone the escort operation until we could deploy a full mine-sweeping effort. After examining the factors involved, our decision was to move ahead. We had a considerable ability to monitor operations in the Gulf, and we could mount intensive surveillance in the vicinity of the convoys using helicopters and small boats. If necessary, we could also bring in anti-mine helicopters, specially rigged to operate against the kind of contact mines the Iranians had in abundance.

Meanwhile, outside the Gulf our carrier and battleship groups would be waiting, and the Iranians knew that we were in a position to mount a powerful strike on their naval headquarters at Bandar Abbas, or on any other target we might choose. We did not know if they would chance laying mines in front of U.S. ships, or how determined such an effort might be. But the general estimate was that the risks did not warrant delaying the operation.

· · ·

---

* Every year since World War Two the Navy has put minesweepers in its budget, but with the exception of the few ships we were building, they had always been cut. The general theory in Congress was that many of our NATO allies had minesweepers. Consequently, looking at the need as part of a total force proposition, there seemed little reason for us to build any. In an era of tight money they were not a priority. The Navy's planners might have been able to talk Congress into it if they had been willing to cut other items. But the fact was that in the last forty years we had only used minesweepers three or four times, so neither the Navy's priorities nor Congress's were unreasonable.

But minesweepers are like so many things. When you need them, you really need them, and you're awfully sorry you don't have them. We quickly discovered that, when we required them in the Gulf, our allies were not at all eager to send theirs, and certainly not on our time schedule.

On July 23 the first reflagged convoy made its way northward through the Strait of Hormuz: the cruiser *Fox*, the destroyer *Kidd*, and the frigate *Crommelin* escorting three empty tankers en route to Kuwait including the 400,000-ton *Al Rekkah*, now rechristened the *Bridgeton*. As the group passed through the Strait, our warships detected the tracking radar at Iran's Kuhestak Silkworm site scanning them. They also picked up two Iranian F-4s flying a racetrack pattern about the launch area. Suddenly the F-4s broke toward the convoy at 5,000 feet. Riding picket just off the twelve-mile limit, *Kidd* locked up on the fighters and warned them off. Three seconds before the *Kidd*'s skipper would have pulled the trigger the fighters dove to sea level and streaked for home.

That night the convoy anchored off Bahrain. AWACS (Airborne Warning and Control System radar planes) reported small-boat activity in the vicinity of Farsi Island, which they would be passing the following day. It seemed as if the Iranians might be planning a small-boat attack. Mines were also in the back of the American captains' thoughts, though they eventually concluded these boats were not minelayers. Nevertheless, when they weighed anchor next morning lookouts were already in the bows and helicopters hovered out in front searching the murky waters.

That afternoon as the convoy was moving through the main shipping channel west of Farsi, the *Bridgeton* struck a moored mine. The explosion was so powerful that two hundred yards back from the point of contact the captain and others on the bridge were bounced up in the air. On the escort ships the underwater blast blanked out the sonar equipment.

A few minutes later my bedside phone jolted me awake with the news. Within twenty minutes I was in the Pentagon war room, where the atmosphere was grim. The only thing known for certain was that one mine had struck the tanker near the bow. First reports indicated no casualties, but two months earlier first reports of the attack on the *Stark* had reported only "light casualties," yet thirty-seven sailors had died then.

The more detailed reports that followed allayed our fears. No one had been hurt and *Bridgeton* was still under way. The rest of the convoy had fallen in behind her and cleared the minefield unscathed. Although the blast tore a gaping hole in the ship's hull and blew out two forward tanks, it had not even slowed the enormous tanker down.

Once it was clear that the convoy had sustained no further damage, the larger implications of the incident began to settle in. That mine, I knew, could as easily have hit one of our escorts as the *Bridgeton*. If that had happened we might well have lost the warship and sustained numerous casualties. The impact of such an event on public opinion would have been dramatic; shock waves would have reverberated through the White House, Defense Department, and Congress. The Gulf policy I had worked so hard to establish might easily have collapsed, whatever its merit.

The truly sobering thought was that evidently Teheran had made a conscious decision to take on the United States despite the risks. That changed the nature of everything. I knew that if the Iranians had the guts to wage a determined effort here—and to take the heavy losses they would incur—they could make our lives miserable. A concerted mining campaign would force us to commit many more assets than we intended or desired. We would have to spend more and make a far deeper psychological and political investment. And with all the resources we could bring to bear, we might still be vulnerable. I knew that if we began to take losses, Congress could easily decide to back us out of the mission. Vietnam was hovering over everyone's shoulder.

While we considered our next step, the newspapers were raking us over the coals about the *Bridgeton*. They lambasted us for not having had minesweepers in place before we started convoying and for not having taken more on-site precautions. Of course this was Monday morning quarterbacking, but the media attacks were not unjust. We had thought our field intelligence on Iranian activity would be more comprehensive, and our patrolling in advance of the convoy hadn't been all it should have been either. I was not in a good position to complain.

With the pressure mounting, I had to decide if we should put a temporary halt to the convoys until our minesweepers arrived. On reflection I concluded that we had sufficient assets in the area to make do while we were waiting. The fundamental error in *Bridgeton*'s case had been an attitudinal one. We had underestimated the Iranian ability to plant a few mines quickly and disappear. But to do this effectively they had to depend on our predictability, and the first transit was nothing if not predictable. The fact was that no one involved had taken the possibility of mining seriously enough. The *Bridgeton* had carried a full load and was at maximum draft, which confined it to the main channel. We learned that day that we had to work out unpredictable routes, vary tanker loads, and take other steps that would permit maximum flexibility—and then we had to make imaginative use of our options.

The forces in the Gulf digested the lesson quickly. Returning from Kuwait, the escorts took different channels. From then on convoys varied routes, speeds, and loads constantly. All reported Iranian boat movements were assumed to be minelaying activity. Surveillance was beefed up. The decision was made to assume the risks and continue a full convoy schedule.

We also began casting around for other expedients. A regular minesweeper does its work by deploying two special cables at an angle off the stern of the ship that are attached at the far end to floats. If the cables engage a moored mine they drive it into a cutter which severs the mine mooring, allowing the mine to float to the surface where it can be exploded by gunfire. Admiral Bernsen's people came up with the idea that the same function could be served by two heavy-duty tugs dragging a cable between them. We borrowed the tugs from the Kuwaiti Oil Company, then installed minesweeping cable that we flew over from the United States. These tugs were not as efficient as a sweeper, but the people on the ships got a tremendous boost from having someone out there in front of them looking for mines. In addition, we brought a helicopter carrier into the Gulf to begin operating in front of the convoys with minesweeping helicopters.* Meanwhile our reserve minesweepers were making their way toward the Gulf from their berths in the States.

At the same time we were working on what we hoped would be a more comprehensive solution. We knew we could not guard the entire Gulf against mining. But we also knew that the Iranians could not set their mines for shallow depths without blowing up vessels they did not want to blow up—the fishing boats and dhows that roamed the Gulf by the hundreds. One solution, then, was to use shallow-draft patrol boats instead of deep-draft warships in the most dangerous channels.

Like minesweepers, patrol boats were at a premium in the modern Navy, but we managed to find and ship over a number of fiberglass boats that had originally been built for Vietnam's rivers. As soon as they arrived, we put them to work as escorts. It was hard duty, the

---

* The reason we had not done this in the first place is that minesweeping helicopters are primarily designed for independent work, not for sweeping in front of moving ships. In the escort mode they are not efficient, and we knew that the harsh conditions of the Gulf would wear them down quickly. Nevertheless, they made sense as a stopgap.

riverboats took a beating from the three- and four-foot swells that filled the Gulf on bad days. But although their fragility made them less helpful than we had hoped, they were not going to be mined and they reduced the risks to major ships. With their machine guns and rapid-fire grenade launchers the patrol boats also gave us added protection against the Iranian Boghammers, and if they found anybody laying a mine they could really do them in.

Here too my ideas did not sit too well with some in the Navy hierarchy, though I was used to it by this time. The Navy's emphasis for years had been on building major vessels with the most advanced electronic equipment and gun and missile technology. It was difficult to persuade senior officers who had spent their careers acquiring and operating a superb blue-water Navy that in the present situation we were better off with three-foot-draft riverboats.

But the small-boat concept was actually part of a larger approach that the Gulf forces were putting into place. Sweeping was one way to counter a mining campaign, but it was not the best way. The best way was to be constantly present in strength throughout the Gulf in such a fashion that we would make life dangerous for the people laying mines. To make our intentions absolutely clear on this subject we announced publicly that we would attack anybody placing mines in international waterways. We would destroy the mines and sink whoever laid them. Realistically, though, we knew we could not be everywhere at once. As bodies of water go, the Gulf is relatively small, but at 92,500 square miles it is still a good-sized area. A warship can cover only so much territory, and if we wanted to surveil every sector a good many more ships would be needed than we had available. That was another reason that helicopters and small boats were desirable; we could deploy a lot more of them with less investment.

Considering the map, it seemed that the area where we were most likely to be mined was north of Bahrain. The Iranians of course could also mine to the south. But there the convoy routes were farther from their bases and substantial traffic plied the waters that they would rather not sink if they could avoid it—shipping of nations that were more or less friendly to them. And while it would be impossible for us to patrol the entire Gulf in strength, there were measures we could take to cover the northern waters fairly well.

Specifically, we developed a plan to anchor large oil barges in strategic locations and base small boats, helicopters, and Marines on them. From these floating islands we could patrol pertinent sections of the Gulf day and night. When convoys came through, forces based on the barges could help with protection, but they would be surveilling and patrolling even when convoys were not there.

Actually, islands would have been better than barges for this kind of operation, and there were several Saudi Arabian islands in the area that would have served the purpose well. The Saudis, however, would not allow us to use them. Nor would they let us use the port of Jubail, except in the most covert way. (We flew the patrol boats in and launched them from Jubail, but we had to arrive after dark and have them out at sea before daylight.) It was often a great frustration to me that the very Gulf states we were protecting at times proved so unhelpful. We could not always count on the support of local naval forces, for example. Even when commitments were made they were often not carried out.*

Some of the Navy traditionalists disliked the barge idea even more than the other innovations. Barges don't go anywhere; they just sit there and act as stationary targets, which was the main criticism I was hearing. The Iranians, I was told, could attack them. I personally didn't know what they might attack them with. Some said Silkworm missiles, but the barges sat low in the water and made poor missile targets. The Iranians might be able to put some small-arms fire into them, I thought, but the barges were a lot harder to sink than a ship. They were highly compartmentalized and practically the size of a football field.

Despite the criticism, we went ahead with the concept as quickly as we could, using two large commercial barges the Kuwaitis rented for us. In short order we made armored islands out of those barges, complete with docking facilities, helicopter decks, hangars, radar, communications, machine guns, and contingents of Marines. We stationed them between Bahrain and Kuwait, just off the Saudi coast. Together they gave us an interlocking protective system for the convoys.

---

* Nevertheless, there were times when we got significant help. Kuwait would not allow us to go ashore, but they paid the barge rentals and they provided the tugs for our minesweeping. The fact was that although the constraints were annoying, they were characteristic of military operations with a high political content, as Earnest Will was. Our own rationale for undertaking the operation was political, as it was also for the Kuwaitis and Saudis. From their standpoint this was not a life or death situation. While they were willing to spend money and make some sacrifices, they were not willing to forgo even the appearance of sovereignty. They had at that point never allowed any foreign forces in their countries, and although Earnest Will was important, it was not important enough to change that principle. (By contrast, when the Saudis believed Iraq might invade their oil fields, their political sensitivities vanished quickly.)

The barges, helicopters, and patrol boats helped give us the ability to conduct an active campaign rather than wait passively for Iranian action. If we were going to counter the mining threat, it was necessary to lean forward. We developed a vigorous intelligence network and attempted to track everything in the Gulf. If suspicious Iranian craft were under way we monitored them. If their attack boats congregated or their communications signaled a possible action, our units closed on the scene in strength. Normally our mere presence was enough to make the Iranians disperse or return home. If they attacked a ship or an American unit, we reacted aggressively. To retain our psychological edge, we would not allow firing on U.S. forces to go unpunished.*

It was some time before the Iranians began to understand the range of measures we were taking. For months all they knew was that an unsettling number of American small boats and helicopters were operating in key areas. It was precisely their confusion about our capabilities that led them to one of their most humiliating moments —the capture and destruction of the *Iran Ajr*.

For several months intelligence had been studying the Iranian mines, minelaying equipment, and methods. One of the ships that had drawn our attention was a small shallow-draft cargo vessel named the *Iran Ajr*. Previously used by the Iranian Navy to transport equipment along the coast, the *Iran Ajr* and several similar ships had now been reconfigured with minelaying racks. On September 20, our monitors reported that the *Iran Ajr* had left Bandar Abbas headed south toward our shipping lanes. As we tracked her course we realized that by nine that night the Iranian would be right in the center of the main channel, where we were at that point running convoys every two or three days.

That night we sent the destroyer *Jarrett* to intercept the Iranian vessel and monitor her with the Special Forces helicopters using their night vision equipment. Sure enough, when the pilots intercepted the *Iran Ajr* they reported rows of "minelike objects" on her deck. As the nearly silent helicopters circled unseen above the ship the Iranian crew began pushing mines overboard. At this, Admiral

---

* Almost five years later, in July 1992, *Newsweek* magazine accused us of also employing decoy and deception operations to lure Iranian patrol boats out so we could attack them. It was a false charge. At no time did we use such tactics. Our main objective was to convince the Iranians to remain in port. U.S. units did not disturb Iranian small craft that were not mining, firing at merchant ships, or otherwise indicating aggressive intentions. If they did attack, though, we did our best to counter and neutralize them.

Bernsen gave the command to attack, and the helicopters swooped down out of the night, raking the ship with machine-gun fire. Panicked by the sudden assault (and terrified that one of the mines would explode), the crew went over the side and into the water. A small task force surrounded the *Ajr,* and at first light they boarded her and took possession. Survivors were rescued from the water and delivered to one of our warships. Among the documents we found on the *Iran Ajr* was the route log, which helped us locate the mines that had already been laid. The only disappointment in the whole operation was that the attack helicopters' low light video equipment had not functioned properly, so we had not caught all the events on tape.*

Once we had captured the *Iran Ajr,* two energetic discussions took place in Washington: What to do with the surviving crew (three had been killed in the helicopter attack and two had drowned), and what to do with the ship. The conclusion was to return the crew to Iran, which we did, using the good offices of Oman and the International Red Cross. In retrospect this was probably a wise decision, though there was considerable debate about it at the time. The possibility existed that they might capture some of our people, and against that prospect it was argued that we should hold some of theirs. Nevertheless, we came to a consensus fairly quickly, if for no other reason than to project a generous image. First, we wanted to convey to the Iranians that we regarded this as a single incident which we had no desire to prolong or escalate. Second, we always had in the back of our minds the War Powers Resolution. We had contended in Congress that the Gulf operation was not subject to the resolution, that for us this was not a war zone. The argument was somewhat dubious, but nevertheless that was our story and we were sticking to it. Consequently, we did not want to lend credence to the idea that we were indeed involved in a real war—by holding POWs, for example.

As far as the *Iran Ajr* itself was concerned, I wanted to keep it. The way I looked at it, a captured warship is a captured warship. If

---

* The same 1992 *Newsweek* article described a second Iranian minelayer, the *Rakish,* which was supposedly captured covertly in an action the Pentagon kept secret. In fact, *Rakish* was the prerevolutionary name of the *Iran Ajr.* While the original military reports referred to the *Iran Ajr,* the name *Rakish* was still painted on the ship's stern when it was taken. It is possible that some Navy documents or log entries called it that, which may have given rise to the error. In any event, the *Rakish* and the *Iran Ajr* were one and the same ship.

we could somehow use it, in a deception, for example, we should. But the political side of the house felt we would be criticized for that. Weinberger wanted to wash his hands of the capture. He did not want to be continually answering questions about it and he believed that blowing the ship up would demonstrate that we were not intimidated by the Iranian rhetoric, which after the incident had become volcanic with threats of revenge. In the end we destroyed the ship, which in retrospect was also the right decision.

The Iranians themselves never did understand how the *Iran Ajr* had been discovered, and it really troubled them. All they could conclude was that we had capabilities that allowed us to know whatever went on at night. Until then the night had always been their favorite operating time; but we took it from them, just as the Vietcong guerrillas had taken it from us in Vietnam. The *Iran Ajr* incident took place on September 21, 1987. As the succeeding months went by and there were no further incidents, the reflagging operation looked more and more like a success. The *Bridgeton* had been our first and (to this point) our last mining incident. Our worst fears had not materialized. Allied navies had now come into the Gulf as well and British, French, Italian, Dutch, and Belgian minesweepers were engaged on patrols that covered the majority of the commercial lanes. Convoy after convoy was escorted to safe harbor in Kuwait, then shepherded back through the Strait of Hormuz. The Iranian threats were still there, in particular the dangerous Silkworms. But at least for the time being Teheran seemed to have backed down from a confrontation. The Gulf was by no means a safe place; Iranians were continuing to hit unescorted neutral shipping, and after a lull the Iraqis had renewed their attacks against Iranian tankers. But despite a rocky start, we seemed well on the way to fulfilling our objectives of protecting American flag shipping, insuring the flow of oil, and demonstrating a strong, durable commitment to our friends in the region.

Nineteen eighty-eight dawned as a year of crisis for Iran. Early in the year Baghdad thwarted Iran's long expected northern offensive; then in a series of aggressive moves the Iraqi Army began taking back territory it had previously lost. On the international scene Teheran saw itself increasingly isolated, and some analysts noted a growing war-weariness among the Iranian people. In various ways the mullahs attempted to rekindle the old anger that had sustained the revolution in earlier days. During the previous holy season a ferocious encounter with Saudi Arabia over the pilgrimage to Mecca had led to a pitched battle within the confines of the holy places and an outpouring of public rage in Iran. Diplomatic ties with the Saudis were severed.

Whether as part of Teheran's effort to reheat the national fervor or not, at the beginning of April 1988 new mines were laid on the convoy routes south of Kuwait, which our surveillance failed to pick up. On the fourteenth of that month the missile frigate *Samuel B. Roberts* was steaming south by herself after having delivered a tanker convoy to Kuwait City. All of a sudden her lookouts spotted mines bobbing on the surface of the water, although at first they weren't positive about the identification. The lookouts initially thought they might be seeing sheep. Giant Australian sheep boats hauling thousands of live sheep bound for Middle Eastern dinner tables sailed the Gulf, and in the sweltering heat scores of sheep would die. When this happened, the Australians just threw them overboard. In the water the dead sheep would bloat up and float upside down with their legs jutting into the air. From a distance the floating sheep often looked very much like mines.

When the *Roberts* found herself in the midst of a minefield, she came to a dead stop and went to general quarters. Then she tried to back slowly out, retracing the course that had led her into danger. At first the skipper, Commander Paul Rinn, thought he was going to clear the area, but as he continued to backtrack the ship was convulsed by a huge explosion that gutted the engine room and sent a flood of water coursing through the machinery spaces. Working feverishly through the night, the *Roberts*'s crew sealed the spaces and brought the fires under control. With the main deck almost split in two, they welded and laced the frigate with cables until they had literally tied her back together. It was a superhuman effort, and it saved the ship.

When the *Roberts* was hit, President Reagan called a meeting in the Oval Office. The subject was retaliation.

The lines of debate on this issue had been drawn during earlier considerations of how to react to the *Bridgeton* mining and to a Silkworm strike the previous October on a tanker docked in Kuwait City. Any time the idea of retaliation was broached, an argument commenced as to what was appropriate, or as the State Department and political people insisted on putting it, "proportionate." Invariably State Department representatives contended that any retaliation should be directly related to the provocation and could not be excessive (although at times George Shultz was more militant than his assistants). Retaliation, they believed, had to be seen as a simple, clear response, not in any sense an escalation, and in this they were usually seconded by the National Security Adviser.

I usually felt the political criteria were overly demanding. My general theory was that if we were going to take any retaliatory measures at all, we should destroy targets that would reduce the Iranians' power to harm us. I wanted targets that had military significance. The chances were good that we would be in the Gulf for some time, and the more we reduced Iran's ability to interfere with us the better I liked it. As in the debate over the Tripoli raid, I was against attacking targets and committing people for strictly political purposes.

The problem with that approach, of course, was that it suggested much larger targets than the politicians had in mind. The President and his immediate advisers wanted to go after something with a low profile. They were dealing in perceptions; what they really wanted was to make something out of nothing. That meant striking a blow that would not hurt the Iranians so much that they would be moved to escalate, but that would at the same time impress the American public as the act of a strong and determined leadership.

This time I pushed hard for hitting a warship. They had gone far enough, I argued. We had to let Teheran know that we were willing to exact a serious price. By that time Frank Carlucci had succeeded Weinberger as Secretary of Defense, and he was inclined in my direction. But all the others at the table argued persistently against the proposal. In the end the President agreed to let us take out three oil platforms the Iranians were using for observation and tracking, but he also went along with what I considered a very good set of rules of engagement. We would limit ourselves to the platforms, but if any Iranians ventured out against us, we could engage and sink them. I was hoping against hope that the Iranian frigate *Zabalon* would get in our way during this action. Of the various Iranian vessels that had been assaulting unarmed neutrals, the *Zabalon* was by far the most aggressive. With any luck we'd see to it that she had assaulted her last helpless victim.

On the morning of April 18, four days after the *Roberts* was hit, we warned the oil platforms, then attacked. Two of the Iranian crews abandoned their stations even before the firing began, but the third fought back briefly. While the assault was in progress a large Iranian missile patrol boat came out of Bushir and fired a missile at the cruiser *Wainwright*. Within a few minutes the Iranian had been hit by three American return missiles and sank quickly.

Shortly afterwards we spotted the frigate *Zahan*, *Zabalon*'s sister ship, steaming toward a group of United Arab Emirates oil platforms that had American technicians and drillers on them. Then radar picked up a squadron of Boghammer patrol boats also headed for the platforms. A-6s from the carrier *Enterprise* were ordered in, and the frigate and two of the patrol boats were hit and sunk. The rest of the Boghammers just managed to race back to their base at Abu Musa in front of the pursuing warplanes.

By then we were going after anything that sortied. The Iranian Navy had decided to fight, but we intercepted their attack orders and started working their ships over as soon as they made it to open water. Late in the day *Zabalon* herself came out—a futile and desperate venture; she was far from any potential targets. A-6s and 7s hit the frigate and stopped her cold. When the planes were out of ordnance they went back to rearm, but by this time it was nearing dusk and the Iranians were taking advantage of the respite to tow the frigate back to Bandar Abbas, her main deck awash. As the light faded in the Gulf we received a request to attack again from one last A-6 pilot who was still in the air. Carlucci had come into the command center and was standing next to me when the transmission came through. By that time we had sunk two or three large ships and several patrol boats. We had destroyed three platforms and badly damaged the *Zabalon*. Once again the A-6 commander asked for permission to attack, but I turned the request down. "We've shed enough blood today," I told Carlucci.

Now the great question became What would the Iranian reaction be to this extremely heavy day? Would this truly create an explosive escalation? (The intelligence people assured us it would.) Over the next few days we stopped convoying, alert for hints of their intentions. But nothing happened. Whatever else was going through their minds, they were also thinking, We went out there and lost half our Navy. Another day like this and we won't have any Navy at all. Which was exactly what we wanted them to think. That was the image we were trying to build in their minds, and that was the reason I had wanted to sink a ship earlier. I wanted the Iranians to understand that any time we felt like it we could start picking off their ships, and there wasn't a thing they could do about it. April 18 had gotten that message across loud and clear. The only options they had left were the Silkworm missiles, but they knew that using those against us would elicit a devastating response.*

Retaliation in the form of terrorism was more likely, but that did not materialize either. By the spring of 1988 the Iranians were not receiving good news from any quarter. On the warfront, the Iraqi Army recaptured territory at Fao and Majinoun Island and launched heavy forays across the border. Unable to respond, Iran appeared clearly to be losing the war, a fact that sent shudders through the Teheran leadership. They seemed almost mesmerized by the vision of their own defeat. While Iranian losses at sea might have impressed us, they were as nothing compared with the tens of thousands of casualties they were suffering on land.

On the hot Sunday morning of July 3, two and a half months after the *Roberts* retaliation, the frigate U.S.S. *Montgomery* was patrolling the western reaches of the Strait of Hormuz. The previous night she had gone to the aid of a freighter that had called for help after being attacked by Iranian patrol boats. Intelligence estimates were predicting a rash of Iranian activity leading up to America's July 4 national holiday, and as the haze cleared that morning *Montgomery* found herself in the vicinity of a group of thirteen Boghammers. On the radio her communications officers could hear the patrol boats querying nearby merchantmen, which often preceded Iranian assaults on neutral shipping. Reporting the situation, the *Montgomery* watched closely, alert for hostile activity or calls of distress.

Earlier that morning the Aegis missile cruiser U.S.S. *Vincennes* under Captain Will Rogers had passed through the Strait en route to Bahrain. Now Rogers received orders to reverse course and join the *Montgomery*. As the big missile cruiser churned into the area, Captain Rogers ordered the ship's helicopter aloft to reconnoiter. Ten miles or so north of the two American ships, the chopper spotted the Boghammers. Flying in to get a better look, the helicopter suddenly found itself under fire.

---

* We put substantial pressure on the Chinese to stop their sales to Iran. It became a very serious issue between ourselves and China. The Chinese eventually claimed they were no longer selling Silkworms, but we had substantial evidence they were not telling the truth. The Chinese needed the income badly, and their unusual military-industrial organization made it difficult for the government to control weapon sales effectively. Many of the arms factories in China are owned directly by the military. If the factories make money, the military can spend more on itself. If they don't, the military budget contracts. Consequently, the pressure to sell arms is immense. In this case it took us a long time to truly get the sales cut off.

Quickly the *Vincennes* turned toward the encounter, its communications linked to the helicopter's radar display. Identifying the Iranians, Rogers approached at high speed, the *Montgomery* following. With the *Vincennes* bearing down on them, most of the Boghammers retreated from the international waters, where the incident had begun, into Iranian territorial waters. But several of them turned toward the *Vincennes* and the *Montgomery*. Considering these boats hostile, the two American commanders radioed their superior, Rear Admiral Tony Less in Bahrain, asking and receiving permission to open fire. As the battle opened, both ships maneuvered radically to ward off the Boghammers and take them under fire, crossing over into Iranian waters as they did so.

In the midst of this melee the *Vincennes*'s radar picked up an aircraft that had just taken off from the Iranian military-civilian airport at Bandar Abbas. The plane closed fast, headed directly at the cruiser, whose repeated warnings to turn away went unanswered. From intelligence reports, Captain Rogers knew that the day before Iranian Air Force F-14s had flown into Bandar Abbas.

At 9:51 A.M. Captain Rogers designated the aircraft as hostile, in all probability an F-14. Electronic squawks were picked up from the plane, in what seemed to be both the civilian and military frequencies, but Rogers knew that Iranian fighter jets often squawked in civilian mode to disguise themselves. What he did not know was that neither Bandar Abbas air control nor the aircraft itself was monitoring the emergency channels over which he continued to broadcast his warnings. From his tactical coordinator the captain heard that the plane's altitude was decreasing, as if it were preparing to fire a missile.* Just then the *Vincennes* swung into a thirty-degree turn to confront the attacking Boghammers. Bullets were hitting the cruiser as she heeled hard into the turn, sending loose objects in the command center clattering to the floor. From the moment the plane was inside twenty miles, Rogers had intended to fire. Instead he continued to hold, hoping for a more definitive identification. Now, with the aircraft nine miles away and still closing, Captain Rogers gave the order to fire two Standard surface-to-air missiles.

Very early that morning reports came in to the Pentagon command

---

* That communication was the lasting mystery. When we analyzed the electronic information later it indicated the aircraft was ascending. But Rogers was not monitoring the screen himself, and those who were told him the plane was angling down. The investigation was never able to unravel this discrepancy.

center that the *Vincennes* had shot down an Iranian F-14. But by 5 A.M. each follow-up was making me increasingly anxious. Clearly there was some confusion aboard the *Vincennes,* and I felt it likely that some of the ship's reporting was inaccurate. Meanwhile, radio broadcasts from Teheran had announced that a civilian Iran Airlines Airbus bound for the United Arab Emirates was missing. From the UAE came an announcement that a scheduled airliner had not arrived. American aircraft tried to get in for a close look at the wreckage, but because the downed plane was in Iranian waters they were unable to do so. What they could see were many boats milling around, as if trying to conduct rescue operations for a large number of people. As the indications accumulated, I became convinced that the *Vincennes* had downed not an F-14 but a civilian airliner.

By now the White House, State Department, and National Security Council, as well as the individual services, were following developments closely. In an atmosphere of tense exchanges among the various parties, I found myself arguing that we should come out and announce the shootdown publicly, even before we had absolute confirmation. If we spent the day denying it and then had to reverse ourselves later on, it would be a public relations disaster. It was tragic enough that this had happened; if we gave the impression that we were trying to cover it up we would compound the damage. Secretary Carlucci agreed, but this decision was not ours alone.

An interagency debate was soon under way, and as the various people talked back and forth there emerged a vague but tangible feeling against going public. Even though the Iranians by now were announcing that we had shot down an airliner, some wanted to stonewall, at least until we knew exactly what had happened. (By this they meant until the *Vincennes* reported that it had fully reconstructed the event and drawn that conclusion—something it was unlikely to do anytime soon.) They argued that the Iranians would say we had downed an airliner no matter what; their announcement did not in any way mean it was fact. We should not admit we had knocked down a civilian plane. If they think we have, went the argument, let them prove it. Why make their job easier?

Others thought we should simply announce that it was possible we had hit an airliner, but that we had no confirmation at the present time. We would provide details when we had them. End of announcement. I argued against that strenuously, even though it was the traditional approach. My feeling was, in general, that taking a "We'll be back to you" stance is a good way to provoke incredulity and criticism. Ignoring the practical problems involved, the media attitude tends to be They have the best communications system in the world and they still say they don't know. The result is that the networks march off with their own stories, and instead of you saying you shot it down, everyone else says it. Then six hours later you have to come back and say, Oh, you're right. We did knock it down.

I opposed doing anything besides disclosing what we all had personally accepted by now, even though I distinctly recalled Phil Goulding's admonishment in his book *Neither Confirm Nor Deny*. "In any crisis," the former assistant secretary for public affairs had written, "ninety percent of the first reports are wrong, seventy percent of second reports are wrong, and sixty percent of the third reports are wrong. It is not until the fifth or sixth reports that you really begin to understand what happened." So it wasn't as if there was no justice in what the others were saying. Nevertheless, I was convinced we knew what had taken place, even without having all the details. And I was certain beyond doubt that we should make the announcement as soon as we could. Finally Frank Carlucci, who had also been in favor of full disclosure from the beginning, made it absolutely clear that the Defense Department was determined to be forthright about this, and that put an end to the discussion. Carlucci got the President and Secretary of State on the phone and told them what we recommended, and although they had a number of suggestions of their own, they approved the basic decision.

The question now was Who would make the announcement? I assumed that the Secretary of Defense would do it, and I was more than willing to back him up. But Carlucci's press adviser did not think the Secretary should be the one to deliver this grim news.* The moment he said that, I knew that though there were several people who might do this, I was the one who would end up on the air. Clearly, this would be a painful experience, and more than a little dicey. I could expect a rough grilling from the press, and many of the facts I would need to answer their questions were still unclear. But there was some appropriateness in having the Chairman deliver the announcement, and I steeled myself.

For the next two hours I was totally consumed by putting together a statement on which we could get agreement around town. In the

---

* Dan Howard was a highly respected veteran public affairs official. He later told me that of all the things he had done in the Pentagon, the decision not to let Carlucci make the announcement was his most serious mistake.

hectic atmosphere of the small conference room off the national command center it seemed to me that all kinds of people were drafting statements, then flashing them to the White House and State, which passed back their own improvements and amendments. In the end I redrafted the entire presentation to make sure it conveyed my personal understanding of the incident. I wanted to clearly state what had happened and express the government's deep regret for the loss of life. I also wanted to place the incident in its total context, describing the action the *Vincennes* was engaged in, the background of attacks on American ships in the region, the ignored warnings, and the captain's ultimate responsibility to protect his ship. I wanted to convey the callous indifference to life the Iranians had demonstrated in flying a civilian airliner directly above an area they themselves had turned into a battle zone and where they were at that very moment carrying out military action against us. We deeply regretted what had happened. The United States had had no intention of harming a civilian aircraft, but the blame was not ours alone.*

In the end it took us more weeks to make a judgment about the *Vincennes*'s action than it had taken minutes for Captain Rogers to arrive at the decision to fire. The day of the shootdown, Middle East Commander General Crist had ordered a full-scale investigation to be conducted under the direction of Rear Admiral William Fogarty of his staff. Fogarty arrived in Bahrain and started work on July 5. Until then we had been attempting to understand precisely what had happened on the basis of the *Vincennes*'s early reports. But once Fogarty got under way, no more information was available. By law and by the Navy's own regulations, investigators are protected from all outside influence. Like everyone else, the Defense Department was forced to await the outcome of Fogarty's inquiry, despite the intense pressure to furnish answers.

---

* Two statements I made during this press conference regarding the actions of the Airbus turned out on subsequent investigation to have been in error. I had, however, taken great care to state that this was a first report and that first reports are inherently sketchy and often mistaken. (In one form or another I had said that eighteen times—I counted them later on.) That did not satisfy some of the reporters, who later took me to task for the inaccuracies. But in general, the bulk of the press and the general audience applauded our decision to be forthcoming.

I had found it a hard job to stand up and tell the American public that we had made a mistake that had resulted in a serious loss of civilian life, but I subsequently received many letters expressing appreciation for the way it had been handled. Some criticism appeared in the press, but there were also quite a few columnists who wrote that though it was hard for the government to do what it had, we had made the right decision.

When the Fogarty report was finally completed, Carlucci and I carefully considered the nature of our endorsements. In the process, we traveled to the Navy's training installation at Dahlgren on the Chesapeake Bay where there is a replica of a cruiser CIC (combat information center). There, with stand-ins playing the roles of captain, executive officer, and fire control team, we ran the tapes that had recorded all communications in the *Vincennes*'s CIC. For fifteen minutes leading up to the missile firing we heard the reports and battle talk and saw the readouts from the Aegis tracking system. We re-created the environment Captain Rogers was in when faced with the decision to either shoot or let the approaching aircraft go. We experienced (Carlucci for the first time) the intensity of the combat bridge, where the world keeps coming at the captain and does not stop, where on that day the Iranian Airbus was closing at 350 knots and not answering the ship's warnings to stay clear.

Afterwards both Carlucci and I had a better foundation to appreciate what had happened. The simulations (we ran the tapes through three times) reinforced my opinion that the Aegis system had functioned properly and that a human error had been made. Given the information at hand, Captain Rogers had made the right decision. It was impossible to forget that little more than a year earlier the commander of the U.S.S. *Stark* had been overly complacent and as a result thirty-seven American sailors had died. The intent of our rules of engagement was to protect American lives. I had briefed the Sixth Fleet commander on them before the Tripoli raid. During Earnest Will I had again made a point of briefing the Middle East Force's major commanders personally. It was a lesson I wanted to be sure they learned. "If the rules of engagement are going to tilt in any direction," I had told them, "I want them to tilt toward saving American lives."

This was a primary factor in the investigation and in my subsequent approval of the decision not to proceed against Captain Rogers. He had obeyed the rules of engagement under which he was operating and had been sensitive to his obligation toward his crew and his ship. The time pressure on him was enormous and there were a number of indications that the approaching plane was an F-14. At the point Rogers fired his missiles he truly believed the aircraft was descending. He had kept his superior fully informed and had good reason to believe he was in danger. If anything, he had probably held fire longer than he should have.

Gross malfeasance on Rogers's part would have brought legal action against him. But barring that, it was vital to reinforce the message that captains were expected to be responsible for their ships and their crews' lives. We had promulgated the new ROEs fully cognizant that an error might someday be made, but also determined that if one were made it would be to protect our own people. The *Stark* and the *Vincennes* bore witness, each in its own way, to the gravity of our intention. I endorsed the formal determination not to take action against Captain Rogers believing that I would be heavily criticized for it. But I was quite prepared to defend my decision.*

Whether the Airbus tragedy significantly affected the Iranians one way or another we could not tell. By the time it happened they were already a depressed and demoralized people, isolated by most of the world and increasingly less capable of achieving their aims through violence. We saw that concretely in the Gulf, where they rarely challenged us anymore and where by the summer of 1988 we had safely escorted more than a hundred convoys.

The American effort in the Persian Gulf was only one of the elements at work in the region during that final year of the Iran-Iraq War. But it was a significant one, particularly in terms of establishing and solidifying bonds of cooperation and trust between ourselves and the Gulf States, in particular Kuwait and Saudi Arabia. On the road to that end we learned a number of lessons, some relevant to the way our nation conducts its affairs in a hard world, others whose truths are narrower.

The Gulf gave us, first of all, lessons in command that paid immense dividends two years later during Desert Shield and Desert Storm. Even though my instincts in this area were good, it still took

---

* It was not until two years after my retirement that any serious criticism surfaced, in a sensationalized treatment of the *Vincennes*'s performance and my own handling of the incident that appeared in *Newsweek* magazine in collaboration with ABC's *Nightline* (the same piece that claimed the American forces had secretly captured a second minelayer and had decoyed Iranian warships). Reporters John Barry and Roger Charles wrote that there was evidence of a "cover-up" and a "conspiracy" against the American people, since in their view Congress had not been kept adequately informed. No sources were cited by name, only "high Pentagon officials," "Navy sources," etc.

It was relatively easy to refute most of the factual errors and to locate actual people who were both knowledgeable and willing to present their views in public. I was called by the House Armed Services Committee to testify and spent three hours addressing the slim evidence *Newsweek* and ABC had presented and the charges they had leveled. Afterwards *Newsweek* acknowledged some errors, though it stood by the more serious claims—still citing no sources. I was content that I had refuted what I considered a series of malicious and irresponsible accusations. The committee apparently agreed and did not pursue the matter further. Of course it was not possible to correct all the damage the article had caused, as it rarely is when the media badly misstep.

some time before all the compelling service pressures of seniority, tradition, and prerogative were resolved satisfactorily. But we established the principle that one man must be in command and that man should be the one closest to the scene of action. Moreover, the line between him and Washington should be as short as possible, stripped of the layers of conflicting authority that have been our bane so often in the past. After a certain amount of thrashing around, that is what we ended up with in Operation Earnest Will. We should have started there. Traditional biases and prejudices will always assert themselves; that is what they do. But a commander must cut them away, ruthlessly if necessary, to make way for a streamlined structure that will work.

In retrospect, the most significant human quality the Gulf demanded was flexibility of mind. We put some individuals in command there who had very fine records and were highly regarded but who turned out to be rigid and dogmatic. They felt that our blue-water ships with their high technology equipment could accomplish every mission. They thought we could manage the problem—not fight a messy conflict on its own terms but manage it on ours. Our ships could be operated to use less fuel, our people could be organized to show up on time, be relieved on time, and get enough sleep. An operation like this, they believed, could be made to run precisely. What they did not see was that all this management makes everything so very predictable—a deplorable approach to warfighting.

Reality demands that a commander evaluate each situation on its own terms and adjust for it. He must have officers who are capable of that, who are willing to do things differently from the way they have been taught. It worries me that our system often fails to tell us if we have people with that quality. The only way to find out is to put them under pressure and observe. Often the kind of individual who does well in situations that require flexibility and innovativeness does not do well in the normal lockstep procedures of the peacetime service and he or she gets winnowed out along the way.

That thought disturbed me deeply at the time and still does. Breeding open-minded commanders is a high priority, yet we often seem to fall short in this regard. So much in service life even militates against it. But not having them is an invitation to disaster. A similar deficiency led to Great Britain's loss of a generation of young men in World War One. During World War Two Eisenhower had to discard a series of commanders before he found some who had the necessary qualities. In the Pacific during that war the Navy sometimes turned rigidity into an art form—in the way we initially used our submarine force, for example, or in the early refusal to acknowledge that our torpedoes simply did not work. Struggling with this problem during the Gulf crisis convinced me that flexibility of thought was our single most crucial need. I have a line that I have used at university commencement exercises ever since then. Your mind, I tell graduates, is a lot like a parachute—it won't help you much if it doesn't open when you need it.

The global lesson the Gulf taught was more encouraging. Initially Iran's leadership believed that despite our words and our commitment we would not be staunch. We could not tolerate losses and we could not stand up politically to the pressure of a long engagement. But despite our recent history, they were wrong. We persisted, and we remained true to our undertaking.

We were able to do that, I believe, because we recognized our strengths and played to them, rather than allowing ourselves to be lured into areas that favored our adversary. To a large extent, we ourselves determined the field of battle. We also found, perhaps to the surprise of some in the military establishment, that there is merit in political sensitivity. It is possible to coordinate military operations and political awareness so they do buttress each other. And while it is not always immediately obvious, if you do that well over time, it will begin to tell in the way events are going and in the way your objectives are achieved. Before and during Operation Earnest Will there was a constant and often vigorous dialogue between the political and military sides of the house, but the results were generally productive. We did not go too far too fast, and we kept Iran in a state of political uncertainty. We never hit them so badly that their government had to hit back to survive. But we never wavered. We stayed; we conveyed the message that they could not drive us out.

It was interesting to watch the Iranians. They could not infuriate us into an explosion that might have unpredictable consequences and they could not pressure us to leave. We kept our heads and walked down the middle, letting other developments persuade them that there was nothing to be gained from what they were doing. They responded with rhetoric and bluster, and eventually they just quit.

That kind of fighting is a hard business though, and difficult to see clearly when you are in the middle of it. Most of all you want it to stop, or to go. You want to know if you are at war or not. You want something tangible that you can get your hands on. The uncertain status drains you emotionally while it saps your resources. But you can make it work, if only you have good people and the strength of will to see it through.

Chapter 12

THE MEDIA
AND DEFENSE

WHILE I WAS CHAIRMAN I once appeared on the sitcom *Cheers* along with Ted Danson, Kirstie Alley, Rhea Perlman, and the rest of the cast. For a long time afterwards I couldn't take a walk without people coming up to me and saying that they had seen me on television. You're doing a great job, Admiral, they'd say. Keep it up. It is unlikely that any of these well-wishers had the foggiest notion of what it was that I actually did. But they were confident that whatever it was, I was doing it well. Forty-five years in the service of my country, I'd think, and I am going to be known for seven minutes on *Cheers*.

That thought was a bit deflating, but the lesson itself was clear. If an individual in a position of responsibility needs public support, then television exposure is essential. (Fifty million people watched that *Cheers* episode, and afterwards one former DOD skeptic said that show had done more to humanize senior military officers than anything else ever had.) Television may be superficial, it may convey a distorted message, but many people will still draw the surprising conclusion that if a person is on television he must be O.K.

Not everyone thought that my appearing on the show was a good idea, although when we scouted opinion in the White House and Department of Defense there were no gross objections either. (One White House aide did say it would be inappropriate for a man in uniform to appear in a comedy show—which prompted a Joint Staff officer to remark that obviously the aide had never been inside the Pentagon.) But though no one seriously demurred, there was still a sense of discomfort.

The same might be said of the armed services' attitude toward the media in general. The services were severely buffeted by the press in Vietnam and came out of that war nursing a strong resentment. In the years since, though, the military has become quite sophisticated.

More information is being released, and everyone understands that the old closed-mouth-and-to-hell-with-them attitude is a thing of the past, that in our open society the Defense Department will never be able to withhold all the information it would like to. Today people accept the fact that the media are part of the military's world and must be accommodated. But that does not eliminate the adversarial essence of the relationship, and consequently the edge of distrust.

I came into the chairmanship determined that I would not be a shrinking violet in my relations with the media. I had already had substantial experience dealing with journalists as CINCPAC and CINCSOUTH, and I saw no reason to change my basic approach. Rather than viewing the press as an evil to be ignored whenever feasible, I would try to be forthcoming as a matter of policy. Eventually I established warm relationships with quite a few journalists, and over the years I developed something of a reputation for candor. But while I came in with some ideas and was perfectly willing to work with reporters, I cannot say that at first I fully appreciated the true impact of the media. It took some time to learn all the ways one might get into trouble with the press, and few fully master the techniques of avoiding danger completely.

Military people have some special problems in playing the rough game of media management. Although like other public figures they can easily find themselves on the receiving end of what they consider unfair stories, they often find it more difficult to mount a defense. This is especially true when fighting back means criticizing political figures; no senior military official is disposed to ruffle the political feathers of his civilian masters. Of course the political side of the house knows this and takes advantage of it constantly.

One of the crucial moments in my chairmanship came after the Reykjavik summit in October of 1986. There President Reagan had proposed the destruction of all ballistic missiles within ten years, a concept that had received none of the thorough study arms control proposals traditionally undergo. The Joint Chiefs were stunned (they had not been informed in advance), and after review I decided to inform the President of our opposition—even though the chiefs' advice had not been solicited. In front of a tense National Security Planning Group I had read out a list of detailed objections. The next day the *Washington Post* published a story by Lou Cannon, the well-connected White House correspondent, saying that the President had consulted with his key military advisers and that the Chairman of the Joint Chiefs had enthusiastically supported the zero ballistic missile proposal. I was incredulous. The White House had felt it necessary to utterly misrepresent my position in order to imply solid military support. Still, in the end I decided to do nothing to correct the record. This happened fairly early in my tenure, and I did not yet feel strong enough to respond in public.

Later I was less reluctant. During the Persian Gulf convoying operation, *Time* magazine covered a retaliatory strike we had made, complete with an inside-the-White-House sidebar on who in the NSPG had favored doing what. There I found that I had been opposed to military action. The truth was exactly the opposite. I had argued hard against the political leadership for a far stronger response than we ended up making. But the White House felt compelled to convey that the military had made common cause with the President. This time I set the record straight in public. The message to the administration was that from here on I would fight back.

Perhaps the major disappointment I had in Washington was to discover very soon after I became Chairman that leaking is not exclusively the pastime of politicians. The military too leaks copiously. Everyone understands that politicians leak to achieve their ends. Political figures and their staffers leak to frustrate their opponents' policies, to cast opprobrium on their characters, and to blow the whistle on their cover-ups. They leak to damage an enemy or a department in conflict with them, and to maximize the prospects for their objectives.

As on the civilian side, military people sometimes leak in order to discredit specific policies—procurement decisions, prioritization plans, operations that the leaker opposes. But this species of leaking is less prominent than among politicians. More often military leakers simply seem to enjoy having the ability to get something in the newspaper. Like graffiti artists who like to see their creations "up," it enhances their sense of importance. Still others leak to curry favor with reporters who might be useful to them at some future juncture. Often people leak out of friendship. George Wilson (or some other reporter) is a friend, so this line of thought goes. He wants to know, and I don't see any particular harm in giving him some help. Besides, bad or good, publicity for the Navy (or the Army, or the Air Force) is always good. Even more depressing, the services also leak discrediting information about each other. A week into the Gulf War, Bob Woodward wrote a lead piece for the *Washington Post* about serious problems with the bomb damage assessment—the BDA— which caused an intense (though short-lived) national furor. Woodward's information damaged the Air Force's credibility, and he may well have gotten it from someone in one of the other services. Such things happen.

But the leaking that bothered me most was of operational information. During Operation Earnest Will I took measures to shut down some of that, only to have the news organizations threaten that they would hire their own ships to trail the convoys and their own helicopters to spot them by air. When I was adamant, they actually did overfly routes and look on their own. And when they found out, they published the names of ships that were being convoyed, ports of destination, and estimated arrival times. During the early period of the operation I was convinced their insatiable curiosity put American lives and ships in jeopardy on several occasions.

Although Caspar Weinberger was a consistent hard-liner with Congress, he tended to take a considerably less aggressive stance with the press, whom he needed in order to make his points in public. He genuinely did not want to alienate them. (In his school days Weinberger was a newspaperman of sorts himself. At Harvard he had been president of the *Crimson*.) The result was that whenever a convoy steamed through the Strait of Hormuz we released an announcement. I took vigorous exception to this policy. We were just then groping for an effective format for our convoying, and the Iranians were searching out the means to keep track of our activities and counter us. We were in the midst of a complicated, deadly dance, and here was the press determined to publish it all, and being helped to do that by our own inability to tell them no.

In debates with the military over the release of information, the media's rationale is primarily constitutional. Exercise and protection of the First Amendment are firmly established principles, and there is little question that the general influence of the press does encourage openness and honesty. Frequently the press performs a high service in revealing official stupidity and mendacity to a public that has not only the right to know but also the need to be educated. There is also more than a little cogency to the ethical argument that people in government will conceal misdoing, misdemeanors, and malpractice if they can, and that the press acts as the nation's watchdog.

For its part, the military's argument for controlling information is based on national security. Information that jeopardizes American lives, the defense establishment maintains, should not be released. Arguments are constant over what does or does not jeopardize, and the press criticism that the military puts too much under the national security umbrella is probably correct. It is also true that the military will take advantage of any loopholes to cover up information that may be derogatory. Nevertheless, the moral argument based on national security is valid—the release of information is not worth endangering lives. As in other cases where two basic principles are in conflict, continuing argument defines and redefines the demarcation line. But the underlying question can never be truly and finally resolved.

Nevertheless, the argument between the principles of free expression on the one hand and national security on the other has little relevance to the daily business of defense reporting. While veteran Pentagon correspondents take great and justifiable pride in their deep knowledge of defense issues, the chief inspiration for a reporter's fervor to ferret out classified information is rarely an irrepressible desire to educate or protect the American people. Rather, the two main factors driving this engine are ambition and competition. The job depends on writing articles every day, and success is partly a matter of pushing and prodding for unusual material. Each journalist wants to report more than his colleagues and scoop his competitors. Similarly, each news organization wants to fill its pages or time slots with interesting, revelatory information—ideally with information that the competition has not yet published, or didn't understand, or doesn't know about. Reporters are under constant pressure from their editors, always hearing "Give me more." The editor invariably says, "I can always delete. But give me all you can and then I'll delete it." Consequently, the news organizations have a programmed-in need for material that is too often heedless of legitimate national security concerns.

This is a need the national security establishment has difficulty coping with. One of the chief problems is that the Pentagon press corps resides *in* the Pentagon; the news organizations have offices right inside the building. Reporters all have passes and they patrol the halls constantly. I would often go outside my office and meet two or three correspondents strolling down the E Ring. On many occasions I went to great lengths to conceal where I was going inside the building and whom I was meeting with. During crisis situations reporters will station themselves in the hall outside the Chairman's office to check on who comes in and goes out. The Secretary of Defense has even more trouble than the Chairman in keeping his meetings private. Whenever a foreign ambassador or minister comes to call, it is known instantly. Under normal circumstances there may not be much harm in this. But in a time of crisis a great deal can be learned and more surmised from knowing who is meeting with whom and how frequently. As one veteran military reporter told me, "I can walk down the corridor there [in the Pentagon] and I'll come back in forty-five minutes and tell you exactly what's going on."

During my tenure I suggested that the way to eliminate this aggravating and potentially dangerous problem was to construct a separate press building in the Pentagon parking lot. If the Secretary or the Chairman or anyone else wanted a press conference he could walk over to the press building and hold it. If a correspondent wanted to set up an interview, he could do it there.

To the objective or unversed outsider such a suggestion might seem reason itself. No one with a hint of perspective would think it logical for reporters to roam freely through the nation's military headquarters. And in fact every person in government to whom I mentioned it thought a separate building would be a good idea. But though they thought so, they would not say so, at least not in public. No political figure would ever be willing to take the heat that would come his way for trying to throw the press out of the building. They will not even take the heat for limiting the press's free access inside the Pentagon. Press access has become embedded in practice, and no Secretary of Defense is eager to irritate the media more than he absolutely has to.

When all is said and done, though, it is still probably true that people in government use the media more than they are used by the media. A tremendous effort and substantial resources go into the public affairs business. The Chairman of the Joint Chiefs has four or five press aides and a special assistant for public affairs. The Defense Department has a large section headed by an assistant secretary that is devoted primarily to crafting a positive image of the Secretary for both the electronic and print media and to persuading the public that the department's positions and not its adversaries' are in the national interest.

Caspar Weinberger understood the significance of exposure well and devoted considerable energy to increasing his air time. He grasped the truth that a highly visible public figure creates an independent constituency, which makes adversaries wary; publicity and a public following strengthen appointed officials just as they do elected officials. It was for precisely this reason that the Secretary's office strove to limit my own press exposure. A chairman with his own constituency would be significantly fortified in the balance between himself and his political masters.*

Nevertheless, once I got my legs under me as Chairman, I consciously became more accessible to reporters. If you want public support, there is no way to get it except through exposure, and media coverage can initiate a public dialogue better than anything else. I could make persuasive speeches to a Rotary meeting in Ogden, Utah, or to the Navy League in Keokuk, Iowa, but for national exposure I had to work with the press. The predilection of many military men of my vintage is to abandon the field and have nothing to do with the media. Unlike elected officials, they believe they can function adequately regardless, and that such an approach is more in keeping with the dignity of their profession. Inevitably, though, the argument that then finds its way into the newspapers is entirely one-sided.

Another reason to maintain open lines with the press is that reporters do have their own leverage and many will not hesitate to use it. An official who is cold toward media people or antagonizes them is likely to find himself the target of unwelcome stories. This too is a spur to maintaining good relations.

In the end I found it easier to be open because I had a natural inclination in that direction—perhaps my Oklahoma roots showing through. Not altogether to my surprise, I discovered that I actually liked some journalists a great deal. I came to feel toward reporters somewhat as H. L. Mencken once said he did toward clergymen, several of whom became his close friends despite, as he put it, their professional enmity to the human race. In addition, I found that listening to journalists was almost as important as talking to them. There was no other group of people around Washington from whom I learned more.

I also proceeded to the next step, which was to look critically at what the military does and does not give out. I concluded very early that too much information is withheld. There are indeed things you can tell the press that are not damaging to security. In particular, I found it useful to distinguish between operational information and policy information. I felt comfortable talking to journalists about

---

* John Vessey, my predecessor, had no separate non-military constituency; he may not have believed it appropriate. But Colin Powell, my successor, has a constituency unique in the history of the chairmanship—among the nation's general population as well as the Washington press corps, with whom he developed close contacts as National Security Adviser.

how decisions were reached within the JCS and why certain policies were adopted. It seemed to me that by being forthcoming in such areas I could help convey something of the substance and meaning behind events. But there was considerable controversy in my staff about this. Captain Jay Coupe, my innovative special assistant for public affairs, encouraged my predilection toward candor; he felt it created a positive atmosphere and diminished reporters' inbred suspicion of their quarry. But others did not think it was right. They did not believe the press had any business having the information I was giving them. But in the long run the approach paid off. Good press contributes immeasurably to the prestige of the office and the stature of the position. Good press reflects on the whole enterprise.

Now, openness does not always work. It is not difficult to make mistakes as to what you give away. An individual who advocates frank relations can suddenly find himself saying something that in retrospect he should have guarded closely. There are dangers also in that speaking to journalists requires a certain amount of faith, and the faith is not always reciprocated. Truman's comment that if you want someone to trust in Washington, you better buy a dog has not yet completely lost its pertinence. Most reporters on the Pentagon beat played fair as a matter of course, but some did not. Others seemed antagonistic purely because I was military, while a few held such a deep dislike for the administration I worked for that they could not seem to help transferring it to me. But pretty soon I determined who the intransigent ones were, and I was either extremely cautious with them or had nothing to do with them at all.

Occasionally too, even careful journalists can get the message wrong, and once something is out, it is out. In this game there are no second chances. The popular conception of George Kennan's containment policy is a graphic example. To this day Kennan, who is now eighty-seven, insists that his policy was misunderstood. He has been saying that for years, and he still says it, even after containment's ultimate success. "They did not understand what I was talking about and they did not do what I advised them to do," he told me prior to my first visit to the Soviet Union. In fact, Kennan believed in containment, but he never thought that the vast military expenditures were necessary to make it work. He simply did not believe the Soviet Union was sufficiently aggressive to warrant the investment, and he may have been right. The point is that Kennan's message was conveyed without the nuances that he considered integral to its meaning.

I had my own experiences along these lines, most painfully when

I testified before the Senate Armed Services Committee prior to the Gulf War, a year and a half after my retirement. In my testimony I recommended allowing sanctions against Iraq to work for a set period of time, but simultaneously to continue military preparations, and to use force if sanctions failed. The press focused solely on my disagreement with the President's timetable and labeled me "anti-administration," with the result that I found myself being praised by people who had not spoken to me in years.* Taking a public position on a controversial subject invites misinterpretation; that is simply the chance you take when you go on the record.

The dangers of press interaction require a studied approach. My natural tendency was to answer directly questions that were asked. Eventually I got over that, but only after a serious educational effort. I had to learn how to provide only information we had decided beforehand to release, regardless of the question. I had to learn how to appear to answer a question without actually answering it. These tricks are used by politicians all over the world, but for some reason military officers often have trouble with them. Both of these techniques I found difficult to master, and sometimes I succeeded and sometimes I didn't. In the end I discovered that for me the most effective way to respond to any question (after screening out dangerous ones) was not to try to control the spin but simply to answer it. In the nation's capital that is enough to attract a high reputation for openness.

A different kind of "candid" response that appealed to me was to admit I did not know an answer if indeed I did not, another approach few Washingtonians avail themselves of. Even less common is the ability to admit a mistake, which I occasionally did when it seemed warranted, even though most of my colleagues frowned on the practice. After the *Bridgeton* was mined on our first convoying venture in 1987, the press attacked us hard, and with some justification. We were all unhappy about this, and one day I told Weinberger that if he would let me I would get hold of the press and kill the story. "How are you going to do that?" he asked. "I plan to tell them that we made a mistake when the *Bridgeton* got mined and that I was the one who made it. We should have had more minesweeping capacity

---

* And spurned by some old soldiers and sailors, who believed that the "code of silence" should restrain even retired officers from openly criticizing the government. The only consolation I had at all from that testimony was that it may have helped spur Congress to actually vote on authorizing the use of force.

out there and we should have looked at our intelligence data more critically." Weinberger's face flushed. "Do not do that," he said. "Never, never, never, never, never admit you made a mistake. They will never let you forget it!" "Okay," I said, and I didn't do it.

Three weeks later I was making a speech in San Diego and an aggressive local reporter got up afterwards and asked a long question about the *Bridgeton* mining, clearly to embarrass me. "Look," I said, "let me put this to rest right now. We were brand-new and we had a lot to learn. I personally made a mistake on the *Bridgeton* mining." The reporter (he was with the *San Diego Tribune*) gave me a strange look—he may never have heard such a response before. Then he sat down. Afterwards he published a story reporting what I had said, and I never heard another word about the *Bridgeton* mining. Honesty often actually *is* the best policy. I always remember reading about Joseph Stilwell after his defeat in Burma. When he finally hiked out of the jungle and got to India, there was a press conference. The correspondents asked, "What happened?" And Stilwell said, "We got the hell beat out of us." The press loved Stilwell. There is a lot to be said for simply saying, I was wrong.

Of course, whoever does that must take the responsibility on his own shoulders. He cannot say, The President made a mistake. He cannot go around including others in the blame. He cannot even use the word "we." He has to say, I did it and nobody else. That is the beginning and end of the mistake routine. And it has to be used sparingly. Otherwise, before too long people will begin asking themselves, What in the world is he doing there if all he can do is make mistakes?

Despite the pitfalls and occasional failures, by and large I was both intrigued and pleased by my relationship with the press. Still, not even my most jaundiced colleagues imagined that I might go so far as to introduce Mike Wallace into the military's inner sanctum. Yet that happened, and no one was more surprised than myself.

If the senior military had a bête noire among media people it was Wallace, who had done a number of programs highly uncomplimentary to the armed services. Then in 1982, he had assaulted General William Westmoreland in a "CBS Reports" special for allegedly falsifying estimates of enemy troop strength in Vietnam. Westmoreland had taken Wallace and CBS to court in a highly publicized trial, and Wallace became persona extremely non grata at the Defense Department. By the time I succeeded John Vessey, a blanket refusal to cooperate with Wallace had been in effect at DOD for five years.

One day in late 1987 Jay Coupe made the startling announcement that he thought he could get me on *60 Minutes*. I was appalled. In the first place, my sentiments about Wallace were more or less the same as those of my colleagues. In the second, I had watched his show on occasion in previous years, and my memory was that Wallace was aggressive, mean, and the subject of various libel suits. I was as thrilled by the thought of being on his program as I would have been by an invitation to jump into a meat grinder.

Coupe's response was that no matter what I might think of Wallace, *60 Minutes* had the largest news show audience in the country. Often it was the top-rated program of any kind. More importantly, Wallace had been frozen out of the Pentagon for years now. He was searching hard for a way back in, but no one would give him an opening. "Everybody in the building is either angry at him or scared to death of him, or both," said Coupe. "It seems to me that if you do allow him an interview he will treat you very well. He knows that if he doesn't he'll be dead forever in the Pentagon. Now, if Wallace gets back in and does twenty interviews, then you can't trust him at all. But he's got a serious incentive to make this first one go well."

Then I started watching old *60 Minutes* tapes, and to my surprise some of Wallace's interviews were not only positive but unusually well done. His interview with Vladimir Horowitz was quite wonderful—sensitive and insightful. So was a probing piece he did with Joe Slovo, the old-line South African communist. Even his Jesse Jackson interview was balanced and fair. Apparently Wallace did occasionally do things with his interviewees other than destroy them. Going on that show would be a gamble, and I pondered it for some time. But I tended to think that Coupe's reasoning was correct. The first interview Wallace did would be positive. There might be one or two terrors, just to keep up his professional reputation, but he would be heavily invested in making it constructive.

So we invited Wallace and his producer Barry Lando for lunch. Quite obviously Wallace was going through the same kind of evaluative process we were. He knew he was warmly disliked throughout the military, and he appeared slightly taken aback that I was not as formidable as he might have anticipated. He himself was friendly and even gracious, not a quality I necessarily expected, and before long we found ourselves hitting it off and trading stories. He was especially interesting when he talked about his early days in broadcasting and the various people with whom he had done programs. But although I found him easy to get along with, I was quite aware that at heart he would be neither deferential nor malleable. More-over, despite the amiable atmosphere, his producer, who did the show's editing, impressed me as someone who harbored a deep-rooted suspicion of the military. (I later discovered that he had deep-rooted suspicions of everyone, not just the military.) Nevertheless, the challenge appealed to me, and on balance it seemed that the opportunity was worth the risk. By the end of the luncheon I had decided to go ahead with it.

I knew my colleagues would not take this decision well. I had not sounded them out beforehand, on the theory that first of all the decision was mine to make, and second, that they would find forgive-ness easier to grant than permission. When I did tell them, the reac-tion lived up to my expectations. Newly installed Secretary of Defense Frank Carlucci was deeply disturbed and Assistant Secre-tary for Public Affairs Dan Howard, while reluctant to precipitate a fight over it, was clearly nervous about this departure from Pentagon press policy. The chiefs seemed to think I had taken leave of my senses. "You're going to regret this," said one of the better dis-posed. "The guy is a son of a bitch and he's anti-military. We're all going to get tarred." Privately I thought that experiencing Wallace would be educational and good for them. What I kept saying was Well, I don't know that I agree with that, but we're going to find out.

When I actually started working with Wallace he asked if he could see the Tank, the conference room where the chiefs met several days a week. I said, "Of course, and how would you like to see the chiefs themselves?" When we walked in, Wallace went to a chair over in the corner to sit down, and I said, "Mike, please come over here and meet the chiefs." Then I took him around the table and intro-duced him. He seemed a little stunned, but the shock was not only his. Air Force Chief Larry Welch told me later that shaking hands with Mike Wallace was one of the two hardest things he had ever done in his life. (I have wondered ever since what the other was.)

Whatever they might have been thinking, the chiefs all greeted him civilly, then he sat down while we conducted some meaningless discussion—not regular business—for his camera crew to film. When we returned to my office Wallace said, "That's one place I never thought I'd be invited to." Afterwards we flew together to Fort Campbell, Kentucky, to visit with the 101st Airborne Division, and from there we traveled to Oklahoma, where I was scheduled to give a speech and where we could do some background shooting in my old neighborhood with a few of my childhood friends. What I did not know until I started introducing him around was that Wallace had earlier done a scathing piece on the Oklahoma City Medical School, and the medical community hated him passionately. I had dragged him all the way to Oklahoma City only to discover that half the people in town held deep grudges against him. But he was still a celebrity, and they managed to make believe they were happy to have him there—at least many of them asked for his autograph.

The centerpiece of all our activity was a three-hour one-on-one interview filmed in the Pentagon's alternate military command center, an impressive but rarely used "war room" with maps of the world covering its walls. I prepared for this extensively with my staff, who put together a list of 120 questions on virtually every issue imaginable, from arms control to Nicaragua to Soviet relations to terrorism, then went over answers with me to ensure that what I had to say was consistent with policy.

The most helpful part of this process came with our discovery of the Air Force Media Training Team, a group of enthusiastic young officers who specialized in preparing senior officers for television appearances. These people were ruthless. They held formal mock interviews in which they asked embarrassing and insinuating questions. They conducted "ambush interviews," accosting me in the hallways when I wasn't ready and challenging my responses. And everything they did they filmed for critical review later. They showed no respect for persons and seemed to take an inordinate glee in sweating the nation's top-ranking military officer. After their relentless attacks, I was convinced Mike Wallace would seem about as terrifying as Mister Rogers.

All the work paid off. With one or two exceptions, we had anticipated every issue that Wallace covered. The resulting segment aired first on March 20, 1988, then again that August. Carlucci, who had originally been so concerned, thought the results were extremely positive, as did everyone else I talked to about it, even the chiefs. My final impression was that the most effective way to deal with Mike Wallace was honestly, that the people he truly goes after are those he thinks have lied to him. When I finished the process and had gotten to know him I was persuaded that Wallace would give a square deal to those who played fair with him, though I was certainly aware that this opinion was not universally held. Many believe he has a personal agenda and treats his subjects accordingly. That was not my experience.

Wallace was also interested in accompanying me to the Soviet

Union when I paid a visit to Chief of Staff General Mikhail Moiseyev in June 1989.

Neither the Soviet nor American bureaucracies were in favor of his request, but I argued that the resulting coverage would be good for everyone concerned. When the Soviets requested my list of wishes for this visit, I provided it. "In addition," I told them, "I would like Mike Wallace to be able to come along. I assure you that you will profit from it." And they agreed.

For Wallace this trip was an opportunity to capture a groundbreaking meeting between the Soviet and American militaries as well as a chance to make his own contacts inside the Kremlin. By this time I knew him well enough to know that it also appealed to his sense of history. There was no doubt in my mind that he would cover these meetings with an eye toward detail, character, and the significance of the event that would be hard to equal. By this time Jay Coupe had retired from the Navy, but I still looked to him for public relations advice. "If you go without Wallace," he said, "it will be a wonderful experience for the fifteen people in your immediate party; if he goes with you it will be a drama shared by the nation."

No sooner did we receive permission for Wallace and his crew to join our party than he began agitating to be allowed aboard the Soviet missile cruiser *Kirov*. My visit to the Soviet fleet at Murmansk promised to be an especially symbolic moment in this embrace of lifetime enemies. The Northern Fleet headquarters, though, was a highly sensitive area, and the Soviets at first refused to allow Wallace and his cameras in. But when we arrived in Moscow I took Wallace with me to see General Mikhail Moiseyev, who had just succeeded Akhromeyev as Chief of Staff. The two of them became engaged in conversation, and Wallace's camera crew got some excellent footage (which eventually appeared on the show). General Moiseyev was new to his international role and seemed somewhat stiff and awkward in our initial interactions, but the camera made him appear amiable and relaxed, and his rugged face and bristling eyebrows conveyed a kind of dignified charm. When he saw the tape he got a big kick out of it; he seemed quite taken with his own image, as so many are when they regard themselves on television.

Shortly afterwards Wallace was given permission to go to Murmansk, and when the day came he and his camera crew spent a large part of it wandering all over the *Kirov* filming everything in view. One of the memorable moments of that day was the sight of Wallace standing on the superstructure while the Soviet Navy band played

"The Star-Spangled Banner" and the American flag fluttered in the Arctic breeze. When I looked up I caught a glimpse of him there with the tears streaming down his cheeks, this most cynical and grizzled of all his cynical and grizzled brethren.

That was a scene rich in ambiguity. Among other things, it suggested the relationship that obtains between press and military— natural adversaries who yet use each other in what has become a complicated symbiosis. Today the public person and the press conduct a two-way affair. Sometimes it is in their interest to play a covert game of leaks and trickery, surprise attacks and retaliation. But not always, or even most often. The fact is that the media, television especially, have become what Hedrick Smith calls "the new political marketplace" with their own rapidly evolving customs and rites. Even now we are in a transitional moment, for the politician, the bureaucrat, and especially for the military man, who has discovered that if he wants to succeed he too had better become a player.

Chapter 13

CONGRESS AND DEFENSE

CONGRESS IS ANOTHER VENUE that professional soldiers often find challenging. Congress does not understand the military well, and the converse is also true. Many officers do not appreciate (or, for that matter, like) congressmen. They deplore the constant political compromises (the heart of congressional proceedings). They often find testifying unpleasant, and they react to the anti-military sentiments with distaste and anger. For there are congressmen who intensely dislike military people and are not shy about saying so.

Nevertheless, an individual who reaches high rank must go beyond his emotions and think hard about his relationship with the "Hill." In my own case, I started out with a strong ambivalence. I appreciated Congress's role well enough, but as a supplicant I often found congressmen a trying group to deal with. To find some workable philosophy that would reconcile this conflict, I found myself going back (as I think many military officers do) to fundamentals.

The Constitution makes senators and representatives full-fledged partners in the security process. They hold the budgetary authority —the whip hand—and they use that to scrutinize and investigate every aspect of the defense endeavor. While this exercise often pits the Defense Department and Congress against each other, the military professional also has to realize that his organization needs the process like lifeblood—a truth not often apparent in the heat of battle.

Congressional scrutiny and budget debates are in fact nothing less than the armed forces' link to the public. Critics occasionally enjoy portraying the military as an institution that rides roughshod over true national needs and desires. But in reality, it either stands or falls on public support. The open budget process develops the necessary political consensus within the Congress and the electorate. It helps ensure that defense policies serve the country's needs through means that the people generally support and that defense is integrated within the whole panoply of societal requirements. From the military's own point of view, congressional control insures the legitimacy of the armed forces and connects the services with the roots of power—the nation's citizenry.

Congress may often prove a poor management organization, but that is not its most essential purpose. (Justice Louis Brandeis insisted that the Constitution's framers were not out to promote efficiency but to preclude the arbitrary exercise of power—a thought I always found therapeutic in times of trial.) If he is to function effectively, the military man has to understand the system's limitations within the context of its basic strength.

Nevertheless, when an officer first arrives in Washington he is often shocked to find that many legislators share neither his values nor his feelings about the significance of military issues. Typically his first reaction (and sometimes his lasting impression) is Well, these people are just not thinking clearly. He is tempted to throw everybody into an "anti-military" category, all the easier to do since there are some who do fit the category well. But that approach is shortsighted and superficial.

The congressmen he objects to may have no specifically anti-military opinions, nor are they necessarily unclear about what's right; it's just that they have different interests and must respond to different pressures. But it is hard for a man who has spent his life dealing with military affairs to grasp that simple reality. The votes go against him and often he cannot understand it. The Navy asks for more carriers and genuinely believes the ships are needed to defend the nation, and yet Congress turns down the request with little heed taken. The tendency for the naval aviator then is to personalize the issue and draw dramatic conclusions about the patriotism of politicians. But in fact he is merely witnessing our pluralistic system at work.

As the senior officer begins to learn the Washington ropes, he understands that pigeonholing congressmen is difficult; there are simply too many splinter groups on Capitol Hill and too many interests working at cross-purposes. Nevertheless, one powerful lever in his and his colleagues' hands is the fact that so many congressmen are beholden to the military in one way or another for the well-being of their constituents. There are production facilities or large bases located in their districts, and the Pentagon is astute at playing on these associations. Indeed, that is precisely where the military gets its most dependable support. Congressmen from the St. Louis area have both General Dynamics and McDonnell Douglas as constituents, and one way or another they are going to be allied with proponents of military air strength. That was the beauty (from the Navy's point of view) of former Secretary of the Navy John Lehman's "home porting" scheme. By building installations in a variety of coastal districts, Lehman created vocal advocates out of congressmen who had not previously identified with naval appropriations. All of a sudden congressmen who had never heard of John Paul Jones were quoting Alfred Thayer Mahan.

For a senior military person interacting with Congress, understanding the political realities has a number of consequences. The first (and most significant for his equanimity) is that he does not get so worked up when he finds his deeply held views ignored or treated harshly. His instincts tell him to become irate and fight back, or maybe to just ignore his antagonists for the rest of time. But when he understands the politics of it, he discovers it's just business, an unpleasant business, perhaps, but still business. The congressmen are addressing their responsibilities just as he is addressing his, and while they may disagree, it is not the end of Western civilization (although at times I thought it was), and he will have to keep working with them.

That is the first stage of the military person's adjustment or, as some would say, the beginning of wisdom in Washington. The second stage starts when he realizes that even if particular congressmen do not have much of an interest in the military, they are still going to vote and there may be indirect ways to influence them. In fact, such people are exactly the constituency the Pentagon lobbyist is looking for. He is never likely to persuade the legislator who has a distaste for the military, nor is he in much danger of losing the one who is dependent on the manufacturers of weapons systems. It is the man in the middle who can most fruitfully repay his efforts.

The great advantage of having high-level military people with long experience in Washington is that they (one hopes) have become practiced in at least some of the political arts. Politically sensitive officers know who is beholden to whom, who is amenable to persuasion, and what kind of persuasion they are amenable to. They know how to muster their allies and constrict the province of their adversaries. That is the great advantage of having a man like Colin Powell at the Pentagon. Powell is a political general (he does not particularly like the term, but I use it in its finest sense) and there is great value in his political expertise. Powell has extensive Washington experience, from the Army staff to the office of the Secretary of Defense to the National Security Council. Having that background is a tremendous strength, especially his knowledge of the White House and Congress. As National Security Adviser he worked closely with the legislature, and he is highly regarded by most congressmen. That is a vital asset to all the services.

But while rapport of this sort can make life easier in many ways, it is not often decisive. During my own tenure as Chairman I testified alongside three secretaries of defense: Weinberger, Carlucci, and Cheney. Of the three, Weinberger was by far the most abrasive. His posture was typically adversarial and a bit condescending. Because of it, many congressmen did not like Weinberger. Nevertheless, he was often a joy to watch in action. To insure that everyone has a chance to query the witness, large congressional committees often set a time limit for each member's questions—commonly ten minutes. Weinberger was superb at framing long answers that would consume a good portion of the allotment. Some would interrupt him, trying valiantly to conserve their time. "Please, Mr. Secretary, I understand. I understand." But Weinberger would just continue blithely, sometimes with an injured expression on his face, commenting, "Senator, please. I'm not through yet."

Once we were testifying before a House committee when Congressman Stephen Solarz was in the chair. Solarz and Weinberger were at opposite ends of the political spectrum and normally disagreed, whatever the issue. This particular day we were discussing the Kuwaiti reflagging proposal, which Solarz was supporting, although Weinberger did not yet know that. At one point the Secretary was rather beleaguered, and in order to help him out Solarz opined that convoying should improve our standing with the Arabs. Weinberger obviously was not listening and immediately took great exception to Solarz, attacking him with his usual vigor. Solarz listened to this, puzzled and offended. Suddenly a light came on. Weinberger hesitated, looked at me with a quizzical smile, and without a hint of embarrassment smoothly turned back to the committee and discoursed eloquently for the next five minutes as to why Solarz was absolutely right.

Frank Carlucci was much more neutral than Weinberger. His style was unemotional and businesslike; he tended to focus more on issues rather than engaging the personalities of the debaters. At the same time, he would not back down if harassed. In many respects he was the ideal witness—knowledgeable and more or less imperturbable. He gave the impression of objectivity and detachment from the political fray.

Cheney, of course, understood Congress very well. He was a political man, at home on his old turf, and he projected a relaxed, easy air. He let everyone know right away that he was a member of the club. Actually, all three were good witnesses, articulate, intelligent, well versed, and quick studies. But Cheney's style was particularly engaging. He was not combative, he never lost his temper, he never condescended.

In fact, Cheney and I talked about his calm approach to testimony, which I had contrasted to my own rather nervous preparations. He smiled and said, "Those guys over there are not genuine listeners. They want to get on the record with their views and we should get on the record with ours. But don't look at testimony as a serious dialogue between questioners and witnesses."

Cheney's approach inspired many comments from members that it was nice to have someone in the job who understood Congress, who was easy to deal with and had credibility. They sure were glad, they said, that Dick Cheney was there. But despite the warmth of Cheney's relationships, he was not any more successful at getting things out of Congress than Weinberger or Carlucci had been. Cheney came in when Congress was talking about restructuring defense and cutting back, and they ended up doing exactly that. Under Cheney they cut the budget dramatically and are still doing so today.

The process is worth contemplating. Cheney, who related to Congress better than almost all his predecessors, rarely got what he wanted. Caspar Weinberger, the most adversarial, was also the most successful; although his achievements, of course, came in expansive times.

My own conclusion was that in dealing with Congress, abrasiveness isn't all bad. When a congressman says, I really like the way that man conducts himself with the Congress, he usually means, He gives us what we want. When the congressman says, I don't like the guy at all, it often translates as, He's really putting it to us and we're having a tough time handling him. John Lehman was confrontational but extremely effective—particularly behind the scenes. You can do worse than play hardball. Maintaining warm relations with Congress is not necessarily the first priority; getting your way is, however. It is also possible to be hard-nosed in the hearings and to fashion close relationships in the back rooms.

As well as I generally got along with Congress, and I got along very well, I never had any positive evidence that I changed a single legislator's mind on any large issue. I was told on occasion that I had, but I could not see much evidence of it. The fact is that by the time the Secretary and the Chairman go to the Hill to testify, almost everybody in the committee room has already made up his mind. All their questioning demonstrates that tendency. Those who oppose your position use the questioning to pick holes in your statement and refute you. Those who support your position use their questioning to display reasons for support. It was rare (not unknown, but rare) to hear someone say, Admiral, I'm really having trouble with this problem. I haven't made up my mind yet. Let's explore issues A, B, and C more carefully. The same process applies across the congressional spectrum, although the Pentagon often believes this treatment is reserved for military issues.

Of course, the chief focus of the Chairman and the Secretary is the general level of the budget, not the specifics underlying it. Cheney, who was so knowledgeable about Congress, was able to sit down before we began our testimony, scratch out some figures on a piece of paper, and say, I suspect the President will eventually approve a defense budget about like this. I suspect the Senate will go for this figure here, and the House will go for that figure. There'll be a conference and they'll end up with something like this figure here. It was amazing how many times what appeared to be outhouse guesses were right on the money. In fact I was seeing a lifetime of political experience at work. He was not guessing, he was practicing the art of American politics.

When Cheney did his figuring, he was not thinking about testimony or debate on specific issues—for or against the B-2, for instance. He was using his politician's instinct to sense the mood of the country and calculate how the national mood would translate itself through the medium of Congress into an increased or decreased defense budget.

The Defense Department knew that if its budget was $300 billion one year (as it often was during my tenure; the 1992 budget was $279 billion) and the next year they put in for $310, there would be no argument at all about perhaps $290 billion of that. All the hoopla and effort during the entire year of developing the budget, then testifying on it, in large part concerned the $20 billion between $290 and $310. And even decisions in this narrow area were almost never made according to the merits of the arguments. Those decisions were arrived at by a process that appeared mysterious and intangible. It had to do with instincts and intuitions, and with an immensely complicated calculus that percolated through the Congress and incorporated all the geographical areas and ethnic constituencies and income distinctions, and all the partisan and bipartisan and nonpartisan views of the members. Congressmen working this calculus were searching for a number: What number, they were asking themselves, would the voters live with? What number would generally fit in with the nation's geopolitical prospects and economic health and at the same time would not jeopardize my reelection by hurting projects dear to my district? (Actually, the latter consideration was usually first.) If the geopolitical prospects were grim, anyone who argued for undercutting the budget would lose credibility, and his peers would not listen. But if there was peace and prospects for more of it, credible arguments could be made for driving the defense budget down to a lower level.

But this is an amorphous process, not amenable to easy definition. What takes place usually follows a certain pattern. Very early in the game the congressional leaders start talking to their colleagues, feeling out the mood from the various constituencies and sensing how far their influence might move people in one direction or another. Then the leaders talk to each other. One will say, Well, I've met with my people and you've met with yours. What do you think can get by? And the second one says, This year we can't get support for more than $270 billion. It's just not in the grass roots. At that point the Secretary of Defense comes over and testifies for $290 billion. He gets some support from his congressional advocates, which precipitates a good deal of marching up and down and sniping back and forth. But in the end, if the Speaker of the House originally said he didn't think there was more than $270 billion in the country, then that is the figure that will most likely wend its way through Congress.

But moods shift, especially when an election year approaches. Suddenly it becomes evident through articles and reports and speeches (as it did during Reagan's first campaign) that the military has deteriorated and international dangers are building up. The sense begins to well up that our security has been damaged and that it is time to reverse the process. Nobody says specifically how much to reverse it, but editorials and analyses are discussing the need. Everyone running for office watches all this closely, and the candidates who are trying to defeat the incumbents start thinking that this is a good issue. They begin making speeches. Look at the facts, they say, and immediately start distorting the facts to support their case.

"In the last four years we've seen a great and harmful deterioration in our capabilities"—this is what Reagan did—"and we are going to correct it." Of course, time doesn't permit detailing the specifics of the deterioration. The point is to build a mood, not a legal case.

Then a Ronald Reagan gets elected. The new Congress meets, and if you listen closely you can hear the thinking as everyone gets busy working out the new calculus. Hmm, they're saying, look at who got elected and who didn't. There's no way we can hold the defense budget down. The President's going to come in big. Our problem is to keep it as low as we can but not upset the apple cart. We're going to have to go higher than we want. And through the mysterious process, conclusions start emerging—He'll come in for 290. We might be able to hold it at 280, but that's all we can do. There's probably 280 in the country. And all this is done through private conversations and back-room jockeying and meetings in congressional hallways and in conference rooms where White House officials, DOD representatives, and legislators sit and intermingle. The Secretary of Defense will have a series of meetings with individual congressmen and one or more breakfasts for the members of the armed services committees. Hearings are held and many pounds of paper generated on both sides of the issue. But these affect primarily the way money will be spent after the top figures are laid down.

In other words, like all other important decisions, those made about the nation's defense are fundamentally political. In any area where we spend such a vast amount of the common treasure, the questions are necessarily political. They have to do with employment and economics and elections as well as with perceptions of our strength and the intensity of outside threats. Congress can call all the experts to testify that it wants; advocates and opponents can build their strongest cases for or against weapons systems. But in the end the overall amount of money spent on the Defense Department budget will be decided by an intuitive process that does not have much to do with strategy, or defense, or the persuasiveness of the Chairman, or the personality of the Secretary.

It is true, of course, that within that budget heated conflicts develop. If the military is going to get $275 billion, there are serious questions about how to spend it. And how it is spent makes a lot of difference to individual congressmen. If the Secretary proposes to cancel the A-12 ground support aircraft, as Secretary Cheney did in 1990, or the Divad high-tech anti-aircraft cannon, as Weinberger did in 1985, the congressmen whose districts are affected will do everything they can to prevent it. The chances are they will not prevail. But at the very least the congressmen who represent those districts have got to look like they are waging a fierce fight to retain the canceled system.

All the constituencies come into play in the business of deciding what is going to fit into this one sock, and battles can be harsh. But in essence they are carried out on the margins of the budget. The center of the budget, monies earmarked for personnel, always takes 45 to 50 percent; there's not much you can do about that. The arguments here are strictly over whether the military is going to be frozen at the current manpower level or go up a few thousand or come down a few thousand. That is normally the range of the argument, although right now we are seeing larger cuts as Congress reacts to the dissolution of the Warsaw Pact and the demise of the Soviet Union. Neither is there much elasticity in the operations and maintenance budgets—which will consume around 30 percent of the whole; that is what it takes to run the military from day to day. The remaining 25 percent includes all kinds of cats and dogs, but is primarily for equipment procurement and research. This is the area where arguments can consume the arguers. Here testimony may well affect whether the Congress will opt for weapon system A or B, or both, or neither.

The Secretary of Defense will play a role in these considerations, but at this level of detail the ball is carried mostly by his lieutenants. Committee staffers will have a lot to say about it, but so will pure partisan politics. The Marine Corps' V-22 Osprey vertical takeoff-and-landing aircraft was a case in point. Faced with great pressure for cutbacks in military appropriations, Secretary Cheney responded by announcing that he had evaluated the competing programs and had decided to cancel the Osprey. But the fact that the Secretary was cutting spending did not precipitate universal satisfaction. Suddenly a whole raft of congressmen were going to be impacted by the V-22 cancellation. As a result, the Osprey stayed in, not, it is true, at the procurement rate originally envisioned, but it was not blanked out of the budget either. The opposition, aided and abetted by Marine lobbyists, whipped up a bow wave, and Cheney was not entirely successful at getting the V-22 deleted. In fact, during the 1992 election campaign the Osprey managed a remarkable resurrection. President Bush became an enthusiastic supporter, for the jobs it would create in Texas (which was considered a pivotal state). Then Secretary Cheney announced that he too thought it was a wonderful idea.

Operations analysis can tell you a great deal about competing weapons systems. Introduced by Robert McNamara as a decision-making tool (he had used it first at Ford Motor Company), operations analysis provides an in-depth method of looking at and comparing physical systems. "Ops" analysis helps frame problems in a more understandable way and prioritize systems more coherently. But it does not eliminate subjective judgment, nor does it necessarily tell you which system is best. It does give the decision makers an array of options suggesting what each alternative might do in certain conditions, but inevitably substantial uncertainty remains, which requires human judgment. Operations analysis may illuminate the problem, but it cannot replace the human decision maker.

For all its strengths, operations analysis is still based on a set of original assumptions. In the process of looking at A, B, and C on the basis of a large quantity of collated data, there is a tendency, particularly among laymen, to conclude that the answer is clear: A is better than B or C. The tables show it. More sophisticated people will go back and examine the initial premises, which may well have tilted the final result. For a while after operations analysis was introduced, many people thought it would solve all the problems, and over the last twenty-five years it has indeed thoroughly changed the way people in the Defense Department view their business. It was a giant step forward in terms of introducing more analytical rigor into the process. But operations analysis does not answer all the questions. For one, operations analysis ignores politics—something our government by its very nature cannot tolerate. We have learned that now, and we have gone back to understanding that subjective judgments are in a sense still primary and so are open to debate and subject to political pressures.

Congressional interest in defense generally focuses on weapons systems and costs and jobs. It does not focus primarily on military strategy. Yet logic would seem to demand that national strategy should drive the defense budget, not the squabbling of congressmen over what is good for their districts. But congressmen find it extraordinarily difficult to concentrate on strategy. First, most do not understand strategy well. More significantly, strategic considerations mask a field of mines waiting to blow up in their faces. Getting committed to a strategy is a tricky business—witness the Iraqi crisis—and generally congressmen will go to great lengths not to commit that sin.

Congressmen think it's interesting to talk about geopolitical strategy and to debate whether Congress, for example, should approve of convoying Kuwaiti tankers. But actually recording votes on the subject is a risky proposition. In the first place, it's a hard question, and congressional debate and resources do not always lend themselves to arriving at a judicious answer. Secondly, a congressman has to be careful what he or she votes for. In 1950 we put Korea outside our defensive perimeter, and look what happened then. If a bad decision is made, those who made it are likely to be blamed. So congressmen generally do not like to make policy decisions; policy decisions can sweep you out of office faster than almost anything else.

Strategic decisions are doubly dangerous because they can also drive some unexpected financial decisions. If a congressman argues that the American global situation suggests a smaller military, that may come out meaning that the A-12 has to go. Then everybody who wants the A-12 will say, Wait a minute. I agreed with that strategy, but I didn't think that strategy meant no A-12. We all witnessed this phenomenon as Congress began drawing down the military in the wake of the Soviet demise. The legislature quickly discovered that radically cutting defense jobs during a recession was a painful business.

Politics (as Professor Harold Sprout taught back at Princeton) turns out to be pervasive. The primary concern of the congressman from Detroit is not the defense of the country, or the national interest (though these may very well be his second concerns). It is how many jobs Defense gives to Detroit and how well he is doing in protecting those jobs. Those considerations bring defense questions right into his backyard, where he can get his teeth into them. And he'd better, or they will come back to bite him.

Given that defense expenditures are so profoundly political, is there any way to inject more efficiency into the system? There is, but it is chiefly in the area of streamlining the relationship between Congress and Defense.

Among the most counterproductive (and intensely aggravating) aspects of this relationship is the congressional proclivity to micromanage programs. The detail level of committee oversight is often absurdly excessive; a stream of reports on the subject have confirmed and deplored this truth that continually plagues Pentagon managers. Congress should not be in a position to second-guess every nut-and-bolt issue. It is neither proper nor effective for congressmen to tell Defense that it should buy a forty/sixty molybdenum-aluminum bolt rather than some other percentage. But they do exactly that kind of thing regularly, and most often because a company in their district produces such a product and needs the order.

There are several culprits here. One is the spiraling growth of congressional staffs. The average senator's staff increased from six in 1975 to over forty in 1985, and a representative's staff from three to eighteen. The large congressional staffs generate work. Their very numbers lead them to get involved in subjects that are not their business and levels of detail that common sense would leave strictly to project managers. Larger numbers of staffers mean more people who have to justify their jobs, which means opening up ever more minute details of programs to oversight.

As Chairman I found it depressing to contemplate the monumental amount of time and effort we put into satisfying Congress. Luckily for my sanity, I had Captain Rick DeBobes working as my congressional liaison. But despite DeBobes's skill, our interaction with Congress was immensely frustrating. If I had believed we were actually influencing decisions or persuading people, I would not have begrudged the time. But the Pentagon files in the neighborhood of 600 reports to the Congress annually. We answered 250,000 phone calls a year from Congress. And I for one was never persuaded that it was worth it. So much was clearly unnecessary.

Often when a congressional committee runs into a problem which cannot be resolved—frequently because the political forces are too evenly divided—it directs the Pentagon to make a study. Rather than admitting that they cannot decide the issue now, the committee declares that the matter needs further examination. There are some extremely important questions here, runs the rationale, that have to be answered before we can deal with this question. So we think, Admiral, that it is necessary for DOD to conduct an in-depth study of the six points spelled out below and report back to us in nine months. Unspoken (though understood by all concerned) is the fact that it may be easier politically to deal with the matter next year.

Normally, little will be learned in that study; its basic purpose is to put the decision off. This is not to say there is anything necessarily wrong with putting the decision off. Perhaps the political forces really will be aligned more favorably for a decision at some later time. But directing a study as a way to justify the postponement is unconscionably burdensome for the Pentagon. These studies have to be taken seriously; the Pentagon responds to Congress's requests as it is charged to respond, with the best resources and effort available.

No one will consciously produce a deficient report. The result is that the Pentagon spends an astounding portion of its time dealing with congressional requests, many of which are unnecessary, and almost all of which concern marginal projects. The huge expense foisted on the Defense Department in this fashion makes a six-hundred-dollar toilet seat seem prudence itself.

So there are things that could and should be done. Congressional staffs should be reduced, Congress should resist the temptation to micromanage programs. Congress should consolidate the overlapping committees that oversee the Defense Department. (At present three different committees in each house perform essentially the same function in reviewing the defense budget.) If these and other congressional reforms were implemented, efficiency would improve dramatically and savings would be substantial.

But even then, Congress would still not be attending to its primary defense function—"to spell out major strategies and purposes," in the words of the Senate Armed Services Committee report. "The Constitution," the report goes on, "intends for the Congress to establish national strategic priorities and to allocate resources toward those priorities." Biting this bullet would furnish the foundation for rational decisions. If only, as most military reorganization studies suggest, Congress would attend more to fundamentals and less to cotter pins and washers.

But that is not likely to happen. Why it isn't is crystallized by an exchange that took place between Senator Sam Nunn and Caspar Weinberger. Nunn was fond of pointing out that the American military is too small to fulfill the nation's strategic requirements. He maintained we had laid out a strategy that essentially declared that the entire world is vital and that we had to be able to protect our interests globally. Clearly we were not capable of doing that with the military we had.

Weinberger's answer went something like this: Senator, I have no quarrel with that reasoning. Where do you want to cut back? Would you be agreeable to cutting Israel out of the strategic interests of the United States? How about Saudi Arabia? We spend an awful lot of money on the Greek-Turkish area, Senator. Do you think we should defend Turkey or Greece? That would be a good place to save; why don't we cut them out of our strategic orbit and leave the eastern Mediterranean alone? Or perhaps we should forgo Pakistan.

The congressional answer to Weinberger's question was usually That's not our job, Mr. Secretary, it's yours. Congressmen will not draw the strategic lines, because doing so would alienate important constituencies. (Administrations, despite Weinberger's reply to Nunn, also suffer from the same disease.) In other words, politics makes such strategic questions extremely difficult for them to deal with. And the truth is that strategic questions are almost always political, no matter who deals with them. Strategic questions are not usually resolved by the light of pure reason but by the lights of human beings who are by their nature political animals. What President wants to say, "I dismantled NATO"?

A good bureaucrat is a man who understands the political process in his bones and manipulates it ruthlessly. One of the best was John Lehman, former Secretary of the Navy, a man I had my run-ins with but certainly an eminently successful bureaucrat. Lehman understood the process, and he possessed an iron determination and a fine sense of timing to go along with his savvy. He had concluded before he was appointed Secretary that the United States should have a 600-ship Navy, and by God we were going to have a 600-ship Navy. It was a simple vision, one that could rally support; it sounded good and it had sex appeal. Whatever the idea's military advisability, in that political environment it was right on target.

From the day John Lehman came in till the day he left, the 600-ship Navy was his theme. He exhibited the spirit of a man who wanted later to be able to declare, I'm the one who built a real Navy. In terms of the political hopes he harbored at the time, he was not eager to be the Secretary who took the Navy from 60 percent spare parts to 95 percent spare parts or from 10 percent of the required Tomahawks to 40 percent. (That would have been a tremendous accomplishment, but it would not have held much attraction for the folks back in Iowa who did not know what a Tomahawk was.) The fact was that Lehman's ships were not nearly as well provisioned and armed as we would have preferred. But we did indeed get almost 600 of them, and in our system there is a great deal to be said for that accomplishment.

But though there might be a lot of appeal in that, it drives the professional military man to distraction. He can seldom get support for the mundane essentials he desperately needs. In all fairness, we had so much military funding under Reagan that we did get lots of those things. And it should never be forgotten that the massive expenditures of Reagan's first term allowed American forces to go into Saudi Arabia in 1990 in better shape than they had been in for many years. But even with an excess of funds we were not able to build up the ammunition and parts inventories until we had made the sexy procurements: more tanks, more artillery, more planes—the big-ticket items that the politicians could get their hooks into.*

Some even argue that supply items should receive a lesser priority in peacetime. John Vessey, my predecessor as Chairman, presented this side of the argument. What deters? Vessey would say. A 100 percent munitions allowance doesn't deter anybody. But if you have ten divisions rather than five, that deters. According to this argument, the military's primary objective is deterrence. It would be nice to have those divisions fully manned, fully armed, and fully supplied. But what do we do in a time of lean budgets when we can't have everything? Keep ten slender or five full? The argument for ten has some justice to it—if you agree that the primary aim is deterrence and that these divisions will never be called on to fight. But the fact is that many professionals would take the five full divisions. They know that they are the ones who will be held responsible if there is a crisis and those divisions do not work, not the congressmen who neglected to vote for adequate spare parts. Congress has a difficult time taking future contingencies seriously; there is, after all, no pressing political need for them to do so.

The process of military funding, because it is at heart a political process, is not easily amenable to reform. Any decision congressmen are involved in—by their very makeup and their most fundamental responsibilities—is going to be resolved in a political fashion rather than by logic or operational analyses. The plain talk about defense is that the process is fractious and messy. But at the same time, I am not so sure that in our complicated pluralistic society it either can or should be any other way.

---

* The munificent military budgets of Reagan's first years apparently precipitated a tremendous internal debate in the Defense Department. It was the time of milk and honey; more money was available than Defense could spend wisely. The question then was: Should we spend it anyway, even if not so wisely, knowing that in five years we won't have it? And the decision was deliberately made—Yes! Spend everything we can for just as long as we can get it. So they did spend it, and not all of it wisely either. But they knew from their bureaucratic experience that five years later it would not be there, and sure enough they were right. It wasn't. In retrospect it is difficult to criticize the decision. Academic arguments can be made that if Defense had spent less in 1981, '82, and '83, the pressure would not have grown to cut expenditures back. But I'm not so sure that is right. The Defense budget levels of the post-cornucopia years depended on that highly complex and mysterious calculus which governs Congress's decisions, and in that calculus the previous years' expenditures do not necessarily have a function.

Chapter 14

THE
ATOMIC GENIE

ON AUGUST 15, 1945, the "Little Boy" nuclear weapon was exploded over Hiroshima, less than a year before I graduated from the Naval Academy. My entire commissioned service was encompassed by the atomic age. One of the landmark events of this terrible and ominous, yet relatively peaceful, period came in 1987 during the time of my chairmanship. On December 8, 1987, the Intermediate Nuclear Forces (INF) Treaty was signed, which for the first time committed the two major Cold War antagonists to destroying nuclear delivery systems. That was the beginning of a disarmament process that has since accelerated dramatically.

The end of the Soviet-American atomic confrontation is now effecting a profound reconfiguration of America's armed forces, but no more profound than that wrought by the dawning of nuclear weaponry more than forty-five years ago. The atomic bomb changed the world. Its implications caught everybody, including the military, more or less unprepared. The Navy's vision of the future was so far removed from the new reality that its very role as a service was threatened.

The story of how the United States Navy entered the nuclear age is a strange one, even in the often surprising annals of military history.* At the end of World War Two there emerged in the Navy a new generation of leaders, most of whom had served as combat commanders in the Pacific, and many of whom were aviators. This group quite naturally shared the view that the carrier force, so immensely successful during the war, had in fact become the Navy's pre-eminent arm and would dominate the service's other component

---

* A detailed account appears in Vincent Davis's fine book, *Postwar Defense Policy and the U.S. Navy, 1943–1946* (Univ. of North Carolina, 1962). The following description draws heavily on Davis.

parts into the future. As Secretary of the Navy James Forrestal put it, "The Navy is becoming an air navy." With this orientation, the new leadership began planning for a large and modern postwar carrier fleet, which they felt would be cheerfully funded by an American people grateful to the force that had annihilated the Japanese Imperial Navy.

The plan phenomenally misjudged the nation's appetite for disarmament. Instead of funding a strong modernized fleet, the budget of 1946 emasculated the Navy. From $16 billion in 1945, funding was slashed to under $4 billion in the years following Japan's surrender. Simultaneously, the Navy faced a powerful challenge from Air Force claims that the atomic bomb had rendered all armed forces other than strategic bombers obsolete. According to the Air Force, war as it had been known was now a thing of the past. The nuclear weapon would dominate all future warfare, and as the service exclusively capable of delivering the nuclear weapon, the Air Force should be given the lion's share of the defense budget while the Army and Navy could safely be de-emphasized.

In the development of the atomic bomb at Los Alamos two naval officers had been closely involved—Commanders F. L. Ashworth and John "Chick" Hayward. Working in an Air Force–run laboratory, these two men had helped weaponize the nuclear reaction and had participated in constructing the first bombs. They had seen from the inside the Air Force's fledgling effort to develop aircraft and weapons and marry them, and they had also seen what the Air Force was planning in terms of its own long-range strategy.

Alarmed, Hayward and Ashworth became the center of a small group of officers agitating for a crash program that would put the Navy into the nuclear business. Concerned that the service's existence was at stake, Hayward convinced Deputy Chief of Naval Operations Forrest Sherman that requests should be made to fund a seaborne strategic bombing capability to complement the Air Force's atomic-bomb-carrying B-29s and the proposed B-36. Sherman was eager to do this, especially since the Navy had a bomber already under development (the AJ) that could be adapted to carry the large atomic bombs of that era. But in light of the Air Force's head start and its strong political support in Congress, the DCNO felt that a Navy request to fund a new program would be doomed from the start. However, Sherman told Hayward, it would be a different matter if the Navy already had a demonstrable nuclear delivery capability. If that were the case, then he could reasonably go to the Hill for funding for a more modern updated aircraft. Unfortunately, as they both knew, no carrier-borne bomber had that capability.

Hayward's answer to this conundrum was a request to let him experiment with a number of the Navy's P2V long-range patrol craft, a shore-based anti-submarine warfare plane whose cavernous bomb bay with some alterations was big enough to accommodate a first-generation atomic bomb. The P2V Neptune was an unlikely candidate to be the Navy's first nuclear bomber. It weighed 60,000 pounds, and its wingspan gave it less than a foot of clearance from the superstructure of even the largest aircraft carrier. Yet Hayward believed that with the right modifications to both planes and flight decks, the P2V could be made to take off and land at sea. It was an expensive gamble, but the stakes were high.

By the beginning of 1948 the flight decks of three *Midway*-class carriers had been strengthened and a number of P2Vs had been stripped down, equipped with tail hooks, and reconfigured to carry a "Little Boy"–type atomic bomb. On April 27, after several months of practice, Chick Hayward successfully took off in a P2V from the U.S.S. *Coral Sea,* thus proving that the Navy had the ability to deliver a nuclear weapon from an aircraft carrier.

Landing the P2V proved to be a different story. After additional training, Hayward finally felt ready to try putting the giant plane down on a rolling flight deck. A superb pilot, he touched down then watched his wing rush by the superstructure with only inches to spare. According to some who were present, his first words as he emerged from the plane were "That's the last time we ever try that!"

Whatever Hayward might actually have said, the effort to make the P2V land aboard carriers was abandoned. But not so the portrayal of the plane as a viable seaborne bomber. Under Hayward and Ashworth's supervision, two P2V squadrons were assigned to carriers, one in the Pacific and one in the Atlantic. With a straight face, the Navy then announced that they represented a nuclear retaliatory force. In the event of atomic war they would take off, deliver their weapons, return to the carriers, and ditch in the water, where the crews would be picked up.

The fleet no more got to sea with these squadrons than DCNO Sherman and his colleagues went to Congress for funding of what was now called the AJ1—a carrier-based twin-jet attack bomber. Ultimately this plane was approved and built, the first aircraft constructed from the ground up to deliver Navy nuclear weapons. The prime purpose of this extraordinary effort to put the Navy into the nuclear business was to keep the service from being overwhelmed by the Air Force. If the prophets of an atomic future turned out to be right, the Navy had now equipped itself with a nuclear rationale. Through a combination of political determination, technical skill, and outright audacity, the service had inserted itself into the fast developing calculus of atomic confrontation.

As the Soviet atomic arsenal developed, the Navy's carriers were folded into the SIOP (pronounced psy-op), the Single Integrated Operational Plan—America's detailed master plan for nuclear war. For years carriers were maintained on station in both the Atlantic and Pacific, always prepared to deliver a nuclear response. To support this strategic deployment the aviation Navy developed its own small cadre of nuclear weapons experts.

The aviators' triumph did not affect the rest of the Navy very much. When I first came in, the average officer had scant knowledge of nuclear weapons; and until the early 1950s he was not particularly encouraged to learn more. The Navy's day-to-day life changed little. In time, though, a family of atomic weapons was developed that could be used on shipboard, and the surface community too began to train its planners and experts. But even then nuclear weaponry was not an especially prestigious line of work in the Navy, as it was in the Air Force. Not until the advent of the Polaris ballistic missile submarine did the Navy acquire a full corps of weaponeers, planners, and targeteers. By the early '70s we had forty-one Polaris submarines deployed, each carrying sixteen ICBMs.

As the nuclear arsenals of both the United States and the Soviet Union expanded, so did efforts to limit the confrontation. The service staffs began actively seeking people for arms control, and individuals with political-military experience (like myself) were always worried about being drafted. Like most line officers, I just did not think that a man whose profession was war should get into an endeavor whose objective was to destroy weapons. The general feeling was that this was not quite a proper line of work for a career naval officer. To an upcoming young commander or captain, arms control also sounded boring and had all the appearances of being a dead end. Most believed that those people who did get drafted into it would probably never be heard from again.

In a similar vein, the people already involved in arms control made great efforts to convince their colleagues that it was an important part of the military, but with mixed success. It was true that many officers who went into those billets did have difficulties returning to the mainstream of the Navy and, indeed, many never were heard from again. That slowly changed during the '70s, but the shift was a long time coming.

Over the years my own thinking about nuclear weapons evolved considerably. As a young officer I looked at them as merely the horrendous end of the scale, the culminating point in a sort of seamless web of weaponry. But while I was doing my graduate work, I came to the conclusion that the threshold between conventional and nuclear really was a meaningful concept, that it would be impossible to use nuclear weapons in any kind of graduated, finely controlled way, because once the barrier was broken, uncontrolled escalation would likely ensue.

Upon becoming a flag officer in 1973, I returned to the Navy's Plans and Policy organization as deputy chief of OP 60 (one of the four main branches of OP 06), which was heavily engaged in strategic requirements and nuclear war planning. In my new post I was immersed in all aspects of the subject, including arms control. All the earlier studies in these areas became part of my background education, and my shop wrote the Navy's papers for the Joint Chiefs of Staff. It was an intense learning experience for me and led me to go back and read much of the theoretical material on nuclear war— theoretical because everything about nuclear war was theoretical. Often the best thinking on nuclear strategy had been done by civilians—academicians and think-tank researchers who had analyzed nuclear war as thoroughly as the military. (The Defense Department kept secret some of the initial research information about blast effects, but even much of that soon fell into the public domain.) In most phases of war the professional derives his authority from the fact that he has studied wars, participated in wars, experienced conditions on the battlefield, been trained by people who knew warfare. He draws on empirical experience for his understanding. But no one had that kind of information about nuclear war, and consequently many civilian theoreticians were as knowledgeable (if not more so) as those in the military.

It was at that point that I found myself involved in the Pentagon's special war games. The Chairman of the Joint Chiefs (Admiral Thomas Moorer at the time) had a staff element that was called the Joint War Gaming Agency. Each year the agency put together four or five political-military games which drew participants from the Defense and State departments and other government agencies. These were not war games as regularly played by the military forces; they were political-military games. In a war game, forces are pitted against forces. Mathematical factors are assigned to each weapon and unit, forces are aligned and maneuvered, and the computer plays a large role in determining the outcome—how many tanks are destroyed, how many planes shot down, and so on, and ultimately which side wins the battle. A political-military game pits government against government. It poses problems that have both a political and military dimension, and it has less to do with who wins or loses than with illuminating potential policy questions and the decision-making process.

In designing a political-military game, the War Gaming Agency would draw up a pre-scripted scenario. It might, for example, posit a situation in which the North Koreans shoot down a civilian airliner. The United States elects to respond militarily, and the North Koreans react in kind. Or perhaps the scenario would involve an incident in Berlin (before reunification). American forces go to high alert and the Soviets blockade Berlin. The scenario sets up the beginning of a crisis, describing the various background events that have precipitated it. Most often the confrontation was between the United States (the Blue Team) and the Soviet Union (the Red Team). A third team run by the agency itself (the Control Team) played the role of the outside world, providing input as well as monitoring deliberations, determining the results of moves, and moving the play to its next stage.

The makeup of the teams replicated the actual political-military command structure of the countries facing each other: a general secretary of the communist party and his advisers on one side, a president of the United States, secretary of state, secretary of defense, and so forth on the other. The War Gaming Agency always attempted to get high-level people to participate; they would usually invite the Secretary of State, for example. The Secretary himself would never be able to devote the time, but the number-four or -five man at State might take his place. The agency also tried hard to get people for the Red Team who knew the Soviet Union intimately.

For the entire four or five days it ordinarily took to play one of these games, the Control Team would watch Red and Blue through one-way glass. Move one would be announced and Blue would deliberate and announce its move, followed by Red, or sometimes the deliberations would go on simultaneously. Control would then assess

what each team had done, make their judgment about the consequences, and move the play along, building a new scenario based on
the moves that had been completed. Here's what has happened, they
would say. These are the events that have subsequently taken place,
and now two weeks have gone by. We are now at move two. Then
the two teams would deliberate and move again. The teams could
send messages to each other; they could send messages to other
countries; they could seek information from a variety of sources:
CIA, KGB, ambassadors, allies. All these messages went to Control,
which provided answers. Likewise, they could generate press releases and individual communications aimed at the opposing government. Control was the outside element in this process. All the
information a decision maker would have available to him came
through Control, which might introduce accidents, misunderstandings, failures in communication, and other elements that served to
make the game more realistic or perhaps to achieve some of the
objectives Control had for the game.

The first game I played was a fairly low level one and I ended up
as number-two man on the Blue Team. I got right into the spirit of it.
We didn't only make moves, we issued press releases, drafted messages, contacted friendly and neutral heads of state. We did all kinds
of ancillary things, many of which evidently were not always done
in these games. Although I was not aware of it at the time, that drew
a certain amount of attention to me as a military person who had
acquired something of a political feel. In any case, I found it exciting,
challenging, and sort of fun.

When the next game was announced, the agency specifically asked
for me to be head of Control. Before it started, Admiral Moorer
called me into his office. "You know," he said, "every time we do
these games in free play [leaving the moves up to the contending
parties] we can never get anyone to use nuclear weapons. No matter
what the scenario, both sides always find some way to avoid it. That
isn't helping us very much to understand what might happen in a
nuclear confrontation. Now I want a game that uses nuclear weapons, so we're going to structure this one differently. What we'll do
is have a Red and Blue team, but the Blue Team won't include the
President of the United States. We'll make head of Control President
of the United States, and the Blue Team's decisions will just be
recommendations to the President for action. I want you to be head
of Control and President. And I'm instructing you to drop some
damned nuclear weapons. I don't care what Blue Team's advice is,
I want some weapons employed."

I found it quite interesting that the players had gone to great lengths not to fire nuclear weapons, even in games that pitted Soviet and Western forces against each other in demanding situations. But whatever plans or strategies might be in place, the fact is that in crisis situations people do not just automatically follow an arranged plan. They reconsider everything. And the participants in these games were determined to avoid nuclear devastation. Of course, there were some individuals who did want to drop weapons and there would be furious debates at the table. The Soviet team was often criticized for not employing nuclear weapons, because many believed that they would use them—that was the American defense establishment's best judgment. And yet in the crunch these Red teams would refuse. The people on the Red teams, who were knowledgeable about the Soviets, would argue back and say, No, in this situation they would not have employed them. You people are just wrong. You think they would, but it's not true, for this, that, and the other reason. Huge arguments would take place in the post-game analyses or "washups."

This particular game Moorer tapped me for was code-named "Scylla II," for the legendary six-headed devourer of men, an appropriately vicious choice. The scenario was a crisis in Iran that led to a Soviet division striking across the border toward the oil fields. The Blue Team recommended a conventional response, but we had no ground forces in the region and only limited air power. As President, I ordered American units to hit the Soviets with tactical nuclear weapons—which precipitated angry protests from the Blue players (who did not know I was acting under Moorer's orders). The nuclear attack decimated the Russian division.

As I watched fascinated through the one-way glass, the Red Team debated ending the war right there. But finally they decided to continue the drive with another division. I thought, My God, what do I do now? We can't let these people have Iran. The Blue Team, already shaken by my first strike, recommended I begin negotiations. But again I struck back with theater nuclear weapons, using naval forces and planes based in Turkey. This division proved harder to stop; it took an astonishing number of weapons to do it. When the dust cleared I had hit the Soviets with over 300 tactical nuclear weapons.

With me on the Control Team was a group of nuclear experts, and with each move I made they would rush out to the computers to calculate the effect. The results were frightful. Moorer had wanted to see what would happen, and I was doing my best, though it was a chilling exercise to say the least. Even though I had limited my strikes to small weapons and had hit military targets exclusively, when the analyses came back I was told that in addition to destroying the Soviet division, thousands of Iranian civilians had died in the collateral destruction. This action was taking place in the middle of a sparsely inhabited area where there were only small villages. I had been aiming solely at the Soviet division, and yet I had killed large numbers of civilians incidentally, citizens of the country we were trying to save. I watched the players' faces as they heard the report. Each one of them blanched.

This time the Soviets hit back with nukes and sank a U.S. carrier with over 5,000 men aboard in the Indian Ocean. Then they brought in fresh troops and kept attacking. In response I mounted strikes out of Turkey and wiped out twelve airfields in the Caucasus, inside the Soviet Union. At that the Soviets took out the air bases I had launched from and also obliterated a Turkish city. According to the experts, over a million Turks died. The casualty figures shocked me, and when they rolled into the teams, they were appalled. (I later participated in a larger game where I was again head of Control. When nuclear weapons were dropped and the casualty reports came in, the drama at the table was so intense and the discussion so over-wrought that one of the State Department players had a heart attack. He died in the hospital the next day.)

Both teams were now in a constant dilemma. Each had its objec-tives and was quite determined to achieve them. But my initial nu-clear attack had upset the original Soviet calculations and forced a searching reappraisal. The Iranian attack was now overshadowed by the fear of escalation. The Red strategists clearly wanted to cap this spiral, but they also had strong domestic imperatives which were impelling them to punish the Americans in a way that roughly coin-cided with their own losses: tit for tat. At the same time, they did not want their response to signal a desire to escalate, nor did they wish to involve other countries. Hence their attack on the American carrier at sea, carried out after a discussion that examined several American island possessions (including Guam) as alternative targets. The carrier's destruction was followed closely by a peace overture.

The next attack on Soviet airfields in the Caucasus depressed the Red planners no end. Conventional wisdom argued that such an attack would precipitate an immediate full-scale nuclear exchange between the United States and the U.S.S.R. The Red Team had an energetic argument, but the main issue was how do we stop this insanity, not how do we get the upper hand. Still, always in the background was the need to "save face." So while they could not bring themselves to stop altogether, the response was restrained. The Soviet attack on Turkey was of such a character. It was followed not only by another peace overture (which Blue wanted to accept immediately) but also by a threat that the next step would be a massive attack into Western Europe. Iran had now all but faded off the Soviet scope as both sides cast about desperately for ways to back off.

In my role as Control leader, I was also bombarding the two teams with national headlines from around the world about the inhumanity of the Russians and Americans and how they were threatening the entire planet with extinction. Within hours I had the prime ministers of England and France in Washington leading a chorus of world figures shouting Stop! which I believe is exactly what would happen. (Some of the military participants later argued with this thesis, but during the Korean War that was precisely what took place. Shortly after the Chinese counteroffensive began, Prime Minister Clement Attlee was in Washington asking Truman not to use the bomb. At that moment American troops were suffering a disaster, but the very thought that we might possibly use atomic weapons had already driven Parliament into a frenzy—not to mention the rest of our allies.)

But despite the pressure to call a halt, my instructions were unambiguous. "Don't let the war stop," said Moorer. "Keep it going. While we're doing this, let's see where it leads." It was the kind of game where I stayed up nights. After everybody had gone home, I found myself working till three or four in the morning getting ready for the next day's play. I was fully involved. I even wrote a speech to the American people to be delivered by the President, in which I incorporated the essence of what I thought then President Nixon would say at such a time.

With no cease-fire, the Soviets did launch a major ground and air conventional attack on Western Europe, which quickly smashed allied defenses in northern Germany. Soviet forces raced across the Jutland plain and occupied almost a third of West Germany before NATO resistance stiffened. I struck back at the U.S.S.R. itself with a tactical nuclear attack that destroyed every Soviet air base in Eastern Europe and a number in the western Soviet Union. The death toll was enormous, civilians as well as military. By then the Soviets had penetrated several hundred miles into Germany, but the latest attack brought their juggernaut to a halt. In retaliation they hit airfields in Western Europe, more American ships, and several islands. But they could not agree on a strike against the continental United States. Then they asked for peace. Their conditions were a cease-fire in place—peace in return for the large chunk of Germany they had torn away from NATO. I accepted the proposal, and that was where Scylla II came to an end.

The Scylla II game affected me deeply. First, I was profoundly sobered by the casualties that were wrought. It was evidently impossible to use even battlefield nuclear weapons and control the damage. No matter how small a nuclear device might be, it will destroy a great deal that was not intended for destruction. Unless the war is taking place in a desert there will be immense collateral damage, even if the weapons are used with the most unlikely precision.

Secondly, I came to the conclusion that the pressure to stop any nuclear battle would mount with great rapidity. Three or four times both teams wanted to desist, and the game would never have become so murderous in the first place had it been free play. One striking feature of this and subsequent games was how many warlike participants suddenly became humanists when the first casualty figures were announced. It was amazing how fast their attitude toward war changed.

I think those conversions were realistic. If there were one atomic explosion and the *Washington Post* headlined pictures of Birmingham, England, going up in nuclear ash, I think people in Washington (let alone England) with a stomach for more would disappear so quickly it would make heads spin. At the same time the pressures from the noncombatant world would be overwhelming. Scylla II itself would have been stopped four times had I not been under orders to keep it going.

In other words, there was no automatic escalation, which came as a surprise to many. The theoretical prognoses regarding uncontrolled atomic warfare were not borne out. (It should be remembered, of course, that we were forced to simulate the Soviet decision-making structure, an important shortcoming.) But though participants revealed profound inhibitions against precipitating a strategic exchange, they did manifest a desire to get even. Both teams kept score and both felt the need to make reciprocal gestures. Observing the deliberations, it seemed to me this was a political as well as a psychological phenomenon. Both sides wanted cover; they needed to be able to go to their people and say, This was not one sided and we did not lose. The Red Team especially made several retaliatory strikes whose chief purpose was to convey a message, for both domestic and foreign consumption. Taking out our aircraft carrier was a 5,000-man signal. Later in the game the destruction of Guam was a 110,000-man signal. Both of these strikes came *after* the Red Team had decided to ask for peace (at different stages of play). They were cold-blooded moves. They said in effect, Don't make the mistake of believing we are not serious. We will do what we have to do. We have just killed 110,000 of your people. But that is all we have done. We have not eliminated San Francisco or spread radiation all over Kansas.

The problem with drawing conclusions from Scylla, of course, was that I had no idea to what extent it might reflect reality. The fundamental purpose of course was to test decision-making reactions in a nuclear conflict. But as good as the War Gaming Agency was, the game was an unsatisfactory attempt to replicate the real world. But while events in an actual confrontation might not go at all the same way, I was still left thinking they might possibly go just this way. I was in enough doubt so that I seriously questioned the more or less accepted wisdom that an exchange of nuclear weapons would automatically spiral out of control and trigger Armageddon. Deterrence might well be effective, even after a first use.

This did not mean that nuclear war suddenly seemed more feasible. (After Scylla II the potential horrors were more vivid to me than they ever had been.) But it did mean that unleashing the atomic genie would not inevitably bring all civilization to a fiery end. Once started, a nuclear battle might possibly be stopped.

A strategic exchange is a different matter. Once one nuclear nation mounts a full-fledged strategic attack on another, the stops are pulled. Had the Soviet Union ever launched a first strike, we would have been forced to utilize our entire available arsenal. I say that although the fact of the matter is that after the first wave both countries would have been so consumed with internal problems that I am persuaded any thought of further nuclear action would have faded quickly. In the theoretical papers and discussions one can find supposedly serious arguments about continuing to fight and making sure we end a nuclear war on favorable terms. But such propositions defy logic. If the United States sustained 80 million casualties (a hypothetical figure), no one would be concerned about hurting the Soviets any further. The first thing we would worry about would be where to get our next meal; the second thing would be how to care for the injured and bury the dead; and the third would be how to begin restoring the nation. The war would be over.

After Scylla II a classified report was drawn up, but I am not aware of what happened to it. It was not high priority. The fact is that these games, as dramatic as they could be, receive little attention in the government. The people who ought to play them seldom do. But no one doubts the games are helpful to people who are thinking about these kinds of problems. At the very least they open up new vistas, as Scylla II (and later games) did for me. They either reinforce or undermine intuitions about war and about how governments might act. They show the people in the command center, the planners at the one- and two-star level, the kinds of circumstances that would arise in that environment. All that is highly worthwhile. But they do not fulfill their most significant function: They do not expose the Secretary of Defense, the Secretary of State, and the President to the problems inherent in such a crisis. They themselves do not play (although they do sometimes make symbolic appearances). The games require the investment of large chunks of time, and crowded agendas always seem to preclude this kind of concentrated reflection on even the gravest potential events. And that is most unfortunate.

For several years I was disturbed by the conviction that President Reagan did not know enough about nuclear issues. I was not at all confident that he had been adequately educated about either the weapons or the plans for their use.

After the 1988 election I made up my mind to do everything I could to impress the newly elected President Bush with his need to know. I was aware that to truly inform him properly we would have to brief him at intervals, as we did the chiefs. (Each year the chiefs are given a thorough analysis of the nation's strategic war plan. When arms control issues are under consideration, they spend substantial time reviewing numbers, dispositions, and options—not that a President should involve himself at that level of detail.) But it is not that easy to get very much of the President's agenda time, not even for the Chairman of the Joint Chiefs.

At my first meeting with President-elect Bush on December 16, I stressed the importance of gaining a working familiarity with nuclear planning so that he could fully understand his range of options. I said that I thought the basic briefing he had received as Vice President may not have been sufficient. Bush agreed, and suggested that we should arrange a session before he assumed office so that we could take the necessary time.

The result of this discussion was a meeting in which we thoroughly briefed the new President on the SIOP and on our assessment of the

Soviet SIOP, including estimates of our attack's effect on the Soviet Union and theirs on the United States. Bush was attentive and engaged. Much of what my planners described was apparently new to him, which did suggest that he had not been adequately informed. Of course, the real question was the extent to which the President would reflect on these issues and take their meaning to heart, and that only he himself would know. But I did feel much better in my own mind, not only because of the President's obvious engagement with the subject, but because his main lieutenants were also present and clearly interested. They would, I hoped, keep the Commander-in-Chief thinking about his nuclear responsibilities.

Chapter 15

DOOMSDAY CALCULUS

AS THIS IS BEING WRITTEN the subject of great-power nuclear confrontation is sliding into history. That, of course, is a profound blessing. Considering it as history is vastly more comfortable than regarding it as current events in the making. Nevertheless, the doomsday anxieties that so deeply marked the collective psyche of the Cold War generation are not yet a thing of the past, and will not be as long as strategic nuclear weapons are in place and ready to use. (Indeed, proliferation may make the future even more dangerous.) The prospect of atomic war with the Soviet Union had about it the triple fascination of horror, mystery, and madness, all subsumed in the inescapable logic of geopolitical reality. Working on the Joint Staff, then behind the Chairman's desk, I used to ponder how it was that we had walled ourselves into such a situation.

In the course of the Cold War the United States acquired an excessive inventory of nuclear arms, although the very fact that in the forty-seven years since Nagasaki we have never used an atomic weapon in anger tells us something about their usefulness. I often asked myself how the country had acquired so many warheads and why it was so difficult to either call a halt to the buildup or to extricate ourselves from our predicament. The dilemma, I eventually came to understand, could not be attributed to stupidity, malfeasance, or even poor judgment, so much as to a combination of compelling political and bureaucratic pressures. It had nothing to do with Democrats versus Republicans or liberals versus conservatives. The answer, at least in my view, had to be seen as an exceedingly complex picture having to do with our system, the decision-making process, and the circumstances of the Cold War.

To begin with, the power of atomic weapons dwarfed previous generations of weapons, and as that truth was absorbed by Americans it took on an inevitable mystique. The specter of nuclear holocaust presented a new order of threat which involved not merely defeat or heavy damage to the nation but the very survival of mankind. It became clear that American voters did not want the decisions for using these weapons in any hands but the President's; the stakes were too high to trust to anyone other than the chief executive. In turn, this consensus view invested the subject with a high political content and opened up a whole new area of political vulnerability for the President, his administration, and his party.

Moreover, although military thinkers could devise a host of new ways to deliver nuclear weapons, they could not in the early period of the atomic arms race suggest an effective defense—against weapons which were so devastating that even a few nuclear explosions in American cities (even one explosion) would be disastrous. The only answer the military could offer was a strategy labeled "deterrence," which threatened an aggressor with the same or greater destruction than he was able to unleash. Unfortunately, deterrence was a rather vague and ill-defined concept which involved large psychological assumptions and a host of uncertainties. The decision about what it takes to deter a potential aggressor was (and remains) highly subjective—especially since we had no experience with nuclear war. This fact alone made every amateur strategist an authority. No one knew with any confidence when enough might be enough. Taken together, these considerations reinforced the tendency of policymakers to err on the side of having more rather than fewer warheads.

Military planners were also part of the problem. As in gauging conventional strength, they were prone to put excessive emphasis on sheer numbers. How, they asked, could we plausibly contend that we had either superiority or parity if our numbers or megatonnage were less than our opponent's? The fact was that in the nuclear business numbers were not by any means the whole story, but that case could only be made to an audience with the substantial technical understanding necessary to comprehend an in-depth argument. The general public had neither the background nor the patience for such a fine and detailed justification, nor did most politicians. From both a psychological and a political perspective, it was more comfortable to make sure that the other fellow was not ahead of us in any respect.

Military people tend to be conservative by nature, and when they are directed to build an arsenal that will bring an adversary to his knees, they will develop a plan to do exactly that. In essence the organization responsible for planning (JSPT—the Joint Strategic Planning Staff) began with an exhaustive survey of the targets in the

Soviet Union, then made judgments about which were significant. These assessments in turn drove decisions about how many weapons to build.

As our intelligence improved and the planners warmed to their task, the target lists expanded. (The fact was that a determined researcher could find an unlimited number of good targets in the U.S.S.R.) With time the lists acquired a mystique of their own. Targeteers became convinced that their lists were sacred; if they were to carry out their charge, then every target had to be covered, i.e., we had to have the ability to destroy it. In addition, our deterrent force had to be survivable. Larger numbers of weapons complicated the Soviet Union's problems and improved the possibility of our nuclear arsenal surviving a surprise attack. In the planners' minds the mandates imposed on them did not square with proposals to limit the number of weapons. On the contrary, assurance and safety demanded more.

The entire process, of course, was subject to political control. But no political leader would willingly open himself to the charge that he had increased America's vulnerability or conceded nuclear superiority to the Soviet Union. That would be tantamount to political suicide. As with so much political discourse in our republic, protracted, technical apologias would provide little defense against blunt emotional accusations by the other party. (The "missile gap" made a powerful broom.)

Here was an issue tailor-made for adversary politics. Few political leaders had the technical understanding or the time to delve into the problem in any depth. For the most part, then, they were inclined to follow the advice of their military advisers. In this, Congress was as much at fault as was the executive branch. To be sure, there were dissenting voices, but they were few and far between. The complexity of the subject, the press of other concerns, and the nature of the political system prevented Congress—the one group that had the ability to stem the tide—from bringing its weight to bear.

At the same time, the Soviet Union was going through a similar process and was making its own constant contribution to the vicious upward spiral in the number of warheads. The Cold War amplified each of the domestic factors that entered into the nuclear calculus. As a nation, we perceived that we were involved in a life-and-death struggle at whose end lay the ultimate catastrophe of nuclear war, a prospect which might well come to pass if we did not exercise every fiber of caution at our command. In this fearful climate voices calling for restraint were easily ignored. For successful deterrence we were willing to pay a very high price indeed. The result was an imposing, hugely expensive arsenal that greatly exceeded any realistic requirement.

With time, of course, the pressure for arms reduction began to grow, slowly at first, but steadily. In the military, too, sentiment in favor of some type of mutual reduction slowly took root. Duty in the arms control field acquired respectability, and planners started looking for ways to reduce the numbers of weapons without sacrificing effectiveness.

Against this background, nuclear targeteers began to view the Soviet Union in terms of systems, much as our planners viewed Iraq during the Gulf War. What must we do, they asked, to disable the electrical power grid? How can the road system best be incapacitated? The railroad system? The communications system? To destroy the communications system it is not necessary to attack every telephone in the land, only certain key nodes. The heating system throughout the country can be put out of commission by bringing down the electrical power grid. This systems approach permitted reductions, but it was not adopted without a fight. During the transition period targeteers continued to argue among themselves about how many and which nodes would best incapacitate the opponent. But reason eventually asserted itself and the lists grew smaller.

But though certain reductions were made, the subject as a whole remained difficult to comprehend. Technically it was complex, but the psychological dimension of nuclear war defied ready analysis. During the 1970s we moved away from the concept of "mutual assured destruction," better known as MAD. After that we claimed that the enemy's warfighting systems were our primary nuclear targets, not his cities or population. This had a far more acceptable sound to it, but probably did little to enhance deterrence. Deterrence is only enhanced when the adversary believes his country will be razed, and the way to shatter a country is to destroy people and buildings and systems. To achieve the maximum deterrent effect, you must prepare to hurt your enemy as badly as you can. But there was something so fundamentally repellent about mutual assured destruction that neither country would admit that was its policy. And in the United States it is extremely difficult to carry on a cosmetic change of this magnitude not accompanied by actual change. The fact is that we did transform our strategy. But this did not change the reality that deterrence was founded on the threat of national destruction.

·   ·   ·

It was during the Reagan administration that arms control gained an unprecedented momentum.* In this area the major development of my watch was the Intermediate Nuclear Forces Treaty (INF). Signed by President Reagan and Mikhail Gorbachev on December 8, 1987, the treaty had its origins eight years earlier in a NATO decision to work for a reduction in the number of intermediate-range SS-20 missiles the Soviets had aimed at Western Europe.

The SS-20 was an accurate triple-warhead missile greatly superior to the American tactical weapons then deployed in Europe. Together with older SS-3s and SS-4s, the SS-20s gave the Soviet Union an imposing inventory of medium-range weapons, far outnumbering the Western deployments. To try to put a cap on this fast-expanding Soviet arsenal, in December of 1979 NATO determined to pursue what was called the "two-track policy." The United States would proceed to put in place 108 advanced Pershing II missiles as well as 564 land-based cruise missiles. At the same time negotiations would be opened with the Soviet Union, the objective of which would be to decrease the number of SS-20s in return for a reduction in the proposed American deployment.

The two-track policy was greeted by a furious Soviet campaign to persuade Germany and other NATO nations not to accept the new American missiles. It was, as political scientist Jeffrey Herf put it, "the last great political conflict of the Cold War in Europe,"† an attempt to drive a permanent wedge between the United States and its European allies. Popular opposition to the missiles grew heated and even violent, especially in West Germany (which would have been the main battleground of a European nuclear war), but also in England, Holland, and elsewhere.

Nevertheless, at the end of 1983 the NATO countries bit hard on the bullet and made the decision to go ahead. The Pershing II and cruise missiles were fielded in Western Europe and took their place as part of the American nuclear warfighting arsenal. The day after the West German Parliament gave its approval, the Soviet Union closed down the "second track" talks that had been under way in Geneva, sending the INF negotiations into what appeared to be a permanent state of limbo. There they stayed until two years later when, in January of 1986, Mikhail Gorbachev suddenly resurrected them.

---

* Curiously, this was a direct reversal of the philosophy President Reagan brought into office: to increase every element of our military strength.
† Jeffrey Herf, *War by Other Means* (Free Press, 1991).

As the new round of talks grew increasingly serious, to our own negotiators' vast surprise, Gorbachev separated the INF talks from other arms control subjects and offered to destroy the SS-20s (and other intermediate-range weapons) in return for elimination of the Pershings—precisely the objective of the original NATO policy adopted six years earlier. We had deployed the Pershings in order to get rid of the Soviet intermediate-range, tactical missiles, and suddenly here it was, right in our lap.

This was a rather startling turnaround, especially considering the scorn which Moscow had heaped on the Reagan administration's original "zero-zero" proposal (zero SS-20s in return for zero Pershing deployments). In some quarters the reversal was attributed largely to the less confrontational worldview of an imaginative new leader, Mikhail Gorbachev. But there was a considerably deeper logic behind it.

In the first place, the Pershing was a heavy-yield, extremely accurate weapon, capable of destroying hardened military sites as well as population centers. Among the characteristics that made it superior to anything the Soviets had was its range. In the Pershing, we possessed a tactical missile that was also capable of hitting strategic targets inside the Soviet Union. There were even some technical changes we could make in it that could potentially bring Moscow itself within range. All of our information indicated that the Kremlin was deeply concerned about this weapon.

Moreover, I was persuaded that the Soviets had come to regard this unfortunate (from their standpoint) deployment as the most recent step in a tactical weapons race that had already outlived its usefulness. Indications had begun as far back as the late 1970s that not everyone in the Soviet leadership was convinced about the logic of battlefield nuclear weapons. Some, including Soviet Marshal Nikolai Ogarkov, had begun talking about "nuclear sufficiency" and putting increasing emphasis on conventional rather than nuclear arms on the NATO front. It looked to us as if the Soviet buildup of battlefield nukes in Europe had begun as a counter to NATO nuclear forces, which themselves had been developed to cancel the Soviets' vast manpower and armor superiority. But now that rationale was being called into question.

By the late '70s the Soviets knew that we were not building missile for missile with them, and that their inventory was far outstripping NATO's. But they were also discovering (as were we) that these battlefield nuclear weapons were highly problematic. Given the prevailing conviction that all nuclear war would go strategic, it was questionable whether battlefield nukes were even usable. My guess (reinforced some years later in discussions with Soviet Chief of Staff Sergei Akhromeyev) was that the Soviets came to the conclusion that they had a large inventory of weapons that they did not know what to do with and had no use for in the kind of warfare their battle plans contemplated.

On the one hand, if any tactical atomic war would go strategic (as was widely believed), then what happened on local battlefields would be moot. On the other, if the Soviets did undertake an aggressive war in Europe for the purpose of acquisition and occupation, they would hardly be able to use many of their nuclear weapons anyway. (By 1986 they had deployed 1,675 SS-20 warheads.) After such a war there would not be much radiation-free territory left to occupy. I was persuaded that the Soviets had studied their war games, examined their logic, and said to themselves, We are wasting resources on a category of weapons that has little practical use.

For our part, we were drawing some of the same conclusions. Our war games repeatedly demonstrated that employing tactical nuclear weapons to cancel out the Soviet manpower and armor advantage was not a sound approach. They had more of these weapons than we did, and every time we went nuclear in a war game, we lost—so did Europe, of course. The way nuclear confrontation works is that if a large power calls a smaller power's bluff, the latter is in grave trouble. If the smaller power uses theirs, they will be overwhelmed by an onslaught that comes back at them two, three, or four to one. For NATO forces, this meant that tactical weapons would not only fail to bring a Soviet offensive in Europe to a halt but would result in far greater damage to ourselves than to our adversary.

Originally, we had considered nuclear weapons a cheap way to counter the Soviets, but they had now decisively cancelled our advantage. This lesson, though, seemed not to have impressed our allies, who still did not want to increase their spending on conventional defense forces. It seemed to me that for decades NATO's political and military leaders had been giving lip service to the horrors of nuclear war, while at the same time demonstrating that they would rather accept the risk of nuclear war and spend less than try to do something sensible about it by spending more. I questioned how many truly appreciated what such a war would do to Western Europe, or to the world for that matter.

Despite the Soviets' new willingness to destroy a great many more weapons than the United States, the proposed INF exchange was not completely one-sided. The Pershing II was now fully integrated into our warfighting doctrine. We had deployed and trained Pershing forces at great fiscal and political expense, and some military men argued that we should not give up so significant a system—especially one that had the ability to reach the Soviet homeland. They believed that, if pushed, the Kremlin would be willing to pay more than we were currently asking.

This was an important question, since the proposed INF Treaty dealt with intermediate-range missiles but left the shorter-range battlefield nuclear weapons untouched. Soviet forces in Eastern Europe deployed hundreds of these ground-to-ground missiles, and it would be highly desirable if the treaty could capture these short-range weapons as well. The question was debated at length within both the administration and the Joint Chiefs of Staff.

There was something to the argument that the battlefield missiles should be eliminated first. Of the three nuclear weapon "bands"— short-range, intermediate, and strategic—logic suggested beginning with the first band and not giving up our major lever (the Pershings) until all the other tactical weapons had left the battlefield. And had we been in a position to start from scratch we would have wanted to do that. But instead we were dealing with the intermediate band, for reasons that were by now submerged in history. Of course, it was far easier for the critics to propose turning our backs on many years of negotiation than it was for an administration that had invested great effort and prestige in the process.

As the INF negotiations proceeded, opposition within the administration and the Congress lost momentum and the issue seemed to fade. But in the last stages General Bernard Rogers, the Supreme Allied Commander, publicly resurrected the argument once again. Rogers was a former Army Chief of Staff, a Vietnam veteran, a Rhodes scholar, and probably our most experienced unified commander. Thoughtful and articulate, he was also known for his forceful manner. Above all, he was a man who had the courage to express his conclusions directly, no matter where they led.

Rogers argued that the U.S. should back away from an agreement now and keep the Pershings until the Soviets were willing to throw in the short-range tactical weapons as well. We could, he maintained, get far more mileage out of the Pershings than the proposed agreement would give us. But with only 108 Pershing II missiles deployed, this was a strategy that hoped to stretch them a very long way indeed. In turning down a proposition that was already lopsided in our favor, we would greatly protract the negotiations. Moreover, there was no assurance that this ploy would succeed.

The debate was rehashed throughout the Pentagon, especially in the JCS, where two of the chiefs, Generals Wickham and Gray, were also reluctant to give up the Pershings. Nevertheless, after comprehensive deliberations the chiefs concluded that we had sufficient capacity in sea-launched ballistic and cruise missiles and forward-based air power so that losing the Pershings would not be consequential. Our forces would retain adequate ability to hit the Soviet Union without firing from the United States. Essentially, the INF agreement was a bird in the hand, and too attractive a proposition to pass up. The administration could see no way to break out at this late date and redirect the whole process. The domestic political cost would have been exorbitant.

Air Force Commander General Larry Welch and I shared the conviction that INF was such a disproportionate deal that it would be foolish to turn it down. Larry had thought deeply about this problem, and he felt that any time we could get a sixteen-to-one trade-off in weapons, we probably ought to grab it, most particularly in an area where we could never hope to achieve parity. It was not what we had that was most significant but what we could get for what we had. Moreover, it seemed likely that the deal we were being offered would pass. In 1986 and 1987 no branch of the government foresaw the dissolution of the Soviet Union. Rather, we were negotiating with what was still very much a cohesive, if troubled, superpower. The Soviets had flipflopped for the moment on INF, but START, ABM, and nuclear and space negotiations were also in process, and it was impossible to predict what tack Gorbachev might take next on this interlocking web of issues.

Perhaps most significant, the INF agreement that was on the table incorporated two historical advances. First, both sides would actually destroy weapons (rather than simply limit them), and second, the Soviets would destroy a disproportionate number. To break those two thresholds seemed to me terribly important, particularly the idea of the Soviets destroying disproportionately. So even though I understood the counterarguments, I never had any serious misgivings about INF.

While our internal deliberations were proceeding, President Reagan and Mikhail Gorbachev agreed to meet in Reykjavik, Iceland, in October 1986 as a preliminary to the full-scale summit scheduled for the end of the year. The general assessment throughout the government was that Reykjavik would be more symbolic than substantive and that it would primarily address the agenda for the later summit. No one expected new issues of any importance to emerge. Looking forward to the full-scale summit, both sides were interested in spurring on the arms control talks taking place in Geneva, but neither would be unnecessarily rocking the boat at this juncture.

Consequently, preparations for Reykjavik were nothing like those for full-dress encounters between heads of state. The several meetings I attended seemed more or less pro forma; the reviews of issues and positions being prepared for the President were sparse and less thorough than usual. When President Reagan and his party left for Reykjavik, no one expected the dramatic weekend that was in store.

At the first session between Reagan and Gorbachev it quickly became apparent that the Soviet leader had come to talk business, particularly in regard to strategic arms limitations. Reagan was responsive, and in a series of face-to-face meetings the two leaders moved much further than anyone had ever anticipated. On the next to last day, Reagan surfaced a proposal to eliminate all ballistic missiles in ten years, and Gorbachev accepted it. The following day Gorbachev came back with a proposal to eliminate not just ballistic missiles but all nuclear weapons. Reagan apparently answered in a positive vein, though no one present seemed quite clear if he meant to do anything more than express his basic sympathy for the idea. Though the press subsequently devoted considerable space to this exchange (their information all came through leaks), for the arms control people the crux of the discussions remained the President's offer to go to zero ballistic missiles in ten years.

During these extraordinary meetings George Shultz was encouraging the President to exploit the breakthrough that seemed to be developing, as was National Security Adviser John Poindexter. Overnight Richard Perle and Colonel Robert Linhard, an NSC staff expert, drew up talking papers for the President. My own representative, Lieutenant General John Moellering, did not know about the ballistic missile proposal until well into the evening. He had had no advance notice and took no part in drafting the talking paper. Nor had anyone seriously discussed such an idea prior to Reykjavik. Neither the Joint Chiefs nor the Secretary of Defense's office had given it any consideration whatsoever. But despite this sudden and ground-breaking development, in the end the Reykjavik summit adjourned with no agreement. At the last moment Gorbachev made all the breathtaking advances dependent on severely restricting SDI (Strategic Defense Initiative, or Star Wars) research, and President Reagan angrily refused.

When the American delegation returned to Washington, the events at Reykjavik were handled in an oddly secretive fashion. Although accounts of what had happened made their way through the rumor mill and into the newspapers, the administration never did inform the Joint Chiefs of what had transpired. No one called to discuss the proposals that had been made, or to ask for an opinion. By inference, I concluded that various people in the President's inner circle had become agitated that he had gone too far, and that the political tacticians had decided the best way to manage the situation was to act as if it had never happened. The President's zero-ballistic-missiles-in-ten-years (ZBM) formula was being treated as a nonevent—the idea apparently being that if it were ignored long and hard enough it would eventually go away (which is essentially what did happen).

However, it did not go away instantly. ZBM was news, and it became the subject of considerable media speculation and commentary. A number of commentators opined that the President was badly off base in not consulting with the Joint Chiefs before making such a radical departure. The fact is, of course, that the President does not have to consult with anybody. Despite the traditional approach of preparing arms control positions with the utmost care, the President is not compelled to consult, and if he finds himself at a meeting where an attractive opportunity suddenly appears to further American interests, he has the right to grasp it. I suspect President Reagan looked at what happened at Reykjavik in exactly that fashion.

At the same time, it always puzzled me that I was not consulted even after the President returned. Caspar Weinberger was also cut out of the official loop. Donald Regan, the President's Chief of Staff, had warned the entire delegation that while the summit was in process nobody was to communicate with his boss back in Washington about anything. As a result, John Moellering did not inform me until he returned, though apparently Richard Perle ignored Regan and did keep Weinberger updated throughout the talks.

Nevertheless, with the continued speculation in the media, I took the subject up with the chiefs. "We weren't consulted about this," I said. "We aren't even sure exactly what happened in Reykjavik, but there are quite a few references to us in the papers, and I think it's incumbent upon us to decide what our position is. If in fact a zero-ballistic-missile offer was made, what is our position on it? Does the proposal we've been reading about appeal to you or appall you?"

The unanimous answer was that from a national security perspective it was completely unacceptable. The chiefs were quite disturbed. For a variety of reasons, the prospect of going to zero nuclear weapons in ten years was unacceptable to all of them. "Think it over," I said. "I want a thorough analysis of this, because I am confident that we are going to be asked about it, if not by the President then by Congress. In my judgment it's going to be necessary for me to convey our views to the President, whether he solicits them or not."

It was unusual for the chiefs to do such a thing. But I was convinced that I would eventually be called to testify by one or both of the Armed Services committees and that I would be asked whether the JCS had been consulted before Reykjavik. When I answered no, Chairman Les Aspin would no doubt then ask what I thought of the idea. And when I told him why I opposed it, he would ask whether I had advised the President to that effect since then. It was important to avoid having to say no to that question. "So if we really feel this way," I said to the chiefs, "we've got to advise the President of it." There were a few mumbles around the table to the effect that it made little sense to volunteer this kind of advice. But my position was that if I was going to have to oppose the President in Congress, I had better tell him about it beforehand. I did not want him hearing our position for the first time on the evening news.

As I agonized over this problem I understood that it was a defining moment of sorts for me personally. There are various nonconfrontational approaches a chairman can take when he feels he has to render advice that may be unpopular with the President (and I had no idea how strongly President Reagan might be attached to the idea of eliminating ballistic missiles). The Chairman can, for example, express himself to the Secretary of Defense, then abide by the Secretary's decision on how to proceed. Alternately, he might couch his advice as one option among several, painting the advantages and disadvantages of each and testing the political waters for support. I was awake for several nights worrying about it and wondering, rightly or wrongly, if I was perhaps taking my chairmanship in my hands.

After reviewing the ZBM proposal with the chiefs, I went to Weinberger and told him that in the upcoming National Security Planning Group meeting I would like to say a word about Reykjavik. "I hear the President may have discussed doing away with nuclear missiles in ten years. If that's the case, then I have to tell him that the chiefs believe it would be a huge mistake."

"Why?" said Weinberger. "Why tell the President that? We all think it's a mistake. But it's going to go away, don't worry about it."

"You may think it's going to go away," I answered, "but it is not going to go away for me. I'm going to be asked by Congress what the chiefs think and whether I told the President what they think. And I'm going to have to say that the chiefs deliberated on the subject and we're against it. There's a hearing scheduled, and I believe that is what Aspin is going to ask."

Weinberger just sort of looked at me for a moment, then said, "Are you sure you have to do this?"

"Yes, I think I do." I was a little put off that he was not being as supportive as I wanted him to be.

"O.K.," he said, "if that's what you think you have to do, it's your privilege."

Ordinarily when I spoke at these meetings, I did so extemporaneously, but I felt so strongly about the importance of this issue that I carefully wrote out the chiefs' objections. I did that for the sake of clarity, and also because if this became a true confrontation I wanted to be able to adduce exactly what I had said. If I was about to gain immortality by being fired, I at least wanted to document my demise. I was really quite apprehensive about what reaction this might precipitate.

The NSPG meeting of October 27 focused on other topics. When it was almost over the President asked, as he usually did, whether anybody had anything else. I said that I did have something I'd like to say, that I wanted to talk about Reykjavik. Discussions at NSPG meetings were most often dominated by the principals—the secretaries of State and Defense and the National Security Adviser, so my taking the floor like this was a bit unusual, and when I announced that I wanted to address Reykjavik the room quieted.

I began reading the statement, to the effect that the chiefs had deliberated on the ten-year zero ballistic missile concept, and that we felt such a proposal, while theoretically attractive, would be ill-advised. I then launched into a four-page description of the problems we believed such a commitment would entail, including the need to vastly restructure our forces and develop new weaponry. Our current posture and strategy had evolved over a long period of time, and a sudden, dramatic change had the potential to jeopardize our deterrent capability and destabilize the equilibrium between Great Power forces. "As your chief military adviser," I concluded, "I do not recommend that you submit this proposal, Mr. President. It is not my intention to make your burdens any greater than they normally are, but this subject is of sufficient significance and the feelings of the Joint Chiefs are strong enough that I feel I would not be carrying out my responsibilities without informing you."

When I finished, Ken Adelman, the young and brash head of the Arms Control and Disarmament Agency, said, "I agree with that." Everybody stared at him, wondering why someone else would gratuitously stick his neck out. Then all eyes turned to the President. I thought to myself, Well I've done my duty, now here it comes.

"Admiral," the President said, "I really love the U.S. military. I have always loved it. Those young men and women do a wonderful job for our country, and everywhere I go I tell people how proud I am of our armed forces. You oversee a superb organization, one that is not adequately appreciated. But I am constantly trying to get the country to recognize and understand the true value of our military."

I looked at him and said, "Thank you, Mr. President," and that was the end of the meeting. I think the most relieved man in the room was Weinberger. All my fears evaporated. If the President was angry, it was not obvious to me. If he had heard my remarks, it was not obvious to me. If he simply did not wish to respond, that was not clear to me either. Nor did I know where the controversial proposal stood now.

In fact the ZBM concept slipped quietly into oblivion and was not heard from again. On the other hand, I *was* called before the Aspin committee, where I was asked about the chiefs' opinions and whether I had communicated them to the President. And I did have the satisfaction of saying that I most certainly had informed the President, face to face. In a number of respects I felt this was the most crucial event of my chairmanship, at least in personal terms. I had weathered a crisis and had decided to take the risk. Afterwards I found it was much easier to speak out at NSPG meetings. It seemed to me that an indefinable but real change had taken place around the table. For the first time as Chairman I felt I had been accepted by the Secretary of State and the others as a full member of the group.

Although the Reykjavik proposal seemed to fade away, the INF Zero Option (zero SS-20s for zero Pershings) gathered momentum. In July 1987 the Soviets formally agreed to eliminate all intermediate missiles in Asia as well as Europe. The talks moved toward closure. But the debate in our own councils had not yet run its course.

At the very end of the process, Bernie Rogers issued a final blast, loudly reaffirming his view that we should not be giving up a weapon that had become so important in maintaining the balance in Europe. Although I disagreed with Rogers, I admired his integrity and courage. He believed strongly in his position and was not afraid to say so, even at personal cost. For several reasons I thought it was imperative that we not ignore him.

In my talks with Frank Carlucci, who was still the National Security Adviser, I suggested that since Rogers was going to make his voice heard during the ratification process, we could put ourselves in the best position by inviting him in to see the President now. Carlucci agreed and Rogers came to Washington, where the chiefs and the Secretary of Defense heard him out. The President was angry about his public blast and did not see him, but Rogers did get to talk to Carlucci. In fact, Rogers's arguments had been fully taken into account during the earlier discussions on INF, but I did want to give him the opportunity to make his points in person. I also wanted the administration to be able to say in the ratification hearings that we had given his position our fullest consideration, even to the extent of having him back for a direct exchange of views.

In the end, the administration accepted the INF principles. Then we fought our way through a variety of verification details and procedures for destruction—very involved and complicated—and reached closure. Although the INF Treaty did not do much to reduce the total nuclear inventory, it was a milestone in terms of breaking the deadlock on nuclear weapons. Happily, many of the issues that seemed so weighty, regarding both INF and strategic arms reduction, have now disappeared with the collapse of the Warsaw Pact and disintegration of the U.S.S.R.

Chapter 16

RUSSIANS

IT WASN'T UNTIL AFTER REYKJAVIK that I first heard anything substantial about Sergei Akhromeyev, Chief of Staff of the Soviet armed forces, and even then it was all secondhand. But I was intrigued nevertheless. The people who came back from Iceland reported that Akhromeyev had headed the Russian arms control delegation that supported the principals. He was, said Richard Perle, who had watched him closely, more open than his political counterparts, more willing to talk, and more willing to compromise. On a number of occasions he had overruled the political people and conceded points. He was clearly confident, receptive, and influential with Gorbachev.

At about the same time I began to hear reports from people who had talked with Akhromeyev in Moscow, among them Henry Kissinger and Davey Jones, the former Chairman. They too described a man who was a tough professional soldier, but who also had a flexible mind and an engaging, friendly manner. Everything I heard made him out to be an interesting character, quite different from the standard run of dour and obstinate Russian military men.

For some time I had been thinking about the possibility of opening a military-to-military dialogue with the Soviets. My natural inclination was to talk problems over, but no avenue existed for high-level contact between the two armed forces. Communication between the Soviet and American militaries was restricted to arms control matters and even then was spasmodic and limited. Considering the potential consequences of friction or accidents, it seemed an almost insane deficiency. There were a host of good reasons for establishing contact with my Soviet opposite number, and when I kept hearing about what an open-minded person Akhromeyev was, the thought began to take firmer shape. I had nothing specific in mind; I did not know where such a meeting might lead, if anywhere. But there were certainly issues I wanted to discuss, and simply meeting with him might open the way for real communication later on.

With this in mind I proposed to Weinberger that I contact Akhromeyev. But the Secretary was not enthusiastic. He did not believe we had any business talking to the Soviets, and certainly not in the kind of setting I was proposing. He was right that it certainly would have been breaking ground. No American JCS Chairman had ever had direct, substantive contact with his Soviet counterpart.

George Shultz's approach differed from Weinberger's. Shultz had met Akhromeyev himself and had told me about him, making his own suggestion that I ought to find a way for the two of us to get together. The idea of making contact made as much sense to him as it did to me. With the overall relaxation of tensions that was gaining momentum, why not just do it?

In the fall of 1987 relations with the U.S.S.R. began improving dramatically. One consequence was that the protracted INF negotiations began to accelerate toward a conclusion. By late October the two sides had reached agreement, and a signing date was set for December 8. Gorbachev would be coming to Washington for the occasion, the first major arms control agreement of the Reagan administration. Akhromeyev, who had been instrumental in the negotiations, would be coming with him. It seemed like a perfect opportunity for the two of us to establish contact. Shultz informally approved the idea, I ran it quickly by OSD (Office of Secretary of Defense), and obtained an oral go-ahead from the White House. It was all rather casual. We simply announced what we were going to do and nobody objected, at least initially. Although Weinberger grumbled a little, he did not want to appear obstinate, since the mood of the administration was clearly changing. (Moreover, he was already in the process of departing from office.) All of a sudden it was no longer fashionable to bash the Soviets, at least not publicly or overtly.

As Chairman I often attended the arrival receptions for visiting heads of state, but Shirley and I both felt particularly privileged to be part of the ceremony for Mikhail Gorbachev. Before his limousine arrived, the White House protocol people were busy arranging us, and right behind me were a group of Soviets. One of them was a short man in an overcoat and homburg whom I did not recognize, and as we were being lined up in the proper order a voice from over my shoulder said, "Admiral, I met a friend of yours in London recently, Admiral Fieldhouse" (Sir John Fieldhouse, chief of the

British Defense Staff). When I turned around, the Russian interpreter who had spoken pointed to the man in the homburg. We
chatted a minute and suddenly I realized that this well-dressed
gentleman was no civilian but Marshal Akhromeyev.

So there he was, the man I had been wanting to meet for a year,
looking nondescript and slightly awkward in his civilian clothes. I
introduced Shirley to him, but in the hustle and bustle we didn't have
much time to talk. After the formalities, though, the whole group
walked into the White House for coffee, and Akhromeyev and I
gravitated to each other. As we sat down with the interpreter we
both said at the same time, I've got some things I want to talk to you
about. Then after a moment of laughter I said, "I've heard a great
deal about you, Marshal." "I've heard about you too," he answered, "and I've wanted to meet you. This is a real pleasure. You
know," he went on, "the two things I'm proudest of in my life are
number one, that I fought in the Great Patriotic War, and number
two, that I'm in Washington attending the signing of this treaty." I
was moved by his genuineness and sense of history. It seemed the
perfect opportunity to make a little history ourselves. "Marshal," I
said, "I know you're here with Gorbachev and you're a member of
the delegation, but do you think you might find time to visit me in
the Pentagon?" That must have come as a bit of a shocker, but
Akhromeyev didn't bat an eye. "I'll make time," he said.

"If you can come, I would like you to meet all the chiefs of service." "I'd enjoy that," he said, looking through an appointment
book he had taken out of his jacket pocket, very businesslike. "I
can't stay long, but I could come for breakfast the day after tomorrow and maybe be there an hour and a half. What do you think,
should I wear a uniform?"

I was treating this as nonchalantly as I could, but we were both
quite aware what a signal event we were talking about—the Soviet
armed forces chief visiting the Pentagon for the first time in history,
as the guest of the Joint Chiefs of Staff. With all the tensions and
antagonisms that still existed, this meeting was going to generate
shock waves. My conservative friends would be dismayed; others
with more naive tendencies would herald it as the end of the Cold
War.

At 7 A.M. sharp on the appointed morning Akhromeyev stepped
out of his car at the Pentagon's main entrance in full regalia. Except
for his interpreter, he was alone—a gesture that conveyed supreme
confidence. His chest was covered with battle ribbons and he wore

the huge visored hat favored by Russian generals. There was no question that he was announcing to all the assembled newsmen and to everyone in the building: "Marshal of the Soviet Union, by God!"

The first moments were stiff and formal, nothing at all like the instant ease that marked our earlier conversation at the White House. It seemed to me that he was a little intimidated by the moment. I know I was, and in a situation like that it is sometimes easiest to take refuge in formality. But when the two of us and our interpreters finally found ourselves alone in my office, the atmosphere softened a little. It relaxed more as breakfast was brought in and we found ourselves in conversation. "I have one subject I'm very interested in," he said. "I want to see if you and I can reach an agreement that will cut down the possibility of friction between our two forces." "Marshal," I said, "that has a lot of appeal to me. I've also had in mind that we should initiate a formal program of military-to-military contacts between our services." "I've been considering that too," he answered. "I think it's got a great deal to recommend it, and I believe we also ought to work on an accord that would put some official stamp on whatever we design."

By the time we finished breakfast the two of us had agreed that we would try to clear these ideas with our governments. If they were willing to go forward we would establish a joint working group to draft a military-to-military program and a "dangerous activities" agreement to resolve problems of inadvertent conflict between American and Soviet forces. (Neither of us, of course, announced any of this publicly.) I was more than a little surprised by how fast this was happening. It was almost as if the Soviet Chief of Staff had been harboring exactly the same fears of miscalculation and misinterpretation I had, and that, like me, he had been searching for an opening to the other side.

As we were getting up to walk over to the Tank so I could introduce Akhromeyev to the chiefs, I asked him if his delegation had any plans to travel in the United States before going back to Moscow. No, he said, they had been invited, but Gorbachev was not able to stay away for very long and they would be returning right after the signing. "Well, I'm glad you're here," I said, "but you know you're not seeing the real America. Washington, D.C., is not the United States. As a matter of fact, Marshal, you haven't really seen my country until you've seen Oklahoma." "What do you mean?" he asked. Oklahoma didn't seem to have rung much of a bell. "That's my home," I said. "It's out west, and you just have not seen this country until you've seen Oklahoma." He laughed at that. He wasn't sure if I was joking or not, but he thought it was funny. "Marshal," I said, "I would like to invite you on behalf of my government to visit next summer as my guest. I want to show you some of the United States." I thought he was going to say something along the lines of Swell, sounds like a great idea. I'll go back and talk to my government about it. But instead he smiled and replied, "I accept." I was a little stunned, but I sealed the deed quickly. "I think that's wonderful. I'll be back to you in a letter suggesting dates, and we'll discuss when you can come and how long you can stay. The longer the better. I guarantee you'll enjoy it, and I will make sure you'll learn a great deal about this country and its people."

In the Tank, Akhromeyev shook hands all around, then said a few words about the INF treaty and talked briefly but warmly about American-Russian cooperation during World War Two and the historic meeting between Americans and Russians on the Elbe in 1945. The chiefs listened to all this politely, but they seemed a little uncomfortable, as if they weren't exactly sure it was proper to have a communist in such a place. (They felt more or less the same way when I brought Mike Wallace into the Tank, though on the whole I think they were happier having Akhromeyev there.) In any event, the meeting only lasted half an hour, and then I took him back to his car.

Summer seemed to approach quickly, and the closer we came to Akhromeyev's visit, the more agitated the State Department grew. Reagan and Gorbachev had held a congenial, in some ways euphoric summit in Moscow at the end of May, but one crux in the superpower relationship where obstacles were not resolved was the Strategic Arms Reduction Talks (START) negotiations. These talks were continuing, though, and Akhromeyev was deeply involved in the process. Our own chief negotiator was Paul Nitze, working under the State Department (in our arms control structure the Joint Chiefs played a strictly advisory role), and various elements at State were nervous about my being in such close, unmonitored contact with Akhromeyev. Some were sure that he and I would get ourselves into the arms control business, that I would be crowding in where I did not belong—or, more to the point, crowding in where they believed only they belonged (another lesson in never underestimating the ability of old Washington hands to protect their turf).

A good deal of sniping went on over this subject, and Rosalyn

Ridgeway (assistant secretary of state for European and Canadian affairs) and I sent a series of talking papers back and forth, though none of the interchanges seemed to calm State's fears. Although it was never bluntly stated, she was clearly worried about letting an Okie military type loose with the Soviet Chief of the General Staff. We were going to be in each other's company for days on end, and it was inevitable that we would end up talking about sensitive subjects, and only "diplomats" can talk to foreigners sensitively. Frankly, I did not plan to exclude anything from our discussions that came up naturally. I fully intended, as I told Ridgeway, to explore with Akhromeyev anything he was willing to talk about. As far as arms control went, he knew and I knew that I was not the spokesman for the United States government on that subject, but the JCS was deeply involved nevertheless, and if I could find out anything about his thinking on it, all the better. "Oh," said Roz, "I don't know about that. That's not a good idea at all." It never ceased to amaze me that as CINCPAC, CINCSOUTH, and Middle East Force commander I visited regularly with heads of state, foreign ministers, and defense ministers, but that as Chairman I had suddenly become too clumsy to be trusted.

In June we sent our proposed itinerary to Akhromeyev. In his return letter he suggested no changes, but he did mention that he would be bringing quite a large group of people with him. My usual procedure in hosting counterparts was to indicate that we would bear the expenses for the military chief, his wife, and two aides. But we had not said anything of that sort to Akhromeyev; we had simply asked who was going to be in his party. Now we discovered that he planned to bring along the vice chiefs of the Soviet Army, Navy, and Air Force, and the commander of the Marines.

That took us by surprise. Immediately, my staff began to wring their hands. Everyone's refrain seemed to be Oh my God, can we afford it? But even those who thought we couldn't were not able to come up with an acceptable way to tell Akhromeyev that his list was too long. My executive assistant Joe Strasser and public affairs assistant Jay Coupe were more realistic. They counseled calm and argued that there should be no dickering about this trip. Anyone Akhromeyev wanted to bring he should bring. In the back of their minds was the idea that the more people Akhromeyev brought, the more we would be able to bring when we returned the visit. Moreover, in the final analysis we wanted to influence the views of the Soviet military, so the more who came the better.

Predictably, the reactions from some in DOD were negative, even distressed. Well, he's just bringing all these spies with him, they said in so many words. He wants that big a group so they can expand their intelligence collection. But my feeling was that they were mainly just curious; they really did want to see us. These people weren't spies, they were more like country cousins going to the big city. It was the chance of a lifetime for them, and I strongly believed that seeing our country is healthy for unbelievers. (After their visit my basic opinion was reinforced. It is true, however, that the Soviet vice chiefs originally regarded the trip as something they were forced into. They considered it much as some of my colleagues did—consorting with the enemy, and they weren't at all positive they should be doing it.)

The Soviets arrived at Andrews Air Force Base on July 5, 1988, two days after the *Vincennes* shot down the Iranian Airbus over the Persian Gulf. It was not an auspicious moment; the shootdown, I thought, might throw a serious pall over the entire visit. Shirley and I went out to meet Akhromeyev and his wife and their party and accompany them back to the Vista Hotel, where we had arranged for them to stay (Akhromeyev in the Presidential Suite). It was all very stiff and more than a little strained. Everybody seemed tense.

But despite the initial discomfort, as soon as we started talking it became apparent that Akhromeyev was absolutely determined that this visit would be a success. My experience around the world over the years had been that Soviet military officers could be arrogant, stubborn, unpleasant people. But Akhromeyev was exactly the opposite. He told me first that the Airbus incident was strictly between the Iranians and ourselves; he felt no need to comment on it at all. He wanted to conduct himself, he said, with complete propriety. He wanted to be on time; he wanted to be dressed properly; he wanted to know what was polite and what was expected. He made it clear from the start that he was putting himself entirely in our hands. Much to our surprise, he had declined to bring his own security. (We were actually quite worried and doubled our already careful precautions.) He did not even bring communicators, which was totally unexpected. I always traveled with global communication capability. Instead, each night he called the Soviet embassy and they would hook him up in whatever way was necessary.

The first day we spent in Washington, kicking it off with a big honors ceremony at the Pentagon. Usually on such occasions we give a commemorative medal to visitors, but nobody could bring himself to even contemplate bestowing a medal on a Soviet marshal, so we quietly skipped that tradition. Afterwards I took the Russians into my office and showed off some of my hat collection. (Akhromeyev presented me with a Russian cavalry commander's hat from the late 1700s.) Shirley and Mrs. Akhromeyev had come to the honors ceremony, but at this point they disappeared to follow their own program. Mrs. Akhromeyev turned out to be a very sweet, very pleasant woman. She had badly wanted to see the United States and was extremely curious, but she was also a bit intimidated, especially by crowds. She had had scant experience of international travel and public exposure and was more than a little terrified by the whole prospect. From the beginning she and her interpreter stuck close to Shirley and Debbie Garretson, a Dartmouth professor and experienced Soviet authority who was acting as Shirley's interpreter. As long as Shirley was with them everything seemed to go well. (Akhromeyev, by contrast, never minded a crowd and liked to wander off and see things for himself.) As a result Shirley stayed close by constantly, and by the end of the trip she and Tamara Akhromeyev had become good friends.

Akhromeyev's second meeting in the Tank with the chiefs was quite interesting. At our request he spoke about the party congress that had just been held in Moscow, the first one in history that had been opened to free debate. He was rather candid and talked not only about the substance but the atmosphere as well. With some bemusement, he remarked that the speakers hadn't been shy about attacking the Soviet military. Then with a wry smile he said, "American officers seem to be more used to criticism than we are."

Afterwards we had a general discussion of the START talks. The American chiefs participated in their usual robust fashion, but the Soviet vice chiefs didn't say a word unless Akhromeyev called on them. On their side he carried the entire conversation.* It was clear that he had fingertip control. That morning before they came over he

---

* Akhromeyev told me later that he was quite impressed by the discussion we had had in the Tank. You noticed, he said, that I didn't call on my people very much. The reason, as he explained it, was that they had little understanding of the political world, either at home or abroad. They knew, for example, nothing about arms control or the Soviet-American relationship. Although they were four-star generals and admirals, their training had been, like his, extremely one-sided. In retrospect he was not happy with his training. It hadn't, he thought, prepared him for higher responsibilities in political circles. He had to learn those skills on the job after he became Chief of Staff. That was what had moved him to bring his vice chiefs along. He wanted to open their eyes to an area of the world they knew so little about. "I thought these fellows ought to get out of town," as he put it.

had held inspection in the lobby of the Vista Hotel. The vice chiefs, all of them four-star officers, had lined up while Akhromeyev looked them over to make sure they were turned out properly. I could just imagine the response I'd get if I ever tried such a muster.

Early the next morning we flew to the Marine base at Camp Lejeune. Before we started our tour I made a point of assuring Akhromeyev that he was free to talk to anybody at any time, and that he could ask whatever he wanted. That must have struck him as something I said for effect, not really to be believed, because at the first unit we visited he saw a Marine and asked if he could talk to him. "Marshal," I said, "you don't have to ask me, you can talk to anyone you like."

The first Marine he actually addressed was an extremely young-looking one. "Son," he said, "who are you?" The Marine told him his name and rank. "Do you know who I am?" Akhromeyev asked. "Yes sir," said the Marine, "I do." "Do you know why I'm here?" "No sir," said the Marine, "but I think it's a real good idea that you are." That kid was eighteen years old. Akhromeyev thought it was a wonderful answer and he quoted it in his speeches throughout the rest of the trip.

At noon we boarded an aircraft to go out to the U.S.S. *Theodore Roosevelt,* the Navy's newest nuclear carrier. The plane was cramped, and it seemed to me that the Russians were a bit apprehensive; they knew we were going to make a wire-arrested landing on the ship. It would be a first for all of them. The co-pilot was a female lieutenant, and when the Russian Air Force vice chief refused to fasten his safety belt, she came back and announced in an authoritative tone that we weren't going to move until he had strapped himself in. That was the first indication Akhromeyev had that there was a problem. He turned around and said abruptly, "Fasten your damned belt!" The problem was solved instantly. The Russian general had flown for decades and apparently never fastened his belt. He was not gracious about it, nor about much else on the trip either. All of the Soviet officers were a little standoffish at first, but as the days passed they began to loosen up. This led to a constant exchange of stories and jokes, and by the end the Army and Navy vice chiefs and the Marine commander had become almost comfortable and very friendly. But the Air Force general never did.

The Russians had watched a firepower demonstration by the Marines at Lejeune and had been suitably impressed, but the demonstration at sea was unlike anything in the Soviet repertoire. I received some criticism for taking Akhromeyev and the others out to the *Teddy Roosevelt,* one of the truly powerful weapons systems in the American arsenal. You're showing that guy all our stuff! was the way several appalled naval officers put it. But what secrets was he actually going to see out there? I thought. Not many. Mainly he would see what I thought he should see.

First the captain took him through the carrier, then we all went down onto the flight deck, right alongside the planes that were taking off and coming aboard. Our party then stepped aside to let the Russians experience this themselves, without any American kibitzing. As they watched they were chattering up a storm. Clearly this graphic demonstration of technical and flying skill knocked their socks off. Catapulting planes off and recovering them on an arresting wire every sixty seconds is an impressive sight. There are few military operations that take the split-second timing and skill of a flight-deck crew. The entire air wing took off, then flew by and dropped ordnance of every kind on targets less than a mile from the carrier: live ammunition, live bombs, live missiles. While the Russians enjoyed that, like everybody else, what impressed them most was watching the landings, seeing those aircraft come in at 140 knots, then hit the wire and stop dead within 200 feet. It is a remarkable and unforgettable sight.

If anything, that visit was too successful; I never heard the last of it. Every time Akhromeyev and I would get into an argument over carriers he'd say, Don't tell me they're not devastating. I've seen them. I know what they can do, and they represent a genuine threat to my country. In a sense we confirmed all his worst fears. But that was not all bad. The fact was that I wanted to impress the hell out of him. I wanted him to see American technology at its best and get a gut feeling for what our capabilities were and what our people could do.

When we flew back from the *Teddy Roosevelt* to the Norfolk Naval Base, the two pilots asked if they might have a picture taken with Marshal Akhromeyev. He was very gracious about it, and when it was done they turned to him and saluted. Akhromeyev returned the male pilot's salute, but seemed unsure what would be the proper protocol with the female officer. Finally he took her hand in both of his and kissed it. He may never have saluted a woman before. From the look on her face she wasn't much more used to having her hand kissed, certainly not by a Soviet marshal.

The following morning on our flight to Fort Hood, Texas, Akhromeyev and I started talking seriously, establishing the format for discussions we would use during the remainder of the trip. With most of our time on the ground closely scheduled (both on Akhromeyev's visit to the U.S. and my subsequent trip to the Soviet Union), the long plane rides gave us our best opportunity to get to know one another and to take up a wide variety of subjects and issues. Sitting opposite each other with our interpreters, we had the time and privacy for exchanges that eventually gave both of us a better perspective on the U.S.-Soviet relationship and where both sides were coming from as we made our way past the rocks and shoals of the Cold War.

Somewhat to my surprise, Akhromeyev had carefully prepared all his talking points on a big tablet he pulled out shortly after we took off. "I don't want to do anything on this flight but talk," he said, "and I want to assure you that everything you tell me, General Secretary Gorbachev will hear." What Akhromeyev was primarily interested in discussing was his view of the process that was going on between the United States and the Soviet Union. He had come prepared to convince me that the Soviet military was not the threatening offensive machine we considered it to be, and to explain why the Soviet security establishment so firmly believed the United States was a genuine threat to his homeland.

The relationship between our countries—how it was reflected in our respective military postures and what sorts of changes might be mutually advantageous—was on my agenda as well. But I felt strongly that this visit was also my great opportunity to help Akhromeyev become aware of elements in American culture and American psychology that constituted the deep background against which a more understanding approach to our nations' geopolitical concerns might be achieved. On that flight and subsequent flights, I found myself talking at length about American history. As the countryside spread out below us, I told him about the wagon trains and their political organization as traveling communities and about the "articles" they wrote and adopted for governing themselves. I described for him how so many of the western cities were founded and about the "boosterism" that had built them up and played such a large role in peopling the land. We discussed the railroads and how our cities were built along the lines rather than the railroads being constructed to connect already flourishing cities, as they were in Europe. I explained why wagon trains didn't stop in the middle of the United States (one of the mysteries that used to bother me as a child), and what the myths of the plains were. He was a great listener; he wanted to know everything.

At Fort Hood they put on a real bang-up tank exercise for the Russians (although not as massive as the one the Russians subsequently staged for me in the Soviet Union). Akhromeyev was impressed, though not in the same way he had been by the *Teddy Roosevelt*. Tanks and artillery he was very familiar with. As we walked by a battery of guns he turned to me and said, "The laws of physics apply to both sides."

That night at the Chamber of Commerce dinner in San Antonio there was quite a bit of bantering, and Akhromeyev picked up the idea that there is a deeply ingrained competitiveness between Texas and Oklahoma. At the final toast, he said he was on his way to Oklahoma the next day, but that he would tell the Oklahomans he had left his heart in Texas. The ovation was deafening. (When I repeated this story in Oklahoma everybody had a good laugh; to them it just proved that Texans will believe anything.)

The next morning we visited the Alamo, then flew to Oklahoma City, from where we drove directly to Oklahoma University at Norman. I had explained to Akhromeyev that I wanted him to see a state university. The United States has many truly fine schools, but I thought that what made the country great was our ability to spread education so widely, and that it was the state university system that had enabled us to do that. I described the land grant system, how Oklahoma University had gotten started, and how my mother and father had graduated when it was still a very young college. I told him about the Land Run, how there had been nothing at all in Oklahoma City on April 22, 1889, and how by midnight of the first day 10,000 people were living on the spot in tents. He got a big kick out of the Run; like many people, he had a hard time imagining it.

That evening with some difficulty I talked the marshal into dressing informally. Instead of his usual suit and tie he put on a cowboy hat and a bandana. "I haven't gone out without a tie in fourteen years," he said. We had been invited to a barbecue hosted by Governor Henry Bellmon at a ranch outside Oklahoma City, and when our limousine pulled up to the front gate we were met by two rows of cowboys on horses who escorted us in. The lead rider on the right hand side was carrying an American flag, the lead on the left a Soviet flag. I didn't believe it myself, especially the Soviet flag. "Oh my God," I said to Shirley, "when people see that Russian flag they'll turn around and go home. There won't be anybody at the party." I couldn't have been more wrong. Four hundred and fifty people showed up, including many old friends I had gone to high school with but hadn't seen in years.

All through the prodigious barbecue dinner a constant stream of people came up to Akhromeyev, introduced themselves, and thanked him for being there. Through all these greetings there ran one constant theme. We appreciate, they said, efforts to improve the American-Russian relationship. On the way home he asked, "Did those people come up to me voluntarily or did you tell them to do that?" "Marshal," I said, "you're in Oklahoma. If we had told them to do that they would have gone straight home instead."

The following morning we shoved off early and flew to Ellsworth Air Force Base. There he met two women who were truly high points of the trip. Standing in front of the first F-16 we saw was Staff Sergeant Marylyn R. Bylander, a black female noncom, tall and imposing. Akhromeyev asked, "What do you do?" "I'm the crew chief for this aircraft," she said in a proud voice. "What does that mean?" asked Akhromeyev. "That means I repair this aircraft, I check this aircraft, nobody touches this aircraft unless I say so." "Well, what does the pilot say about that?" "Why don't you ask him?" she replied. "He's standing right there." Close by was a major standing quietly but with a wry grin on his face. Laughing, the marshal turned to him and said, "What about it, Major?" "My life is in her hands," came the answer. The marshal looked at me and said, "We have no women in all the Soviet military with that kind of responsibility."

Now I was sure that Ellsworth had run out their best personnel (although the CO vigorously denied it). Word had obviously preceded us that Akhromeyev especially liked to talk to female troopers, and it seemed to me that they had sandbagged him. From the jets we rode over to a missile training installation commanded by a young woman, First Lieutenant Jill Nagel. She was extraordinary. In describing what she did, her presentation was precise, articulate, and immensely knowledgeable. Competence flowed out of her every pore. He was visibly intrigued. "How many men do you have working for you?" he asked. "A hundred and forty," came the answer. "Do they do what you tell them to?" "They damned well better." "You really boss all those men?" "Yes, sir, I'm the boss. I'm the commanding officer."

Akhromeyev was warming to the exchange. "Tell me about yourself," he said. "How did you get in the Air Force?" And she told him an inspiring story. She had joined the Air Force as an enlisted person after dropping out of high school. While working as a missile technician she attended night courses and got a high school diploma. Then she went to college at night. By then she was a sergeant, but after she obtained her college degree the Air Force sent her to Officer Candidate School. Now she was taking graduate courses, right at Ellsworth. During her time in the service she had married, had two children, then divorced. Now she was raising her children and running this impressive training operation. Akhromeyev asked her a number of detailed questions about the work, and she answered each one concisely and skillfully. When we got through he turned to me and said, "You ought to promote her early." General Richard Burpee, her boss, was standing there, and I said, "Dick, did you hear that?" "I've got it," he said. That woman may be the only U.S. soldier ever promoted by a Soviet marshal.

That week seemed to fly by. Two days later we were in New York driving out to the airport to put our visitors on their plane. In the car Akhromeyev and I had a very touching conversation, though he capped it off with a remark so disturbing that it gave me shivers for a moment. "You know," he said, "I've had a wonderful visit. I've seen marvelous things and I've achieved what I wanted to achieve. But, Admiral, I still must tell you—you know, you and I have become very friendly. I think you and I can talk to each other. But I must tell you, I still believe the prospects for your country attacking mine are very high."

I was still mulling that over when we got to Kennedy and drove out to the waiting aircraft. To my astonishment, Mrs. Akhromeyev threw her arms around me and kissed me. Then she was crying and saying goodbye to Shirley. Akhromeyev and I had a very warm farewell. Then all the vice chiefs went marching up the gangway. The vice chief of the Army was quite a joker, the most pleasant one of the bunch. "Admiral," he said, "number-one place in United States—Oklahoma." Then he laughed and disappeared into the plane.

Before Akhromeyev went up himself, he repeated his invitation to me to formally visit the U.S.S.R. "Of course I'll come," I said. "I'm really looking forward to it. I'll come for ten days." Akhromeyev had only been able to stay with us a week, but ten days sounded better to me. I had never been to the Soviet Union, and I figured that maybe I'd never visit again.

So much had happened it was hard to absorb everything. It took a little while to step back and reflect on all that had taken place. My own hopes for this trip had been modest. I thought that the two of us might develop a relationship that would allow us to start talking and maybe sweep away some of the cobwebs that blinded the two sides' vision of each other. In fact that was very much our mutual theme. We wanted to have enough of a dialogue so that eventually we would feel comfortable telling each other the truth. In many ways American and Soviet vital interests clashed; we knew we could not change that. But we did think that at least we might be able to right some of the misunderstandings.

In retrospect, what really took place was that two lifetime military men who had spent their careers as antagonists had begun to grasp the profoundly different assumptions that had shaped each other's perspectives. Akhromeyev literally believed in his mind and heart that the U.S.S.R. needed to maintain a huge military primarily to prevent the United States from attacking. NATO he also regarded as an offensive threat. When I described it as a defensive alliance, his response was vehement. "Nonsense," he said. "I know a defensive alliance when I see one, and a defensive alliance doesn't gather forces on my border. That's what they told us about Germany in 1941, that it was a defensive deployment. They were doing it for defensive purposes. The next thing I knew they were marching through Minsk and surrounding Leningrad. There isn't anything at all defensive about NATO." As far as he was concerned, NATO had never been defensive, and it was propaganda to maintain otherwise. In his view the buildup of the Soviet military had been solely a response to NATO's aggressive posture.

Although some of this was clearly designed to sell the Soviet party line, I was convinced that a sizable element of it was genuine. My sense was that at bottom he was sincere in this belief. Like me, he was a product of his background—right or wrong—and he had acquired some deeply distorted views of the United States over the years. In turn, I was beginning to understand that some of my perceptions of the U.S.S.R. were not necessarily accurate either.

Akhromeyev also laid out his conception of the U.S.S.R.'s general military strategy, a very defensive one in his view, designed to do nothing but protect the Soviet Union. Some of my incredulity about this, he insisted, was due to the fact that the Soviet-American relationship had been strained for so long that pervasive misapprehensions had built up on both sides, and candor between us meant understanding thoroughly each other's underlying perceptions.

Despite our differences, I felt that Akhromeyev's basic premise about the extent of Soviet-American misunderstanding was sound. In many ways we had been for forty years two railroad trains rushing by in the night, and all that time we may in truth have posed substantially less of a threat to each other than either nation supposed. But of course that was not the same as accepting the assertion that Soviet strategy has been defensive, a notion wildly out of keeping with virtually all of the concrete evidence as well as with so much of the Kremlin's rhetoric over the years.

I told him this. I had prepared a rather elaborate review of the postwar history of the United States vis-à-vis the Soviet Union and I went through it in detail, focusing on all the events that signaled the Soviet Union's aggressive intent: Eastern Europe, Greece, Berlin, Korea, Cuba, the decades of penetration into the unstable regions of Africa, the Middle East, and Latin America, Nikita Khrushchev's banging his fist on the table at the United Nations and declaring, "We will bury you"—to which the unanimous response was Like hell you will. This was a history, I said, that we did not regard as either benign or defensive. On the contrary, the Soviet Union's policies had suggested to the average American as well as to the political and defense establishments that its antagonism toward the West was profound and relentless, and that confronting this hostility required strength.

I was as straight and hard as I knew how to be in describing basic American views and the reasoning behind them, but at the same time I made every effort to invite his own views and encourage discussion of the issues. Akhromeyev was no less straightforward. He talked at length about America's offensive orientation, and in particular about the United States Navy, whose strength seemed almost to mesmerize him. He described how the U.S. Navy had surrounded the Soviet Union with its carrier forces, how his country had been encircled since the end of World War Two. To bolster his contention he gave me a carefully prepared chart that supposedly pinpointed our global system of military facilities. The map was thick with flags—a sobering visual representation of the Soviet view of American naval deployment worldwide. The problem was that a good 60 percent of the flagged locations were not American bases at all. They were ports that our ships visited, places like Haifa and Alexandria, but they were not U.S. bases. Nevertheless, that was Akhromeyev's view of America's ability to roam the world and control the seas, all of it designed to surround the U.S.S.R. and intimidate the Kremlin. "How can you look at this map," he said, "and say that we shouldn't be building to deter and face down the Western threat? How could any thinking man?''

My overall impression was that Akhromeyev had not given the thought to naval warfare that he had to other matters. One result was that he overrated our power significantly, and he undersold the Soviets' own capabilities. But at the same time he never attempted to shade or distort the asymmetry between the two sides in tanks, artillery, and ground forces. He did, though, maintain that the West greatly exaggerated the readiness of Soviet ground forces, and my impression was that this argument had substantial truth to it. The U.S.S.R. always had a conscript army, and consequently faced severe problems of constantly changing manpower. More important, while Soviet units in Eastern Europe were at full strength, only three of the 115 divisions they maintained inside the Soviet Union were, and those three were research divisions that field-tested new equipment. Many of the divisions in the Soviet Army were cadre units, and some were little more than shells. The Red Army's ability to attack westward from a standing start, Akhromeyev stressed, had been widely misconstrued. They would have had to mobilize their Army, and that was a much longer, more laborious and difficult process than Western analysts made it out to be.

Akhromeyev was himself truly a man of the Second World War. It was the great experience of his life, and he alluded to it constantly. On the outskirts of Moscow is a small monument made of tank traps that shows the high water mark of the German invasion. He told me that he drove by that monument every day to work, and each time he thought of Hitler's tanks in Moscow. Not a day in his life had passed that he hadn't thought about it. I understood that very well. When I was living in Pearl Harbor as CINCPAC I had a house right on the water, and each morning when I came out of my front door to go to work I pictured those Japanese planes flying down the lochs and dropping their torpedoes.

Despite strong disagreements between us on a number of specific issues, Akhromeyev's view of the overall direction of arms control was quite positive. As he described it, the Soviet Union under Gorbachev had concluded that the assertive foreign policy of the previous decades had been counterproductive. On balance it had led to more alienation for the U.S.S.R. than alliances, more enemies than friends. Gorbachev, he said, had made a fundamental decision to change the direction of Soviet foreign policy; that was the single most significant message he wanted to convey to me. Among other things, Akhromeyev said, the U.S.S.R. would be making unilateral reductions of land forces as evidence of good faith, on both their southern and eastern borders. That was the way they were going to play the game; they wanted the United States government to know it and they wanted the U.S. military to know it.

We were quite interested in those unilateral reductions, although most people to whom I reported his statement did not find it credible. When you start upsetting long and deeply held beliefs, skepticism runs high. The first time Colin Powell was in on a debriefing his reaction was "I don't believe it. You can't take a guy like that at his word. It's just not Russian." And Colin was right. Akhromeyev was, I think, not at all typical of the Soviet military. He was an aberration, one of those rare people, like Gorbachev himself, who had the courage to break through at least some of the confines of his dogma.

My visit to the Soviet Union was scheduled for June 1989. During that year talks on military-to-military contacts proceeded without a hitch, as did negotiations on reducing dangerous activities. In November 1988 Akhromeyev retired. His retirement was announced right after Gorbachev promulgated the unilateral troop reductions; and it was widely interpreted in Washington as Akhromeyev's objection to those reductions. But he assured me by letter that this was not so, and the fact that shortly afterwards he was appointed special assistant to Gorbachev ended the rumors.

Before I left for Moscow I got a message from Akhromeyev saying that he would be on a state visit in Germany with Gorbachev when I arrived, but that he would join my party just as soon as he returned. I would be met by my official host for the visit, General Mikhail Moiseyev, who had replaced Akhromeyev as Chief of the General Staff. As Akhromeyev had done, I took the vice chiefs of the four services along with me. They seemed a little reluctant to go, but I sort of sent out a press gang which brought them aboard. Afterwards I think to the man they were glad they had been shanghaied. It was their first look at the U.S.S.R. As it turned out, it was also a final opportunity to observe the military machine of the Soviet Empire in the last flush of its great power.

That first day I called on Defense Minister Dmitri Yazov, and Alexander Bessmertnykh, the deputy foreign minister.* At Moise-

---

* Bessmertnykh later was named ambassador to Washington and subsequently Foreign Minister. He was replaced after the August 2, 1991, coup attempt.

yev's office we signed the Dangerous Military Activities Agreement, which we had now concluded. We also signed a military-to-military contacts agreement, formalizing the arrangements that had been worked out. In practical terms, these documents established procedures for military communication between Soviet and American forces when they were operating in each other's vicinity. They covered such topics as inadvertent violations of territory, jamming, and lasing each other's units. The broader significance was that we were stepping back from confrontation. An important psychological shift had taken place, a willingness to entertain the thought that perhaps our traditional enmity could be softened.

From Moscow our party flew to Murmansk, and from there to Minsk, where Akhromeyev joined me, having just returned from his trip to Germany. I was interested in what it would be like when we saw each other again; I thought it would be a defining moment of sorts. I had not seen him for a year, and while we had an intense week together in the United States, I did not know how our friendship had weathered the time. I needn't have wondered. When Akhromeyev arrived he walked up, threw his arms around me, and kissed me on both cheeks, in the Russian fashion. I wasn't quite ready for that, and the rest of my party was more or less shocked. It was a clear signal that he felt himself a friend—as opposed to Moiseyev, whom I had just met. (Moiseyev was also an easy person to get to know, though much more bluff and defensive than Akhromeyev.) From that point Akhromeyev took over as host and Moiseyev returned to Moscow. My impression was that while the two of them got along well enough, there was also some concealed resentment. In any event, they preferred not to share the limelight.

The military stops on the tour were fascinating—the Northern Fleet, the rocket command headquarters (where we had the unnerving experience of watching them run through a launch exercise with missiles we knew were targeted on the United States), a giant armor exercise outside of Minsk in which enemy forces were represented by real radio-controlled tanks which were all destroyed in the course of the day.

Minsk was the last military stop on my tour. But I also had asked to visit Stalingrad. There Akhromeyev took me first to the war museum. Our guide, an Intourist woman in her late thirties, hadn't been alive during the war and did not have an intimate feeling for the battle. But she knew what she had been taught, and she was quite militant about it. "This," she would say, pointing to a display, "is where our brave troops stopped the fascists, and this is where the courageous Red Army threw back the Hitlerian dogs and crushed them.'' That was the nature of her monologue throughout the tour— the heroic defenders of the fatherland on one side and the cowardly fascist dogs on the other.

Akhromeyev was walking next to me through all this, and though he had fought in the battle he never said a word. When we left the museum and were in the car I mentioned how pleased I was to have seen the displays; they conveyed a good idea of what a watershed struggle it had been in world history and how fierce the fighting must have been. Akhromeyev laughed. ''That guide spoke a lot about Russian bravery,'' he said. ''But let me tell you who was really brave in that battle. We trapped 360,000 Germans there. To do it we brought in twenty-two divisions. We surrounded them and we fought for five months. They didn't surrender until they were out of food, out of blankets, out of fuel, and out of bullets. And when they finally did give up there were only 90,000 of them left. They were utterly tenacious.'' This about people he had profoundly detested. When the war was over, he said, he harbored a searing hatred of Germans. It had taken him decades, Akhromeyev said, to get over his anger at the Germans, and I wasn't totally persuaded he had yet shed it. ''The damage they wrought on my country,'' he told me, ''and the cruelty they inflicted, was such that you had no choice but to hate them.''

The picture Akhromeyev painted of Russian fear and loathing seemed to me quite real, not a propaganda picture at all, but an ingrained part of his psyche. He himself was born in 1923, and the staggering fact is that 80 percent of the men born in the Soviet Union in 1923 lost their lives in World War Two. ''I went to high school with thirty-two other boys,'' he told me, ''and from my class only two survived the war, myself and one other.'' That 1923 age group was called up to a man. They were eighteen years old when the Germans attacked, and they were utterly decimated. Their death rate was far worse than equivalent classes of British and French in World War One—though not a lot worse than the Germans' own figures for World War Two. The Russians may have lost 25 to 30 million people during the Second World War (the official figure is 20 million, but that is probably low), but the Germans also lost about 20 million, out of a far smaller population.

In many respects the Soviet Union was still living in World War Two. For almost everyone who experienced it, the war was in one way or another the formative event of their lives. But another reason the national memory of that cataclysm was so assiduously kept alive is that winning the war was the only major achievement of the communist party. Under communism the Soviet Union experienced an endless trail of moral and economic disasters. But it did win the war. That is the main reason the regime never let it die, but instead made such tremendous capital out of it. World War Two was the single bonding experience between the party and the people.

In Stalingrad I laid a wreath at one of the lesser monuments in the center of town. As Akhromeyev and I walked down from the little podium toward our car, an older woman, her head covered by a black babushka, suddenly darted out of the crowd. When she got close she started shouting at me in Russian. The interpreter turned to me and said, "She was obviously alive during the battle and she is asking you if there's going to be war." (I was wearing my uniform and was likely the only American military man she had ever seen.) I was nonplussed for a moment. By now she was right in front of me, still talking excitedly, agitated and in tears. Akhromeyev was taken aback too, but he was gentle with her and didn't tell her to go away or even to keep quiet. "No," I told her, "I don't believe there's going to be war. The United States wants peace, that's one of the reasons I'm here." When she heard that she started weeping. "The people of Stalingrad don't want another war," she managed to blurt out. They had seen what war could do, and they didn't want it. She wanted the Americans to know, she hoped they would understand.

Later the press speculated that the woman may have been a plant of some kind to get my sympathy. One or two reporters even wrote about how I had been taken in by this old woman in Stalingrad. At a press conference back in the States someone asked me how I could be fooled by something so transparent. I told him I didn't think I was fooled. I thought that woman was sincere. "And I'll tell you," I said, "that very same thing happened many times to Marshal Akhromeyev in America. People came up to tell him how much they wanted peace, and the CIA didn't put them up to it." One aspect of the relationship between ourselves and the Soviets that had already deeply impressed me during Akhromeyev's visit was how quickly Americans' hostility toward the Russians had dissipated, despite all the decades of antagonism.

I came away from Moscow convinced that the converse was also true. That was high among my thoughts as the Air Force 707 flew westward toward Washington at the end of the ten days. Something else that stayed with me was a remark Akhromeyev had made while we were at the military's vacation resort on the Black Sea. A year earlier he had stunned me with his opinion that he felt the probability was still high that my country would attack his. He had revised his thinking about that, he said; he had come to believe that the chance of a major war between our nations was now the lowest it had been in his lifetime. The past year had also clearly turned his thoughts inward. This ebullient man seemed to have become less confident and more reflective. "Isn't it depressing," he said, "to conclude that what you've worked and fought for for fifty years is wrong." Then, after a pause, "And even more depressing to find out at my age that you have to start all over."

After I retired in October 1989, Akhromeyev and I kept in touch. I saw him when he came to the United States to testify in front of the House Armed Services Committee and I accompanied him on visits to a number of cities. After that we tried to arrange other meetings, but our schedules never seemed to coincide. Finally he wrote me a letter and said, "Why don't you just come to the Soviet Union as my guest. You can testify in front of the Supreme Soviet, then we'll have a chance to visit some places you didn't get to last time."

I left for Moscow on March 16, 1990, this time accompanied by a small group of civilian foreign policy specialists. The first order of business was to speak to the Defense Committee of the Supreme Soviet in the Kremlin. I had visited this center of Soviet government on my first trip, and I found it equally striking this time around. Inevitably the majesty of the Kremlin intimidates an outsider. This complex of buildings was originally a fortress, and the visitor has the impression that all the ghosts of Russia's bloody history are lurking in the shadows.

Akhromeyev was still working very hard as Gorbachev's special assistant, and I thought that after my testimony he would probably send me around the country and that I would not see that much of him. But instead he came with me and we spent the next seven days together. From Moscow we flew to Novosibirsk, Kiev, Odessa, then back to Moscow, a tour of a land in the throes of ferment and doubt.

Outside Kiev we visited a large collective farm that seemed to be doing quite well. The manager was a PhD in agriculture who had been running the farm for a long time, both as its chief executive and as mayor of the self-contained farming community. He was an impressive individual, and not shy about expressing himself. When we sat down to talk he started right off. "I'm going to tell you about some of our problems," he said to me, "and what we can do about them." Then he looked at Akhromeyev, "You may . . ." and he cocked his finger against his temple. Akhromeyev said sharply, "We don't shoot people anymore!" "Well," said the manager, "whether you do or not, I'm going to say this. If I had International Harvester or John Deere tractors our efficiency would go up by a factor of ten. It's not that they do things our tractors can't, but they don't break down. We spend half our time repairing tractors." From there the discussion focused on the private ownership of land, the manager arguing strongly for it. "If my people owned this land," he said, "we'd produce many times what we do now." Akhromeyev took vigorous exception to that, and a huge argument started between the two of them about private ownership.

Few of our subsequent meetings gave Akhromeyev more comfort. We met with Valentina Shevchenko, the chairwoman of the Ukrainian Supreme Soviet. She had decided not to run in the recent elections and was scheduled to leave office three days later. She had spent her whole life in the communist party and now all these other parties and groups were emerging and taking power. One of her chief complaints was that the quota system for women that had been established by the party was failing. Under communism, 25 percent of all officials were women. But now they had held free elections and only 1½ percent women had been voted in. Women simply had not filed for office, she said. They did not want to run. "I'm worried that women won't run," she said, "and that if they do, no one will vote for them." She did not seem overly bitter that her own career was ending, although she was still relatively young. Instead she appeared resigned and philosophical. The communists had been defeated. Now, she joked, it had become fashionable to camouflage any communistic leanings a person might ever have had.

From Kiev we flew to Odessa, where I visited the 26th Motorized Rifle Division. We ate lunch with the officers, and afterwards I gave my standard short speech in which I described the cutbacks the U.S. had already made and our plans for far deeper cuts. Hearing this always upset Akhromeyev, who maintained that, on the contrary, we were spending as much as we had been and that while we wanted the U.S.S.R. to cut back, we ourselves had no intention of doing so. When we opened the floor to questions, the senior officers asked (as they always did at that period) about Germany, whether Germany would be unified and whether the former East Germany would join NATO. Then one young lieutenant said, "I don't understand why we just can't do away with NATO and the Warsaw Pact both. What would be wrong with that?" I said, "Well, the idea has a lot of appeal to it, but it's my understanding that the Warsaw Pact has already disappeared." Whereupon Akhromeyev erupted. "That's not true, that's not true." One of the Russian speakers in my party, Steve Sestanovich of CSIS, was sitting at the other end of the table and heard one officer say, "No, there's still a Warsaw Pact, but we're the only member."

Back in Moscow I met with the editor of *Izvestia* and watched while he and Akhromeyev got into a vociferous debate about freedom of the press. The editor was outdoing Ben Bradlee on the subject, while Akhromeyev sounded like an old time Brezhnev-style communist, though on reflection it seemed to me that his tone was less Stalinist than it was that of an English aristocrat of the late 1800s arguing against liberalization.

Then I called on a large peace organization which had a subcommittee made up of retired military officers. These retirees had asked to see me, and though I did not think Akhromeyev would come to that meeting, he did not flinch. When he surveyed the crowd (everyone in civilian clothes), he said, "My God, this room is full of admirals." At their request I also met with a group of Afghan war veterans, who asked for American help in persuading their own government to take a concerned approach toward the Soviet prisoners of war still in the hands of the Afghani mujahedeen. They believed that the mujahedeen were still holding two to three hundred Soviet prisoners out of an original thousand (they had allegedly killed the rest). Apparently the Soviet government was not doing anything about those who were still alive. It was an odd request, to say the least, asking an American to encourage the U.S. government to influence the Kremlin to take a deeper interest in its own prisoners of war—another sign, I thought, of how truly paralyzed the Soviet leadership had become.

All through this trip, Akhromeyev and I talked in the airplane, as had become our habit. He was in a bad mood, edgy and irritable (as he had demonstrated in so many of the meetings we had attended), to such a degree that I was surprised he had chosen to spend so much time with me. One afternoon we even got into a furious argument and did not speak to each other for a couple of hours. I had been trying to talk to him about arms control and he did not want to discuss it. When I suggested certain directions I thought the Soviets should be moving, he told me he didn't take orders from Americans.

What was clear was that he was profoundly disturbed about the way things were going in the Soviet Union.

There was a great deal, he said, that was wrong with his society. He and I had already talked at length about that, so I knew how he felt. When Gorbachev came along and wanted to liberalize the country, he, Akhromeyev, had seen it as a great opportunity. In a sense what he wanted was a gentler, kinder Soviet Union. Gorbachev was doing that; at least he thought Gorbachev was the right man to make the effort. He was younger. He was energetic and bright. He did not have the Stalinist baggage. In Akhromeyev's view he had the right idea about liberalization. But Akhromeyev had had no concept of how far it was going to go. And now he thought that Gorbachev had not had an idea either. "In retrospect," Akhromeyev said, "Gorbachev had no vision of where he was heading. Very shortly after it started we were improvising. We were traveling with the times, with no game plan, just trying to keep it stuck together—one problem at a time.

"I wanted a lot of these abuses to go away," he said. "But I didn't want the communist party to disappear. My God, you didn't kill the communist party. NATO didn't kill the communist party." He was alive with frustration. "We killed it ourselves! We killed it! My heart broke a thousand times a day when we were doing that. And now it's gone. It's just gone."

He had not had that in mind when he signed onto Gorbachev's reforms. Nor was he enchanted with the disappearance of the Warsaw Pact. "That just shouldn't happen," he said. "This country has been through too much. We've paid with too much blood to protect ourselves. But there it went. And all these republics that want autonomy! We can't permit that. We'll fight over that. [This was in the spring of 1990.] We're not going to let them go. The idea that we have no claims on those countries is just wrong. We can't live with that, at least I can't."

He was equally upset at the way the American-Soviet relationship was evolving. "I had in mind a moderated relationship between our two countries. Fifty-fifty. You give, we give. And it hasn't been fifty-fifty at all. It's been ninety-ten. Everything you want has transpired. You wanted the Warsaw Pact to disappear; it's gone away. You wanted Estonia and the others to get their independence; they're trying like hell and the world's supporting them. You wanted free market economics; we're trying it. You wanted Germany to join NATO; it looks like they're going to. That isn't fifty-fifty." And he blamed us bitterly. He did not blame Soviet policies for producing a situation that could not go any other way. He did not think it was inevitable. He believed that these developments were at least in part due to the manipulation and maneuvering of the United States government.

Throughout the visit Akhromeyev seemed bitter and disillusioned. He did not look good and was obviously not sleeping well. Clearly he was depressed, perhaps, I thought, in a serious depression. He seemed down on everything and caught in the throes of a thoroughgoing pessimism, an attitude that was totally foreign to him by nature. His was not a Kismet psychology. "All my life we've done something about problems," he said. "But these problems we are doing nothing about."

On March 25 we parted amicably and I flew back to Washington. When I returned I briefed National Security Adviser Brent Scowcroft and Dick Cheney on my trip. The conversations between Akhromeyev and myself were, I knew, far more candid than what ordinarily passed between American officials and their counterparts. And Akhromeyev was important. He was a member of that moderate group that had gone along with Gorbachev but was becoming disillusioned. And since he was so high in the leadership of the Army, it seemed to others as well as myself that the tendencies of his thinking might have some more general significance.

Subsequently I received several letters from Akhromeyev. Then he came to the U.S. again with Gorbachev for the last stages of START. At first I did not get to see him, though we talked often by phone. But one day his interpreter Popov came over to my new offices at the Center for Strategic and International Studies. The marshal, he said, was upset about how things were going at home. He was very worried about nursing his connections with the military back to health, that he had damaged them when he threw in his lot with Gorbachev. Many military people apparently felt they had been let down by Akhromeyev. He had spoken throughout the military on Gorbachev's behalf, and when much of what he had promised did not materialize, his fellow officers had blamed the marshal.

Then one day Akhromeyev sent a message that he would have an hour free before business started the next morning. Could I come over to the Madison Hotel at seven. We hugged when we met. Or he did. I had never learned how to do that. He was very friendly for those few minutes and seemed in a good mood. START was going well. He was sure it was going to come to pass and he was quite pleased with that achievement. Before he left, I asked, "Are you going to stay with Gorbachev?" "Well," he said, "I really don't have much choice." Then he added, "But I don't support any man unconditionally." That was the last time I saw him.

After he returned to Moscow I received a letter from him. It did not sound good. Conditions in his country, he said, were rapidly deteriorating. His own state of mind did not sound healthy.

My last contact was through Debbie Garretson, the Dartmouth professor who had been Shirley's translator. She was in Moscow and saw Akhromeyev just a few days before he committed suicide. She thought he had seemed extremely sad. He said to her, "My daughter doesn't understand me. She thinks I'm all wrong. She thinks I ought to shut up and get out of the way. I'm outdated. Even my own family doesn't agree with me." Then the day before his death I was told that while he was walking down the street a crowd threw things at him and somebody spit on him. He had been wearing his marshal's uniform.

I do not know if Sergei Akhromeyev was one of the anti-Gorbachev conspirators. After the coup Sam Nunn called me. He had just come back from Moscow and had talked to several people in the Ministry of Defense, all of whom told him that Akhromeyev had had nothing to do with it. But there was disagreement; a number of Akhromeyev's detractors, including Georgi Arbatov, insisted he was involved. The military attaché in the Washington embassy told me he had had nothing to do with it, as did the embassy's KGB officer. Whether they knew or not, or whether they were covering up or not, I had no idea. But I knew that Akhromeyev was in such poor emotional shape that in a sense it was irrelevant.

I was still stunned by his death. I did not really think he would commit suicide. On the other hand, when I began to think about it I was not too surprised. The basic problem was that Akhromeyev could never bring himself to the conclusion that most of the bad things that were happening so quickly in his last year were the fault of the system, the fault of communism itself. This required one intellectual leap too many. He had an open mind in certain respects. He wanted conditions to improve, but he could not get over the last hurdle and say, We have done this to ourselves. He could not bring himself to admit that their troubles were due to a system that just would not work. Like Gorbachev, he remained a communist. He believed in common ownership of industry, resources, and land. And he believed in dedication to the state. He thought that if everyone was as loyal to the state as he was and worked as hard as he worked, then the world would be wonderful. He took great pride in being a military monk. He told me on my last visit that he had 7,000 rubles in the bank. That was all he had to his name. Beyond that he owned nothing.

But he could not make that last intellectual transition. He was too old, in the final analysis, too frozen. He had a fine mind, an agile mind, far ahead of most of his contemporaries. He was by degrees more flexible than the average general officer of the Soviet Union, far more objective and far more patient. I liked him for that. I admired him. He was a significant figure in creating the breakthrough that ended the Cold War. But like Gorbachev himself, he never had in mind the final denouement.

Chapter 17

DEFENSE AND THE ADMINISTRATION

IN DEALING WITH THE SOVIETS some sparks of friction had flashed between myself and the State Department. A more serious contention lurked in the relationship between the Chairman's office and that of the National Security Adviser. Here the problem was institutional.

Even before the Iran-Contra affair, I knew that National Security Adviser Vice Admiral John Poindexter occasionally substituted his military judgment for that of the chiefs. Not that such a thing was unusual for a military man serving as the security adviser. When issues with a military dimension were discussed in closed White House councils, the President of course asked questions. If the adviser was an admiral or general, the President would naturally feel that he had received a competent military opinion. The possibilities for conflict between the JCS Chairman (by law, the President's senior military adviser) and the National Security Adviser were high. There was always the chance too that with a military man as security adviser, the President might be tempted to use the National Security Council to circumvent the normal Defense Department channels, avoiding the check on action the standard procedures provided. That, I thought, held a significant potential for danger.

But although I had long opposed the practice of appointing active-duty military professionals to the council's top slots, early in my tenure I was not prepared to bring the problem to a head. It was not until after the 1986 arms talks at Reykjavik (on which the chiefs had not been consulted) that I girded my loins to do battle. The summit wonderfully sharpened my views about the issue, and I resolved that I would no longer passively accept the situation. But I had no more made the resolution when the unfolding Iran-Contra affair plunged John Poindexter into deep trouble.

Iran-Contra vividly illustrated what could happen when the National Security Council attempted to carry out military related policy in secret. The Joint Chiefs of Staff were bypassed completely in both formulation and implementation, as was the Secretary of Defense. Eventually, of course, Caspar Weinberger did find out what was going on. As careful as Oliver North tried to be, he had to involve others in the scheme, among whom were the security assistance specialists responsible for delivering arms to other nations. The security assistance is in the domain of the Secretary of Defense, and ultimately Weinberger learned about the sales of additional equipment to Israel. When he discovered that this assistance was part of an attempt to exchange arms for hostages, Weinberger immediately saw President Reagan and registered his objections in the strongest terms. But he did not inform me. When the news began coming out later on, I was livid. I felt that on such a delicate issue as arms transfers the chiefs should have been informed. When I vented my feelings, Weinberger just shrugged his shoulders in resignation. "Bill," he said, "I was against it. But the decision had been made and the President wasn't going to change his mind. I saw no point in bringing you in."

While I raised a little hell about it, the Iran-Contra machinations did not surprise me. If people in the White House want to do something improper and hold it close, they can do it—particularly when the impetus comes from the President. There will always be an Ollie North to carry out what he believes the President is asking, legal or not. Some restraint, of course, is stimulated by the threat of media discovery and adverse publicity. A media blow-up, even of far lesser magnitude than Iran-Contra, does considerable political damage. It also tends to have a cleansing aftereffect. Among the consequences of the Iran-contra affair was that a new security adviser came in who announced that from now on business would be done differently. Frank Carlucci replaced Poindexter and made it clear that although bringing issues to the National Security Planning Group might be clumsy or inefficient at times, that was the procedure they were going to follow. The NSC was not going to substitute its judgment for the Pentagon's. That's what Carlucci said, and (to my vast relief and gratitude) that was what he practiced.

Among other things, the ease with which the Iran-Contra conspirators circumvented the JCS points up the tenuousness of the Chairman's policy role. He may be the nation's top military officer, but his authority is largely undefined. Technically, the Chairman is not even part of the military chain of command. His influence depends principally on the relationships he can forge with those he advises and his effectiveness as a contender in the occasionally bloody jousting among Defense, State, and the White House.

My own initiation into this truth began the moment I walked into the Chairman's office. Prominent among the subjects that provided the introduction was SDI, popularly known as "Star Wars."

President Reagan was wedded to the Strategic Defense Initiative, stirred by a sincere horror of nuclear war and a dream that American technology could make the prospect vanish. But the concept had quickly fallen prey to ideology, and by 1985, when I became Chairman, the antagonists were deeply dug in. On one side were the conservatives, in particular a group of Republican senators including Dan Quayle, Malcolm Wallop, Pete Wilson, and Warren Rudman. Among their strongest allies in the administration were Secretary Weinberger, Assistant Secretary Richard Perle, and Director of Arms Control Kenneth Adelman. On the other side stood the liberals, prominent among whom were Senators Ted Kennedy, Alan Cranston, and Brock Adams.

The conservatives were enamored of SDI. They had always detested the idea that the United States could do nothing to actively defend itself against the Soviet nuclear threat. Deterrence had worked for years, but in their minds deterrence was a fragile defense, relying as it did on Soviet notions of mutual preservation. As the conservatives saw it, any approach that depended on communist restraint was flawed in its heart. The Strategic Defense Initiative offered hope that by building a space-based anti-missile shield, American creativity and resources could eliminate the need to trust either Soviet psychology or Russian signatures on arms limitation treaties. In fact, a working SDI could render the whole subject of arms control moot—a goal held dear by some in the Reagan administration. The conservatives did not always put it that way in public, but those were their sentiments. The public argument they preferred was that SDI offered a non-nuclear defense against nuclear weapons. The proponents were against nukes; in this matter at least they were on the side of the angels, interested in protecting American citizens rather than avenging them. As SDI's scientific godfather Dr. Edward Teller once put it, "I'd rather shoot missiles than shoot people." When it became fully operational, SDI, they maintained, could well lead to the elimination of the (now rendered obsolete) intercontinental ballistic missile.

SDI's opponents were convinced the opposite was true. They be-

lieved that an anti-missile defense would fuel a proliferation of nuclear weapons. The Soviets, they argued, would try to counter SDI
by deploying more missiles than the system could handle. And in
fact, this was exactly what Soviet Chief of Staff Sergei Akhromeyev
told me they would do. "We can't match you on SDI," he said when
we discussed the subject. "But we'll do something we do know how
to do. If you build SDI, we'll build more missiles. We'll overwhelm
it." Between the Soviets increasing their offensive capacity and the
United States thickening its defensive shield, the liberals foresaw an
arms race on a larger scale than ever before. The already massively
inflated number of nuclear arms would spiral upwards. Far better to
accept the Soviets as negotiating partners and rely on the admittedly
slow and unsure progress of arms limitation compromises.

But the liberals too did not always choose to articulate their inner
feelings. Instead they poured abuse on the concept. SDI was "Star
Wars," a preposterous fantasy with no scientific validity. It would
squander vast sums of money to prove nothing more than that the
proponents didn't know what they were talking about. Technologically, they argued, we were nowhere near being able to say that such
a futuristic scheme even might work.

There was a good deal of scientific testimony backing the opponents' charges. But the SDI men were determined to get the nation
committed—not only committed to the idea but committed to what
type of system we would ultimately have and committed to the
money involved. They were afraid that if we took the time to do
extensive preliminary research, people would lose interest. SDI
might become (like a lot of other Washington ideas) a shooting star
that burned brightly, then evaporated in the night. In doing the research we might even discover that a space-based missile defense
was not technically feasible. And they did not want that to happen;
the political and military stakes were far too high. They argued that
with America's five-trillion-dollar economy and unmatched technological resources, what the government needed at this juncture was
vision and faith.

Most of the political advocates had little understanding of the technology SDI would require. But they believed they knew a good idea
when they saw one, and acquiring the ability to eliminate a Soviet
first strike seemed like a capital objective. Moreover, endowing the
country with a non-nuclear defense would give the Republicans a
political achievement of great and lasting power (a truth which also
stimulated SDI's Democratic opponents considerably).

But there were also a lot of people in the middle on SDI, and I was one of them. So was General Robert Herres, the JCS vice chairman. Herres had come to the JCS from the U.S. Space Command, and he was well versed in the relevant technologies. As a space and electronics enthusiast, he might have been expected to be a vigorous SDI supporter. But in fact his feelings and mine on this subject were virtually identical. Neither of us was opposed to SDI, but we did think we should have more information before we went riding off into the space age sunset. In our opinion, SDI was not a cut-and-dried issue that had already been decided.

This put us in an uncomfortable position vis-à-vis Caspar Weinberger, who did not consider SDI as a program in question. As far as the Secretary was concerned, President Reagan had made a decision to go ahead with it; the only job left was to figure out how. But Weinberger did not have any more of a grip on the technology than did the other political advocates. And though the state of anti-missile art had advanced substantially since the early 1970s (when the Army's Safeguard program was scrapped), the problems to be solved before a workable SDI could be deployed were daunting.

The basic concept of SDI was that space-based interceptors could be used to attack ballistic missiles shortly after they were launched, that is, before they entered the stratosphere and deployed their nuclear-tipped multiple independently targeted re-entry vehicles (MIRVs). To do this, the interceptors (powerful lasers were favored at first) would have to hit their ballistic missile targets within five or six minutes from the time of launch. Destroying one booster rocket would neutralize ten or twelve re-entry vehicles. (The Soviet SS-18 could technically carry as many as twenty MIRVs.) Once the MIRVs were released in space, the problem assumed a different magnitude. At that point the only time to attack them would be when they re-entered the atmosphere and came down toward their targets, which didn't take long, since by then they would be moving at hypersonic speed, Mach 20 or 25.

Given only a five- or six-minute leeway, detection, identification, targeting, and interception constituted a very tight loop. And each of these functions required a significant stretch in the available technology. Then there was the problem of the interception mechanism. Very powerful lasers, for example, required huge power plants to drive them. Other options, "kinetic kill" vehicles, for example (called "smart rocks" by initiates), had their own difficulties. Whatever interceptors were used, they would have to be able to hit very fast moving targets under all conditions and simultaneously cope with a variety of deceptions and countermeasures. Because they might not be orbiting over the right location when a Soviet strike was launched, there would have to be enough of them up there to cover all the threatening missile fields at all times. That led to the calculation of four to six thousand interceptors in orbit, which, of course, would have to be regularly replenished.

The science required was formidable. So was the expense. SDI advocates estimated the cost at somewhere in the neighborhood of $80 to $100 billion over six or seven years. The JCS considered this extremely low. To really go to a full space-based SDI as we saw it in 1986 and 1987, the rough estimates (nobody could even say to what extent they might be accurate) were huge. Most of us thought we were talking about several hundred billion dollars—although, of course, these were all gross figures and depended on such factors as how large a percentage of a strategic attack the system was designed to wipe out.

Among other problems, committing the necessary funding would have seriously unbalanced the military's non-SDI programs. From my point of view, that alone was enough reason to move carefully. But the advocates did not seem to care much about the cost. I sometimes thought that the Defense Department had been spoiled by President Reagan's first term, when they had more money than they could spend.*

But I did favor SDI research. I believed we should start exploring the technologies in order to determine what might be feasible, how much it actually would cost, and how long it would take. In public I made such profound announcements as "I think we should pursue the research as vigorously as we can afford and still keep a balanced military. If we're going to spend so much money, we're going to unbalance our forces, and I don't want to do that." Privately I pushed Weinberger to bring SDI into conformity with the standard Defense Acquisition Board procedures.

---

* To put this problem in perspective, one major goal of the Air Force at that time was to build a "beyond the horizon" air-to-air missile, based on technology far less sophisticated than that required to shoot down ballistic missiles. This program had been through several iterations in an attempt to keep the cost of these "beyond the horizon" missiles below five or six hundred thousand dollars each. Planners had been back to the drawing board three or four times, and on several occasions Congress had been on the verge of cancelling the program because of potential cost overruns. So here were people who were trying to solve a far less challenging technical problem in an economical way, going carefully through all the detailed acquisition requirements, and all of a sudden they were being told how easy and affordable it would be to put SDI in space.

The Defense Acquisition Board procedures required that all new weapons under development had to pass through a series of detailed steps (known as "milestones") that forced its managers to rigorously explain and justify their work at significant stages. Before 1987 the Strategic Defense Initiative had been carried on without reference to these guidelines. SDI had such great political significance that Weinberger wanted to handle it personally with the President. As a result, the Strategic Defense Initiative Office had been established as a separate shop, distinct from all other defense activities. And SDIO reported directly to the Secretary of Defense.

In our effort to subject SDI to the regular review process, Bob Herres was the JCS spear carrier. But he spoke for a united group of chiefs. We knew that almost every weapons program that had suffered large cost overruns or fallen short of performance expectations had gotten into trouble because it had not gone through the DAB stages meticulously. All too often program advocates were eager to start building hardware prematurely. That was clearly what the SDI lobby had in mind, a prospect that seriously worried us. To the extent we were able, the chiefs meant to hold the SDI program officers' feet to the fire and demand compliance with the DAB milestones. After some fencing, we succeeded in getting a commitment from Weinberger.* In retrospect, that may have been the chiefs' most significant accomplishment on SDI.

Overlaying the differences between the chiefs and the Secretary's office was the thorny issue of the Anti-Ballistic Missile (ABM) Treaty. Signed in 1972, this treaty strictly limited the development that either the United States or the Soviet Union could put into antiballistic missiles. In particular, neither country could test or deploy any defensive missiles based on "new technology." While this phrase was amenable to different interpretations, a highly plausible case could be made that it barred SDI.

The Joint Chiefs had backed the ABM Treaty when it was negotiated and had never abandoned their support. We still did not want to get rid of ABM. We believed ABM worked to our advantage because in restricting defensive weapons it also had the effect of limiting offensive missiles. With ABM in place there was no motivation to build more ballistic missiles in order to overcome defenses, and consequently the door was opened to mutual reductions in offensive weapons. The Soviets had the capacity to turn out larger num-

---

* This was shortly before he retired. SDI actually went into the DAB process for the first time under Frank Carlucci.

bers of missiles than we could, and the chiefs saw no advantage either in giving them an incentive to do that, or in spending more of our own limited defense money on nuclear missiles in order to keep deterrence believable.

The chiefs were also in favor of START, the Strategic Arms Reduction Talks whose goal was to substantially reduce the American and Soviet strategic nuclear stockpiles. We were working hard to support this initiative, and we knew that the Soviets could not accept both an American breakout from ABM and a START treaty. If an American defensive system became a reality, the only way the Soviets could counter it was through building additional offensive weapons. A deployed SDI would mean abrogating ABM, and abrogating ABM would mean putting an end to START. They were all interwoven. Secretary Weinberger, though, had never liked the ABM Treaty himself and he knew that President Reagan did not like it either. To both men the treaty embodied a supine acceptance of America's helplessness and consequently of a reliance on the balance of terror—that is, on the idea of mutual assured destruction. It was never quite clear to me which came first—whether Weinberger's enthusiasm for SDI had been stimulated by his dislike of ABM or vice versa.

Part of Weinberger's dilemma was that George Shultz was intent on achieving a START treaty and had already persuaded President Reagan to his point of view. That made SDI a difficult problem. You could not have it both ways. Shultz assumed that if ABM were abrogated, START negotiations would come to a screeching halt. The chiefs agreed. It was utterly illogical to think that the Soviets could accept a limitation of offensive systems and also the elimination of the limits on defensive systems.

We had a number of sessions with Weinberger on the ABM issue, making it clear to him that we did not favor ABM Treaty breakout until or unless a clear military advantage would result. If at some point research gave us the possibility of deploying an effective SDI, a treaty breakout might be justified. But we were many years away from that point. Under the most optimistic conditions imaginable, we could not foresee deployment until the end of the 1990s.

All this cautiousness upset the SDI advocates considerably. Here a powerful new weapons system was being proposed and the professional military was not clasping it to its bosom, even though their civilian masters were leading the way. The chiefs were invited to lunch with the principal proponents. I was called over to see Senators Quayle, Wallop, Wilson, and Rudman on several occasions and Bob Herres received close attention as well. We were lobbied hard and frequently. We knew we were regarded as naysayers and pessimists, men with neither the imagination nor courage to move ahead into something new and bold. Although none of them had much technological understanding, they were all sure that SDI could be carried off far sooner than was possible. At times it seemed they thought of SDI as something that was sitting in a parking lot waiting to be driven off. Whenever I tried to make what I considered a sensible statement which wasn't in full support, I would get angry phone calls.

One of the problems was Air Force Lieutenant General James Abrahamson, who had been brought in to run SDI. Abrahamson had a superb record in program management. He had overseen the Maverick air-to-surface missile and several space projects. He had also managed the international F-16 program, one of the most successful we had ever had. He was an outstanding technician and a powerful advocate who could deliver highly polished presentations with a sophisticated yet genuine air. If his listeners didn't know anything about SDI they would come away from an Abrahamson briefing talking to themselves, which is exactly what congressmen were doing. The trouble with Abrahamson was that he believed it was his job not just to run the SDI program but also to sell it.

Abrahamson reported directly to Weinberger, but Herres and I would often be present when he briefed the Secretary. During these sessions an upbeat atmosphere always seemed to prevail in Weinberger's top-floor office. Here Abrahamson was playing to a friendly audience. Herres would always ask a few hard questions to try to keep the enthusiasm at least partly in check. But neither Weinberger nor his policy advisers liked to hear them. Their primary reaction seemed to be dismissal: Well, you could practically hear them thinking, just consider the source. Herres was viewed as a conduit for the negative views of the chiefs.

I was certainly not getting the same thing out of these briefings that Weinberger was. I had a lot of questions about what was going on, and I wanted Herres, Air Force Chief Larry Welch (who also had a strong technical background), and some of our own staff experts to hear Abrahamson in a more neutral setting. As a result, we started inviting him to brief the chiefs in the Tank. These briefings bore little resemblance to what was going on in Weinberger's office. Here the chiefs and specialists would take vigorous exception to much of what Abrahamson was describing. This sounds great, they would say, but it isn't exactly right. Before long it became evident to me that Abrahamson was slanting his briefings.

I finally reached the point where I no longer relied on his reports. Then we started looking into the situation more carefully. We would have a scientist who worked for Abrahamson come in, and he would tell us, I know he said that, but the real situation is . . . Or, You know, we didn't do as many tests as that, and that test really was pretty artificial. We discovered, in fact, that we were hearing only about the small percentage of tests that worked, and not the majority that didn't. To put the best face on it, we knew that Abrahamson himself was under great pressure from the advocates to put developments in the most optimistic light. I complained to Weinberger about this, but he just sort of brushed me off.

By now it was clear that SDI had become so highly politicized that some people were quite ready to misinterpret test results to further their interests. Every time we ran a modest test—not a real test of what we were ultimately going to have to solve, but a first step—the advocates would point to it as a sign that SDI "worked." Then the scientist who conducted the experiment would say, Wait just a minute. You can't give too much credence to this yet. It worked and we're encouraged, but look at what remains to be done. That kind of remark would draw angry glances, then would quickly be disregarded.

The National Security Planning Group provided its own distinctive venue for the SDI conflict. All the NSPG members lived in fear of those occasions when a big issue would give rise to a roaring argument in front of President Reagan. When that happened, the meeting would normally close without a decision. Members would walk out wondering whether they had been on the winning or losing side, sure that somebody opposing them would get in to see the President and convince him in private. We're in trouble, they would think. Shultz was against us, and Shultz will get in to see him personally tomorrow and bring him to a decision. SDI was so significant that the jockeying among the principal NSPG players was unusually vigorous.

One of Weinberger's ploys in this game was to sidestep his opponents altogether. Instead of taking new information to the NSPG, he would call up the President and tell him he wanted to update him. Could he come over with a few of his key people and tell him about the most recent developments? That'd be fine, Cap, the President would say. Come on over.

Of course that would infuriate George Shultz, Jim Baker, and practically everybody else. SDI was so big it concerned them all, and here Weinberger was going to have not only the first word but possibly the last as well. Moreover, he was not going to provide a balanced report. I understood this better than most, since on occasion I accompanied the Secretary to see the President. One day I was with Weinberger when he was telling Reagan about all the promising developments on SDI. After relating some recent test results Weinberger said, "Mr. President, your dream is here." I thought I was going to choke. The dream was not anywhere close to being "here." But the President really and truly seemed to buy it.

This kind of thing was not unusual in the effort to keep the SDI program going. The conservatives believed the President had to be regularly encouraged. If you were reasonable and described the true, complicated picture, his enthusiasm might flag. I did not think that what was going on was right. I understand well enough the need to carefully craft your phrasing when there was a chance your remarks might see daylight in the *Washington Post*. But inflation and exaggeration within the highest policymaking circles seriously disturbed me. It seemed to me that, at that level, decision makers needed to have an accurate view of where we stood and what our prospects were. But when it came to SDI, that was rarely the case in the Reagan White House.

In the development of SDI, the chiefs took a stance that allied them much more closely with the State Department than with the civilian leadership at Defense. Though neither of us might have said it out loud, George Shultz and I were allies on this issue. But though I considered myself one of Shultz's strong admirers, that was not always the case.

The year 1987 drew to a close with a major foreign policy triumph for the administration—the signing of the INF Treaty. To some in Washington it seemed as if a new age might be dawning. After years of surly recalcitrance, the Soviets had finally accepted the American position on intermediate nuclear forces. The treaty had broken through formidable historical barriers and had resulted in the full realization of a negotiating strategy the West had initiated eight years earlier. There were good reasons for the euphoria some administration officials were experiencing. If the Soviets had agreed to this, other more ambitious arms reduction goals might also be in reach.

George Shultz was one of those infected by the prevailing excitement. Shortly after the INF signing he suggested in a closed meeting with the chiefs that we should be able to conclude the START treaty before the upcoming 1988 elections (which would have given President Reagan an even bigger coup with which to close out his term). That sent a tremor through everyone at the table. START, the Strategic Arms Reduction Talks, was many degrees of magnitude more complicated than the INF Treaty. Moreover, there were a large number of significant issues we had not even begun to explore in depth. We had just had the experience of watching the last minute rush to close INF gloss over several questions the JCS thought warranted additional study. And now the Secretary of State was proposing that we could conclude a START treaty in less than a year.

I genuinely believed that was not possible. It was also highly dangerous, and all the pressure to put together the pieces before the President's departure would make it doubly so. This kind of haste violated everything I knew about the arms control process; it was almost calculated to result in mistakes, perhaps major mistakes. And it was evident that Shultz was serious. His statement was not just propaganda meant to add the light of good intentions to the INF glow already bathing the administration. He started energizing the bureaucracy to move quickly on START.

Secretary of Defense Frank Carlucci, who in November 1987 had succeeded Caspar Weinberger, was as skeptical as I was. So were Bob Herres and the four chiefs. All of us had supported INF, and we were prepared to support a carefully crafted START as well. (The operative words were "carefully crafted.") Personally, I would have been quite happy to see an even larger reduction in strategic nuclear weapons than the START negotiators were proposing. But arms control treaties with the Soviet Union were of a different character than other international agreements. They struck to the heart of the country's security, and consequently they required the utmost care and patience. In this field, errors could result in intolerable consequences.

The INF Treaty itself had been tricky to negotiate, in part because of the verification regime. But the verification problems associated with START were vastly more complex. (In the course of the INF ratification hearings, Senator Phil Gramm of Texas remarked to Bob Herres, "General, it looks to me like this one [INF] is pretty much for practice; the next one [START] is going to be for real.") START covered more weapons and a greater variety of weapons, including Soviet rail-mobile and road-mobile ICBMs, which presented special difficulties. Soviet manufacturing and support facilities for strategic missiles were far more widespread than those for intermediate-range weapons, and a significantly more secretive environment surrounded them.

Some in State felt that even with the difficulties a quick framework agreement was still feasible. At the very least the Soviets and ourselves could agree on reducing missiles to a given number, leaving the verification and other details for more deliberate consideration. But while that approach might have seemed logical to a layman, from an American arms negotiator's perspective it would have proved a nightmare.

The problem was that the Soviets could verify our force structure far more easily than we could verify theirs, if only because of the differences between the two societies. In the relatively open American system, gathering intelligence on missiles was in large part a matter of going to hearings on the Hill and to industry gatherings where defense contractors showed off their capabilities. This is exactly what people do who write books such as *All the World's Aircraft* and *All the World's Missiles,* which are full of such extraordinary detail. Obtaining equivalent information within the closed system of the U.S.S.R. meant breaking through walls of secrecy.

Consequently, in order to arrive at an acceptable verification regime, we needed considerably more concessions from the Soviets than they needed from us. But the only leverage we had to gain these concessions was in our positions on ceilings, subceilings, deployment options, and so on, precisely those items that would be set in concrete by a framework agreement. Numbers and verification procedures were thus linked; agreeing on a framework would have eliminated our ability to achieve the verification we needed.

The bottom line was that the stakes were just too high to not go about this whole process very carefully and methodically—regardless of domestic political objectives. Consequently, the chiefs dug their heels in. Persuaded that we could not negotiate a safe treaty in the amount of time available, we made our objections clear and prepared to fight it all along the line.

Shultz and I talked at length about this. I pressed constantly the difficulties and the time frame, and he would answer, Well, this is of such moment, it's worth a try, isn't it? I considered that terribly unrealistic. Similar discussions were taking place between other Pentagon representatives and their counterparts at State and the National Security Council, where our people pressed hard questions and insisted on answers. Where issues needed research, I instructed the experts to do their jobs thoroughly. I wanted these staff studies handled with the usual care, and I was not particularly concerned if they did not meet the time frames State was pushing for.

George Shultz was in the same bind all leaders face. He wanted this to happen quickly, but he was an extremely busy man, unable to personally follow all the details of arms control progress. State would set deadlines, but I took a firm position that our first obligation was to furnish right answers rather than fast answers. Every three or four weeks when Shultz was briefed on arms control he would be told that certain things had not been completed and informed what the problems were. Listen, he would say, not pleased, I want to catch up with the schedule next month. But inevitably (given the nature of the problems) by next month the delays would have grown even longer.

Shultz and I did not have any knockdown-dragout fights over this. Instead he eventually came to the realization that though it might be nice to push START, it just was not going to move as rapidly as he wished.* In a sense, Carlucci and I had thrown our bodies across the tracks. The Secretary of State no doubt understood that at the time, and it was not likely that he was happy with what was happening. It may be that he appreciated our reasoning more after he himself retired from political life.

It was in the nature of the Chairman's job that I occasionally found myself fighting against Defense Department positions as well as for them. With the dawning of the Bush administration in early 1989, though, events placed me in a position different from anything I had previously experienced.

At the beginning of George Bush's tenure, the Secretary of Defense's office was in turmoil. Frank Carlucci had resigned, and Senator John Tower's nomination was in serious doubt. At a crucial moment, just as the new administration was finalizing its budget, the Pentagon suddenly had no representative in the highest councils. With no one else around, the role seemed to have devolved on me.

From where I was sitting, the 1989 change in administrations seemed almost like a Democrat-Republican shift. The Bush administration was determined to distinguish itself from its predecessor,

---

* President Bush and Russian President Boris Yeltsin eventually signed the START agreement in June of 1992, four years later.

and though the new President himself was one of the kindest and most courteous of men, that could hardly be said of some of the people handling the transition. Many Reagan appointees were ushered out with barely a nod of appreciation, and they left harboring resentments. There was considerable whispered bitterness over this rough changing of the guard, though not much out loud, since the new President was, in any event, a Republican.

I did not know how Frank Carlucci felt in his heart about leaving, but I thought he was treated shabbily. In my view he had been a highly competent Secretary, but he was neither given the courtesy of a reason for being cut loose nor consulted about his successor. If he had been a Democrat that would have been normal, but he had served a Republican administration loyally and well. The transition team, though, seemed to care little about amenities.*

With Carlucci gone, Deputy Secretary William Taft became acting Secretary of Defense. But he was not much consulted. Instead, I began to get phone calls from the White House on items that would not usually come to me. "Well," I would say, "you know we do have a Secretary of Defense." "What do you mean?" would come the answer. "Taft is the Secretary of Defense." "I know," the voice on the other end would say, "but we don't know him and he's right on the verge of leaving." †

Given this state of limbo, one item I was watching with special attention was the proposed defense budget. The biggest immediate question for the new Bush administration was what to do about the budget. Should they submit the proposal that had been prepared by their Reagan predecessors or should they try in the short time available to retool the Reagan budget and put their own stamp on it?

Whichever they decided, under ordinary circumstances I would not be engaged with it. I had already participated in working up the budget with Carlucci. At this point the Secretary of Defense's office would make whatever refinements were necessary through the service secretaries, submit it to the Office of Management and Budget, and try to get the President's signature on it so it could go to Congress—none of which involved the JCS.

I soon learned that even though there was little time before the

---

* The insensitivity that characterized some of President Bush's people came back to haunt them later in his term, nowhere more evidently than in the scorn heaped on John Sununu for his use of government airplanes.
† Taft was subsequently appointed ambassador to NATO.

budget had to be submitted, Richard Darman (the new director of OMB) and John Sununu (the new White House chief of staff) had taken it in hand and were reworking it, including the defense portion. I had hoped, of course, that President Bush would accept the 3 percent increase embodied in the Carlucci proposal. But on a Friday afternoon shortly before the deadline I got word from the people I had following budget developments that OMB was going to propose a four-year defense budget with zero growth, in government short-hand, zero, zero, zero, zero.

That got me excited. Given inflation and several other uncontrollable factors, zero growth actually meant a sizable decrease in funding. Moreover, the administration's budget proposal would, as always, get worked over by the Congress and end up with even lower figures. The worst part of it was that the budgeteers were hoping to get the President's imprimatur on this without even consulting the Defense Department. That is, Darman, Sununu, and their colleagues wanted to cut the budget without the vaguest notion of how the cuts would affect the country's forces, or what the consequences might be for the relationship between our military strength and foreign policy positions. Even if the administration was bound and determined to reduce the budget, this struck me as an obtuse way to go about it. The President's budgeteers were looking for a quick political fix without even attempting to understand what the deeper consequences might be.

That afternoon I called National Security Adviser Brent Scowcroft to confirm what was going on. "My sources tell me that this budget is now in the White House and you're seized with it." "That's correct," said Scowcroft, a retired Air Force three star. "But the four zeros aren't true. As I understand it, the President has decided on a zero for the first year, but hasn't made up his mind on the rest." I complained to Scowcroft that the chiefs had not been brought into these deliberations and insisted that we had to be given a chance to defend our judgments. The President also needed to be protected, I said. Whatever happened, he had to be able to say that he had given the chiefs a voice and understood the military ramifications. It sounded to me very much as if this side of the story had not been presented to him.

Scowcroft sounded distressed, like a man beleaguered. I knew that he was the main advocate for the Defense Department inside the administration, not necessarily because he was a military man but because he believed that a strong military was necessary to support a strong foreign policy. "You're right," he said. "I need some allies over here. They've got their knives sharpened." "How bad is it?" I asked. "It's very bad," he answered. "The prospects are grim." "Well, can I come over and talk to somebody about it?" "Absolutely. Why don't you come over tomorrow morning." "You understand," I said, "this really isn't any of my business. You actually should have Taft over there." "Well, Taft's a caretaker, and I don't know how much good he'd do. Besides, we should hear what the chiefs think about it." "How about if I bring Tower with me?" I asked. "O.K.," said Scowcroft. "Bring Tower if you can."

A short time later I was sitting with John Tower in the Pentagon office he had been given while his nomination was in process. Tower and I were not bosom buddies, but I knew him. He was a hardball politician, feisty, with a bantam rooster approach to life. There was a lot of Texas about John Tower; tact and diplomacy were not his strong suits. But despite his lack of the niceties, he was an astute politician. He had been around the political game long enough so that he knew where a lot of skeletons were buried.

A man of great self-confidence, Tower had chaired the Senate Armed Services Committee before Barry Goldwater and in fact did know quite a bit about defense. But as committee chairman he had had a tendency to treat people in a high-handed way and shove issues through. As a result, he had made a lot of enemies, people who would now be voting on his confirmation. There seemed an even chance that his abrasiveness was going to come home to roost.

Tower had not been following the budget. What he was interested in was whether he was going to get the Secretary's job or not. He was under heavy attack, primarily for his drinking habits, and he was totally consumed by writing statements, defending himself, and lobbying. Sometimes I would go up to see him late in the afternoon after he had been through one of these strenuous days. He would be completely exhausted but still defiant. I was amazed that he held up under that fire. Tower was a very tough cookie.

"I think you better get in this," I told him. "It's really going to affect you. It looks like they are trying to emasculate our budget over there and the whole organization is in such disarray that nobody is making much of a defense on it." Tower implied (without actually saying it) that he had in fact sat in on a number of the budget discussions but had not been totally aware of their importance. "O.K.," he said, "I'll come."

The next morning early I got a call from Scowcroft. He had been mistaken the previous day, he said, it was not just a zero for the first year. OMB was pushing for four zeros and they thought they had agreement on it. "Agreement from whom?" I asked. "From the President," said Scowcroft. A little later in the morning I mustered the chiefs in the Tank. I described the situation and told them Tower and I were on our way over to the White House to meet with Scowcroft, Darman, Sununu, and some others. "If we can't get any relief from this," I said, "I'll be requesting a meeting for all the chiefs with President Bush. You might start thinking about what kind of presentations you want to make."

That afternoon found Tower and me in Brent Scowcroft's West Wing office facing Richard Darman, John Sununu, and Treasury Secretary Nicholas Brady. From the start it was clear there would be no easy meeting of minds. With Scowcroft running the meeting and casting himself in a sort of arbiter's role, Darman led off with some strong talk about President Bush's campaign promises to reduce spending and how they were determined to zero the budget. Even if Defense was zeroed, we would still have a lot of money to spend, so it was unclear to him why there was all this unhappiness.

Tower interjected that campaign promises had also been made about having a strong defense, and he gave a forceful little speech that was long on patriotism and on the prematurity of making dramatic military cuts. After some stiff words between Darman and Tower, I took up the cudgel. "Are you saying," I asked Darman and the others, "that it's evident to you that Gorbachev is going to survive and succeed? Is it already clear in your mind that we are going to get a START agreement and that we are going to cut nuclear arms fifty percent? The chiefs have testified to their assessment of the nuclear threat and that if we cut more it's going to go higher. Are you telling me that's not true? Instead of addressing these issues, what I see here in the budget is your statement that we are now going to get 'more defense for less money,' which I take vigorous exception to.

"You have not made clear to the President two or three fundamentals. One, you get less defense for less money. That's like a law of physics. You can lie about it and manipulate it all you want. But if you spend less money, you're going to get less defense.

"Now there are smart and dumb ways to cut down, and if the President insists on cutting, the chiefs will do everything they can to advise him what risks we can best afford to increase. If the President wants to say, My number-one priority is the deficit and we need to accept increased military risk in order to take care of the deficit, O.K., that makes a lot of sense to me. But say that. Don't tell him there are no downsides to doing this, because there are downsides."

As the discussion went on I emphasized that we were just at the beginning of meaningful arms control, that SDI research was part of the budget, that the military now was funding substantial intelligence costs for INF verification, that we had entered into the drug war and had beefed up our anti-terrorism commitment. The Brookings Institution estimated that a 2 percent increase was necessary just to stay even; our own estimate was 3 percent.

None of this visibly moved my opponents. Brady weighed in with a discussion of the economic problems facing the administration, and Darman and Sununu backed him up with what I thought was a good amount of hand wringing and hair pulling. Finally I said, "This is just totally unacceptable. I think that before the President makes a decision, he should see the chiefs."

The reaction to that announcement was not enthusiastic. Darman suggested that since this was part of the budget process I did not really need to see the President. We were all talking about it right now, and they would make sure that all my views got to the President. "No," I said. "That's not satisfactory to me, particularly if you're going to zero this. If that's what you plan to do, he had better hear what we have to say. Regardless of what decision he makes, he has to know what impact this will have on his armed forces and what we feel the risk is. At the very least he has to be ready to defend himself against some of the charges that are going to be leveled at him by the pro-defense people. You're not able to give him that. I have to give him that, and I want to bring the chiefs with me."

That was motherhood, I thought, and they couldn't argue with it. But Sununu was getting agitated. "Well," he said, "I hope you're not going to be too pessimistic." I could feel my own annoyance rising, though I tried not to show it. "That's irrelevant," I said. "We'll tell him the facts. Are you telling me you don't want the President to know the facts? I would think he'd want to know the facts." "No, no," said Sununu. "I want him to know the facts."

"O.K.," said Scowcroft, turning to me. "I think it's your privilege to see the President. I don't have a problem with that. We'll try to get you in early next week, even Monday." "Well," said Brady, "I still don't think it's absolutely necessary."

By this time it was all too obvious how much we were suffering the lack of a Secretary of Defense. They would never have attempted to shove Caspar Weinberger around like this, I thought. He would simply have said, Screw you. I'm going to call the President and get on his calendar for Monday. Not that I minded seeing the President and defending the budget, but I was a little out of my element. The truth was that I had just butted into the budget process because there was nobody else ramrodding it. I also believed that President Bush was more or less being steamrollered by his advisers, who neither knew anything nor cared anything about defense.

At this late stage of the budget (or at any stage) it was highly unusual to have the chiefs in full regalia parading into the White House, as we did at nine-thirty on Monday morning. Normally the Secretary of Defense would have been there himself, nor would he have wanted any of the chiefs around. As a politician himself, the Secretary is closely attuned to the administration's political concerns. He will give the military budget his best effort, but he does not want too many people privy to the discussion. However the internal arguments are resolved, he is going to have to support the budget proposal that eventually goes to Congress.

The chiefs, on the contrary, were essentially saying, We are not going to support this. We were not about to rush out into the streets screaming that we were robbed, but our presence in the Oval Office that morning was a way of letting the President know how we felt. Everyone in the room understood that we were positioning ourselves so that if Congress got excited and wanted to question us, we were going to differ with the President. In effect, we were announcing to all concerned that our hands were untied when the argument started over in Congress. Everyone in the room also understood that if we did take issue, it would not reflect well on the administration, especially on a brand-new administration. That was one of the reasons Darman, Sununu, and Brady had not wanted us to see the President.*

The meeting offered no great surprises. I made many of the points I had made the previous Saturday, while Brady painted a general economic picture that indicated the need for defense reductions.

---

* There are implicit conventions governing conduct in this area. The Chairman and chiefs of service are expected to support the President's budget right down the line—until a congressman says, That's very well, Admiral, but I want your personal opinion. If he says that, you cannot refuse to answer. In fact, when a Chairman or chief is confirmed, he is often asked specifically, Can you assure us that no matter what the administration has done, this committee will have access to your personal views on important issues? And the confirmee answers yes.

This time, though, Secretary of State James Baker was present, and he insisted that this was not the time to appear weak, either in the eyes of the allies or in confronting the Soviets, who were entering a crucial period in their own national and international policymaking. I seconded Baker, pointing out that our strength was the reason the Soviets were at the bargaining table in the first place. Indeed, our military strength had been instrumental in supporting our foreign policy around the world. It had had a high payoff, and I harbored deep concerns about prematurely cutting back, as it seemed to me we were about to do.

The meeting ended without President Bush either saying anything or making a decision. But just before lunch I got a call from Scowcroft. The President, he said, had decided on zero, zero, two, two. But if I preferred, he would agree to zero, one, one, two. I said I preferred the latter. Everybody in the business knows you can promise an increase in the future to get you something in the present without necessarily ever having to make good on the promise. That will be reevaluated when the future arrives. It's a safe bet that adding on the big numbers at the end means you are never going to get anything.

All in all, I thought we had done fairly well, especially considering how late we had been brought in (fought our way, some might have said), and what the administration's original position was. I knew that we were going to get cut; we all understood that. But I thought that at least as far as the weekend's events were concerned, we had done pretty well. The President had given us our day in court and, to a certain extent, had gone with us. We didn't win it all. But we were a lot better off than we might have been. Tower called it a "Texas standoff," which isn't all that bad.

Chapter 18

WINGWALKING

THE ANCIENT CHINESE HAD A BENEDICTION: "May you live in interesting times." I have sometimes regretted that my professional life was lived during an era when American foreign and military policy was shaped by a single factor: the challenge of the Soviet Union. But the times have not been uninteresting. For the whole of my career the U.S.S.R. was constantly in the forefront of our minds as our one formidable military adversary. What American forces should be doing and building, how large our military should be and how deployed—these were all dictated by the Soviets. For almost half a century American strategic thinking rose and set on the Soviet Union.

Curiously enough, even though the U.S.S.R. dominated American military thought during this period, the engagements we fought were never against the Soviet Union. Our fighting was done in Korea and Vietnam, in various limited actions in Latin America and the Middle East, and then in Desert Storm, which in its way marked the end of the era. None of those was a direct confrontation between the United States and the Soviet Union, but lingering always in the background was the Kremlin's long shadow.

Desert Storm was fought against a country that had been one of Moscow's staunchest regional allies and only the dramatic reorientation that preceded the Soviet Union's collapse allowed that confrontation to take the course it did. As it was, in the Gulf War we utilized weapons and tactics developed to confront the Warsaw Pact. The Gulf War also marked the emergence of the United States as the one superpower of the post–Cold War world and signaled a short-term future, at least, in which regional turmoil has replaced big power confrontation as the great threat to mankind.

Desert Storm suddenly focused the country's attention on the art of war that America's military had perfected during the Cold War years. Directly afterwards there was a tendency to feel that we had tested our warfighting concepts and found them good. But the euphoria receded when we began to realize that some of our weapons did not work as well as we had thought and that our military decision making was at times less effective than it had appeared.

In strictly military terms, the outstanding accomplishment of Desert Storm was logistical: We succeeded in moving large numbers of troops and vast quantities of material over great distances. But it is also true that we grossly overestimated Iraq's strength and consequently deployed far too much material and manpower. Over 300,000 tons of ammunition were stocked for battle, but only 30,000 tons were used. While prudence always requires overpreparation, this hardly excuses estimates so unusually wide of the mark. In other areas top leadership was difficult to judge, in part because the Iraqis provided so few real challenges. The ground campaign, billed as brilliant, was, frankly, the obvious option, and most military commentators were predicting the "left hook" weeks before hostilities began.

Nevertheless, General Norman Schwarzkopf proved to be a well-grounded planner, a solid battle commander, and (to many people's amazement) a good coalition diplomat. His post-hostilities performance, however, left something to be desired. The Iraqis seem to have gotten the better of some of the agreements that were intended to limit their ability to intimidate their own people. Additionally, Schwarzkopf was apparently inclined to continue hostilities—at least long enough to destroy Iraq's elite units. But there is little evidence that he pressed the point with any vigor. This is, perhaps, a lot to ask. But he was the commander on the scene, and if he felt strongly he should have persevered. A military commander is expected to obey his political masters, but he does not have to acquiesce to their thinking without arguing his own views as convincingly as he can.

In retrospect, the decision to stop hostilities so quickly was probably a mistake, though we will never be able to say definitely. To change another nation's political system or its deeply entrenched leaders requires total, not partial, victory, especially in the Byzantine labyrinth of the Arab world. Of course President Bush would have received criticism both at home and abroad had he done what was necessary to remove Saddam Hussein. But the alternative was the resuscitation of Saddam's regime and all the dangers that has entailed. It is difficult to justify deploying 400,000 troops 6,000 miles from home and winning a decisive military victory if a year later such grave political troubles remain. When the large number of Iraqi wartime casualties are thrown into the equation (somewhere between 70,000 and 100,000), and also the postwar atrocities against Kurds and Shiites, Saddam's survival becomes a travesty of the first order. These considerations throw a shadow over what was otherwise an example of masterful presidential leadership.

In retrospect, we went into major hostilities with no firm idea of how to translate a military triumph into beneficial long-range political consequences. Our postwar approach to Iraq, for example, was laden with contradictions. We hoped for a different government in Baghdad (or at least a change in leadership) but did not know how to achieve that. We wanted to protect the Kurds and Shiites but were unable to prevent savage atrocities. Our leverage over Tel Aviv in brokering a Palestinian settlement turned out to be far less than the administration imagined it would be. Even the idea of injecting a dose of democracy into Kuwait's political life proved a passing fancy.

In a sense, these failures did not condemn the Bush administration for lack of foresight so much as they demonstrated the complexity of the Middle East's politics and cultures. The same can be said of our painfully inconsistent Iraqi policy in the years preceding the war. Despite constant references throughout the region to "Arab brotherhood," the Arab world is not one, but many contrasting peoples with their own histories, loyalties, and interests. Throw in Islam, oil, and Israel and the result is a mélange neither easily sorted out nor easily managed. In this region particularly, gauging the future is a risky business. Nevertheless, as the globe's number-one consumer of crude oil and its greatest military power, the United States will necessarily be closely involved here for decades to come. Most of the Middle East's governments themselves expect and desire us to be. In the process, our future policies will no doubt undergo a variety of twists and turns, just as our past policies have.

Among its other effects, the Gulf War dramatically illustrated the unpredictable nature of international events. It reminded us that the disappearance of our most powerful adversary does not mean that the world will suddenly forgo violence. If anything, warfare and its associated human suffering is more widespread today than it was during the American-Soviet confrontation. It is, then, especially important to understand that the decisions we are currently making about the military are fundamental ones; in the years ahead they will undoubtedly affect global stability as well as our own security.

In this post–Cold War world we are faced with the need to determine what size military we can afford and what balance we are going to have between ground, naval, and air forces. In addition, each of the services has to decide about its own mix of elements. Each of them is being forced to make painful trade-offs against the background of defense cuts steeper than any serving officer has seen.

In making these decisions, the Gulf War was an important testing ground, even though it may well be that in the future we will face scenarios that resemble Southeast Asia far more than they do Iraq. Civil wars, guerrilla actions, and terrorism in such places as Eastern Europe and the former Soviet republics bear little resemblance to Iraq's invasion of Kuwait and have considerably more potential to bog intervening forces down in Indochina-style quagmires. It may be aggravating to have the shadow of Vietnam still dogging us, but we can hardly afford to discard the lessons we learned there so traumatically.

Having said that, it is nevertheless true that Desert Storm has unquestionably had a great impact on conventional military thinking. The major achievement in that war was our success in transporting 400,000 troops and their equipment to a distant region and putting a logistics bridge in place that could sustain them. The effort was considerably facilitated by the military infrastructure already existing in Saudi Arabia, particularly the large airdromes, landing strips, and seaports. But that does not diminish the logistical accomplishment, which was the cornerstone of both Desert Shield and Desert Storm.* There is an old military adage that the layman worries about tactics, the professional about logistics.

---

* It would have been vastly more difficult, for example, to build up a capability to fight Iran than it was to fight Iraq (as we contemplated doing during the Teheran embassy hostage period). Iran could have given us serious problems bringing ships into the Persian Gulf through the Strait of Hormuz. Instead we would have had to go around to the west coast of Saudi and truck everything across the peninsula—assuming for a moment that Saudi would have permitted such a thing. That would have been a different order of problem. In fact, one of the reasons Jimmy Carter did not do anything about the embassy hostages, for which he was always criticized, is that he knew that in order to hit somebody it is necessary to have a place to stand. And we could not find any place in the vicinity where we could stand. Probings and soundings were made all over the region, but no one was about to support us in an action against Iran. Neither Kuwait nor Saudi Arabia would entertain the idea. Nor would Bahrain. Oman was a longtime ally of Iran. So while it was pleasant to talk about what we were going to do, or should have done to Iran, actually doing something would have posed prodigious logistical difficulties.

Still, even with the advantages we enjoyed, it took 116 days to build up for the attack on Iraq. That is a long period of time, and it is unusual that an opponent will allow that. (In the war we were planning for against the Soviet Union in Western Europe, we assumed that our ability to get across the ocean would be attrited, our ports of entry would be under bombing attack, and moving up to the line would be costly.) I suspect that afterwards Saddam Hussein asked himself why he did allow it. If he had known what he knows today, he probably would have marched straight into the Saudi oil fields. We would have thrown him out eventually, but the process would have been far more painful. Iraqi occupation would have made a substantial dent in global oil production, and extinguishing fires in the Saudi fields would have been a Herculean task. We proved we can get along without Iraqi and Kuwaiti oil, but without Saudi oil the United States would have suffered.

The Gulf War also demonstrated the significance of having good people. The main reason we did so well once we got there was the skill of our personnel. That was the result of many factors, but primarily it is the great benefit of having a volunteer professional force. The men and women who participated in Desert Shield and Desert Storm were members of the oldest, most experienced (in length of service) fighting force the United States has ever fielded. It was also, not incidentally, the best-trained force we ever deployed. The outcome of Desert Storm attested to the wisdom of the services' emphasis on realistic training: the live-fire training centers we have at Fort Irwin and Twenty-Nine Palms and Red Flag; the simulations we do; the computers that allow people to practice running tanks and flying airplanes twenty-four hours a day without expending fuel. All those investments were justified in great measure by Desert Storm.

Desert Storm also proved instructive about the makeup of the different services and the effectiveness of various weapons systems. Few question that air power received a tremendous boost from its performance in the Gulf. Before Desert Storm, critics were in the habit of faulting air power on two major grounds: It was not effective at night, and it was not accurate. But those criticisms have now disappeared. No future enemy can contemplate fighting the United States in any kind of conventional war without control of the air (although that may still be possible in a guerrilla war). In Normandy and afterwards the Germans had little in the way of air strength, yet they managed a tenacious retreat and significantly extended the war. Similarly, in Korea we dominated the skies yet were often hard pressed on the ground. But those days are gone. Desert Storm demonstrated that no one could do that today. Of the 4,000 Iraqi tanks destroyed, 3,587 fell victim to air assault.

Desert Storm also demonstrated that Stealth—aircraft designed to thwart radar—is the wave of the future. Critics notwithstanding, there is significant merit in this technology. In the coming decades Stealth will play heavily in the chess game between offensive and defensive systems. No country whose forces depend on technology can ignore this reality. Currently the United States leads the world in this area, and we should not allow our predominance to erode.

At the same time, some of our advanced systems did not work as well as we would have liked (or as well as we originally thought). Early assessments, for example, of Patriot and Tomahawk missile performance were too optimistic. But, this is normal, and although reports of problems made headlines later on, those familiar with combat were not surprised. Post-action analyses performed with more data and away from the heat of battle always deflate combat accounts.

This is not to say that no questions remain about anti-missiles or "smart weapons." Some precision weapons can be countered. Lasers, for example, do not operate through smoke, and the Iraqis did not use smoke intelligently. Moreover, precision weapons are expensive. There is a serious question about how long our precision guided weapons would have lasted if we had been in a more protracted campaign. Against Iraq we used them profligately, but in a large-scale war we would have had to decide carefully what targets were worth precision guided weapons and use them selectively. But those issues are open to analysis, and that is where the debate over arms procurement should center now.

As to heavy ground forces, the most serious problem we had with them in the Gulf was that it took so long to position them. They are cumbersome to lift and deploy and they require a large logistics tail. Given the military environment toward which we apparently are moving, questions arise about their affordability. Defense spending is likely to remain at a premium for some time, while the most probable military contingencies will be thousands of miles from home. At the same time our overseas base structure will be shrinking. In such circumstances, heavy tanks may not be a priority. We will no doubt need some, but not in the proportion to other elements that we have maintained in the past or that some tank advocates are suggesting today.

One of the more serious arguments that has come out of Desert Storm revolves around the Navy's participation. Since the war, unflattering comparisons (from the Navy's perspective) have been made between the contribution of seaborne and land-based air. Some analysts have even drawn the conclusion that, given our substantial force of land-based aircraft, carriers are no longer needed.

These assessments seem to me both misguided and shortsighted. In bringing superior air power to bear against a determined enemy, land-based air is always preferable—providing that airfields and the infrastructure to support them can be emplaced behind the ground troops, as they were in World War Two and in Desert Storm. But in the past fifty years we have fought in many places where air bases were not available. Carriers can project force where land air is not feasible.

When a carrier arrives, it brings with it aircraft, ammunition, food, repair facilities, barracks, and mess. It provides its own security. A carrier is self-contained, enclosed, and prepared to fight, unlike the Air Force, which may stream in for several days or weeks or months, depending on how much work is necessary to build its air base into something workable. The carrier's power is only modest, but it is ready to go. It can support itself and fight indefinitely. That is a tremendous advantage in many parts of the world, and Desert Storm did nothing to disprove any of that.

On the other hand, the Gulf War did reveal deficiencies in our naval operations. In common with Earnest Will (the Kuwaiti convoying operation) and recent actions off Syria and Lebanon, Desert Storm required that American ships operate close to shore, sometimes in mineable waters. In these situations the Navy has used oceangoing men-of-war to fight in shallow waters, primarily because deep-draft ships are what we have. Now, with the Soviet Union gone, our concentration on control of the high seas will recede to an extent. In turn, more emphasis will probably be placed on the ability to operate inshore, including minesweeping capability. This trend argues the need for shallow-draft patrol boats that are not as vulnerable to mines and that involve less risk to people and equipment.

The reason we did not mount an amphibious operation against Kuwait during the Gulf War was primarily the mine threat. It is true that our feinting and maneuvering off the coast caused the Iraqis problems, and the value of deception was, of course, emphasized in the postmortems. The fact is, however, that we would have liked to have had the option of mounting an amphibious assault, but the mine danger was too serious.*

The fundamental point is that we need more countermining capability than we now have. We also must have the ability to operate in close waters without risking capital ships. (During the Gulf War the Aegis cruiser U.S.S. *Princeton* was incapacitated by a mine.) If there is going to be a shift of attention to inshore areas, we will need more of an inshore Navy. We would have been much better off with smaller ships in the Persian Gulf, not only in Earnest Will, but also in Desert Storm. This lesson argues not for a dramatic change in the way the Navy is configured but for an intelligent reorientation.

However the services choose to reconfigure, the great fact all of them face is the large reduction in force size that is now under way. The first axiom that should guide us through the downsizing process is that it is not possible to redirect the military establishment quickly. Military affairs are unlike foreign policy, where decisions can be made and implemented in relatively short order. Reshaping the military in a rational manner is a long-term enterprise. Building new weapons, for example, requires considerable time. It takes eight years to build a carrier; we were developing the M-1 tank for twelve years; to truly change the base structure will take a generation.

As we reshape the nation's armed services, that is the sort of time scale we must consider. To truly redesign a modern military built on sophisticated technology, ten, fifteen, or twenty years will pass between conceptualization and implementation. This remains true even though events rarely provide such leisure. While we attempt to search that far into the future, there is also the possibility that we may have to actually fight someone in the next four or five years. If we do, we will go into that battle with what we have today. One or two new systems may be on line, but for the most part we will be waging war with today's weapons.

The development time for new weapons and technology indicates the need for a careful rather than a rushed reappraisal. It is equally important to recognize the practical political difficulties involved in re-forming the nation's security posture. The fact is that building up is substantially easier than building down. The United States has

---

* Political inhibitions prevented us from stopping the Iraqi minelaying effort. We did nothing about it prior to January 16 because they were operating inside Kuwaiti and Iraqi territorial waters. I still found it mind-boggling that we allowed them to do it.

gone through the builddown process many times, and most often we have handled it miserably.

Our experience has largely been that once circumstances precipitate a builddown, the political temptations to move rapidly are hard to resist. In the rush to harvest a dividend—either in money or in returning people to civilian life (the post–World War Two demobilization, for example)—funds are cut, contracts haphazardly cancelled, units arbitrarily dismantled. It is an approach that time and again has proven inefficient, wasteful, and shortsighted. The more gradual the drawdown, the more rational its planning and execution can be and the more opportunity there is to grasp the new strategic realities. Political and military leaders have the chance to better understand changing geopolitical circumstances and adapt the force structure to meet emerging needs. Moreover, the heavy impact military cuts have on the civilian economy can be better controlled and the lives of newly separated servicemen disrupted less.

Curiously, cutbacks often do not even save money right away. There are substantial near-term costs associated with closing bases, mustering out troops, and cancelling partly completed contracts. Real dividends do not begin to accrue until several years have passed. This phenomenon is another argument for proceeding deliberately rather than precipitately.

Planners must also find ways to overcome significant political hurdles. The congressional tendency to retain bases and other military activities that furnish civilian jobs becomes especially acute during a drawdown (even more so if the economy is in recession). Objectively, the most economical approach is to reshape forces to support new missions and reduce personnel levels accordingly. But that philosophy does not necessarily fit congressional priorities and is normally ignored. Preserving military bases, for example, is often a high political priority, but the smaller the overall defense establishment the more wasteful is an inflated base structure and the more of a drain it becomes on fighting strength.

In a similar vein, congressmen's ties to reserve forces may unbalance the downsizing effort. State National Guard organizations and regular reserve formations often carry considerable political weight in local affairs. In any builddown, the argument immediately emerges as to whether the reserve forces will undergo cuts similar to the regular forces. Certainly reserve formations assume more importance in a dramatically shrinking establishment that may have to expand rapidly under extreme pressure. But at the same time it makes no sense for the active forces to bear the brunt of the draw-down. Ideally, trade-offs should be made to reach a reasonable balance between the two elements. But in hard economic times the reserves can generate more political clout than the regulars. No congressman wants to give up the local armories, jobs, and units associated with the reserves. These working people, reservists, and their families are constituents he or she accounts to every day. Against such considerations, strategic and management concerns may not rank high in the debate over what to reduce.

Perhaps most important—increasingly so during budget decreases—is the congressional funding cycle. The inability to predict future funding has played havoc with the Defense Department for years. With a few exceptions, Congress votes and appropriates funds annually. As a result, there is no long-range assurance that weapons production, even once contracted, will be continued or completed. Congress cannot abdicate its responsibility for controlling expenses. But multi-year funding (even twenty-four-month funding) would facilitate efficiencies in planning and producing weapons systems. Some procurement experts estimate that multi-year funding would provide 25 to 40 percent savings in buying new systems. One can hardly overemphasize the difference this one change would make. But in this area, too, considerations of efficiency and thrift are unlikely to dominate the debate.

In this transitional period the defense establishment will be groping for new benchmarks, new criteria to judge what the nation's military posture ought to be. For the past half century, from World War Two through the Cold War, the United States has been used to building its military to meet specific measurable requirements. Perhaps that habit of mind is no longer so useful. A different, broader kind of decision-making process may be called for—one that is not totally oriented to meet a particular threat. Former Secretary of Defense James Schlesinger suggested that the basic question is "How much strength does a superpower need?" The answer seems to lie in several areas. Even in a world free of an antagonistic Soviet Union, it seems obvious that we still need to maintain a level of power adequate to oversee our vital interests, to buttress our position of leadership, and to protect against our inability to foresee all challenges.

For the first time in fifty years we live in a world with no superpower adversary. Third World threats, while real, are more ephemeral, less dangerous, and not especially predictable. These new strategic circumstances should allow the United States more flexibility. Without the global confrontation between two camps, not every crisis or every challenge will require American reaction or intervention. In the future Washington's primary international relations problem may be to determine when American interests are genuinely at risk. This will be a perplexing task, and history suggests that our pluralistic system of government has difficulty coping with ambiguous, relatively low-stakes, political-military conflicts.

Such challenges already abound. In many parts of the world traditional enmities are thriving, and local rivalries have the capacity to blossom into international dangers. The possibility of one or more Third World countries employing nuclear weapons on their neighbors is also increasing. In potential nuclear crises Washington will undoubtedly be called on to act as an international policeman, as it will in less catastrophic confrontations as well. That is a burden of our role as the world's one superpower.

The chief mechanism by which American military power has supported our foreign policy over the years has been the strategy of forward deployment. Although the armed forces may need less strength to fulfill this role in the post–Cold War world, it is hard to imagine that the mission itself will change. The Far East is a case in point now that the Russian Fleet has withdrawn from Camranh Bay and deploys out of its home waters infrequently. Under these new circumstances, many are asking if there is a reason to remain strong in the Pacific, and if so, what it is. This is a question Alan Romberg and I explored in a *Foreign Affairs* article written in the waning days of the Soviet empire. The conclusions we arrived at I believe make good sense from a foreign policy perspective (though perhaps not from the point of view of environmentalists or social service advocates). There is no doubt that the sense of security Asian nations have felt and the contribution this has made to their political, economic, and social development has been of enormous benefit to American national interests. To sustain this climate, we must keep enough of a presence in the region to assure mutually suspicious nations that the United States is not withdrawing and has no intention of contributing to the creation of a security vacuum. There is, in other words, still a need for the United States to convey to its allies that we are determined to continue supporting them and that we are prepared for uncertainties either in the foreign policy or military sphere. The forces required to achieve these ends will be smaller, will be deployed somewhat differently, and will be working with a less clearly defined mission. But we will need to have them.

The process of restructuring the American military was already under way in the last year of the Bush administration. Secretary Dick Cheney and Chairman Colin Powell laid out a long-term program and began defending it before Congress and the public. They accepted that reducing the size of the military was fitting and appropriate. Their plan called roughly for mustering out 25 to 30 percent of the current force by 1997. Many of the weapons procurement programs would likewise be cut back—some drastically. Gradually, overall expenditures would decrease to somewhere around 3 percent of our gross national product. As these changes were fully implemented, the nation would ultimately realize the highly publicized "defense dividend." But that, Cheney and Powell argued, should represent the base level of expenditure. We should spend about that portion of our GNP on defense no matter what the threat, because below that we would be unable to maintain an adequate professional force to meet contingencies or to sustain our role as a great power.

The background to this is that by the end of 1991 (when the Soviet Union officially lowered its flag for the last time) the United States had already reduced its expenditures from about 5.7 percent of the GNP to 4-plus, on its way to 3.5. By contrast, during World War Two approximately 35 percent of our GNP went to the military, and during the Korean conflict 19 to 20 percent. After that crisis settled down, peacetime appropriations ran between 8 and 9 percent, then eventually drifted down to 5 or 6. With the onset of the Vietnam War, military expenditures returned to the 8 and 9 percent bracket, but afterwards President Carter decreased it to 4 percent (though he reversed the decline just before leaving office). When the Reagan buildup started, we went back up to 5, then 6, but we have been reducing since 1985. Three percent, Powell says, is the ne plus ultra.

The ultimate fate of the Bush administration's proposals is not yet clear. Secretary Cheney argued fervently (and I believe convincingly) that these drawdowns would create what he called a "base force" and would represent the minimum strength we should maintain. In his view, irrespective of threats, the leader of the free world should be prepared to support the "base force" as a matter of security insurance as long as we face an uncertain international climate.*

From a historical standpoint, it is curious that in the hundred years of the Pax Britannica, when the Royal Navy reigned supreme, Great Britain spent approximately 2 percent of its annual GNP on defense

---

* At this writing President-elect Clinton has not yet announced his intentions regarding force levels.

(there was no air force, of course, and the Army played only a small role in the British military posture). By modern standards 2 percent is an exceptionally low figure, but the point is that the British government was employing a base force concept. The 2 percent a year was more or less a given; the debate was over how that 2 percent was to be spent. This practice eliminated much of the uncertainty that otherwise would have accompanied the budget process, and from a security standpoint it served Great Britain well.

The primary reason Great Britain sustained this steady expenditure was that the country was run by a relatively homogeneous elite. Deriving from the same stratum of families and educated at the same institutions, upper class Englishmen shared a basic worldview. It was their common conviction that Great Britain should have a strong Navy. In that day and age the social movements as yet had no real clout, and anybody who might have been an environmentalist (if there was anybody) had no influence whatsoever. The power elite admitted little in the way of competing demands for that 2 percent. Opinions differed as to the most desirable of the competing weapons systems, and the balance between Singapore and the Mediterranean could raise hackles, but the arguments rarely strayed beyond such issues.

Our pluralism (as opposed to Great Britain's former homogeneity) suggests the problems any administration will have in gaining approval for a base force concept. Committed members of the Sierra Club, for example, will not readily embrace the concept of a steady level of military appropriations. Their position is likely to be that no agency should be able to fence off 3 percent of the GNP. The idea of a sacrosanct Defense Department (even at a low level of funding) is alien to single-interest pressure groups and to every other vested interest that is vying for a share of the budget. The military, in their view, has no special call on the nation's resources, and Congress in the past has not hesitated to ignore the security benefits of fencing off funds in order to meet other demands—no matter how short-range they might be.

That position impresses me as unrealistic. It ignores the history of war generally (one is tempted to say the history of human behavior, or at least the behavior of nations) and two hundred plus years' worth of American experience in particular. I find the concept of a base force sensible on several levels. It eliminates the compulsion to frame particular long-term rationales in an unsettled, rapidly evolving geopolitical environment. It does not leave us at a loss regarding our orientation toward defense after the Soviet threat disappears or if a Chinese threat should rise up, or if China subsides and Indonesia comes up. If we can agree that we should have a military of a certain size to meet future threats realistically, it simplifies the world and, more to the point, provides an effective way of handling a necessarily complicated and unwieldy system. From the standpoint of a career military man, and I believe from the standpoint of the nation as a whole, this is much to be desired. On the other hand, our country has not historically supported the base force concept.

Cheney and Powell understood these realities and attempted to make the most convincing case they could. They had the testimony of history on their side. Today's problem is in no sense new. For the past 150 years it has been a consistent pattern to demobilize rapidly once a truce was signed and to neglect our defenses until the next crisis was upon us. Then suddenly the country would be energized, hastily assemble forces, and throw them into the fray—inadequately trained, shabbily equipped, and poorly led. Four times in the last hundred years we have entered major hostilities grossly unprepared: the Spanish American War, World War One, World War Two, and the Korean War. We have paid exorbitantly for this lack of foresight in terms of national treasure and in the lives of our young people. It is heartbreaking to read the congressional testimony of professional military people in the years before each of these conflicts and to note how it was comprehensively ignored. One can still hear echoes of the flurry of high-sounding speeches that have been made after each armistice declaring, We will never make those mistakes again. And then the mistakes are duly repeated. "In war," as one military commentator said, "we remember the Alamo, the *Maine,* and Pearl Harbor. In peace we forget."

With this in mind, I would argue that the Defense Department's initial approach was well founded. It called for appropriate decreases carried out not precipitately but logically, gradually, and deliberately. It envisioned a schedule that would buy time to observe the trends in the former Soviet Union before making dramatic and irrevocable reductions. Moreover, the resulting force level five years from now would leave the United States still the pre-eminent global military power—an objective that the great majority of Americans genuinely share. The base force concept would achieve all this; it deserves the most careful attention.

In the bygone days of barnstorming air shows, daredevil pilots in biplanes sometimes performed a stunt called "wingwalking." The first rule of wingwalking was: Never let go of anything until you've got hold of something else. That advice has a certain pertinence for today's defense dilemma. As we grope over the next few years to chart our long-term security policies (and the process will take several years), it seems sensible not to lose our grip entirely on what we have.

My great concern is not that we are decreasing the size of our forces. In peaceful times that is to be expected. But there is also a tendency not to stop there. In a period where no major threat looms on the horizon, Congress may be tempted to cut to the point where military forces become "hollow." I fear this outcome more than any other. Appropriations steadily diminish; training, spare parts, and munitions are pared down (especially likely because these are not items with great political sex appeal). Units gradually become less and less effective. In turn the military loses its attractiveness to capable individuals thinking of making a career in the services.

Equally powerful is the tendency not to restructure and modernize forces. In the post–Cold War world, the military is not likely to need fleets of heavy tanks. But heavy tanks are all we have, and building a new lightweight tank involves substantial research and development, experimentation, and testing. That is an expensive proposition, even though the new tank will be lighter and cheaper than the M-1. The same is true of other new generations of weapons that will be necessary to stay technologically abreast and meet new strategic requirements. If we do not develop them, we will find ourselves ill-equipped for whatever mission does come along. Lack of modernization is the primary reason armies historically tend to fight the last war, but democracies typically find it difficult to modernize in periods of peace.

When equipment becomes obsolete and training deteriorates, the only people who join the military are those who cannot do anything else and have no true professional interest. At that point the country has grave problems, particularly when it is relying on a volunteer force. Given the military's magnificent performance in the Gulf War, this kind of development may seem unlikely. But it is not an improbable hypothesis. Exactly this happened between the two world wars, and because it did the nation found itself in dire trouble. It was little less than miraculous that a few officers of great ability—people like Omar Bradley, Matthew Ridgway, Lyman Lemnitzer, and Raymond Spruance had stuck it out for twenty years and were available for the new military to build around when World War Two came along.

It was a salvation that men like Dwight Eisenhower and George Marshall were still in the Army, that people with gifts had stayed in at all.*

The first way to deal with this potential problem is to recognize that draining the military of talented people is a genuine possibility. It is vital to our national health that whatever military we have retains the wherewithal to do what militaries are supposed to do. Even smaller forces can remain attractive. And they will if they are active and modern, if the aviators fly and sailors sail and soldiers train, if we continue to provide military education so people can keep updated and we still have a modicum of money to put into research so they can stay on the edge of technology.

The bedrock position, it seems to me, is that while we can spend less, we still must make a sufficient investment to maintain a healthy cadre, around which we can expand if necessity strikes. If we do not have that, we will be wasting whatever money we do spend. This brings the argument back to Colin Powell's theory that there is a certain level below which we cannot reasonably go. To have a viable military we have no choice but to attract and keep good people. And that is really our national insurance.

The essence of the question, of course, is whether the military has a mission that the country accepts. That is a difficult prospect, especially now that our vision depends on careful thought rather than on the existence of a clear and present danger. But the morale of the services depends in large part on the attitude of the civilian world toward the military. I have seen in my own career what happens when people no longer honor or respect their armed services. When the public no longer regards the profession as worthwhile, the psychological underpinnings of the institution begin to wither and decay. One of the reasons our military is so good today is that we have turned around the Vietnam syndrome. Parents tell their children who want to go into the military as a career that their choice is all right, that it is an honorable and worthwhile calling. (Desert Storm, of course, did wonders for that.) It is a shame to see that dwindle away, which of course it will; it's in the nature of things. But we do not want to see it die. Those who have the guts of the military in their

---

* Of course, the Depression played a significant role in this phenomenon. The lack of outside jobs was a strong incentive, to the degree that people with college educations were often found in the enlisted ranks. When World War Two came along, large numbers of these men were immediately commissioned.

hands have got to realize that there are ways to keep it healthy, and that it is terribly important to do so.

The United States is on the brink of making fundamental decisions about the future of its armed forces. These judgments are not matters in which just President Clinton, the new administration, and the Congress have an interest, they are a subject for the entire nation. It is impossible for the military to be capable if the country does not want it to be. It is impossible to make people enthusiastic about what they are doing if the country does not believe that what they are doing is worthwhile. It is impossible to inspire people to risk their lives if the nation is uninterested. There are few occasions our military has not risen to. We have made mistakes, yes, but in general the men and women of the armed forces have risen to challenges time and again. As a nation we have needed our military on occasion, and we have typically found that when there is a need, there is really a need. Rudyard Kipling put it movingly in the last verse of his memorable poem "Tommy Atkins," about the archetypal British soldier who is given short shrift in peace, but expected to perform feats of valor in war.

> You talk o' better food for us, an' schools, an' fires, an' all:
> We'll wait for extry rations if you treat us rational.
> Don't mess about the cook-room slops, but prove it to our face
> The Widow's Uniform is not the soldier-man's disgrace.
>   For it's Tommy this, an' Tommy that, an' "Chuck him out, the brute!"
>   But it's "Saviour of 'is country" when the guns begin to shoot.

The essential lesson, perhaps, is not that we need Patriot missiles or M-1 tanks. The essential lesson is that we need good people, and that good people pay rich dividends when circumstances grow perilous. Whatever else we do, we must have an enlightened policy that offers capable individuals a satisfying career in a prestigious profession. If we have that, they will compensate for many of the material deficiencies we may ask them to endure.

EPILOGUE

IN MARCH OF 1989 President Bush asked to see me. With my second term as Chairman drawing to a close, he wanted to discuss the future and my staying on. We were living, he said, in interesting times. I would be sorry to miss out on them, and he would be sorry to have me leave. Could I remain in the job for another term?

For a tough few weeks I contemplated my decision. In Washington few people choose to give up office. Power, it's been said, is a tonic. It drives the government. When you have it, you don't give it up voluntarily. I was not insensitive to this particular call. Moreover, the President was right: We were living in interesting times. On the other hand, I had to ask myself exactly how much power the Chairman really had. Influence, yes, and as I gained experience in office my influence had expanded, but perhaps not power.

The Goldwater-Nichols Act of 1986 gave the Chairman more authority, but by 1989 it ws clear that this authority would extend over less and less. With the U.S.S.R. fading, the armed services would soon be under great pressure to cut back. A significant change of character was in the wings. For the Defense Department, the next four years would be trying, filled with tilts against Congress over how much and where the budget would be reduced.

I recognized that after almost half a century in the Navy, the last nine years of it in high command, I was tired. I also was not sure that a sixty-five-year-old man with arthritic knees was precisely what the job called for (though one of my friends said that such a man might not be so eager to run into battle, or to run away either). But more than anything, I was eager to have a look at the world as a civilian. I had spent my entire adult life inside the military culture, sometimes chafing against it but always conscious of the divide between those within and those without. I vividly remembered Admiral George Crawford coming back to his office one day at the New London submarine base when I was his aide and saying, "Bill, I met a civilian today, and you know what? He seemed like a nice guy." For Crawford, civilians were a somewhat exotic group one did not often run across.

Admiral Crawford's attitude was far more characteristic of his Navy generation than mine, but I have also been all too aware that military people are different, that as cognizant as they might be of the larger world, they are still separated from civilians by certain intangibles of psychology and outlook. While I had grown intimate over the decades with the military enterprise, I had seen less than I might have of how the rest of the nation works and produces and consumes. Although my academic and social contact with the civilian world had been extensive, I had never experienced that other culture from the inside.

Since retiring I have found my new life quite fascinating, particularly my transition into the corporate world, where for the last several years I have served on several boards of directors.

American business is marked by constant competition and relentless judgments. As an officer I knew this, of course, but in a somewhat academic fashion. Now I see firsthand the competition with Germany and Japan, where industry is sustained by government in ways that give them significant advantages. I see the infrastructure problems our country has, how they affect our ability to produce and compete. In retirement I am getting a far better perspective on such problems than I had as a serving officer. There would be great benefits in finding a way for people who are moving into senior leadership positions in the military to experience the practical challenges that face the private sector every day. Once you have laid down your tools, it is easier to become detached from specific interests, more relaxed about the ongoing debate, and more tolerant of opposing views.

Essentially, the larger perspective rests on the understanding that the nation's true security (and its influence) derives from its overall economic and social health as well as its military strength. Every political science course teaches that security is a great deal more than guns and bullets. But it is one thing to know this intellectually, quite another to experience it and be involved in it firsthand. As a nation we are in the midst of digesting that lesson right now. Speaking as one who spent a career in the defense establishment, I am deeply concerned that cutbacks may proceed too quickly and go beyond what is safe. But it is also true that given global developments, this is probably the best opportunity we have had in my lifetime to concentrate more on our pressing domestic problems. And frankly, one of the reasons our domestic problems have gotten out of hand is that we have been forced to focus on defense requirements and overseas problems for so long. For several decades we have been extending our global role, while at the same time our economy has become steadily less dominant.

Our great competitors, Japan and Germany, have been able to concentrate the bulk of their energies on the economic side of the house. Japan has not had to be in the business of defending itself or even contributing to the stability of its region. That luxury has paid off handsomely for the Japanese. For years Germany was in a somewhat similar situation, although Bonn is now in the military business in a big way. But Germany has not allowed her defense endeavors to jeopardize her other interests. The United States shoulders the global burden, and consequently these countries have been largely spared a similar drain on their resources.

The potential consequences of increasing military investment against a background of limited national resources is evidenced nowhere better than in the fate of the U.S.S.R. The Soviets overextended themselves fiercely. They literally destroyed themselves. I do not believe, though, that we too are inevitably fated to decline and fall, or even to yield the mantle of leadership. America possesses a wealth of human and natural resources that we have yet to tap. But at the same time we must realistically assess our situation. Societies, like individuals, do make choices that affect their health and, in the end, their survival. One of the reasons for the fall of great powers has been the reluctance to acknowledge or comprehend the loss of relative economic strength and retrench accordingly. For the United States, the time for prudent retrenchment may well have arrived.

During the 1992 presidential race I unexpectedly found myself an adviser to Governor Bill Clinton. My decision to get involved with the campaign had nothing to do with military issues. While I had had some occasional disagreements with the Bush administration on specific national security issues (particularly the plan to abandon sanctions against Iraq and rush to military action before laying out long-term regional objectives), on the whole I was more than satisfied with the direction it had taken.

There were other considerations, however. In my postmilitary life at the Center for Strategic and International Studies, and on various corporate boards and several national commissions, my attention had been drawn to the nation's economic and social problems. I was dismayed by our lack of a sensible industrial policy, by our educational failings, and by the terrible divisiveness isolating so many citizens from the great American community that makes us a people rather than an assortment of factions. I found myself increasingly disturbed by the Republican party's tendency to exclude certain groups from the mainstream of American life and exploit antagonisms within the society. It seemed to me that our economic and industrial deterioration had replaced superpower confrontation as the greatest threat to our national security. Moreover, I was witnessing a determined effort to shift the country's attention away from these issues to peripheral concerns, such as Bill Clinton's leanings during the Vietnam War some twenty-five years earlier. After considerable reflection, those considerations persuaded me to get involved in a political race for the first time in my life.

Governor Clinton seemed to me to be the candidate most capable of shaking off the inertia of Cold War habits and addressing the challenges of a vastly different world, and by mid-August I had begun advising him. The connection came about through Dick Klass, a retired Air Force officer who was working in the Clinton campaign. Klass was troubled that the governor was not talking regularly with anybody on military affairs, and when he mentioned this to campaign officials he was asked to organize a solution. In short order Klass arranged a meeting in Philadelphia with four retired senior officers: Marine Lieutenant General Bernard Trainor, Air Force Major General Perry Smith, Army Lieutenant General Jack Woodmansee, and myself. Clinton's scheduler said there was an hour available for the meeting, but the governor quickly reversed him. "You have as long as you want," he said. "If you want three hours you'll get three hours."

Clinton was very impressive. He was an uncommonly good listener and a quick study. He was able to focus completely and absorb quickly. Although he was in the midst of a grueling election campaign, he gave himself completely to our discussion. I'd met a lot of politicians in my life and he was refreshingly different.

As I got to know him better over the succeeding weeks, my initial impressions were reinforced. I was talking to him because I believed that he was entitled to high-level military advice and that he should be aware of the military's concerns. But, increasingly, I found that I admired the breadth of his vision, his knowledge, and his obvious caring for people. He came across as someone interested in defining problems and willing to listen to those with ideas and potential solutions. He was especially impressive in small-group settings. He generally delivered his speeches from memory; he had a powerful and retentive mind.

It was also clear that, contrary to some opinions, Clinton was in no sense antimilitary and was genuinely interested in retaining an effective defense establishment. As for his alleged draft resistance, I thought Ross Perot was right on the mark. Perot said that a man should be judged on his performance and conduct as a mature adult, especially in positions of high responsibility, rather than on something he did when he was twenty-three years old. Looking back on my own career, I wouldn't want people to judge my contributions to the country or my philosophical foundation on the basis of what I did as a young man. I am a far different person today than I was at twenty-three.

I also thought that Clinton was much more forthright about his draft status than he was given credit for. He did not handle the question well at the beginning, but he finally decided he had better go back and find out exactly what he had done and then release that information. When he did, his critics carped, Well, his story is changing and he's not coming clean. When *Newsweek* made some allegations about my role in the alleged "cover-up" of the shootdown of the Iranian airliner by the U.S.S. *Vincennes*, I discovered that all you can do is go back and look and then tell the truth. If you discover that you originally made some inaccurate statements, you correct them. Of course, not everyone will accept the concept of "honest mistakes." Your adversaries will say, He still hasn't gotten his story straight. He's waffling. But most people will understand that this is nothing more than partisan politics.

The issue of Bill Clinton and the draft was another indication, as if one were needed, of the intense emotion that Vietnam still arouses. That was a war in which neither America's survival nor its future was at stake, and millions of Americans opposed it. I did not like that at the time, but I have put those divisions behind me. I do not believe that anyone who avoided the draft during the Vietnam War should be excluded from the political life of the country for all time. I don't think George Bush believed that either, despite his campaign rhetoric. Had he felt that way, he would not have selected Dan Quayle (who opted for the National Guard) as Vice President or Dick Cheney (who received numerous student deferments) as Secretary of Defense. Quayle, I thought, was a creditable Vice President and Cheney a fine Defense Secretary.

Eventually I decided to endorse Bill Clinton publicly, and I did so in Little Rock on September 19. Afterward, some critics raised questions about the propriety of a former Chairman involving himself in the political process. Not surprisingly, most (though not all) of the objections came from Bush supporters. At the same time, I received many letters and phone calls thanking me for my decision—a number of them from younger military people who complained that, while they too supported Clinton, they could not say so out loud without risking their jobs. One woman's remarks were especially moving. She said that she could not speak out because her bosses were Republicans and she was intimidated. "It's scary," she said, "being one of the little people."

I was trained to believe that a professional military officer expresses his opinion, then carries out the orders of his political leaders regardless of whether he agrees with them. If he feels he cannot do so in good conscience, he resigns his commission. But once he leaves active service, he is then completely free to express his opinion in any legitimate fashion and to participate fully in the country's political life. I wasn't surprised that some of my diehard Republican friends were unhappy or that a few truly had reservations about military people mixing in politics, but I never doubted my right to do it.

A few weeks before the election I addressed a combined meeting of the Naval Academy Association and the West Point Alumni Association. I knew that many in the audience were suspicious of my endorsement of Governor Clinton, and a few minutes into the question period someone raised the issue. I spoke about it for forty-five minutes. I said that some people join the military because they like to fight. Others join because they need a job. The majority, though, have something more in mind, and most career people spend time during their professional lives reflecting on the path they have chosen, questioning the fundamentals of their service and the larger purposes behind it.

Among the variety of answers, it is generally accepted that career military people defend the country's ideals and institutions. In so doing, we defend the rights even of those who are opposed to the military or who disagree with the government. After spending our lives in this endeavor we cannot then retire and allow ourselves to feel that anybody who disagrees with us is unpatriotic or does not have the right to dissent. That seems to me to make a mockery of why we served in the military. I held that opinion when I was in uniform, I told the service academy alumni, and I am practicing it now that I am retired. And I believe that people should accord me the same privilege. When I finished speaking there was a standing ovation.

My endorsement of Governor Clinton was based on my belief that he was the best candidate. However, there was another reason as well. It seemed to me that the conventional wisdom was that nobody in the American military was a Democrat; the uniformed leaders seemed so conservative that they were simply assumed to be Republicans. But that just wasn't true, and I thought that my endorsement might go some way toward exploding the myth. My experience was that many military people believed that the country was going in the wrong direction. In that regard they pretty much mirrored the general population. They did not conform to the stereotype of the military as a caste discrete, separate, and distinct in its views.

My opinion of Clinton as a candidate was strengthened when I traveled to Little Rock to make my endorsement public. Before I went out to face the press, some of the governor's aides were talking with me about possible questions that might be raised. One said that I would probably be asked my views on homosexuals in the military. I was not prepared to talk about that, I told him. I had not yet thought the question through adequately. "Oh, they'll ask you," he said. "And you know the governor has spoken on that subject."

"What exactly have you said, Governor?" I asked.

"That's not so important here, Bill," he answered. "If they ask you that question, you tell them what you think. If you're against gays in the military, say it. Some reporter will pop up and say, You know, Governor Clinton disagrees with that. If that happens, you're welcome to tell them that you and I disagree on a number of things, but that you are one of my advisers and you will be discussing the subject with me. And incidentally, you do that on *any* subject. You don't have to agree with me. You're an adviser. If you have a view, tell them. If we disagree on an issue, we'll talk about it."

I thought that was a solid indication of strength of character. It was particularly welcome because President Bush had made character and trustworthiness such a major campaign focus. As I got to know Clinton somewhat better, it seemed to me that what you see with him is pretty much what you get. The idea that he is somehow "slick" or deceptive did not mesh with the reality I saw. Moreover, his feeling for people was obviously genuine. I would call him a humanist.

In our meetings together to discuss security issues, he came not so much with an agenda as with an open mind. He wanted to know what I thought the major problems were and where the country should be going on defense. Curiously enough, he did not ask a single question about what Bush was doing wrong, or where the President was vulnerable. He was interested exclusively in understanding the larger problems: To what extent can we decrease our NATO commitment? In what ways would decreasing our commitment damage us? At what point will personnel reductions begin to jeopardize the country's security? How much and in what way can we wisely cut defense spending? We talked at length about what I consider the biggest problem—maintaining a viable defense-industrial base in the face of sharply reduced government spending. On this issue he seemed far more sensitive than the Bush administration, which to that point had refused to tackle the problem of rationalizing the defense industry.

I was not involved in coaching Governor Clinton for the debates, though I was asked to review some questions that his staff thought might arise. I wrote a memorandum on the subject, but said in the first sentence that I did not anticipate defense being much of an issue in the campaign, as indeed it was not. I did advise him to stay away from specifics if he could; you don't want to commit yourself to programmatic decisions in a campaign only to find when you are President that you have to change your mind. The governor did not necessarily take that advice. He came out for the V-22 Osprey aircraft, and the Sea Wolf submarine. The political pressure in the locales of their manufacture was simply too great to ignore.

Overall, it did not seem to me that Clinton had great disagreements with Bush in the area of national security affairs. But there were some variations of emphasis: He favored a deeper cut in American troop strength in Europe than did Bush; he was more inclined to emphasize the Far East; he was less bullish on the Strategic Defense Initiative; and he favored somewhat greater reductions in defense manpower and funds. Clinton was clearly more amenable to unconventional proposals for protecting the industrial base. And while it might surprise some people, I received the definite impression that he would take a hands-on, activist approach to the needs of the armed services.

Throughout my service career I took sustenance from the military's role in the nation's affairs. I enjoyed being part of an organization I thought was important, one that served the nation well and was progressing technically and socially, one that was constantly honing itself to fulfill its role. The Navy was close knit and believed in what it was doing; it offered a way of life in which relationships were strong, which gave its sons and daughters enough yet was not materialistic.

Just as important, the Navy was a manly profession (an old-fashioned word)—manly in the sense that we were warriors, that our lives involved risk. You did not just commute to a desk each day and hope you didn't get killed on the bus. There was physical skill involved in taking a ship to sea, and mental skill too. You were apart, doing things that ordinary people did not do. Most important, perhaps, was the conviction that you were serving a good cause, that the job of defending the nation and its institutions was a high calling indeed. Whatever failures or troubles might have intruded into my life from time to time, I could always find solace in that thought.

In retrospect, what I enjoyed most about the Navy is that I was able to do so many different things. I've run a ship, dived a sub, commanded men in combat, participated in international negotiations. I've defended people in courts-martial, testified in front of Congress, and participated in some of the high councils of government. I was able to sample a wide variety of life.

One of the reasons being retired from the Navy is different from being retired from a large corporation with its own corporate culture, say, IBM, is that the Navy is so all-consuming. A business executive may start out with AT&T, go to General Foods, then end up at IBM. You can't start out with the U.S. Navy, then go to another navy; you spend forty years in the world of the U.S. Navy, and that is the sum of your professional life. And it is not eight to five. There is no Navy man who cannot remember the ships he was on and their unique personalities, often in great detail. He has vivid memories of shipmates and his experiences with them. His family has been intimately involved in his postings and adventures, his successes and failures. It has been an encompassing experience. And in the end the journey seems to take on an ever greater importance (my friend Ken Sears tells me that I can look forward to increasingly vivid memories of events that never happened at all), as it does for all those who spend more time recalling and less time creating as they grow older.

I am going through that very process now. During my last ten years in uniform my jobs involved not just the Navy but all the services. In some quarters I was known as the high priest of jointness. I believe strongly in jointness and have long held soldiers, Marines, airmen, and coast guardsmen as well as sailors in the highest regard. Perhaps my proudest accomplishment is that I protected the interests of all the services without bias or prejudice. Yet in the end the Navy demands a special place. Whatever its shortcomings, over the years the Navy grows strong in your soul. No matter what you do after you get out, some of the old-timers say, no matter what you make or where you go, it will never be as satisfying as what you did when you were in the Navy. I couldn't put it better.

ACKNOWLEDGMENTS

THIS HAS BEEN THE STORY of my professional life, a memoir in more or less the traditional sense. But in considering how to thank the many individuals who have given me strength for this endeavor, it strikes me that something essential remains to be said. For all the intensity of participating in the military life of the United States of America at the zenith of its power, I was always acutely aware of what I owed to the people and places I grew up among. Those who know me at all know that I am an Oklahoman (even though I was born in Kentucky), and the voices of that exceptional part of the country seem to be calling out loudly for acknowledgment.

Oklahoma was wonderful territory for a youngster's imagination to roam around in. Past and present, the state was filled with characters and events that drew the mind. It made you feel that you belonged to a place that was very distinct and very American. The great Jim Thorpe was an Oklahoman, as were Wiley Post, the first circumnavigating pilot, and America's beloved humorist Will Rogers. The Cherokee alphabet giver Sequoya died in Oklahoma after traveling the "Trail of Tears" his people shared with Choctaws, Creeks, Chickasaws, and Seminoles.

Other trails crossed Oklahoma too, the Great Western, the Shawnee, and the Old Chisholm, made famous by Texas cattlemen driving their herds north to the Kansas railheads. For a while the Jesse James gang hid out in the Arbuckle Mountains, near where I used to go camping as a boy with my YMCA group. In the 1890s the notorious Dalton brothers operated out of Indian Territory, as did the Doolin gang. Little Dick West was gunned down in Guthrie and U.S. marshals ran the Jennings boys to earth outside Muskogee, fifty miles north of McAlester, where my mother's father, Fred Russell, owned a hardware and supply company. It was no wonder my grandpa always went armed.

I still think about my grandfather often. I can see his straight, wiry figure, his sunburned face, intense dark eyes, and the stub of a cigar that was always clenched between his teeth. I used to stare at the pistol stuffed into his belt and the callused skin above the belt line where the butt had been rubbing him all those years. I like to picture him as he must have been on that bright, hot morning of April 22,

1889, the day of the Oklahoma Land Run, riding alongside his two brothers and their father, my great-grandfather, on their way to stake a claim in what was about to become Oklahoma City.

I have the most vivid memories of my father's father too, as unlike my other grandfather as could be. Fred Russell was a hard-drinking pioneer; James Crowe, my father's father, was a semiretired Methodist minister, white-haired, frail, and hunched over from years of battling asthma. An intellectual, cultured man, he read voraciously and was as comfortable speaking off the cuff as he was delivering lengthy sermons to parishioners. He also had a sharp sense of humor. Though he had given up his own church before I knew him, he still preached part-time on invitation from other ministers. He didn't mind, he told me, when members of the congregation looked at their watches while he was sermonizing, but it did upset him when they started tapping on them and holding them up to their ears to see if they were still working.

We lived with my father's parents for a while during the Depression, when my father's health failed and he lost his law practice. But even in the worst times my dad kept the wonderful sense of humor he shared with his father. My mother also laughed easily, and would join in the joke telling around the kitchen table, though she couldn't really do it. She'd always forget the punch line, which by itself would send my father and me into gales of laughter.

Northwest Oklahoma City was in many ways an ideal world during the 1930s, at least if you were young and didn't have to worry about supporting a family. It was a place where doors were never locked, where whatever their pocketbooks might be telling your parents, their hearts (and yours) told you to believe in the country, that eventually things would get better. We were always in straitened circumstances, but until I went to high school I never met anybody who wasn't. To help make ends meet I delivered *Liberty* magazines, and until 1936 I delivered the *Literary Digest* too. That was the year the *Literary Digest* went out of business after predicting a landslide victory for Alf Landon in the presidential election. I was eleven years old, and that was the first attention I had ever paid to politics. Roosevelt was elected and half my livelihood vanished.

In our house, election nights were a special event. My father would have a bunch of his cronies over and they'd cook hot dogs and sauerkraut and sit around listening to the radio all night long until the results were announced. Politics fascinated him. In Kentucky he had served as a Democratic party county chairman several times and had been elected county attorney twice. He was a staunch party man who voted for Roosevelt in 1932, then again in 1936. But when FDR ran for a third term it made my father mad. In the end he switched parties, blamed the deterioration of the country on the Democrats, and became a diehard Republican till the end of his days.

Both my parents were devoted to education. (My father and mother were University of Oklahoma graduates and intensely proud of it.) My father also had a particular love for language. He memorized and recited poetry, long sections of the Bible, patriotic speeches, Shakespeare—anything that impressed him seemed to stick in his mind. For a small western community he was something of an intellectual, a cut different from most of the other fathers I knew.

One consequence of that was that I grew up not only reading but being read to, which was an education in itself. He loved Sir Walter Scott, and the Rafael Sabatini books were also special read-aloud favorites—*Captain Blood, Scaramouche,* and the others. They were rousing adventures, and they were also, not so incidentally, anti-Catholic. My father was a thirty-second-degree Mason with a streak of anti-Catholic prejudice in him. I often wondered why he had those feelings. Almost everyone we knew was either a Methodist or Baptist, or else belonged to one of the fringe groups of Christians, like Lutherans or Episcopalians. As far as I could see, there were extremely few Catholics around to be prejudiced against. Years later when I was a young lieutenant based in New Haven I almost married a Catholic girl who was attending Connecticut College. During the entire course of that relationship my father kept sending me anti-Catholic literature, hoping against hope that I'd eventually see the light. I never did, though to his vast relief we never got married either.

We ourselves were Methodists. My mother was active in the church, and especially in church charities, always far more interested in doing good than doing well. My father was religious too, though not in a churchgoing way. My mother took me to services with her, and our problem in Oklahoma, despite my father's biases, was not Catholics but Baptists. My grandfather used to say during especially hard times, "Well, at least the Baptists aren't any better off." Other Methodists felt the same. For many years I thought that one of the main purposes in life was to keep up with Baptists.

To much of the country, Oklahoma was the Bible Belt (Prohibition was not repealed there until 1957), dust bowls, cowboys and Indians, oil rigs, and schoolboy sports. A much less well known state phenomenon was high school debate. Debate was a kind of institutionalized version of arguing, the local pastime, and it was popular. I had already had some public speaking experience in junior high. I was motivated largely by having been exposed to oratory and notions of eloquence by my father. But my speaking career was also helped along by the junior high school music teacher. In seventh grade I was forced to audition for the school operetta, which was having trouble recruiting enough performers. The song I chose for the occasion was "La Cucaracha." When I was through the teacher in charge of auditions was thoughtful for a while, then said, "Maybe you ought to stick to public speaking."

So I became a debater. At Classen High School, Charles E. "Pop" Grady was the coach, in fact the most successful debate coach in the United States. Of twelve National Forensic League debate tournaments, Oklahoma had won eleven, beating teams from states like New York, California, and Massachusetts. Grady's teams had won three, and when I was a junior we won the national championship again. Tournaments were held all over the state, and some would be in Missouri and in Kansas. Like Oklahoma, these were big highschool debate states, and their teams, like ours, were made up of hard-bitten competitors. In those days there was precious little child psychology; no thought at all had been given to the idea that too much competition might damage young egos, that children might be crushed by defeat. Every match had a winner and a loser, and every debater was scrapping for all he was worth. You knew who the good teams were. You knew their strengths and weaknesses and you were laying for them, just as they were laying for you.

Oklahoma City, like the rest of the state, was a place of contrasts, a place where governors could regularly mix up "was" and "were" but where learning and even culture coexisted on a friendly basis with Midwestern accents and Stetson hats. I grew up at a time when Oklahoma was changing from a frontier state to a modern sophisticated one. There were still a lot of people, including my mother, who had been raised in what was really a pioneer world, a tough place where life's amenities were often primitive or nonexistent. But despite the jokes and yuks, Oklahoma was not a backwater. I debated, traveled, I had even worn a tuxedo. People from my high school class went to Ivy League schools, some of them, and although many of us couldn't understand why someone might want to do that, the fact was that their education enabled them not only to get in but to do well.

But it was still in essence a small-town world, where people knew each other and had an abiding belief in the goodness of the country. My wife, Shirley, grew up in Okeene, Oklahoma, and graduated from high school there, in a class of fifty-two people. Several years ago when I was still Chairman of the Joint Chiefs, I gave the graduation address at her high school. It was such a big event they had to move the ceremonies from the auditorium to the gymnasium. The weekly newspaper ran a huge headline, "Welcome Shirley!" then in small type next to it, "and her husband the Admiral." That was a great day. We said the Pledge of Allegiance three times that day. Twenty-five kids graduated, and they all received awards. I never saw so many awards. Some of them got three or four, and everybody got at least one.

It was a day that reminded me in some ways of the kind of place Oklahoma had been to grow up in. The Oklahoma tradition wasn't really cowboys and pioneers, though they certainly colored the state's history. The Oklahoma tradition was independence and straightforwardness and a kind of rough honesty. It was putting down roots and not quitting. It was a faith in the nation, an ingrained conviction that for all its failings the United States was good, its underlying values admirable. Not that other places couldn't give that to you too. Oklahoma never had a corner on those qualities, but it certainly did pass them on.

Among the many Oklahomans and non-Oklahomans whose skills and enthusiasm contributed to this book, I would like to mention first Jay Coupe, my long-time associate and public affairs adviser. Shortly before he left the Navy in 1988, Jay wrote a long memorandum outlining the things he thought I should be concentrating on for my own retirement, about a year away. He mentioned a public speaking career, a teaching assignment, television work, association with a think tank, some corporate directorships . . . and a book.

While I really didn't have much time to consider all those future activities in my busy last year as Chairman, I was pretty sure that I did not want to tackle a book. I knew how difficult a project that would be, especially if I was going to be engaging in the other pursuits, and I certainly did not want to have anything with my name on it that didn't meet my own standards.

The one thing I didn't count on was Jay's persistence. In our first meeting after my retirement, he brought the subject up again. This time he had an agent in mind—the brilliant Washington lawyer Bob Barnett, literary agent to many serious writers. The two of them,

Coupe and Barnett, worked on me for several weeks about the project and, before I knew it, we had an outline and a list of interested publishers. Without their perseverance this book would simply not have been written.

Along the way I have become indebted to many others. David Chanoff has been a superb collaborator, patient and insightful. My assistant at the Center for Strategic and International Studies, Brooke Jaffe, has labored long and hard to organize my infamous chicken scratches into legible paragraphs. Her good humor and efficiency have meant much to this project. My former executive assistants, Rear Admiral Joe Strasser and Rear Admiral Tony Maness, were extremely helpful in recalling and reconstructing specific events from my days as Chairman.

Others whose kindness and generosity I am most grateful for include Petty Officer Don Harrison, Master Chief Eddie Cesa, Darla Patton, my assistant at Oklahoma University, Captain Bill Kelley, Rear Admiral Roberto Hazard, Captain Dan Murphy, Rear Admiral Hal Bernsen, Vice Admiral Tony Less, James Blackwell of CSIS, and Carolyn Piper of the JCS staff. Also my aunt Ruth Bozalis, Rowdy Sanger, John Lovett and Bradford Kaplowitz of Oklahoma University's fine Western Collections, and William Pitts of the Oklahoma Historical Society. My thanks go as well to Vince Davis, Director of the Patterson School of Diplomacy, Steve Sestanovich of CSIS, Marty Haugen, Ellen Simmons, William Chanoff, Nigel Hamilton, Raphael Bouganim, General Bob Herres, Captain Rick De-Bobes, Irving Jaffe, and Bob Sims.

At Simon & Schuster I would like to express my appreciation for the fine work of George Hodgman and most especially my editor, Alice Mayhew.

Of course, as with virtually every important undertaking in my life, the contribution of Shirley Crowe has been enormous. She has been a major part of this project in every way and I am, as always, so grateful to be "Shirley's husband, the admiral."

WJC
Norman, Oklahoma, and Washington, D.C.
October 27, 1992

INDEX